JOHN XXIII
POPE OF THE CENTURY

Peter Hebblethwaite

Continuum
London and New York

Continuum

Wellington House, 125 Strand, London WC2R 0BB
370 Lexington Avenue, New York, NY 10017–6503

First published in Great Britain in 1984 by Geoffrey Chapman as
John XXIII: Pope of the Council
First published in the USA in 1985 by Doubleday as
Pope John XXIII: Shepherd of the Modern World
Revised edition published by Fount in 1994
This abridged edition published 2000

ISBN: 0 8264 4995 6

Typeset by YHT Ltd, London
Printed and bound in Great Britain by Biddles Ltd, Guildford & King's Lynn

Contents

Acknowledgements

The author and publisher wish to acknowledge especially Mgr Loris Capovilla for his help and support without which this book would not have been possible. We are grateful to him for permission to quote from the many documents and publications listed in *Bibliography and Sources*. We wish to thank also the Italian publishers of his books especially Storia e Letteratura, Rome; Messagero, Padua; Grafica e Arte, Bergamo, and Istituto Paolo VI, Brescia. Thanks are also due to all those indicated in the sources to extracts quoted especially Libreria Editrice Vaticana (Actes et documents); Queriniana, Brescia (Alberigo); Vatican Polyglot Press (DMC); Cittadella Editrice, Assisi (Utopia).

Preface

To this abridged edition

My late husband originally dreamed of calling his biography *Blessed Pope John*. Such a title at the time would have been premature. But this new edition has been produced precisely for the happy event of John's beatification, on 3 September 2000, to which Peter had looked forward with so much anticipatory hope.

I have reduced the original length by some forty per cent to make a tighter, more accessible, and, I hope, even more readable version. In this shorter edition, the ordinary reader ought to find all she or he requires, without loss of the colourful anecdotes which gave such character to the original work. While serious scholars of the period will still wish to refer to the 1994 edition for maximum information, I have preserved here all the references and sources.

One important addition which has been made to the Bibliography was not available at the time Peter wrote: the magisterial *History of Vatican II*, edited by Giuseppe Alberigo, which is coming out in five volumes

M.H., April 11, 2000

From the Preface to the 1994 edition

A book written about Pope John XXIII in 1977-1983 and first published in 1984 obviously needs revision. One form of 'revision' occurred naturally as translations into various languages got under way. Easily the most important was the Italian translation *Giovanni XXIII, il Papa del Concilio* (Rusconi, Milan, October 1989) by Marco Roncalli, Pope John's nephew. Living at Sotto il Monte, John's birthplace, he is close not only to tangible memories of his uncle but also to Archbishop Loris Capovilla, John's secretary in Venice and Rome, who had retired there to chronicle his life and works.

Not reading English, Capovilla had to wait for a translation before he could judge the book. He kindly sent me fifty-five dense pages of observations and corrections (January 30, 1989) which were taken account of in the Italian version and have been incorporated into this edition. Capovilla insists that although here and there he produces 'documents' to support what he says, for the most part he was relying on 'memories' rather than 'archives' which have been duly deposited in the Vatican. I thank him again, adding that he is not responsible for what I have written.

Pope John, knowing death was near, entrusted Capovilla with an 'historian's mandate' which he carried out with great faithfulness. Without Capovilla's publication of the *Journal of a Soul* in 1964 within a year of Pope John's death, the world would have had a very different and incomplete picture of him and his pontificate; and would have been a poorer place.

P.H., Feast of the Ascension, May 12, 1994

From the Preface to the 1984 edition

The danger of biography was well put by John Henry Newman in a letter to his sister, Jemina: 'Biographers varnish; they assign motives; they conjecture feelings; they interpret Lord Burleigh's nods; they palliate or defend' (Martin, Brian, p. 152). Except in the Prologue, I have tried not to interpret 'Pope John's nods'. It would, however, be a bloodless biography that offered no interpretation. The worst effects of subjectivity can be mitigated by letting Pope John speak for himself. Hence the copious quotations from his letters, diaries and reported conversations.

To avoid cumbersome footnotes, references have been simplified as far as possible. A quotation is usually 'sourced' by the name of its author. Since the numerous works edited by Pope John's literary executor, Mgr Loris F. Capovilla, could not be usefully listed under his name, they have been given abbreviated titles. Capovilla's version of texts of sermons and addresses has been followed where available: in AAS and DMC Pope John was zealously over-edited.

Pope John developed throughout his eighty-two years. His name changes with him. He is successively Angelino, Angelo, Don Angelo, Canon Roncalli, Mgr Roncalli, Archbishop Roncalli, his excellency, his eminence, Patriarch Roncalli, Pope John. I have not thought it disrespectful to call him plain Roncalli sometimes and plain John when he becomes pope. He never had much use for titles.

P.H., Whitsunday, June 10, 1984

Prologue

Introducing
Angelo Roncalli

I picture you, Pope John, in your vast bedroom on the top floor of the Apostolic Palace, not long before your eightieth birthday on November 25, 1961. Don't ask how I got in here. Let's just say your secretary, Don Loris Capovilla, fixed it (*Letture*, pp. 138–40, where John's room is described). He also tells me that your eyes are 'autumn-brown'.

You are standing at your window, overlooking St Peter's Square. Mgr Loris claims you never made that remark about 'opening the windows of the Vatican' that every journalist in the world has felt obliged to repeat. You didn't like draughts. Still, it was spiritually true, which is why they will go on saying it.

There goes the clock, chiming the hours with the Lourdes hymn – *Ave, ave, Maria*, part of the furniture left behind by Pius XII. Your light goes on at four a.m., sometimes three. You said to Cardinal Antonio Bacci: 'I always get up at four in the morning: it's my time'. 'That's too early', he said timidly, 'even your holiness needs sleep'. And you replied: 'Yes, yes, sleep. But I also need to work ... Anyway, one prays so well at first light, when everything is silent' (Bacci, p. 93). In your eightieth year you don't need so much sleep. But you like a nap in the afternoon, always in an armchair, never in bed.

You keep your diaries and personal notes in this drawer over here, carefully catalogued. You started keeping a diary in 1895 as a record of graces received and to check if you were keeping your resolutions. Mgr Loris tells me you have given him permission to publish your diaries after your death, because you believe they will help people. They will, no doubt, but it's a terrible risk, exposing yourself to the derision of the sophisticated, revealing your vulnerability, your naïveté. Some will fail to see that it is a record of growth in which the end crowns and explains the beginning. It will be known – not by your choice – as the *Journal of a Soul* on the model of St Theresa of Lisieux's *Story of a Soul*. I hope people will realise it is the *journey* of a soul, and that it is only a tiny selection from what you called 'sixty years spent with pen in hand'.

You never throw anything away, do you? You have your Mass intentions for every day of your life, and all the dog-eared passports and visas you ever collected. Is this the peasant in you, squirrel-like hanging on to everything 'in case it might come in handy some day'. Or is it rather your historian's instinct for the *document*, however apparently insignificant? It's the latter, obviously.

Then there are all these statues which make your room look like a shop for religious bric-a-brac, if you'll forgive me. But they all have a meaning for you. Opposite the crucifix is St Mark, patron of Venice. Mark is flanked by the two Johns, the Baptist and the Evangelist. It was to honour them, and your father, that when for the first time in your life you could give yourself a name, you chose John. At least that was what you said.

Madonnas abound, icons picked up in Turkey and Greece, mediaeval paintings from France. 'Through Mary to Jesus': how many times have you preached on that theme? You had it inscribed above the door of your chapel in Istanbul.

We've still not finished with pictures. Sts Peter and Paul: obvious why they are here, the pastor and the missionary. St Joseph: that is your middle name, and very soon you are going to surprise the Council by including his name in the canon of the Mass. St Charles Borromeo: your whole life was bound up with him: he was archbishop of Milan, he visited your diocese of Bergamo, you were ordained in his church on the Corso here in Rome where his heart is still kept, and your five volume edition of his episcopal visitations – over there on the shelf, proudly displayed, was the main literary work of your life. Unless, of course, you have something else up your sleeve, like a letter about peace to the whole world.

Then, of course, the obligatory portraits of your immediate predecessors. Pius X and Pius XI both died in this very room. Benedict XV died next door. Pius XII died at Castelgandolfo. So much for statues.

The photographs are less daunting and more intimate. Your parents: Giovanni Battista Roncalli and Marianna Mazzola; the three deceased sisters, Teresa, Ancilla and Maria, to whom you were so close; your three surviving brothers, Zaverio, Alfredo and Giuseppe who came to Rome for your coronation and fidgeted with their Sunday hats, stolid peasants astonished to find themselves brothers of a pope. There's Giovanni, who died on September 18, 1956.

Now some clerics you'll have to explain for the uninitiated. Don Francesco Rebuzzini was the parish priest of Sotto il Monte. He baptised you the day you were born, taught you better than most of your teachers, and left you his copy of *The Imitation of Christ*. To be more accurate, you just took it as a memento. Canon Giovanni Morlani who helped pay for your studies. Mgr Vincenzo Bugarini, rector of the Roman seminary, who died in your flat in 1922. Fr Francesco Pitocchi C.SS.R., invalid and spiritual director at the seminary. Then a group photograph of your class looking earnest and puddingy. The layman with long flowing beard is Count Giovanni Grosoli, advocate of 'Catholic social doctrine', and owner at the start of the century of a newspaper chain.

But pride of place goes to Giacomo Radini Tedeschi, *your* bishop, whose secretary and biographer you were. You still describe him, with capital letters as 'il Mio Vescovo'.

This lot of photographs show people you met in the East, and here are pictures of the presidency of the French bishops on your arrival as Nuncio. Finally, a painting of the cemetery at Sotto il Monte where most of your family is buried, but you will not be.

So much of Pope John was gathered in what Capovilla calls his 'gallery'. His love for the saints of the Gospel, and the saints of the Counter-Reformation. His loyalty to his modest family. His fidelity to the past and Bergamo. The sheer length of his life and diversity of his experience – he had lived for long periods in five different countries.

His neglect of his own achievements – none of the photographs are of himself – and his attentiveness to others. His need for 'models' of the priestly and episcopal ministry. His sense of continuity in the office he now held.

But this collection was in the room of the man who happened to be pope. Anywhere else one might have been tempted to regard it as the dusty debris of a lifetime or the self-indulgence of a very old man who could not let go of the past. But he had already called an Ecumenical Council that would launch the Church on an adventure of hope. Far from being buried in the past, the old man had a keen eye for the contemporary world. He was always looking to the future, right up to the end. He was open to the Holy Spirit, whom he believed to be at work, burrowing away in the modern world. That was why he could surprise people.

His 'gallery' was like the iconostasis of an Orthodox church: the bond between earth and heaven in the communion of saints. So here he was in the room where he will die, surrounded by saints, relatives, friends, and spiritual guides who were all involved in the onward rolling story of salvation.

Dates, anniversaries, birthdays were important to him. John entered salvation history in 1881. Also born in that year were four boys whose lives were to intersect with his own: Pierre Teilhard de Chardin, Jesuit, paleontologist, mystic; Ernesto Buonaiuti, his fellow-seminarian who was driven out of the Church as a 'Modernist'; Alcide De Gasperi, who spent the Second World War in the Vatican Library and emerged to lead the Christian Democrats; and Augustin Bea, another Jesuit, who became the founder-president of the Secretariat for Christian Unity. Angelo Giuseppe Roncalli came last in this vintage year. He was born on November 25.

Chapter 1

A village boyhood

Great things are done when men and mountains meet.

(William Blake, *Gnomic Verses, 1*)

Angelo Giuseppe Roncalli was born at 10.15 a.m. on Friday, November 25, 1881, in the matrimonial bed at Via Brusicco 42, in the village of Sotto il Monte, ten miles from Bergamo, just off the road from Bergamo to Lecco. The 1,200 inhabitants worked on the land, and lived in scattered, roomy but spartan houses, which mostly had individual names. The Roncalli house was known as the Palazzo. But there was nothing very grand about it. They shared the ground floor with their six cows.

Giovanni Battista (John Baptist) Roncalli and Marianna (née Mazzola) were contemporaries, both born in 1854. They had grown up together in Sotto il Monte and were married on January 23, 1877 when they were twenty-three. Their model was the Holy Family of Nazareth whose actual house was believed to have been angelically transported to Loreto on the Adriatic coast, sometime in the twelfth century. Their honeymoon treat was to walk to Bergamo and back.

Ten months after the wedding Marianna had her first child Caterina (1877–83), quickly followed by Teresa (1879–1954) and Ancilla (1880–1953). Above the matrimonial bed hung a large picture of Our Lady of Sorrows. In the earliest surviving photographs Marianna looks prematurely aged, and she went on to have nine more children after Angelo; but she out-lived her husband by nearly four years. He died on July 28, 1935, and she followed him on February 20, 1939.

Angelo was born in the first-floor bedroom. The single window does not let in much light. The walls are four feet thick and outside runs the three-arched gallery which gives on to an inner courtyard. Next door, at right-angles, was 'the girls' room'. It was somewhat larger and boasted a cut-down version of a steeply inclined 'Renaissance' fireplace. A large kitchen and storerooms completed the other sides of the quadrangle. The house was better adapted to the summer months, when life could be lived out of doors.

On Angelo's birthday a bitter wind blew down from the Alps, and rain and hail made the roads muddy and impassable. Giovanni, his father, was delighted that, after three girls, he now had a son and heir, someone to help him in the backbreaking work in the fields.

Equally delighted was 'Uncle' Zaverio, the brother of Angelo's grandfather. In this patriarchal society, he was the senior male, the *reggitore*, the man in charge. Unmarried, literate and pious, his first concern was to have Angelino – the diminutive was used throughout his childhood – baptised as soon as possible. Naturally, Zaverio would be his godfather. He went off to find the parish priest, but he was away in Bergamo. Zaverio decided to wait for him in the cold and empty church. He had recited all fifteen decades of the rosary and the litany of Our Lady before Fr Francesco Rebuzzini got back. So as darkness fell Angelo was wrapped in shawls, carried down the wooden steps and taken the eighty yards to the church of Santa Maria di Brusicco. It belonged to the parish, but was not strictly the parish church (Cugini, p. 23). So not yet a day old Angelino was baptised. Uncle Zaverio joined the men for a glass of wine. 'Tonight we are thirty-two', he announced. He meant that there were already thirty-one members of this distinctly 'extended family'.

This hasty baptism was not due to anxiety about his state of health. Angelo Roncalli was baptised on the day of his birth not because he was a weakling but because it was the custom in the diocese of Bergamo. It was 'the way things were done'. Of the Roncalli children, ten were baptised on the day they were born; the remaining three, having been born during the night, were baptised the next day (*Secolo*, p. 23). His civil existence began four days later when his birth was officially registered. The mayor's secretary distractedly got the order of names wrong and called him Giuseppe Angelo. This strengthened his bond with St Joseph.

Throughout Angelo Roncalli's life this nondescript church of Santa Maria di Brusicco remained his own church in a special sense. There his parents had been married. There he was baptised, and would make his first communion. And there he sang his first solemn Mass on August 15, feast of the Assumption, after his ordination in Rome. Built about 1450, it is, as Roncalli later said, 'not much to look at, but inside what richness' (*Letture*, p. 47). The walls bear traces of early frescoes that have not quite vanished. Now a plaque commemorates Sotto il Monte's most famous son.

The Roncallis had lived in the same village, though not the same house, since the fifteenth century. Angelo's historical researches later showed that the family had arrived in Sotto il Monte from the Valle Imagna to the north-west in the year 1429. A certain Martino Roncalli had built a solid-looking house which still exists. It was known as Camaitino, the dialect form of *Casa Martino*, Martin's house. Angelo's sense of history led him to rent this house and use it as a summer retreat – except when prevented by war – between 1925 and 1958.

The name Roncalli is said to derive from the Italian word *ronchi*, a terrace for vines cut into a hillside. It was an appropriate name because from the back of Camaitino Angelo could see the rising ground, vineyards below, woods above, which gave Sotto il Monte its name: beneath the mountain. At the top of the hill was the tower and church of San Giovanni, the earliest parish church. From what became his study at Camaitino Roncalli could see the new parish church and then the plain beyond, known as the 'island' (*l'Isola*) because it lay between the two rivers Adda and Brembo. The River Adda had once been the border between the Duchy of Milan, ruled by the Spaniards, and the Republic of Venice, to which Bergamo belonged until the French Revolution. It remained, in opera scenarios and sometimes in fact, the frontier between tyranny and liberty.

Like most of the inhabitants of Sotto il Monte, the Roncallis were sharecroppers. Their landlords were Count Ottavio, Guido, Maria and Don Giovanni Morlani of Bergamo. Don Giovanni Morlani was prior of Santa Maria Maggiore in Bergamo. Later he became Angelo's patron and financed his seminary education. He ended his days as a canon of St Peter's in Rome.

The share-cropping system meant that the Roncallis led a precarious life. Half their produce went to the landlords, and they had to live off the rest. They extracted what profit they could from their five hectares. Their cows produced milk and veal. Their vines yielded a rough, non-exportable wine. They grew kale as animal feed. But the silkworms were their most important and fluctuating asset; mulberry bushes provided the leaves to feed them. Male and female tasks were clearly distinguished. The women looked after the silkworms, the kitchen-garden, the piggery and the chicken run (*Secolo*, p. 28), as well as the cooking. The men looked after the farm. It may sound like a formula for self-sufficiency, worked out over so many centuries.

But there were so many mouths to feed. The number sitting down to *polenta* –a dish of maize flour – was rarely less than thirty. Besides Giovanni Battista and his brood, there was his cousin Luigi who had ten children. Then there were the survivors of an earlier generation like Zaverio. Their whole economy was vulnerable to the hazards of the weather, price fluctuations, and to international trade factors that were entirely beyond their control. They were poor because they were dependent.

The main consequence of their poverty was that there were too many of them in too small a space. They lived on top of each other, and there were sometimes demarcation disputes. Without some sense of Providence, they could hardly have borne it. Another child meant another mouth to feed. But Angelo liked to recall the old Lombardy proverb, 'God blesses the pots when they are big'. And he exhorted them in one of his earliest letters home to see the hand of God in their poverty. 'We must never feel saddened by the very straitened circumstances in which we live; we must be patient, look above and think of paradise . . . Think of what the good Jesus did and suffered for us. He endured great poverty, he worked from morning to night' (*Journal*, pp. 253–4).

The Roncallis worked 'from morning to night', being woken in the morning by the Angelus bell from the village church or the Franciscan convent at Baccanello. His mother Marianna was the chief waker-up: 'Time to get up, Angelo, "The Angel of the Lord declared unto Mary"' (*Secolo*, p. 27). He gave the ritual answer: 'And she conceived by the Holy Spirit. Hail Mary, full of grace . . .'

As pope, Roncalli looked back on his childhood with affection but without romanticism:

> We were poor, but happy with our lot and confident in the help of Providence. There was never any bread on our table, only *polenta;* no wine for the children and young people; only at Christmas and Easter did we have a slice of home-made cake. Clothes, and shoes for going to church, had to last for years and years . . . And yet when a beggar appeared at the door of our kitchen, when the children – twenty of them – were waiting impatiently for their bowl of *minestra* [vegetable soup], there was always room for him, and my mother would hasten to seat this stranger alongside us (*Familiari*, I, p. 8).

The Roncallis knew their bible: 'Do not neglect to show hospitality to strangers, for thereby some have entertained angels unawares' (Hebrews 13.2). They treated the stranger as a Christian brother.

It was a traditional, patriarchal society that would change more in Angelo's lifetime than it had in the previous 400 years. Life was monotonous and laborious. But it had the rhythm of the changing seasons and took colour from the liturgical year. They celebrated the great feasts of the Christian calendar and went annually on pilgrimage by donkey-cart to the Madonna del Bosco (Our Lady of the Woods) across the River Adda (*Secolo* p. 27). But besides the feasts of Christmas, Easter and Pentecost, almost every month had its special 'devotion'. January was for the child Jesus; March, St Joseph; June, the Sacred Heart; July, the Precious Blood; October, the Rosary; November, the 'faithful departed'.

They were a close-knit family, the Roncallis, the largest in the village, but they were undemonstrative. 'Our old people were a little gruff [*burberi*]', Angelo later wrote to his brother Giuseppe, 'but they were serious-minded and good' (*Familiari*, I, p. 565). The same day he wrote to his sisters: 'In our family we are not much given to external shows of tenderness. And it's better that way' (*Familiari*, I, p. 566). The men of Sotto il Monte had a practical, matter-of-fact attitude to marriage and children. They expected their women to be industrious and reliable. Emotion was diffused in daily fidelity.

The first important date in Angelino's life came when he was eighteen months. His brother Zaverio was born on May 12, 1883. Each Roncalli baby slept and was suckled in the matrimonial bed, moving out only when the next child came along. So, as Roncalli put it, 'when the child [himself] no longer needed his mother, it was grand-uncle Zaverio who looked after him and shared with him, by word and example, the attractive power of his religious spirit' (*Secolo*, p. 25).

Henceforward, Zaverio took charge of him. Zaverio was already fifty-nine (he lived to 88), had never had a family of his own, and, says Angelo, 'devoted himself to his godson, without intending to make a priest of him' (*Secolo*, p. 25). Zaverio, more usually known as Barba, was a reading man, and through him the whole family was kept in touch with a wider religious world. He was involved in the beginnings of Catholic Action in Bergamo. He read the *Bollettino Salesiano* published by Don (later Saint) John Bosco in Milan and was a 'cooperator' of the Salesians, a member of their 'extended family' (*Secolo*, p. 25). Zaverio cut out of the *Bollettino Salesiano* a picture of 'Our Lady Auxiliatrix' and placed it above Angelo's bed (*Secolo*, p. 34).

But Angelo's mother, Marianna, still played an essential role in his life. His earliest distinct memory is of her. It can be dated very precisely: November 21, 1885, feast of Mary's Presentation in the Temple. She set off for the shrine of the Madonna delle Caneve (or delle cantine). It was only about a kilometre away, but the track towards it wound slightly uphill, and she had to coax along Teresa, 6, Ancilla, 5, Angelo, 4, while carrying Zaverio, 2, in one arm and Maria Elisa, 1, in the other. She was also pregnant again. By the time they reached the shrine Mass had already started and the tiny chapel was packed out. Unable to enter, she lifted up her children one by one and let them look through the grille of the window so that they could see the Madonna (*Secolo*, p. 47). Seventy-six years later, the whole episode was still fresh in the mind of Pope John. He recounted it to a group of pilgrims:

> The shrine of the Madonna in my native village is at the end of a rough track, among the
> trees, at a point where one can go no further. It is still a place of pilgrimage today,
> especially for young people going off for military service or emigrants setting off to
> look for work. And old people go there too, so they can remember the kindness of Mary
> and renew their hope . . . My mother lifted me up and said: 'Look, Angelino, look how
> beautiful the Madonna is. I have consecrated you wholly to her'. This is the first clear
> memory that I have of my childhood (*Rosario*, pp. 15–16).

Marianna was then 28. He loved her with simplicity until her death and beyond: 'What a mother! what a simple and lucid conscience, that she kept into extreme old age, loved and venerated by her ten children and the whole parish' (*Secolo*, p.25).

At the age of five (or six) Angelino learned his first poem by heart:

Quanto è soave al cuore	How sweet to the heart
il nome tuo, Maria.	is your name, Mary.
Ogni dolcezza mia	Every joy I have
Da quel tuo nome vien,	comes from your name.
Che bella idea di amore	What a fine idea of love
da quel tuo nome appresi	I learned from your name.
che bei desiri accesi	What fine desires are kindled
mi vien destando in sen.	and awakened in my breast.

He still knew it by heart in the last year of his life. A month before the Council began, he wrote it down in his Journal and explained:

These lines are the beginning of the first poem I knew as a child, and I learned it from the Second Reader then in use in the village school. I did my first year's schooling in the old village schoolhouse at the right-hand corner of the so-called Piazza, as you come from Guardina. Opposite was the shop of Rosa Bonanomi and her sister, Marianna, who was an invalid. That must have been in 1886 or 1887. The next year, with the completion of the school buildings, the new school was opened at Bercio, and I was among the first to attend it (*Journal*, p. 347).

The 'new' school was the result of the Casati law on public education. Primary education, but for three years only, became in principle universal and compulsory; and state schools replaced the hit-or-miss system of parish schools.

Thus in 1888, when nearing seven, Angelino unwittingly found himself caught in ideological cross-fire. The new state schools were designed to forge a new national consciousness. While raising educational standards, they would also overcome the 'regionalism' that flourished in Italy and transform it into a truly modern state. The physical unity of the peninsula had been achieved with the final collapse of the Papal States in 1870; it remained to bring about its psychological unity. Thanks partly to the intransigence of Pius IX who declared himself 'the prisoner of the Vatican' and forbade Catholics, in a famous phrase, to be 'either electors or elected', the new Italian 'Establishment' was liberal and anti-clerical. Garibaldi, a notorious Freemason, had called his horse Mastai – Pius IX's family name. Schoolteachers were in the front-line of the battle for a new Italy, freed from ignorance and superstition.

The man entrusted with this mission in Sotto il Monte was Oprandi Guerrina complete with monocle and side-burns and nicknamed Orbì. It was uphill work. Orbì had to teach the first three years together. He found the peasant children stubborn and slow on the uptake. His brightest pupil, Angelo Roncalli, was already under the spell of the parish priest, and preferred church to school. One incident is recorded. An essential feature of the Casati law on education was that schools should be regularly inspected. The inspector arrived at Sotto il Monte and asked the class: 'Which is heavier, a quintal of straw or a quintal of iron?'

'A quintal of iron', chorused the class, except for Angelo who said they weighed the same: a quintal is a quintal (Cugini, p. 37). It was not evidence of any great precocity. But he was different.

Signor Orbì was fighting a losing battle. Angelo was already serving early morning Mass daily. In 1888 'Uncle' Zaverio was the only member of the parish to go to Rome for the fiftieth anniversary of Pope Leo XIII's priestly ordination. Angelo begged to be allowed to accompany him, but was considered too young (Cugini, p. 37). This was one of the first mass pilgrimages, made possible by the spread of the railways, which persuaded Leo that the workers wanted him to say something on 'the social question'; three years later, he published the encyclical *Rerum Novarum*, the 'workers' charter'.

Eighteen eighty-nine was a most important year for Angelo. On February 13 he was confirmed by Mgr Camillo Guindani, bishop of Bergamo, at Carvico, the next-door parish. Two weeks later, March 3, *Laetare* Sunday, he made his first Communion. This was an exceptional privilege, since it was only later, in the pontificate of Pius X, that children were encouraged to make their first Communion so young. He remembered the day well:

> I was allowed to make my first communion at the age of eight, without any special ceremony, on a cold Lenten morning, in the Church of Santa Maria di Brusicco. Only the children, the parish priest, Rebuzzini, and his curate, Don Bortolo Locatelli, were present. I like to recall one detail which remained in my heart.
>
> After the ceremony the neo-communicants went to the presbytery to be inscribed one by one in the Apostleship of Prayer; and Fr Rebuzzini gave me the honour of writing out the list of names of my companions. This was the first writing exercise I can remember doing, the first page of so many that would proliferate in half a century of living with pen in hand (*Secolo*, p. 26).

The Apostleship of Prayer had been founded by the French Jesuit, Henri Ramière in 1861. Its members pledged themselves to say the 'Morning Offering' every day. They offered all the 'prayers, works and sufferings' of the coming day for some intention (e.g. the 'foreign missions') approved by the Pope. It was another bond with the 'lonely prisoner of the Vatican'. It was also a way of sanctifying everyday happenings.

One of Angelo's playmates was a girl cousin, possibly Camilla, daughter of Luigi. One day, as an adventure, they crept up a creaking staircase to see a dead old woman. They found her lying there in a darkened room, lit only by an oil lamp, her mouth agape, the last remaining tooth visible. Curiosity turned to terror. They fled (Cugini, pp. 32–3).

Angelo's father, Giovanni, played little part in his life. He was eclipsed by other 'father-figures', first Zaverio and then, increasingly, by Fr Rebuzzini. Giovanni, with his crew-cut hair and moustache, was austere and the least demonstrative member of the family. Angelo remembered him as an exemplar of industry and goodness: 'My father is a peasant who spends his days digging and hoeing, among other things, and I, far from being better than my father, am worth much less, for my father is at least simple and good, while I am full of malice' (*Journal*, p. 92). This remark, made in the fervour of a retreat at the Roman seminary in 1902, tells us more about himself than about his father.

But there is one sun-lit memory of his father which remained with him till his death. On August 6, 1889, they walked together the six kilometres to Ponte San Pietro for the eleventh feast of the Bergamo Catholic Action. The church was large, resplendent with gold, lit by innumerable candles. For a child it was a magical spectacle. But Angelo was too small to see the parade, so his father hoisted him onto his shoulders. Pope John recalled the incident when, for the first time, on November 4, 1958, he appeared on the *sedia gestatoria* (or portable papal chair): 'Once again I am being carried, carried aloft by my sons. More than seventy years ago I was carried on the shoulders of my father at Ponte San Pietro . . . The secret of everything is to let oneself be carried by God, and so to carry Him [to others]' (*Letture*, pp. 53–4).

The Catholic Action rally at Ponte San Pietro on that sweltering August day is a reminder that the diocese of Bergamo pioneered this form of Christian 'presence to the world'. Catholics, on papal orders, had withdrawn from the official political life of Italy. But they remained concerned about 'social problems' and invented a network of movements to work for justice. Italian unification had not brought prosperity to the peasants and the working-class. High taxation and growing unemployment in the 1880s led to emigration, and the statistics in Angelo's boyhood told the grim story: 1880, 20,000 emigrants; 1887, 127,000; 1888, 196,000. When Catholics pointed out that the lot of peasants and workers was worse than before unification, they were accused of 'clerical demagogy' (Fonzi, p. 80). An alliance began to develop between the 'intransigents' – those Catholics who felt that the Pope had been ill-treated – and the peasants and workers.

Thus, although Italian Catholicism of the 1880s was still associated with the reactionary conservatism that had marked the pontificate of Pius IX, it was beginning to have a potential for changing society. Angelo wrote the following note for Zaverio's funeral card: 'He was truly the "upright man" of Holy Scripture . . . Throughout the vicissitudes of a turbulent age, to the end he held fervently and affectionately to the enthusiasm of his youth: devotion to the Sacred Heart, the cause of Christ, the Church and the Pope, and he was a humble but convinced apostle of Catholic Action in this rural milieu' (*Familiari* I, p. 34).

A typical institution of rural Catholic Action was the credit bank. It took the Roncallis twenty more years to save enough to get a mortgage on their own house and farm. Some critics thought that Pope John's encyclical, *Mater et Magistra*, gave a disproportionate amount of space to agricultural problems. Now we know why.

Angelo later confessed that 'he could never remember the time when he didn't want to be a priest'. The first person he told about it was his cousin Camilla. Angelo was both alarmed and delighted at the idea. He had observed Fr Francesco Rebuzzini very carefully, noting the way in hot weather the rigid white collar pressed round the neck and sweat gathered. But Rebuzzini had also been observing Angelo. One day he said to him: 'Don't be a priest, Angelino. You see how high and sharp this collar is. It digs into the neck and sometimes really hurts' (Cugini, p. 33). So he'd already guessed.

Rebuzzini had been at Sotto il Monte since 1872 and was to die there. Angelo never forgot the text, alleged to be from St Bernard, which hung on the wall of Rebuzzini's study:

> Peace within the cell; fierce warfare without.
> Hear all; believe a few; honour all.
> Do not believe everything you hear;
> Do not judge everything you see;

> Do not do everything you can;
> Do not give everything you have;
> Do not say everything you know.
> Pray, read, withdraw, be silent, be at peace (*Journal*, p. 440).

Christian faith is here turned into a 'practical wisdom'. Rebuzzini was not to know it, but it was the perfect formula for a Vatican diplomat.

Meanwhile in 1890, Rebuzzini looked on as Zaverio arranged for Angelo to have Latin lessons with Don Pietro Bolis, parish priest of Carvico. An impressive and rather frightening man, with huge hands, he spared neither rod nor child. Angelo remembered this year with dread: 'After a few Latin lessons the merciless Don Bolis invited me to translate Book I of Caesar's *Gallic War*. I had to translate and find the nominatives and the accusatives, and if I made a mistake, he gave me a slap. Sometimes he made me kneel down outside as a punishment for an error' (Cugini, p. 39). After a year of blows and Caesar, Angelo, nearly nine, was considered ready to go as a day boy to the episcopal college at Celana, founded by St Charles Borromeo as a pre-junior seminary. This meant leaving home for the first time and staying with relatives at Ca' di Rizzi di Pontida. Even though he came back home for the weekends, he felt keenly the pain of parting and described it fifty years later to console a cousin who had left home to become a Sacred Heart sister: 'My father came with me as far as the Faida woods, just before the Villa d'Adda, where he left me to make my own way to Celana. I was alone in the woods and it was cold and, thinking of the warmth of the family I had just left, I felt for the first time the pain of separation' (*Familiari* I, p. 561). He pulled himself together. But he added that each time he returned home to Sotto il Monte

> My heart was endangered, and I had to leave as quickly as possible so as not to reveal my inner emotion. And it is right that this should happen. We are made to love each other eternally. It goes without saying that this feeling should find expression and be a cause of sorrow. Thus we merit the sweetness of final reconciliation (*Familiari*, I, p. 561).

It was an unhappy year. Angelo was younger than the rest of his class. He still had to walk six kilometres daily there and back. His Latin master, he recalled, 'managed to make me forget what little I knew: it was a disaster' (Cugini, p. 47). So to spare him the humiliation of failure in the end-of-term exams his parents brought him home.

At this point Don Rebuzzini took over. Throughout the summer of 1892 he acted as Angelo's tutor and prepared him properly for entry into the junior seminary at Bergamo. It now became apparent that he had a taste and an aptitude for study that his previous teachers had failed to awaken. This period also brought them closer together. Rebuzzini had before him a ten-year-old who was setting off to the seminary just as he had done in the 1840s; and Angelo had found his father-figure.

Even so he remained deeply attached to his family. In 1930 he wrote to his parents: 'Ever since I left home, towards the age of ten, I have read many books and learned many things that you could not have taught me. But what I learned from you remains the most precious and important, and it sustains and gives life to the many other things I learned later in so many years of study and teaching' (*Secolo*, p. 28).

Chapter 2

A Counter-Reformation seminary

In the art of your native city, you had already found all the lessons needed by
a diplomat. Your painters, above all the great portrait painter Lorenzo Lotto,
had taught you psychology; the statue of Torquato Tasso, reminding you of
the beauty of your hills, evoked the poetry of far-away lands; and the tomb
of Colleoni contained the remains of a man of heroic wisdom. Your love of
history led you to interest yourself in the glorious series of Bishops of
Bergamo. (President Vincent Auriol, January 15, 1953, *Mission to France*,
pp. 181–2)

Hardly anything remains of the Bergamo seminary, junior and senior, where Angelo Roncalli arrived as a boarder in November 1893, shortly before his twelfth birthday. It was rebuilt on a lavish scale in 1964. As pope he was to have consecrated the new chapel, but he
died before it was completed. But the old chapel remains, its dome the highest point of
the hill-top city. Inside it has been much re-arranged, the position of the altar has been
changed, and so Our Lady in Glory now looks down from the painted vault sideways on.

Yet the old chapel, with its heady evocative smells of incense and flowers, remains the best
link with Angelo Roncalli and the seminary founded by St Charles Borromeo, archbishop of
Milan, who had been canonised in 1610 as 'the model of a bishop according to the Council of
Trent'. Roncalli later wrote the history of the Bergamo seminary: work on it plunged him into
his favourite historical period, the Counter-Reformation in Lombardy. After all, the city of
Trent was only a hundred kilometres away. But what he later wrote about, he first experienced.

Trent brought about a revolution in studies for the priesthood. It invented the seminary
or 'seed-plot' as a place of formation, spiritual and theological, for future priests. It caught
them young. It segregated them from 'the world'. It tried to protect them from whatever was
troublesome or tempting. The very first entry in Angelo's journal is a transcription of Trent's
Decretum de reformatione, canon 1, on the 'model priest':

It is in every way fitting that clergy who have been called to the service of the Lord
should so order their lives and habits that in their dress, gestures, gait and conversation
and all other matters they show nothing that is not grave, controlled and full of religious
feeling; and let them also avoid minor faults, which in them would be very great, so that
their actions may win the respect of all (*Journal*, p. 4).

The second entry in Angelo's journal is a quotation from Ecclesiasticus 3.27: 'It is good for
a man to bear the yoke in his youth' (*Journal*, p. 4). He began his journal in 1895, at the age of
fourteen, and kept up the practice for the rest of his life. Eighty printed pages are devoted to
the minor seminary at Bergamo. It is the most fully documented period of his life. He began

9

his journal on the advice of Canon Luigi Isacchi (1839–98), who held the office of spiritual director. Its purpose was three-fold: to remind himself of his resolutions, to record his moments of grace or spiritual insight, and to maintain a critical weather-eye on his faults and back-slidings. The latter function tended to prevail.

He was not writing for posterity. We can only eavesdrop on his inner conversation. The portrait that emerges is of a serious-minded, intense, painfully scrupulous adolescent, tempted only by gossip or *gourmandise*. His aim in life is to become a holy priest. The only 'events' were the tonsure, June 28, 1895, by which he became officially a 'cleric'; the minor orders of door-keeper and reader, July 3, 1898; the minor orders of exorcist and acolyte, June 25, 1899. He led a sheltered life on which public events hardly impinged: no newspapers were allowed. The seminary was a fortress, a self-contained world of its own.

But his self-portrait is incomplete. Simply to live in Bergamo was a liberal education. History lay about him as he walked round the city, never without a companion. The seminary was at the highest point of the upper city with its narrow streets, tiny squares, massive sixteenth century walls, plashing fountains, and everywhere the lion rampant of St Mark as a reminder that Bergamo had known Venetian rule for 350 years. Looking down from the seminary garden, Angelo saw the new city, with its broad, tree-lined avenues, the railway station linking Bergamo to Milan and Brescia, and the textile factories beyond.

Roncalli came to love Bergamo and would talk endlessly about its beauties. In his walks around the city, in cassock and soup-plate hat, he was laying the foundations for that intimate knowledge of its churches and piazzas that would console him in exile and sustain his research. It is true, that, as a seminarian, he had to keep 'custody of the eyes', another form of self-discipline. He resolved to behave 'with the greatest decorum when I am passing through towns or other places full of people, never looking at posters or illustrations or shops which might contain indecent objects, bearing in mind the words of Ecclesiasticus, "Do not look around in the streets of the city; nor wander about its deserted sections" ' (*Journal*, p. 17).

The bishop of Bergamo, Camillo Guindani, lived at this date in the seminary fortress. Looking out from its ramparts, he saw rather more than Angelo. He knew that the problems of contemporary Bergamo were not knife-drawing or gaming in the streets so much as strikes and lock-outs. Guindani was a leader in social action. In 1893 he published a full commentary on Leo XIII's *Rerum Novarum* which stressed the novelty of this somewhat ambivalent encyclical and applied it to the local circumstances.

It really was astonishing. Bergamo's claim to lead Catholic Action in Italy was vindicated. Professor Niccolò Rezzara, put in charge of social action, reported that the diocese had over 200 associations with over 40,000 members. They included 50 study circles, 104 mutual assistance projects, 43 co-operatives and credit banks (Dreyfus, p. 32). In this way the Church in Bergamo, though still excluded from politics, demonstrated that it was concerned for justice as well as charity. It sought to serve the poorest members of society, victims of the unrestrained *laissez-faire* capitalism deplored by *Rerum Novarum*. If, in the process, it dished the socialists, that was a bonus, not the aim. Angelo was already inscribed in the diocese of Bergamo as a 'cleric'; if he wanted to be a priest in the diocese his theology would have to have a social dimension. 'Uncle' Zaverio had disposed him to understand that. There was already talk of 'Christian democracy'.

From the time he began to think about it, Angelo was spontaneously 'conciliarist', a term used for those who held that the pope should cease sighing for the *ancien régime*, accept the loss of the Papal States as a liberation for the Church, and permit Catholics to take their place in Italian political life. Seen in this light, Catholic Action and the lay movement known as *Opera dei Congressi* were a dress-rehearsal for the return to full political involvement. But that was not the mood in the Vatican where 'intransigence' still prevailed.

Angelo caught a glimpse of the Italian Church as a whole in September 1895 when he visited Milan for the third National Eucharistic Congress. It was a display of Catholic muscle as well as an act of piety. There he saw for the first time Cardinal Andrea Ferrari, archbishop of Milan, his metropolitan and later spiritual guide. Also present among a galaxy of cardinals was Giuseppe Sarto, patriarch of Venice and the future St Pius X.

Back in the seminary after this excursion, Angelo devised his own 'Rules of Life'. He maps out what he has to do daily, weekly, monthly, annually, concluding with a final section devoted to 'at all times'. Angelo's 'Rules of Life' were rules for life. Capovilla says: 'He copied them out by hand, in minute writing, kept them always by him and constantly observed them, even when he was Pope' (*Journal*, p. 4). So however fastidious the exercise, some account of his 'Rules of Life' must be given here. They mattered so much to Angelo.

Daily he devoted 'at least a quarter of an hour to mental prayer' on rising. He heard or preferably served Mass, read 'thoughtfully' a whole chapter of *The Imitation of Christ*, examined his conscience and prepared the next day's meditation before going to bed. In addition there were visits to the Blessed Sacrament, five Hail Marys and Our Fathers 'between six and nine o'clock in the evening in honour of the five wounds' (of Jesus on the cross), not to mention 'brief, fervent invocations'. He says nothing about his studies in the 'Rules of Life' but in 1896 seemed to regard them as an opportunity for ascetical self-denial: 'As regards studies I will apply myself to them with love and enthusiasm to the best of my abilities, taking care to give due attention to all subjects without distinction, never offering the excuse that I do not like any of them' (*Journal*, p. 14).

His *weekly* tasks included confession and communion. The fact that he went to Mass daily but to Communion only weekly was a relic of Jansenist influence in Bergamo: Pius X opened the way to daily communion a decade later. He fasted on Fridays and Saturdays, when he would also perform some penance.

Monthly he saw his spiritual director, set aside a day 'for more profound recollection' and reflection on how well he was keeping his rules. He invited one of the most 'exemplary and zealous youths' to tell him 'with frankness and charity about any faults he had noticed'. He also chose a special patron saint for each month.

Annually, he would make a retreat in the seminary, choosing Carnival time in order to be praying harder while the world revelled. He would make an annual general confession. A touch of humanity comes in with the resolution at the end of term 'to give some souvenir to his companions and accept one from them, to help us all pass the time profitably in the Lord' (*Journal*, p. 7). Roncalli was, in fact, always good at remembering anniversaries and feast-days, and performing small thoughtful kindnesses. Life, as the spiritual writers said, is made up of little things.

Angelo stated his project in his 'Rules of Life'. But it was threatened on all sides. 'Occasions of sin' lay in wait to entrap him. Life became a kind of obstacle-race in which coming through unscathed was the goal. His seminary companions posed the first threat, because dangerous 'particular friendships' might arise. So he counter-attacks: 'On no account or pretext must you use the intimate *tu* in talking together or lay your hands on each other, or run after, push or strike each other, even in jest' (*Journal*, p. 7). He exhorts himself to avoid 'those whose speech contains impure suggestions, filthy or cynical words, or dialect expressions' (*Journal*, p. 7). Later he relented a little about dialect and the intimate *tu*, but he remained punctilious in such matters.

Women generally represented a major source of trouble. So they too were simply to be avoided, *vitandae*. Nor was he talking merely about seductresses, *femmes fatales* or women of the streets. The ban also applied to relatives and 'holy women': 'I will be particularly cautious, avoiding their familiarity, company or conversation, especially if they are young women. Nor will I ever fix my eye on their faces, mindful of what the Holy Spirit teaches us: "Do not look intently at a virgin, lest you stumble and incur penalties for her" '(*Journal*, p. 18). This was yet another quotation from Ecclesiasticus (9.5).

Even his sleep was supervised. He dealt with the problem of what moralists called 'involuntary nocturnal emissions' in the recommended manner:

> I will likewise observe the greatest modesty with regard to my own body at all times . . . To remove any occasion for these movements, however innocent, at night before falling asleep, I will place the rosary of the Blessed Virgin round my neck, fold my arms crosswise on my breast, and see that I find myself still lying in that position in the morning (*Journal*, p. 18).

In this way, he believed, he would remain 'pure as an angel'. And since self-indulgence in one realm of physical appetites so easily leads to laxity in another, he will be austere in eating and drinking as well: 'Wine and women lead intelligent men astray' (*Journal*, p. 18). Inevitably this is another quote from Ecclesiasticus (19.2).

Clearly Angelo had a long way to go to reach spiritual and human maturity. But his mature spirituality was a development, not a rejection, of his seminary formation. He led a rigorously structured and regimented life, but he was also assimilating values. At the age of fourteen he already knew that fidelity to the discovered will of God was at the heart of the Gospel. So he could write: 'Let your will be mine, and let my will ever respond to yours, in perfect harmony. Let me desire what you desire and hate what you hate, and let me desire and hate nothing but what you desire and hate.' (*Journal*, p. 11). In maturity he would quote St Gregory Nazianzen: *Voluntas Dei, pax nostra* (God's will is our peace). In adolescence he characteristically preferred to quote Thomas à Kempis: 'You are the true peace of the heart, you are its only resting place . . . In this peace, in this very peace which is yourself the one, supreme, eternal God, I will sleep and rest' (*Journal*, p. 11; *Imitation*, Book 3, ch. 15). On this point he never wavered; it provided the contemplative ground-base of his life.

There is no evidence to suggest that Angelo was miserable at the seminary. Life was austere, but he was where he wanted to be. On the other hand the long summer holidays spent with his family at La Colombera – they had moved to this nearby but larger eighteen-roomed house on November 21, 1893 – proved increasingly irksome. He had a growing sense of misunderstanding and alienation. The root of the trouble was that some members of his family thought he 'wanted to be a priest to escape having to work on the land' (*Familiari* I, pp. 482–3).

The first sign of trouble came in June 1898. A busybody Franciscan from Baccanello, who was always dropping in at La Colombera, picked up the domestic gossip. It was said that Marianna was giving her eldest son preferential treatment and choicer food. Angelo was not enjoying his holiday anyway. He resented the constant bickering, and was frustrated at not being able to write for two days running, first because he had no candle and then because he had no ink (*Journal*, p. 38). The Franciscan took it into his head to delate Angelo to the rector of the seminary. Angelo noted: 'My superiors have received an account, I think exaggerated, of my having behaved arrogantly during the vacation, and I have been duly rebuked. So I have had to humble myself against my will' (*Journal*, p. 25). The atmosphere of La Colombera was subtly poisoned. Home was no longer the same.

He could always turn to Don Rebuzzini, his old teacher, the parish priest. On Saturday evening, September 24, 1898, he met Rebuzzini and exchanged routine greetings with him. But next morning, while preparing for Mass, Don Rebuzzini tried to kneel down, fell back on his head, and died. Angelo saw him lying there on the ground, 'his mouth open and red with blood, his eyes closed' (*Journal*, p. 49). He seemed 'like a statue of the dead Jesus, after he had been taken down from the cross'. This was not just pious hyperbole: the theme of the priest as *alter Christus*, another Christ, was commonplace in Counter-Reformation piety.

Angelo felt orphaned by the death. The expression occurs three times within a few pages of his journal. 'I am left an orphan to my immense loss' (*Journal*, p. 51), he wrote. In 1962, rereading his account of the death of Rebuzzini, he added a heading in which he called him 'the saintly guardian of my childhood and vocation' (*Journal*, p. 52). Don Rebuzzini was his first 'model' of the priesthood – and he found that he could not improve on it. Rebuzzini had spent the last twenty-six years of his life at Sotto il Monte. The life of an obscure diocesan priest, living contentedly in this insignificant pre-Alpine village, could be a path to holiness that put into perspective ecclesiastical ambition and careerism.

Don Rebuzzini bequeathed to him his copy of the *Imitation of Christ*, a Latin edition, published in Venice in 1745. Or to be more truthful, Angelo managed to purloin the book while the effects were being cleared up ('I have succeeded in obtaining' – *Journal*, p. 51). The *Imitation of Christ* is the most widely diffused and translated book of spirituality ever published, and Angelo treasured this well-thumbed copy because Francesco Rebuzzini had used it since he was a seminarian.

Angelo returned to the seminary and began his theology on November 3, 1898. On May 21, 1899, he preached his first sermon. It was largely a stylistic exercise, intended only for his peers. It was the eve of Pentecost. His appointed theme was 'Mary in the Cenacle'. He began:

> This place, which gathers us for prayer and study, our seminary, *is* the upper room, the cenacle. We who live here in the exercise of ecclesiastical virtues, our gaze fixed on the altar, *are* the new apostles who, renewing the miracles of the first Pentecost will lead back the scattered sheep to the sweet embrace of Jesus, the Good Shepherd (*Rosario*, p. 89).

No great claims need be made for this, but he anticipates his prayer for the Council so many years later: 'Renew thy wonders in this day, as by a new Pentecost' (Abbott, p. 793). Thereafter his sermon wanders off into a prose poem about the dawn breaking over the

Vatican Hill to illumine the white hairs of a valiant old man – Leo XIII – and then, sweeping over the Mediterranean, it lights up a grotto in a hillside. We have arrived in Lourdes, and this is Mary, arising like the dawn. Angelo was quoting the Canticle of Canticles 6.10: 'Who is this that looks forth like the dawn, fair as the moon, bright as the sun?'

September 17, 1899, was a turning-point in his life, though no one knew it at the time. He had escaped from the oppressive atmosphere of La Colombera and walked the five kilometres to Ghaïe di Bonate Sopra for a celebration in honour of Our Lady of Sorrows. The parish priest, Alessandro Locatelli, had befriended him after the death of Don Rebuzzini. While he was there, Mgr Giacomo Radini Tedeschi, a canon of St Peter's Rome at the age of forty-two, turned up. He and Locatelli had taught together in Bergamo. Locatelli, forty-nine, was a modest parish priest, while at forty-two Radini Tedeschi already had an important national role: he was animator of the *Opera dei Congressi*, the umbrella movement for Catholic social action, and he was organising the mass pilgrimages for the coming Holy Year of 1900. He radiated energy and excitement. In Rome he was talked about as a future Secretary of State. If Angelo were to go to Rome he could join Radini's study and action group, the *Circolo dell'Immaculata* (Our Lady's Club) (*My Bishop*, p. 32). But at this stage going to Rome was a distant mirage. It wasn't something he could choose to do. Still, he had made his first contact with an influential member of the Roman Curia. Since there was no orderly 'career structure' in the Church, much depended on the old-boy network and chance meetings.

In the seminary he was beginning to pick up minor posts of responsibility. Early in 1900 he was put in charge of Gregorian chant or plain-song. He was also 'prefect' which meant that he had to keep an eye on his companions. One of his charges, referred to only by his initials, A.G., later abandoned the ministry, and Roncalli traced the beginnings of trouble to the Bergamo seminary. A.G. in 1900 was spending 'entire days with eyes cast down so much so that he would not look his companions in the eyes at recreation' (*Pasqua*, 1976, p. 51). Angelo intervened:

> I warned him that custody of the eyes could never be excessive while out walking or in his contacts with the outside world, but that the rigorism he practised was out of place within the seminary; that it would not last; that it would be a tyranny to live for ever in this way; and that he should avoid excess in everything other than the love of God (*Pasqua*, 1976, p. 52).

This was written in 1932. Hindsight may be at work in the editing of his memories. But it suggests that his assimilation of seminary values was neither wooden nor mechanical. He knew about the perils of inhuman 'straining'.

But while Angelo was advancing on all fronts at the seminary, at home a crisis was brewing in the summer of 1900. While everyone else was out in the vineyards, he was at his books but 'although I racked my brains to try to study with some profit, I could not get anything done. I felt out of sorts with everything, bored stiff with sermons and reading, with everything in fact' (*Journal*, p. 80). Five days later, on August 29, 1900, a most painful incident occurred. The precise details elude us, but the journal conveys the feeling:

> My mother was rather hurt by something I said (which, I confess, might have been put

more gently) rebuking her curiosity about a certain matter. She was deeply offended, and said things to me that I would never have expected to hear from my mother for whom, after God, Mary and the saints, I bear the greatest love of which my heart is capable. To hear her tell me that I am always uncivil with her, without gentleness or good manners, when I feel that I can say with all sincerity that this is not true, has hurt me too deeply; she was distressed because of me, but I was very much more distressed to see her grieving and, to put it bluntly, giving way like that. After so much tender love, to be told by my mother that I dislike her, and other things that I have not the heart to remember any longer, oh, this was too much for the heart of a son, and of a son who feels the most profound natural affection (*Journal*, p. 82).

From now on he would be less dependent on his mother. It is interesting that he did not think of appealing to his father to smooth out the misunderstanding. He was growing up, and growing away.

Perhaps to cheer him up, the curate at Sotto il Monte, Don Ignazio Valsecchi, subsidised a Rome journey for the Holy Year pilgrimage from September 12 to 19, 1900. For the first time he saw Rome and the ninety-year-old Pope Leo XIII. It was a particularly tense moment. As September 20, thirtieth anniversary of the breach of Porta Pia which signalled the end of the Papal States, came round, the anti-clericals intensified their campaign against the Pope. Rival demonstrations were organised round the statue of Giordano Bruno in the Campo dei Fiori where he had been burned as a heretic in 1600. It was enough to make anyone intransigent. But Angelo reflected on the papacy in the light of St Gregory the Great: 'Before this majestic figure, I feel renewed enthusiasm and affection for the Pope, the great Leo XIII, against whom the most grievous, wicked and diabolical insults are being hurled these days' (*Journal*, p. 83).

On his way back from Rome he stopped at Assisi with its vivid memories of St Francis, and at Loreto. On the eve of the Council, in October 1962, he redid these pilgrimages and recalled his first visit to Loreto in 1900. On September 20 he received Communion at two o'clock in the afternoon and 'poured out my soul in prolonged and deeply moved prayer'. But the 'painful circumstances of the time . . . turned the pilgrimage to bitterness'. He had to shut his ears to the mocking gibes coming from the square outside the basilica (*Rosario*, p. 138).

Good news awaited him when he returned from Loreto. He was invited by Bishop Guindani to sit for a Rome scholarship exam. This had been founded in 1640 by Canon Flaminio Cerasola to provide for ten to fifteen Bergamesque theology students at the Roman College (*Secolo*, p. 120). Angelo passed and was accepted. His fellow-students, as a thank-you gift for the way he had fulfilled the office of prefect, presented him with the four Latin volumes of the *Treatise on the Church of Christ* by Fr Louis Billot S.J.

After the safe haven of Bergamo, Angelo hoped to find 'the stimulus of research' in Rome. We do not know what his exact feelings were. His seminary journal, unaccountably, dries up at this point. Its last words had been written on September 7, 1900: 'Recollection, prayer and, for the rest, holy joy' (*Journal*, p. 84).

Chapter 3

A Roman education

There is no other social organism which so attracts and absorbs a man as the
Church of Rome. Rome remains always greater than any Roman, whether
he be Roman by birth or Roman by service. (Don Giuseppe De Luca, *Il
Cardinale Bonaventura Cerretti*, p. 89)

Angelo arrived in Rome by the overnight train from Bergamo at 6.30 a.m. on January 4,
1901. With him were two other Bergamo scholarship winners, Achille Ballini and Gugliel-
mo Carozzi. At this time there were two Romes which stared at each other uneasily. There
was the Rome that had become the capital of Italy in 1871. It was symbolised by the new
public buildings on the Via Nazionale and the frock-coated statesmen who strutted in stone
along the Corso Vittorio Emanuele. On the Capitoline Hill the monument to King Victor
Emmanuel, known officially as 'the altar of the nation' but popularly as 'the wedding-cake',
was already rising allegedly to challenge the dome of St Peter's. This 'Rome of the Freemasons' contrasted with ecclesiastical Rome, city of the catacombs, drenched in the blood
of martyrs, endowed with innumerable baroque churches (one for every day of the year,
said legend) and religious houses, home of the popes and their civil service, the Roman
Curia. The two Romes were not on speaking terms with each other. That, in essence, was
'the Roman Question' which was not resolved for another thirty years.

Angelo and his two companions clip-clopped along in a horse-drawn carriage from the
station to the Roman seminary in Piazza Sant'Apollinare, just to the east of Piazza Navona
and a good stone's throw from the Tiber. He had a room to himself. The bed was rather hard,
but he thought that no bad thing. He had all he needed: a table, a wardrobe, bookshelves *and*
running water. With a radiator in his room and electric lighting on the streets, introduced
only the previous year, it seemed to him that Rome was in the van of progress and modernity. That, at least, is the impression he gives in his first letter home (*Familiari*, I, pp. 3–5).
Because of his youth – he was only nineteen – he was enrolled in the first year of theology.
The lectures caused him no bother. He already felt like 'an old hand' (*'una persona vecchia del
Seminario'*).

It was not all study. They were allowed out for walks around the city in their purple cassocks, looking like the bishops that most of them, except by misadventure, eventually became. They learned the archaeology and geography of Rome. They sometimes had
meetings with students from other ecclesiastical colleges. On January 10, less than a week
after his arrival Angelo tells his astonished family about going to Propaganda Fide, the missionary college in the Piazza di Spagna, where 'forty clerics recited their own compositions
in forty different languages' and 'some were white, some yellow, some red, and some had

hands and faces as black as coal' (*Familiari*, I, p. 4). If that sounds like Babel, harmony was restored on January 31 when he attended a performance of Lorenzo Perosi's *Il Natale* (Christmas), the Italian answer to Georg Friedrich Handel's *Messiah*.

They even attended special productions of plays which expressed Christian values. On February 17, 1901, Angelo saw a dramatised version of the novel by the Polish writer, Henryk Sienkiewicz, *Quo Vadis? (Cronologia*, p. 518). St Peter, fleeing Rome during Nero's persecution, meets Christ along the way. Peter asks, '*Quo vadis*, where are you going, Lord?' Jesus replies: 'I am going to Rome to be crucified a second time'. Crestfallen, Peter returns to Rome to stand in for Jesus. In 1901 Sienkiewicz's message seemed to be supremely topical. Although in fact Pope Leo XIII would die tranquilly in his bed, it suited Catholics to regard the 'insults' to which he was daily subjected in the liberal press as a form of persecution, unparalleled since the time of Nero.

Angelo rather enjoyed the pomp and pageantry of the Vatican. He liked his ceremonies to be long and grand. He was present in April 1901 when Pope Leo created ten new cardinals, including the Bergamesque, Felici Cavagnis (*Cronologia*, p. 518). Though Leo was unbelievably ninety-one, Angelo learned from him how a proper pope should behave. He tells his parents how, on his first Sunday in Rome, he received a personal blessing from the Pope in St Peter's. He wrote home: 'In that solemn and moving moment, I thought of all of you, and all our relatives, benefactors and friends; and he, the good old man, included all of you in his blessing' (*Familiari*, I, p. 4).

Although Leo XIII, the 'good old man', repeatedly foiled those who predicted his proximate demise, it was evident that he could not live for much longer. 'Informed circles' (that is, clerical gossip) said that his successor would undoubtedly be Cardinal Mariano Rampolla, then Secretary of State and general factotum. Mgr Radini Tedeschi was a protegé of Rampolla, who made him ecclesiastical assistant (in effect chaplain) to the Mary Immaculate Club. Angelo naturally gravitated towards this '*circulo*'. Radini Tedeschi's initiatives included soup kitchens and hostels for the poor as well as recreation centres for soldiers. Angelo found life in Rome exhilarating.

He found the staff of the Roman seminary welcoming. He became a life-long friend of the rector, Mgr Vincenzo Bugarini, and the tutor and from 1902 vice-rector, Mgr Domenico Spolverini. There were 'characters' too, who provided the stuff of anecdotes for later reunions. Don Ignazio Garroni, the bursar, was a 'grumpy but kindly man' who prowled round the refectory vainly urging the students to 'Eat less, eat less' (*Lettere*, p. 86). Angelo was humiliated by having to borrow from him from time to time even though they were only 'small debts' (*Journal*, p. 136). His poverty was real and meant that he had to make do with second-hand reach-me-downs: 'Since I became a seminarian I have never worn a garment that was not given to me out of charity by some kind person' (*ibid.*, p. 94).

Roncalli recalled these memories on November 27, 1958, when he visited the Roman seminary next to the Lateran Athenaeum. He could still reel off the names of his eleven professors. The most famous was Riccardo Tabarelli (1859–1909) who contributed to the revival of Thomism stimulated by the encyclical *Aeterni Patris* (August 4, 1879). His most notorious professor was Umberto Benigni, later to mastermind the spying campaign against the 'Modernists'. But at this date he appeared to be —and probably was — a serious historian. We will meet him again. He contributed to Angelo's choice of history as his special field.

The first semester sped by. 'Here in Rome, I can say I have all that I need', he noted (*Journal*, p. 86). He was happy and spiritually fulfilled. Twinges of social inferiority sometimes afflicted him; but he used them as 'rebuffs to my pride'. He had no sense of intellectual inferiority. On June 25, 1901, he sailed through his exams and was awarded a prize for an optional paper in Hebrew (*Cronologia*, p. 518). But then the comfortable world he was fashioning crashed about him.

He was ordered to report to the Umberto I Barracks in Bergamo for compulsory military service. On November 30, 1901, he became plain Private Roncalli, Angelo, Number 11331-42, sir, in the 73rd Infantry Regiment, the Lombardy Brigade. The fact that clerics had to do military service at all seemed to him 'an unjust and barbarous imposition' (*Journal*, p. 94). It was one of the irritants that kept 'the Roman Question' alive. By paying 1,200 lire the diocesan Curia in Bergamo at least got his service reduced to twelve months. But he hated it from the start.

He called it 'the year of Babylonian Captivity' and 'the year of conflicts' (*Journal*, p. 88 and p. 108). After less than a month he wrote despondently to his Rector, Mgr Bugarini: 'My life is one of great suffering, a real purgatory; and yet I feel the Lord is very close to me, with his holy and provident care, beyond all expectation' (*Journal*, p. 357: December 23, 1901).

Yet his military purgatory had some redeeming features. He was stationed in Bergamo, and so could return to the seminary on week-end leaves and at Christmas. The army appreciated him. He was promoted corporal on May 31, 1902, and sergeant on November 30. He scored high marks on the rifle range (*Cronologia*, p. 518). Angelo reports also that his fellow conscripts, mostly from Bergamo or Brescia, gave him 'marks of respect and affection', and 'compete in doing those little services that at least save me a lot of bother' (*Journal*, p. 358). Did they clean his boots? So what was the problem?

Bluntly, the 'brutal and licentious soldiery' confronted him with the raw facts of sexuality for which he was not prepared. He simply did not know how to handle barrack-room boasting about brothel exploits. This explains his wildly extravagant language when he was rid of it all:

> O the world is so ugly, filthy and loathsome! In my year of military service I have learned all about it. The army is a running fountain of pollution, enough to submerge whole cities. Who can hope to escape from this flood of slime, unless God comes to his aid (*Journal*, pp. 92–3).

He wrote that in December 1902 shortly after he was demobbed.

His chastity had been tested. He realised that priests and future priests were not immune to temptation: 'And the priests? I tremble when I think that not a few, even among these, betray their sacred calling' (*Journal*, p. 93). He resolves to be 'more scrupulous than ever about this matter, even if I become the laughing-stock of the whole world' (*ibid.*). He said goodbye to 1902 with a sigh of relief and a sense of providential protection:

> I shall always remember 1902: the year of my military service, the year of conflicts. I
> might, like so many other poor wretches, have lost my vocation – and I did not lose it. I

might have lost holy purity and the grace of God, but God did not allow me to do this. I passed through the mire and by his grace I was kept unpolluted . . . Jesus I thank you, I love you (*Journal*, p. 108).

On his return to the Roman seminary, Angelo began a ten-day retreat directed by Redemptorist Fr Francesco Pitocchi, who had just arrived as assistant spiritual father. It followed closely the *Spiritual Exercises* of St Ignatius as they were then conceived both by Jesuits and Redemptorists. This method of retreat was often highly effective, despite a somewhat mechanical use of the *Exercises* that was, as subsequent work has shown, entirely foreign to Ignatius. Angelo, despite being preached at five times a day and told how to feel, responded to the *Exercises* in a personal way. Ignatius had been a soldier and cast his meditation on the Kingdom of Christ in military imagery. Fresh from his army service and just twenty-one, Angelo welcomes this aspect of the *Exercises* with enthusiasm: 'I am the King's page, and go with him everywhere; I am admitted to his secrets' (*Journal*, p. 89). He pictures himself as a knight, called to fight in the battles of Christ the King:

I boldly enlist in the ranks of your volunteers. I dedicate myself to your service, for life or death. You offer me your cross as a standard and weapon. I place my right hand on this invincible weapon and give you my word, swearing with all the fervour of my youthful heart absolute fidelity unto death. So I, whom you created your servant, have become your soldier. I put on your uniform, I gird on your sword, I am proud to call myself a knight of Christ. Give me a soldier's heart, a knight's valour (*Journal*, p. 93).

And so on. The motto of the 73rd infantry regiment had been *Acerrimus hostibus* ('Most fierce to the foe'). He transposed this easily enough into the spiritual realm. But since the signal for battle had not yet been sounded, he was waiting in his tent, where the chief enemy was the relentless ego (see *Journal*, pp. 93–4).

But there was in this retreat something more fundamental, which Angelo derived not from Fr Pitocchi but from his own experience: he thought of God not as Father so much as Mother:

It really looks as though God has lavished upon me his most tender and motherly care . . . (*Journal*, p. 91).

He (God) took me, a country lad, from my home, and with the affection of a loving mother he has given me all I need . . . and he still cares for me without respite, day and night, more than a mother cares for her child (*ibid.*, pp. 95–6).

No doubt this reflected relationships within his own family, where the busily caring mother was contrasted with the taciturn father; but it is more important as an instance of the way Angelo exploited his own experience to understand God better. In fact, at this stage, his actual mother, Marianna, was more alarmed at the idea that he was out on the streets of Rome at night when there were thieves about. He gently tells her not to worry (*Familiari*, I, p. 12). Marianna had been transcended; the essential lay elsewhere.

He came closer still to it on the evening of December 16, 1902, when he had his first conversation with Pitocchi:

He gave me a kind of motto as the conclusion of our first meeting. He repeated it often, calmly but with insistence: 'God is everything: I am nothing'. This became like a touchstone which disclosed to me a new and unexplored horizon, full of mystery and spiritual fascination (*Giornale*, 5th edition, p. 471).

He returned to his studies in January 1903 with renewed enthusiasm: 'Tomorrow the lectures begin again: I feel a need and a passionate desire to study' (*Journal*, p. 110). His mind had lain fallow throughout his military service. Now it was hyper-active: 'I feel a restless longing to know everything, to study all the great authors, to familiarize myself with the scientific moment in all its manifestations' (*Journal*, p. 111). No one at this date was talking of 'modernism' or 'modernists': for that we have to wait until the encyclical *Pascendi* condemned them (September 8, 1907).

That Angelo was on the side of those who wanted to reconcile faith and contemporary thought becomes clear in his reflections after the funeral of Cardinal Lucido Parocchi (1833–1903) who had been archbishop of Bologna and then, since 1884, cardinal vicar of the diocese of Rome. In other words he looked after the diocese of Rome on behalf of the Pope who, because of the 'Roman Question', could not set foot in it. Parocchi was a learned man, who had founded the review *La Scuola Cattolica*, and had worked for reconciliation with Italy through the *Opera dei Congressi*. He was one of Angelo's heroes:

> The bare mention of his name was enough to silence those who accused the Church of ignorance; before him even unbelievers reverently bowed their heads, and men of science faltered when they had to speak in his presence ... Opinions may differ about Cardinal Parocchi's political views: I know that some malicious insinuations have been made – but no one will ever question his courage and his enthusiastic loyalty to Church and Pope (*Journal*, p. 114).

'Conciliarists' like Parocchi were accustomed to being accused of 'disloyalty to the Holy Father'.

But now a new generation of Catholic scholars was emerging. At the Roman seminary, the most brilliant student was Ernesto Buonaiuti. Chance had thrown them together during Angelo's first semester, January to July 1901. The custom was to draw lots for places in chapel and the refectory and companions for walks. Buonaiuti drew Roncalli, so they had many walks together around Rome. Buonaiuti was already a scholar and conscious of his worth. He was impatient with the petty restrictions of the Roman seminary. One piece of idiocy caused him great amusement. He had asked permission of the vice-rector, Spolverini, to read Augusto Conti's *History of Philosophy*, a safe and reputable work, graced even with an *imprimatur*. Spolverini thought about it and eventually gave his permission, but only after tearing out the pages concerning Peter Abelard: his love for Héloise and subsequent castration were not fit reading for a seminarian. Buonaiuti was later excommunicated as a 'Modernist' and later still hailed as a 'prophet'. That may account for the ambivalence of Roncalli's attitude towards him. To some he later admitted that he had learned a lot from 'Don Ernesto' (Andreotti, p. 66). But to Capovilla he edited his memories of 1901–4 and claimed that he 'never discussed theological, biblical or historical questions with him, and never read any of the underground works of his that were circulating' (*Dodicesimo anniversario*, p. 118).

Now Umberto Benigni (1862–1934) was professor of Church History at the Roman seminary. In his early period, Benigni was fascinated by the social impact of Christianity and strongly favoured 'Christian democracy' which he said should be called 'Christocracy'. Thus Léon Harmel, the French industrialist who introduced profit-sharing into his factory in the 1890s, says of Benigni:

> He has managed to prove from contemporary sources that the spread of Christianity depended on the social movement. It was through the development and application of democratic ideas that the Christians recruited so many followers among the slaves and humble people. So much so that the priests who today are concerned with trades unions and co-operatives are doing no more than follow in the footsteps of their early predecessors (Poulat, p. 178).

Volume I of Benigni's *Storia sociale della Chiesa (SocialHistory of the Church)* did not appear until 1907. But he had tried out the material in lectures long before then. Angelo was enthusiastic about this aspect of Benigni's work. He retained Benigni's optimism, and never followed him into pessimism. But he saw Christian democracy as another way of expressing the priest's mission of service: 'Jesus stooped to wash the feet of the twelve poor fishermen. This is *true democracy*, of which we ecclesiastics should be the most eloquent examples' (*Journal*, p. 97).

Angelo's spirituality was maturing under the double impact of his military service and his progress in theology. He decides that his idea of holiness as the literal imitation of the lives of the saints, was mistaken:

> I used to call to mind the image of some saint whom I set myself to imitate down to the smallest detail, as a painter makes an exact copy of a Raphael picture. I used to say to myself: in this case St Aloysius would have done so and so; he would not have done this or that. It turned out, however, that I was never able to achieve what I had thought I could do, and this worried me. The method was wrong. From the saints, one must *take the substance, not the accidents, of their virtues*. . . I must not be the dry, bloodless reproduction of a model, however perfect (*Journal*, p. 113).

Angelo was approaching ordination to the sub-diaconate which took place on April 11, 1903 in St John Lateran. He was now, at twenty-one, irrevocably committed to celibacy. The 'angelism' he had professed in the Bergamo seminary was abandoned. Instead of suppressing emotions, he seeks to harness them to the love of God:

> I must not let my head be turned in good fortune nor let myself be soured by the bitter moments of life. This does not mean denying that the senses or impulses of nature exist. The enjoyment of God's love, the sweet and total abandonment to his will, must absorb all else in me or, rather, *transform and sublimate* all the desires of my lower nature (*Journal*, p. 136).

Without some such positive idea of sublimation, Angelo's celibacy would have been nonsense. His remaining sixty years must be seen in this light.

Meanwhile, in the spring of 1903 international events began for the first time to engage his attention. On February 20 Leo XIII celebrated the twenty-fifth anniversary of his pontificate. On April 29, 1903 and then on May 2, the streets of Rome were alive with 'flags, festoons, decorations, glittering uniforms, plumes, soldiers, military reviews' (*Journal*, p.

128): first King Edward VII, of Great Britain and Ireland, and then Kaiser William II of Germany, were on their way to see the Pope. This was dramatic and unprecedented. Angelo reads both visits as Providential events:

> It is highly significant. . . that an heretical King of Protestant England, which has persecuted the Catholic Church for more than three centuries, should go in person to pay his respects to the poor old pope, held like a prisoner in his own house. It is *a sign of the times* that, after a night of storms, we see the new dawn rising from the Vatican, a slow but real and sincere return of the nations to the arms of their common father (*Journal*, p. 130).

> It is truly an act of Divine Providence, a real triumph for the papacy. A Protestant Emperor, after centuries of hostility, ascends the Vatican staircase with unusual, almost unique ceremony and splendour, and humbles himself before the greatness of the papal throne (*Journal*, p. 132).

One thing was clear at this date: 'The Roman question had ceased to count in international diplomacy' (Seton-Watson, p. 331). No one, not even Leo XIII himself, imagined that Italy was about to be broken up and the Papal States restored. So Edward VII and William II could pay their courtesy visits to the Vatican without annoying overmuch their brother King Victor Emmanuel III.

Then, within three months of the crowning triumph of his pontificate, Leo XIII died. Instead of going to the villa house of the Roman seminary at Roccantica, Angelo stayed on in Rome to follow, from afar, the conclave. The central issue was: continuity or change? Rampolla was the candidate of continuity. Leo XIII's heritage was impressive. First there was reconciliation with the nations of Europe. Secondly, he had contributed to the revival of Catholic scholarship, opened the Vatican Library, made John Henry Newman a cardinal, encouraged an enlightened Neo-Thomism, and declared that 'the Church has nothing to fear from truth'. Thirdly in his encyclical *Rerum Novarum* he had displayed a qualified interest in democracy and defended the rights of workers to band together in trades unions. Rampolla was the standard-bearer of these causes. He was prepared to take up and develop this inheritance. Angelo – not that, as a seminarian, he mattered – supported the same line.

At first (though none of this was known at the time) Rampolla carried all before him. There were 63 cardinal electors. He needed therefore 42 votes. In successive ballots Rampolla got 24, 29, 29 and then 30 votes. There comes a time in a conclave when a candidate gets stuck: being unable to rise any further, he is condemned to sink. That is what happened to Rampolla. His defeat is usually attributed to the veto of the Austro-Hungarian Emperor Franz-Joseph conveyed through the cardinal archbishop of Kraków, Kniaz de Kolzielsko Puzyna. But there was also a curial faction implacably opposed to Rampolla which sought a change from what they saw as the weak and accommodating policies of Leo XIII. This opened the way for Giuseppe Sarto, patriarch of Venice, who made a great point of stressing his humility. After the fourth ballot he declared: 'I shall renounce the cardinalate and become a Capuchin friar' (Falconi, p. 13). However, he did not carry out this threat and strolled home with 50 votes in the sixth ballot (*Quale Papa?* pp. 132–4). Asked the ritual question 'By what name do you wish to be called?' he replied without hesitation: 'Pius, trusting to the help of the holy popes who have honoured this name by their virtues and defended the Church with strength and gentleness' (Falconi, p. 14). This was ominous. The last Pius, Pio Nono, had turned his back on the modern world and in his *Syllabus of Errors* (1864) denounced those who fondly hoped to reconcile the Church with 'progress and modern civilisation'.

Angelo had been present at the 'white smoke' in St Peter's Square on August 14, 1903. Special editions of the papers were rushed out within half an hour. On his way back he passed by the church of San Giovanni dei Fiorentini, just across the Tiber. There he found an old woman intently studying photographs. 'I don't know anything about this Pius X', she said, 'but at least he's handsome' (*Corriere della Sera*, January 3, 1959: Pope John told this story at an audience). But Pius X was not just a pretty face. There were other aspects of his character that were less agreeable. Angelo was present at the coronation in St Peter's on August 9, 1903. He never forgot the impression the new pope made on him: 'The Pope came in to a hurricane of applause and *vivas*. For a moment he lowered his head a little, and when he looked up again his eyes were filled with tears. And the crowd fell silent' (*Letture*, pp. 51–2).

Angelo did not comment in his journal on what he called 'these grave and extraordinary events' (*Journal*, p. 145). He was more immediately concerned about his ordination to the diaconate at St John Lateran on December 18, 1903 and his ordination to the priesthood, due in 1904. Pitocchi had the good sense to forbid him to make any additional 'retreat resolutions' (*Journal*, p. 145), and assigned him the desultory task of producing a summary of the autobiography of Maria Celeste Crostorasa, a seventeenth-century nun who founded an institute that eventually became the female arm of the Redemptorists (Battaglia, p. 4).

Angelo was becoming aware of a tension between the 'scientific movement', into which he had plunged with so much ardour, and his ambition to be a 'good priest'. He stated the dilemma clearly on March 7, feast of St Thomas Aquinas: 'In our enthusiasm for study, it often happens that piety has to take second place; we behave as though we thought the time given to devotional exercises was wasted. And yet St Thomas, before becoming the greatest scholar of his age, was a saint; and it was because he was a saint that he reached such a lofty height of wisdom' (*Journal*, pp. 122–3). The dilemma was sharpened with the new pontificate. There were already signs that Pius X would conduct an offensive against what he considered 'excessive' criticism. In December 1903 Angelo was looking for a *via media*, a middle way between intellectual integrity and compliance:

> On very doubtful points I shall prefer to keep silent, like one who does not know, rather than hazard propositions which might differ in the slightest degree from the Church's orthodoxy. I will not be surprised at anything even if certain conclusions, while preserving intact the sacred deposit of the faith, turn out to be rather unexpected. Surprise is the daughter of ignorance (*Journal*, p. 153).

He swings dialectically to and fro, torn between 'the atmosphere and light of the modern age' (*Journal*, p. 153) and the example of the 'good old Bergamesque priests of old ... who neither saw or desired to see further than could be seen by the Pope, the Bishops, the common sense and mind of the Church' (*ibid.*). It was a cruel and, some would think, an unnecessary dilemma. But Angelo felt it deeply.

If 1902 had been the testing year of military service and 1903 the exhilarating year of intellectual expansion and international events, 1904 was the year of immediate preparation for ordination. On July 13 he was awarded his doctorate in theology – easily come by in Rome – and his written exam was supervised by Eugenio Pacelli, the future Pius XII.

He made his pre-ordination retreat at the house of the Passionist Fathers on the Coelian Hill. There he reread the words he had written two years before and would underline in red when he became pope. He felt that he had been brought to Rome so that 'I may live under the protection of his Vicar, alongside the very fountain of Catholic truth and the tomb of his apostles, where the very soil is stained with the blood of his martyrs, and the air is filled with the holiness of his confessors' (*Journal*, p. 95). Every afternoon he practised saying Mass in the room where St Paul of the Cross, founder of the Passionists, had died. On the eve of his ordination he prayed in St John Lateran, mounted the 'Holy Stairs' on his knees, and then went on to St Paul's without the Walls (*Journal*, p. 169).

Early in the morning of August 10, 1904, feast of St Lawrence, the vice-rector, Spolverini, collected him and they went by cab to the church of Santa Maria in Monte Santo, on the Piazza del Popolo. The ordaining bishop was Giuseppe Ceppetelli, titular patriarch of Constantinople. Throughout his life, Angelo, now Don Roncalli, always celebrated the anniversary of his ordination. In 1912 he recalled it in this way:

> When all was over and I raised my eyes, having sworn the oath of eternal fidelity to my superior, the Bishop, I saw the blessed image of Our Lady to which I confess I had not paid any attention before. She seemed to smile at me from the altar and her look gave me a feeling of sweet peace in my soul and a generous and confident spirit (*Journal*, p. 170).

He had no anxiety about the irrevocable step he had taken. He was in his right place.

He wrote letters to his parents and 'Uncle' Zaverio to thank them and share his joy. They had been unable to scrape together the money for the train fare. He would be in Sotto il Monte by August 15 to say Mass in the church of his baptism on the feast of the Assumption. He wrote to Camillo Guindani, bishop of Bergamo, pledging obedience. Then he went on a round of churches – he lists seven but says there were 'many others' (*Journal*, p. 171).

The next day, August 11, Spolverini accompanied him to the crypt of St Peter's where he celebrated his first Mass. He was not to know that he would himself be buried where he said his first Mass. 'I came out of the church as if in a dream. On that day the marble and bronze popes aligned along the walls of the Basilica seemed to look at me from their tombs with a new expression, as if to give me courage and confidence' (*Journal*, p. 171). Spolverini had arranged an audience with the living Pope, Pius X, which took place towards midday. Kneeling, Angelo stammered out a few words. Pius placed a hand on his head, and almost whispering in his ear said: 'Well done, well done, my boy . . . this is what I like to hear. I will ask the good Lord to grant a special blessing on these good intentions of yours, so that you may remain a priest after his own heart' (*Journal*, p. 172).

He spent the months of September and October with his Roman seminary friends at Roccantica, savouring his priesthood and the daily intimacy with Christ in the Eucharist. He began further studies in canon law on November 4, 1904. But his first months as a new priest were not a period of unalloyed happiness. His mother was complaining that he did not love her any more. He had not written to her and, what is more, she alleged that her husband was withholding Angelo's letters. He had not sent her any money. And he had sent a photograph to the parish priest but not to the family. Don Angelo patiently tried to clear up these misunderstandings in a long letter. He refused to believe that his father had with-held any letters. He did not have any money: he had to buy new shoes and a soutane for his ordination, and canon law books were particularly expensive. He advises patience and pro-mises to send a photograph (*Familiari*, I, p. 19). He protests: 'Even if I were pope, you would always remain for me the greatest lady in this world. So, I beg you, please don't doubt my love and the tender memories that I will always have of you. Believe me, distance, far from weakening filial love, makes it more vivid, gentle and affectionate' (*ibid.*, p. 18). The purpose of this letter dated January 1, 1905, was to reduce the growing gap between himself and his mother; yet it provides evidence of how deep the estrangement was becoming.

Nor were his first attempts at public speaking back in Rome a great success. On Decem-ber 8 Fr Pitocchi had prevailed upon him to give a talk on the Immaculate Conception to the Children of Mary in a rich Roman suburb. He wrote it out in advance, but on rereading it, found it 'too fancy, too flowery and full of high-sounding words' (Pepper, p. 41). So he tried to make it simpler, but got confused and lost his way:

> My talk was a disaster. I mixed up quotations from the Old and the New Testaments. I
> confused St Alphonsus with St Bernard. I mistook writings of the Fathers for writings
> of the prophets. A fiasco. I was so ashamed that afterwards I fell into the arms of Fr
> Francesco and confessed my mortification (*ibid.*, p. 41).

He still remembered the fiasco as Pope, and told the story to the sculptor, Giacomo Manzù.

Then something happened that made him forget his mother's grumbles and his oratorical failures. Without any initiative on his part, his life suddenly took a new and wholly unex-pected direction.

Pius X had stunned the Roman Curia by appointing a thirty-seven-year-old Spaniard educated in an English seminary, Rafael Merry del Val, as his Secretary of State. He made it clear that he was repudiating both the policies and the men of the previous pontificate. The first victim was the defeated candidate in the conclave, Cardinal Rampolla. He re-signedly prepared for death (it did not come) and lived 'like a king in exile' (De Luca, p. 90). He was too close to the spirit of Leo XIII for comfort. In his *Memoirs*, Merry del Val cruelly explains that Rampolla would not have been elected pope, even if the Austrian veto had not operated (Newman Press, Westminster, Maryland, 1951, p. 1). Pius dealt with the institutions as harshly as with the men of Leo XIII.

In July 1904 he dissolved the *Opera dei Congressi*. This was 'the hardest moment in the life of its chaplain, Radini Tedeschi' (see Gabriele De Rosa in *Linee*, p. 51). Angelo said later that 'it came like a thunderbolt in a clear sky'. Pius X was not interested in social doctrine and de-spised democracy, whether Christian or not (see his encyclical *Vehementer*). He saw the *Opera dei Congressi* as 'modernism' in its social form. Since the main goal of his pontificate was the suppression of 'modernism', the *Opera dei Congressi* had to go. And with it had to go Radini Tedeschi, another 'Leo XIII man'. Bishop Guindani of Bergamo had died in October 1904. Radini Tedeschi was appointed to succeed him.

Pius X contrived to pass off Radini Tedeschi's banishment to Bergamo as a promotion. It was nothing of the kind for someone used to being at the decision-making centre. But Radini Tedeschi accepted the appointment with good grace and his obedience, so creative in its results, had a profound effect on Roncalli. The bishop-elect needed a secretary. He asked the rector of the Roman seminary, Bugarini, to bring along to his flat, Corso Vittorio Emmanuele 21, his Bergamesque students. They imagined they were merely going to present their homage to the new bishop. He took two of them, Roncalli and Carozzi, and tried them out for a week, setting them to deal with the abundant correspondence that followed upon the news of his appointment. He selected Roncalli. Thus at twenty-four Angelo, the village boy, became secretary to an aristocratic bishop exactly twice his age. On January 29, 1905, Pius X ordained Radini Tedeschi as bishop. Angelo acted as chaplain, holding the Book of the Gospels on the bishop's shoulders to signify the burden he would have to bear. For Angelo it meant the end of canon law; and it meant going home.

Chapter 4

Into the whirlwind of Modernism

Controversy, at least in this age, does not lie between the hosts of heaven,
Michael and his angels on the one side, and the powers of evil on the other;
but it is a sort of night battle, where each fights for himself, and friend and
foe stand together.

(John Henry Newman, 'Faith and Reason contrasted as Habits of Mind', in *Sermons,
chiefly on the Theory of Religious Belief preached before the University of Oxford*, 1843)

Angelo left Bergamo for Rome as a hopeful young seminarian in 1901. He returned at the
start of April, 1905 as secretary to the newly appointed bishop It was a post requiring the
utmost tact. Though he had so far 'done nothing' as a priest to justify his early promotion, his
regular contact with the bishop led the Bergamesque clergy – including his old seminary
professors – to suppose that from now on he would have some 'influence'. On closer analysis, they were a cliquish lot. Opinion in the diocese, already divided under the two previous
bishops, was far from unanimous about the appointment of Radini Tedeschi, who could be
malevolently regarded as a Roman careerist whose career had unexpectedly gone wrong.
Roncalli was to write the biography of Radini Tedeschi whom he always called, with pride
and affection, 'My Bishop'.

Radini Tedeschi was authoritarian, and something of a martinet; 'In the government of
his diocese this military spirit was very apparent in his insistence on discipline which was to
be maintained in everything, down to the smallest detail' (*ibid.*, p. 106). He was not in the
habit of turning a blind eye. He was convinced that 'a strong and vigorous government does
less harm than a weak one' and 'abhorred popularity won by compliance and surrender'
(*ibid.*, p. 106). Angelo, whose own temperament was very different, was able to observe at
close quarters the way Radini Tedeschi exercised his episcopal authority. It was part of his
ecclesiastical education to discover that holy men could differ among themselves, and that
obedience and loyalty, though essential, did not magically solve all problems. But he was
'the Bishop's shadow', as he was nicknamed, and learned discretion the hard way.

The bells of Bergamo echoed from the upper town on April 9, 1905, when Radini Tedeschi entered Bergamo in triumph and took possession of his cathedral. Angelo wrote an
account of it for the local paper, *l'Eco di Bergamo*. It was his first piece of journalism, and for
the next decade he wrote regularly for this staunchly Catholic paper.

But having taken possession of his diocese, Radini Tedeschi, accompanied by his secretary, immediately departed on a national pilgrimage to Lourdes. They set sail from Genoa
on April 29, 1905, stayed in Marseilles, Lyons, Paray-le-Monial and Montpellier as well as
Lourdes. They returned via Rome where Radini Tedeschi addressed the 13th National Eucharistic Congress on June 5. They had an audience with Pius X on June 29 and in July Don

Roncalli spent a few days at the Radini Tedeschi family home in Piacenza. It might be thought that Radini Tedeschi was reluctant to take charge of his diocese. But as the Bergam-esque clergy waited apprehensively for his first move, he was laying his plans.

The visit to France was a pilgrimage, of course. But it also gave the pilgrims an opportu-nity to measure the impact of Pius X's policy towards France. Leo XIII's attempt to rally French Catholics to the Republic had been rejected as 'appeasement'. The new policy was one of confrontation. It was expressed with admirable clarity by Merry del Val:

> If only one could persuade the French that their salvation lies in battle . . . They are on the
> battlefield and the front line. Men in that position are generally only too anxious to
> fight. But they just want to surrender. I am thinking particularly of the leaders, the
> intellectuals who are actively involved (Larkin, p. 124).

So France became the testing ground of the new pontificate. Pius X saw France as a coun-try where bishops were feeble, Catholic political leaders like Marc Sangnier compromising, and theologians like Loisy were undermining the foundations of faith. He challenged all three groups. The French government responded with increasing petulance, culminating in the 'Law of separation of Church and State' on December 9, 1905 (Text in Larkin, pp. 227 *et seq.)*. The religious orders were expelled. Pius lost the battle with the French state. He then fell back on the battle within the Church.

These were alarm bells for a not very distant future, but they did not affect Radini Te-deschi as, in the autumn of 1905, he at last began to put his plans for the diocese into effect. Angelo sincerely admired his methodical energy. He discreetly noted: 'His fiery apostolic eloquence, his determination, his innumerable projects and extraordinary personal activity may have given many people at first the impression that he intended to make the most ra-dical changes and was inspired only by the desire to introduce innovations' (*My Bishop*, p. 48). Was this first impression, then, mistaken? No and yes. He explains: 'He did not concen-trate on carrying out reforms so much as on maintaining the glorious traditions of his dio-cese, and interpreting them *in harmony with the new conditions and needs of the time*' (*ibid.*, p. 48). This was precisely Roncalli's own ambition when he became Pope more than fifty years later, and he expressed it in the same language: the revivifying of tradition through *aggior-namento* (a word only inadequately rendered by 'adaptation' or 'up-dating').

Radini Tedeschi's first priority was the pastoral visitation of the diocese. It had 352 parishes and a population of half a million. The Bishop began his visitation with the cathe-dral in Bergamo on December 8, 1905 and concluded it in 1909. In that time it was calcu-lated that he had distributed Communion to a good third of his flock. Angelo was always at his side. Those priests who 'had dreaded his arrival' were won over (*ibid.*, p. 49).

Radini Tedeschi was a great builder. He restored and redecorated the cathedral – rather too ornately for Roncalli's taste. He had a purpose-built retreat-house set up at Martinengo. Finding his episcopal palace 'an ugly, inconvenient and insanitary building', he had a new one designed and moved into it on November 21, 1906. There Roncalli lived for the next eight years. He thought it was 'a noble and graceful building' which did not clash with 'the jewels of Renaissance art, the Colleoni Chapel and the Baptistery' among which it was set. But inside it was very simple, 'the home of one who must set an example to others' (*My Bishop*, pp. 51–2). Radini Tedeschi also modernised the seminary, installing running water and central heating. Physical education, unheard of in Angelo's time as a student, became compulsory. Chemistry and other science labs were added. Around the diocese tumble-down parish churches were rebuilt. Roncalli learned to care for ecclesiastical plant.

Radini Tedeschi, finally, was an organiser of great ability. He laid particular emphasis on Catholic Action in the social sphere. In other words, he carried on exactly where the now suppressed *Opera dei Congressi* left off. Roncalli says this explicitly: 'He grieved for the disappearance of the Opera, but always remained faithful to its ideals . . . He shared with his friends the desire . . . to direct its rejuvenated energies into new social organisations required by the new conditions of the times' (*My Bishop*, p. 77).

In June, 1905 Pius X, with his encyclical *Fermo Proposito*, dispensed Catholics from the *non expedit*, that is, allowed them to vote in the November elections wherever Church interests demanded it. As Italian Catholics re-entered Italian political life, the role of the Catholic press became more important than ever. Pius X was an avid newspaper reader, scrutinised articles for their orthodoxy, and was not above 'planting' pieces written by himself or his private secretary, Giambattista Bressan. He favoured papers like *Riscossa*, edited in Milan since 1890 by three priest brothers, Andrea, Gottardo and Jacopo Scotton. It was the organ of the 'intransigents'. Their proud motto was *Frangar, non flectar.* They would rather break than bend before the winds of change. Don Roncalli repudiated this attitude, and modified the motto to *Flectar, non frangar* (I will bend, but not break) (*Letture*, p. 397). But in 1906 the 'intransigents' were in command, confident that they had the support of the Pope. They specialised in attacks on 'modernism', and their principal local target was Cardinal Andrea Carlo Ferrari, archbishop of Milan.

Don Roncalli first met Ferrari on September 4, 1905, and despite the difference of age – Ferrari was fifty-five, Roncalli twenty-four – and rank, they became friends. Ferrari had been Archbishop since 1894. They met almost once a month until Ferrari's death in February, 1921. He was not technically a spiritual director, but Angelo consulted him on important decisions. Ferrari was no 'modernist', but he was a 'conciliarist' in Italian politics. He believed that only adaptation would permit the Church to reach the dechristianised working class, and encouraged theologians, clerical and lay, to work for the reconciliation of faith and learning (see Carlo Snider, *L'Episcopato del Cardinale Andrea Carlo Ferrari*, vol. I, Vicenza, Neri Pozza, 1981). Roncalli shared in all these ambitions, and remained faithful to Ferrari. The proof is that on February 10, 1963, in the presence of a large number of pilgrims from Lombardy, he signed the decree introducing the beatification cause of the cardinal.

But in 1906 it was dangerous to be associated with Ferrari. Pius X did not like him, set his watch-dogs on him, and made leaden-footed jokes about the tediousness of his sermons: 'Preach away, preach away, and it won't even be noticed if you bore the pants off everyone' (Snider, p. 361). Pius X, with his 'peasant simplicity', could be crude as well as unjust. Jesuit historian Domenico Mondrone claims that further study of the relationship between Pius X and Ferrari would show 'how far a well-orchestrated campaign of calumny can take over the mind and affect the judgement of a saint' (*Civiltà Cattolica*, July, 1981, p. 159).

The contact with Ferrari led him to make an important historical discovery on February 23, 1906. Don Roncalli was browsing in the archiepiscopal library, full of memories of St Charles Borromeo. He describes what happened:

Suddenly I was struck by thirty-nine parchment bound volumes which bore the title: *Archivio Spirituale – Bergamo.* I explored them: I read them through on successive visits. What a pleasant surprise for my spirit! To come across such rich and fascinating documents concerning the Church of Bergamo at the most characteristic period of its religious renewal, just after the Council of Trent, in the most ardent period of the Counter-reformation (*Atti,* III).

The Borromeo archives showed that the constitutional way to reform a diocese was by meticulous episcopal visitation of all its parishes and religious houses followed by a diocesan Synod. In the mind of the Council of Trent, the bishop, not some curial interloper from Rome, was the proper agent of reform. 'History', Roncalli liked to say, is the teacher of life'. He quoted this in his opening speech to the Council on October 11, 1962.

Roncalli, at any rate, had discovered his scholarly vocation: editing thirty-nine volumes of St Charles Borromeo. It took a lifetime. The volumes appeared in 1936, 1937, 1938, 1946 and 1957. The patient, steady work suited his temperament. The fact that it was local history did not make it unimportant. This work meant that Roncalli saw the Council of Trent not as an anti-Protestant polemic, but as a reforming Council in a world he knew well. As he plodded round after Radini Tedeschi on his pastoral visits to parishes, notebook in hand, he was reliving the pastoral visitation of St Charles Borromeo.

In September and October, 1906 there was a national pilgrimage to the Holy Land. It was no jet-age four-star hotel joyride. Much of it was done on horseback. The *Spiritual Exercises* had taught him to visualise in imagination the places where Jesus had lived. Now he is seeing them for real. They were up at 4.30 one morning to take a boat across the Lake of Tiberias:

I shall never forget the enchantment, the heart's ease, the spiritual relish I discovered this morning floating upon these waters. Little by little, as our small boat stood out into the lake, the first light of dawn lent colour to the water, the houses and then the surrounding hills. We did not speak, but our hearts were stirred. It was as though we could see Jesus crossing this lake in Peter's boat. Jesus was before us and we could see him; unworthy though we were, we sailed towards him and our prayer, silent though it was, was eloquent and spontaneous . . . As we touched the shore the sun appeared (Elliott, p. 53. Translation modified).

Christological controversies were raging in Europe. The Holy Office was already extracting propositions from the works of Alfred Loisy, author of *L'Evangile et l'Eglise,* in preparation for the decree *Lamentabili.* One condemned error stated: 'It may be granted that the Christ shown by history is much inferior to the Christ who is the object of faith' (DS, 3429). Roncalli's pilgrimage to the Holy Land helped to preserve him from the ruinous disjunction (later developed by Rudolf Bultmann) between the 'Jesus of history' and 'the Christ of faith'.

But this interlude was soon over. The new academic year was beginning, and he had to lecture in the Bergamo seminary on Church history. He could hardly have begun to teach the subject at a less propitious time than in November 1906. Far from being a quiet grove of

Academe in which dusty scholars exchanged even dustier papers on topics that concerned only themselves, history was at the fiery heart of the contemporary philosophical debate.

Alfred Loisy was reputed to have said that 'God is not an actor in human history', a remark which was, to say the least, ambivalent. The difficulty of the enterprise at that date was that historical science was held to be 'critical', while orthodoxy was often 'uncritical': it was enlightenment versus obscurantism.

To overcome that false dilemma, Don Roncalli remained faithful to a central insight: the 'Christian idea' works itself out in human history, not without ups and downs, and not without human collaboration. The 'prophets of gloom', denounced at the start of Vatican II, 'behave as though they had learned nothing from history . . . They behave as though at the time of the former Councils the *Christian idea* was fully vindicated' (Abbott, p. 712). If God is at work in human history and all history is *Heilsgeschichte*, salvation-history, then this presence ought to be detectable through the 'signs of the times'.

However, this was not a view of history that was fashionable, or even understood, at the court of Pius X. It believed that the modern world was riddled with errors. Pius went over to the attack. On July 3, 1907 the decree *Lamentabili* listed sixty-five unattributed errors (though fifty-three of them were derived from Loisy). It was difficult, indeed impossible, to deduce a positive content from *anathemata* cast in a negative form. Error 65, for example, stated: 'Modern Catholicism can be reconciled with true science only if it is transformed into a non-dogmatic Christianity, that is to say, into a broad and liberal Protestantism.' Did that leave room for other attempts to reconcile 'modern Catholicism with true science' that did not fall into this manifest error? The answer was by no means clear. But an atmosphere of anxiety and suspicion was generated in which the presumption was that 'errors' were omnipresent, and menacing.

But *Lamentabili* was mere skirmishing compared with the encyclical *Pascendi* which appeared on September 8, 1907 (AAS, 40, 1907, pp. 593–650). It acted as the Syllabus of Errors for the early twentieth century. It may be said to have invented 'Modernism' as a system in order better to condemn it. *Pascendi* recognised this in its introduction: 'It is one of the cleverest devices of the Modernists (as they are commonly and rightly called) to present their doctrines without order and systematic arrangement, in a scattered and disjointed manner, so as to make it appear as if their minds were in doubt and hesitation, whereas in reality they are quite fixed and steadfast' (Daly, p. 195). The author *of Pascendi* (in fact Fr Joseph Lemius OMI, working to the orders of Pius X conveyed by Merry del Val) claims a remarkable insight into the hidden motivations of those he seeks to destroy. He credits them with a synthesis they had not previously achieved, and obligingly spells it out for them. The two errors at the heart of the system are agnosticism, defined as 'the restriction of knowledge to phenomena', and its correlative, 'immanentism'. Since the source of religion cannot be found outside humanity or in the objective order, it must necessarily be sought within humanity, in therefore the wholly subjective needs, impulses, aspirations, or so-called 'religious sense' of the human person. *Pascendi* did not deign to argue to try to refute this position. Its author appeared to believe that mere statement would be sufficient repudiation.

That is not, however, what happened. 'Modernists' (some now began to accept the label) declared that they could not find themselves in the incriminated system. *Pascendi* was talking about someone else, possibly some imaginary theologian. They had not been hit; they had not even been grazed (*'Nous ne sommes pas même effleurés'*, wrote Maurice Blondel, Daly, p. 205). Where the encyclical was precise, it did not concern them; where it was vague, it was so indiscriminate that no one at all need feel wounded by it. 'The Modernist', *Pascendi* confidently explained, 'includes in himself a manifold personality; he is a philosopher, a believer, a theologian, an historian, a critic, an apologist, a reformer'. Few could escape belonging to one or other of these categories; no one could embrace them all. Everyone had a bolt-hole.

The discussion about who was or was not condemned by *Pascendi* could have gone on for a very long time, with all the suspects protesting their aggrieved innocence. But Pius X had thought of that, and included in the encyclical a *disciplinary* section of the utmost severity. It said:

> Anyone who is in any way found to be tainted with Modernism is to be excluded without compunction from those offices, whether of government or of teaching, and those who already occupy them are to be removed. The same policy is to be adopted towards those who openly or secretly lend countenance to Modernism, either by extolling the Modernists or excusing their culpable conduct, or by carping at scholasticism or the *Magisterium* of the Church, or by refusing obedience to ecclesiastical authority or any of its depositories; and towards those who show a love of novelty in history, archaeology or biblical exegesis; and finally towards those who neglect the sacred sciences or appear to prefer the secular sciences to them.

Pascendi was a catch-all net in which anyone in any scholarly field could be trapped. So that these harsh provisions would not remain a dead letter, other measures were taken: 'councils of vigilance' were set up in every diocese; Umberto Benigni was encouraged by Merry del Val to create a secret network of informers; 'apostolic visitations' (what Ferrari called 'apostolic vexations') began in suspect dioceses. That meant, in the first place, Italy, which was always more immediately affected by Vatican decisions.

In November 1907 it was announced that those who opposed *Pascendi* would be excommunicated. The ordinary process of 'reception' of an encyclical was short-circuited. Even those who agreed that there was a need to condemn some of the wilder theories that were circulating might have thought that *Pascendi* was badly drafted, ill-conceived, and wrongly timed. Was that 'disagreement'? The witch-hunt drew perilously close to Bergamo. The Milanese review, *Il Rinnovamento*, was condemned and the reforming group led by Tommaso Gallerati Scotti was dissolved (*Utopia*, p. 393). It is not unfair to speak of a reign of terror.

In this context the lecture given by Don Roncalli at the Bergamo seminary on December 4, 1907, to commemorate the third centenary of the death of Baronius, was dramatic (text published as Angelo Roncalli, *Il cardinale Cesare Baronio*, Edizioni di Storia e Letteratura, 1961). He was just twenty-six. He had been professor of church history for only a year. Trip-wires abounded. He knew exactly what was at stake: a loose or incautious phrase might have wrecked his career for good. His appointed theme was 'Faith and Scientific Research'. So although Baronius was the pretext, his real subject was the place of historical scholarship in the Church in the year 1907, just four months after *Pascendi*.

This was Roncalli's finest hour to date. He defended 'historical criticism' and spoke of the 'wonderful progress that has been made in scientific history in the last few years' (Alberigo,

p. 401). He claimed that Baronius 'has quite rightly been hailed as the founder of historical criticism'. This was a shrewd and legitimate move. It meant that he could assert that the Church had been the first in the field of historical criticism. Not content with this defence of 'historical criticism', he went out of his way to use the now suspect language of 'renewal' (*rinnovamento*). He drew an analogy between the late sixteenth and early twentieth century and made it plain that he considered the 'general renewal of Catholic scholarship' promoted by Baronius, to be still on the agenda. It was precisely this capacity for 'renewal' that made Baronius 'a man of his time – we would say today a "modern man" – in that he had intuited profoundly the needs of the Church and the society of his time' (*Linee*, p. 64).

This was quite enough to arouse the interest of the delators who, he knew, were somewhere in his audience. So, dialectically, he offered them a 'pound of flesh'. He talked clearly about 'Modernism', though without actually naming it. He did not need to.

> It seems to me that the abandonment of these deep convictions of faith (i.e. that history has a supernatural factor) is one of the main causes of the strange movement of ideas which until recently troubled Catholic consciences and caused grave concern. Certain poor deluded souls – I think it right to call them so –judged the Church and Christianity by criteria that were all too human . . . Woe to the day on which such doctrines prevailed (*Linee*, p. 66).

That could be considered as an endorsement of *Pascendi* in the broadest sense.

Don Roncalli could not have spoken in this way and risked Roman censure unless he had allies. His first ally was his bishop, Radini Tedeschi. In Milan, his ally Cardinal Ferrari went public. In a pastoral letter in 1908, he denounced the 'anti-Modernists' who, he said, were just as bad and just as 'modern' (the word now having lost all meaning) as those they attacked: 'These anti-modernist zealots discover Modernism all over the place, and even manage to throw suspicion on those who are very far removed from it' (Tramontin, I, p. 72). That did not endear him to Pius X.

From June 1 to 3, 1908, Roncalli spent three days with Bishop Geremia Bonomelli of Cremona, one of whose pamphlets, *Italy and the Reality of Things*, had been placed on the Index of Forbidden Books in 1889. The old volcano was not yet extinguished. He had tried to persuade Cardinal Rampolla that the intellectual crisis 'should not be met with repressive and negative measures' (Tramontin, I, pp. 85–6). Rampolla agreed, but was powerless to influence events. Even more remarkably, Bonomelli, already in 1908, looked forward to an ecumenical council: 'Perhaps a great ecumenical council, which would discuss rapidly, freely and publicly the great problems of religious life, would draw the attention of the world to the Church, stimulate faith, and open up new ways for the future' (*ibid.*, p. 86). Almost exactly fifty years later, Roncalli took up Bonomelli's idea in almost identical terms.

In June 1908 there was an 'apostolic visitation' of the Bergamo seminary and another for the whole diocese in July and August. Don Giuseppe Moioli, the New Testament professor, was sacked. The others including Don Roncalli survived; but they became uncomfortably aware that there were spies in their midst. One of them was Giovanni Mazzoleni, a cathedral canon. The best he could do was to report on the senior common room at the seminary. The priests are reading newspapers of a 'modernising tendency'. He has heard disloyal remarks such as: 'The Vatican is merely stumbling forwards and doesn't know what to do', and 'Another pope would not behave in this way' (*Disquisitio*, p. 172). None of these remarks was particularly outrageous and, with hindsight, we can say that they were all true. But they were dangerous at this time, and Mazzoleni judged them worth delating.

In autumn 1909, 800 workers at a textile factory at Ranica, just outside Bergamo, went on strike to secure a guaranteed 'contract of employment' for the future. It began on September 21, 1909. There was very little in the union coffers. After a month *l'Eco de Bergamo* started a fund to support the strikers. Radini Tedeschi made the first contribution of 500 *lire*. The right-wing press was furious. 'The Bishop's alms', thundered *Perseveranza*, 'is a consecration of the strike, a blessing given to a frankly socialist cause (Dreyfus, p. 50). Pressure was put on Pius X to disavow this somewhat improbable candidate for the role of 'red bishop'.

Don Roncalli sprang to Tedeschi's defence with an article in *La vita diocesana* in November 1909 (text in *Pasqua*, 1976, p. 17 *et seq.*). It is a mini-treatise on the right and duty of the Church to 'intervene in politics'. 'The priest who lives in the light of the teachings of the Gospel', he writes, 'could not pass by on the other side of the road.' The Bishop led the way because he had 'a duty of charity towards the weak who were suffering for the triumph of justice'. In the Gospels 'Christ's *preference* goes to the disinherited, the weak and the oppressed' (*ibid.*, p. 19). Here he adumbrated one of the main themes of 'liberation theology' in the 1970s.

During Roncalli's 1910 retreat made at Martinengo he passed the severest and most conventional judgement on 'Modernism' that ever came from his pen. When set alongside his Baronius lecture it is puzzling. Our Lord had shown him in prayer 'the wisdom, timeliness and nobility of the measures taken by the Pope to safeguard the clergy in particular from the infection of modern errors (the so-called Modernist errors), which in a crafty and tempting way are trying to undermine the foundations of Catholic doctrine' (*Journal*, p. 188). 'Many, some of them good men, have fallen into error, perhaps unconsciously... (*Journal*, p. 189).

Word for loaded word, especially adjective for adjective ('infection', 'crafty', tempting'), he was echoing what Pius X wanted good seminary professors to believe. How could he be so supine? The answer can be seen by looking at the dates. The retreat was made from October 2 to 10, 1910. On September 1 the 'Anti-modernist Oath' had been published (DS nos. 3537–50: trans. in Daly, pp. 235–6). Don Roncalli was due to take it the following November. It was a fiercely uncompromising text. 'I submit and adhere wholeheartedly to the condemnations and all the prescriptions which are contained in the encyclical letter *Pascendi* and in the decree *Lamentabili* especially those which bear on the history of Dogma.' As Archbishop Mignot of Albi wrote in private to Baron von Hügel: 'They are organising a white terror... We used to believe that in order to be a good Catholic it was sufficient to believe all the truths which God revealed or the Church taught... It seems now that more is needed, namely that the Church should tell us not only what must be believed, but *how we should think*... (De la Bedoyère, pp. 210–11).

In such a crunch-situation, Don Roncalli inevitably had to side with the Pope. He quotes the maxim of St Alphonsus Liguori, 'The Pope's will: God's will' (*Journal*, p. 190).

Don Roncalli asked to be admitted to the diocesan Congregation of the Priests of the Sacred Heart on November 4, 1911, feast of St Charles Borromeo. It had been set up two years earlier by Radini Tedeschi to be closely modelled on the Oblates of St Charles Borromeo, to be 'of special help to the bishop in the fulfilment of his pastoral ministry', especially in 'missions to the people, in the *Spiritual Exercises* for clergy and laity' and in 'the Christian education of youth'. Two days later he made his vow of obedience to the bishop and promised to live in poverty of spirit. These were temporary vows. He renewed them annually until 1917 when they became 'perpetual'. When he became a bishop himself, he remained an 'honorary' member and continued to correspond with the Superior throughout his life. So from November 1911 Don Roncalli was a diocesan religious (see *Pastore*, p. 43), a fact which has escaped most of his biographers.

'Uncle' Zaverio died in May, 1912, at the age of eighty-eight. Radini Tedeschi's health became a source of concern; he needed longer periods of rest. But in the summer he was fit enough to set off on a journey to Munich and Vienna for a eucharistic congress. They stayed at nunciatures; Don Roncalli made his first contacts with Vatican diplomats, without any feelings of envy.

Nothing was changing in the anti-Modernist campaign. On June 1, 1914 Don Roncalli was in Rome with the seminary rector to discuss finance with Cardinal Gaetano De Lai, head of the all-powerful Consistorial Congregation which dealt with the appointment of bishops and supervised the administration of dioceses. As they were leaving, De Lai called him back and said: *'Professore*, please be careful in the teaching of Scripture'. Roncalli was too flabbergasted to explain that he had never taught scripture and that his work had been in church history, apologetics and patristics. Perhaps it was a case of mistaken identity. Roncalli was deeply distressed and rushed straight to the Gesù, the Jesuit church, where he renewed all the vows of his youth. He wrote a reply to De Lai at the Albergo del Senato the next day, June 2, and had it delivered by hand. He corrected the mistake about the teaching of Scripture and protested his fidelity 'to the directives of the Church and the Pope always and in everything' (*Decimo anniversario*, pp. 63–4).

On June 12, 1914, De Lai answered apparently in friendly fashion: 'I am sorry you were so disturbed by my advice to you. It was not a reproach but a salutary warning'. But then he revealed the real cause of his displeasure:

> According to information that has come my way, I knew that you had been a reader of Duchesne and other unbridled authors, and that on certain occasions you had shown yourself inclined to that school of thought which tends to empty out the value of tradition and the authority of the past, a dangerous current which leads to fatal consequences etc. (*Decimo anniversario*, p. 65).

De Lai had written that letter a hundred times. The mechanical phrases fell from his pen, illuminating nothing, creating a mood of apprehension in the receiver. He signed off: 'I bless you in the Lord, Yours most affectionately in Jesus Christ, ✠ G. card. De Lai, Bishop of Sabina'.

Don Roncalli did not find it easy to reply. Louis Marie Olivier Duchesne's *History of the Early Church* had been placed on the Index on January 12, 1912. Roncalli's letter went through several drafts and had many corrections – all of which he preserved. By June 27 he was ready to post it. 'I do not believe that the information comes from anyone who knows me' he began. He was prepared to deny all the charges *on oath*. In particular:

I have never read more then 15 to 20 pages – and even then just as a sampler– of volume I of the *History of the Early Church* (second edition, Paris, 1906). I have never seen the other two volumes. I have therefore *not read a single line* of Duchesne's history translated by (Nicola) Turchi, and never had them in my hands or among my books. I knew the French prelate a little, but I never had any sympathy with him even when he made corrections intended to put to rest doubts about his orthodoxy. I was fairly familiar with the ideas of Turchi who for some months was a fellow student at the Roman seminary, but he never confided in me. I remember more than once expressing my feelings of mistrust and antipathy towards him to my fellow seminarians (*Decimo anniversario*, p. 67).

There is only one word to describe Roncalli's letter to De Lai: grovelling.

In 1914 Don Roncalli was like a soldier who, having come unscathed through a long and arduous war, narrowly escapes being wounded on the eve of the armistice. For the whirlwind of Modernism was blowing itself out. It ended with the death of Pius X, on 20 August. From the whole tragic episode Roncalli drew the conclusion that there were other and better ways of dealing with 'error' in the Church. But another whirlwind was brewing up, the whirlwind of war.

Chapter 5

The Great War

What candles may be held to speed them all?
Not in the hands of boys, but in their eyes
Shall shine the holy glimmers of good-byes.

('Anthem for Doomed Youth', Wilfrid Owen)

The First World War, known to contemporaries as the Great War because it surpassed all previous conflicts, broke out on August 1, 1914. Italy was not involved until May of the following year, but already the dark shadow fell across the whole of Europe. On August 20, 1914, the day Brussels fell to the advancing Germans, Pius X died broken-hearted, it was said, by a war he had foreseen but had been unable to prevent. Two days later, Don Roncalli was kneeling at the bedside of the dying Radini Tedeschi:

As the curfew sounded from the tower, Monsignor lay on his death-bed with as much dignity as if he were seated on his episcopal throne during a solemn ceremony. As I knelt beside him . . . I remembered the first service I ever performed for him when, on the day of his solemn consecration in the Sistine Chapel, I held the Book of the Gospels, representing the yoke of Christ, against his shoulders, while the august hands of Pius X were laid upon his head to confer upon him the fulness of the priesthood and the strength of the Holy Spirit. Ten years had been spent in his company since that day, and it seemed to me a great privilege and blessing, that I shall never forget, to be able to assist him to the end and to witness a death so precious in the eyes of the Lord. The last prayer we heard him murmur was . . . 'and for peace, and for peace' (*My Bishop*, p. 142).

Shortly before his own death, Pope John noted in his diary: 'I reread in my volume on Mgr Radini, written in the thick of the World War in 1916, the account of the last days of my Bishop and his final prayer, peace, peace . . . I would like that to be my last prayer as Pope' (*Letture*, p. 497).

The deaths of Radini Tedeschi and Pius X added to the feeling that the lights were going out all over Europe. Shrewd old Fr Francesco Pitocchi, his spiritual director at the Roman seminary with whom he still corresponded, said that Don Roncalli would suffer more from the death of Radini Tedeschi than from that of Pius.

The truth was that many were glad to see the back of a pontificate which had been a disaster for the intellectual life of the Church. To a senator who wondered at the impressively devout crowds who flocked to pay their last tribute to Pius X as he lay in state in St Peter's, Cardinal Andrea Ferrari of Milan remarked: 'Yes, but he will have to give an account before God of the way he let his bishops down when they were attacked' (*Disquisitio*, p. 129).

Cardinal Désiré Mercier of Malines-Brussels, who embodied the heroic resistance of 'gallant little Belgium', wrote a pastoral letter in which he spoke of the 'wounded souls' and 'human wretchedness' to which the pontificate had led; and he denounced the 'free-lance knights of orthodoxy who imagine that, in order to obey the Pope more humbly, one has to attack the authority of the Bishops' (*Per Crucem ad Lucem*, pp. 66, and following). So Ferrari and Mercier were among those cardinals who hoped that the September 1914 conclave would produce a pope who could put an end to the atmosphere of repression. In the midst of a fratricidal European war, the Church had to have a different set of priorities.

The Curia, however, did not agree, and with Cardinal De Lai acting as kingmaker, supported Cardinal Alberto Serafini, a Benedictine and assessor at the Holy Office, who could be relied upon to continue making orthodoxy, narrowly conceived, the most important task of the papacy. So the Curia bitterly opposed first Cardinal Maffi of Pisa, believed to be close to the House of Savoy, and then Cardinal Della Chiesa of Bologna, who began to gather in the 'Austrian' vote. The Curia said that Della Chiesa was a mediocre man and a mere bureaucrat (he had been *sostituto* or substitute in Rampolla's time). They argued that his election would be an insult to the memory of Pius X. Even when Della Chiesa managed to reach the thirty-eight votes needed to win the election, the curial faction accused him of voting for himself. The accusation was shown to be groundless. So Giacomo Della Chiesa became Pope Benedict XV.

Two days after an economy-style coronation in the Sistine Chapel – pomp would have seemed blasphemous at such a time, Benedict announced his intention of making peace his main concern: 'We are firmly resolved . . . to leave nothing undone which may lead to the speedy ending of this calamity' (Holmes, pp. 2–3). In his first encyclical, *Ad Beatissimi*, he called for a halt to the anti-modernist campaign: 'There is no need to add epithets to the profession of Catholicism. It is enough for each to say, '*Christianus mihi nomen, Catholicus cognomen*' ('Christian is my name, and Catholic is my family name'). (*Popes of the Twentieth Century*, p. 132).

The election of Benedict XV helped to console Roncalli for the death of Radini Tedeschi. The loss of his father-figure was hard to bear, and Roncalli had a sense of being orphaned once again. His whole priestly life had been lived out as the bishop's secretary. Now his life seemed empty. It was highly unlikely that the new bishop, whoever he was, would want him to continue as secretary. Secretaries were expendable. In his September 1914 retreat he drew the obvious conclusion: 'I have entered this new period of my life' (*Journal*, p. 200).

He resolved to get up at half-past five every morning and to 'make a point of giving my new bishop, whoever he may be, that reverence, obedience, and sincere, generous and cheerful affection which, by the grace of God, I was always able to feel for his unforgettable predecessor' (*Journal*, pp. 200-1). He went to pray at the tomb of St Charles Borromeo in the Duomo (cathedral) of Milan, reminded himself that as a priest of the Association of the Sacred Heart he was bound in a special way to his bishop, renounced 'fantastic dreams, . . . thoughts of honours, positions *etc.*', and steeled himself for sacrifices to come (*ibid.*).

Freed from his chores as Bishop's secretary, Don Roncalli gave courses not only at the seminary but also at the *Casa del Popolo*, an adult education centre. The titles of his lectures reveal the range of his intellectual interests: The Church, Science and the School; Christianity and Graeco-Roman Science; Schools in the Barbarian Period to Charlemagne; Astrology, Alchemy and the Intellectual Aberrations of the Middle Ages; the University and Scholasticism; the Church and the Renaissance; the Church and Modern Scientific Thought; Modern Struggles for Freedom in Education; Origins of Modern Universal Education; Great Christian Educators. It was a typical reflection for a time of crisis, when values were in the melting-pot and the foundations of society seemed to be shaken: to improve the quality of education often seems to be the answer.

There was intense debate between the 'neutralists' and the 'interventionists'. For Italy to join the war on the side of the *Entente* (Britain, France and Russia) would mean abandoning the Triple Alliance with the Central Powers (Germany and Austro-Hungary) to which it was pledged. The Treaty of London was secretly negotiated as an inducement to Italy to come into the war on the side of the Entente: post-war territorial gains were promised. This strengthened the hand of the 'interventionists' in the government, but since the arrangement was confidential, it was of no help in winning over public opinion. Pope Benedict XV was a 'neutralist'. So was Don Roncalli. He remained deeply sceptical about 'the gains' of war.

If Italy joined the Entente, its bedfellows would be Protestant England, free-thinking France and autocratic Russia; and its potential enemy would then be Austria, the only combatant with which it had a common frontier. But Bergamo and Venice, especially, had strong cultural links with Austria, and had been part of the Austria-Hungarian Empire between the fall of Napoleon and the unification of Italy. For Roncalli's grandparents, war with Austria would have been a civil war.

So Italy stumbled into a war that could hardly be called popular. Mobilisation was ordered in May 1915. On May 19 Don Roncalli was called up, and became a hospital orderly stationed in Bergamo. On May 24 Italy declared war on Austria-Hungary, though not on Germany, and there were sharp engagements on the north-eastern front. Bergamo was tranquil and unchanged. Don Roncalli began to grow a moustache which soon bristled formidably on his upper lip. Though there was no question of 'hiding his priesthood', he did not want to appear odd or singular among his peer-group. Despite his portliness, he cut a fairly dashing figure in his uniform.

But he was not very warlike. His first wartime letter is to his brother, Zaverio, who was two years younger. It gave fraternal advice on how to get invalided out. As a hospital orderly and a scholar, Don Roncalli had time to master the regulations. But by September 17, 1915, he learned that all his efforts had been in vain: Zaverio was passed 'fit for war-service' (*ibid.*, p. 42). By December 12, 1915, Zaverio was in Brindisi, possibly about to embark for Albania or Macedonia. Don Roncalli, as usual, recommends calm: 'If the Lord is with us, who can be against us? We won't fear either hunger or cold or malaria or Albania or the Germans, will we?' (*Familiari*, I, p. 43). But Zaverio never set sail from Brindisi. That's war: order, counter-order, disorder.

On May 6, 1917, Don Roncalli wrote to Zaverio about how he sees 'duty towards our country': 'We know that love of our country is love of our neighbour, and that this implies the love of God. That's really all there is to say (*Familiari*, 1, pp. 48–9). It is not a very sophisticated argument; but he is trying to give his brother at the front a motive for hanging on. Moreover, Zaverio was a peasant like most of the men whose wounds he was tending, and he was learning from them. Angelo knew how resentful they sometimes felt at being merely cannon-fodder while urban munitions workers enjoyed the luxury of discussing 'war aims'.

Don Roncalli no longer sees the conscript army as a sink of iniquity, as he priggishly did during his military service in 1901. He came to know these simple men and appreciate their unnoticed qualities. Caring for the troops is his entire life, he tells Zaverio, and 'I have learned that with a little patience and the grace of God, they can all be won over' (*Familiari*, I, p. 49). The wounds of anticlericalism were superficial and could be healed.

While still close to the events, he spoke about the war in an address given on September 9, 1920:

> Oh! the long vigils among the bunks of our dear and brave soldiers spent in hearing their confessions and preparing them to receive the bread of the strong in the morning! The hymns to Mary that rose up around simple, improvised altars; the sublime solemnity of the Mass celebrated in the fields; the hospital feast-days, especially Christmas, Easter and the month of May, where the poetry of one's own village church flourished again, and the tender memories of distant wives and mothers mingled with the anxious hope for an end to the harsh sacrifice!
>
> Humble priests, generously fulfilling their duty towards their motherland, but still more aware of a higher duty towards the Church and souls, how many times did we lean over our dying younger brothers and listen to the anguished breathing of the nation expressed in their passion and agony. It is impossible to say what the priestly heart felt in such moments. It often happened – permit me this personal memory – that I had to fall on my knees and cry like a child, alone in my room, unable to contain the emotion that I felt at the simple and holy deaths of so many poor sons of our people . . . No, it is not true that Christian Italy is dead. *Non est mortua puella, sed dormit* [The child is not dead but sleeps: Matthew 9. 24] (*Rosario*, pp. 126–7).

Pulpit-rhetoric apart, the text is faithful enough to experience to show that Roncalli, unlike many military chaplains in the First World War, never glorified war or justified it because of its bracing and stimulating effects. He says: 'War is and remains the greatest evil'. Yet somehow God was present in it.

Pope Benedict XV had never wanted Italy to get involved in the war, foreseeing (correctly) awesome consequences. On the Western front in 1917 a stalemate had been reached. The allies and the Germans were pounding each other for a few yards of muddy trenches. Benedict tried to profit from the sense of having reached an *impasse* by offering an honourable way out. On August 1, 1917, he addressed a note to all the belligerents urging them to accept 'a just and lasting settlement', to abandon the empty hope of 'victory' as a war aim, and to put an end to 'the useless slaughter' (*ibid.*). One of Benedict's agents in this diplomatic initiative was forty-one year old Mgr Eugenio Pacelli, the future Pius XII. He liked to recall – much later – that he had been ordained archbishop on May 13, 1917, the very day on which Our Lady appeared for the first time to three peasant children near Fatima in Portugal.

But Benedict's well-meant initiative not only failed; it rallied everyone against him. In Italy, his remarks about 'the useless slaughter' undermined national morale and suggested that Catholics were unpatriotic and disloyal. Benedict was dubbed Maldetto XV (Accursed instead of Blessed) and charged with 'defeatism'. Nor was he any more acceptable to the Western Allies.

In October 1917 the Austrians, now stiffened by seven hand-picked German divisions, broke through with overwhelming force, took 300,000 prisoners in two weeks, inflicted heavy casualties, and drove the Italians back to within fifteen miles of Venice. This was Caporetto, the greatest battle on the Italian front during the entire war. It was a rout, later compared by General Cadorna's wife to the collapse of France in 1940 (Seton-Watson, p. 480). This was an exaggeration, but one sees the point. The seventy-mile retreat had left a million and a half Italians under Austrian occupation. Four hundred thousand refugees clogged the roads and had somehow to be housed and fed. The Italian commander, General Cadorna, blamed the defeat on the lack of fighting spirit among the troops ('they cravenly withdrew without fighting or ignominiously surrendered' said his communiqué). The retreating troops were 'decimated' (that is, one in ten was taken out and shot) *pour encourager les autres*. Despite this, one witness reported that the retreating men 'gave the impression of people returning home at last after a long job of work, laughing and chattering'. The soldiers 'naively imagined that this was the way to end the war, and there were shouts for peace and for the Pope' (Seton-Watson, p. 479; also Ragonieri, pp. 2038-41).

The shock of Caporetto brought about a revival of patriotism. *L'Osservatore Romano*, the Vatican newspaper, now editorialised about the Catholic's duty to resist the enemy. Prayers were offered not merely for 'a just peace' but for 'victory' (Seton-Watson, p. 482). Don Roncalli shared in this changed mood. He wrote to Zaverio on November 22: 'Now the enemy is in the house, he has to be chased out at whatever cost, otherwise things will be bad for us. Everyone should stay in his own house. We are all guilty, but today it is our duty to make every sacrifice to see that the Germans clear out of Italy' (*Familiari*, I, p. 60).

As the Bergamo hospitals filled up with the wounded of Caporetto, he had a more personal cause for worry. His youngest surviving brother, Giuseppe, was missing. (Luigi, born in 1896, had died at the age of two.) He was twenty-three, thirteen years younger than Angelo, who felt very protective towards him. He wrote to Giuseppe, always known in the family as Pino or Giuseppino, on November 5, 1917:

> A sacrifice for one's country is a sacrifice for God and for our brothers; and when you come back – soon, I hope – you will see that nothing, nothing at all has been lost by your sufferings . . . . Where are you? In a trench on the Tridentine front? Let me know, if you can, without failing in your duty (*Familiari*, I, p. 61).

But this letter to Giuseppe was never delivered. A month later, on January 6, 1918, there was still no definite news about him. Angelo told Zaverio that 'tears well up in my eyes when I think of Giuseppino, and I cannot resist the impulse of tenderness that comes over me' (*Familiari*, I, p. 63). His enquiries about Giuseppe have led nowhere: he could be 'already in paradise, but is more likely in a prisoner-of-war camp'. Sergeant Roncalli fights back the tears with the brisk command: 'Yes I must, I want to be strong'.

There is a three month gap in his correspondence at this point. It starts again with a letter to Zaverio on April 17, 1918, with the good news that Giuseppino is a prisoner-of-war somewhere in Austria. Pino's routine postcard (cross out what does not apply) was dated February 19, 1918. His only complaint was that he was hungry and lacked bread.

Apart from the fate of Giuseppe, the war now faded out of Roncalli's correspondence until it was over, and he began to pick up the threads of his future. He saw Cardinal Ferrari in Milan on January 31, 1918, and stayed on to give a lecture to the Union of Catholic Women on St Catherine of Siena. Normality, it seemed, was flooding back. The war was being settled elsewhere.

Don Roncalli was given his post-war job. On February 27, 1918, Bishop Marella decided he would become warden of a Student Hostel (*Casa dello Studente*) to be housed in a *palazzo* not far from the Seminary. This was a new venture. He had to start from scratch. Roncalli threw himself with enthusiasm into the novel task of setting up his own place at the age of thirty-seven. He started to buy furniture, paying a 5% rate of interest on the loan he took out to pay for it. He hoped that his sisters Ancilla and Maria would come and keep house for him (*Familiari*, I, p. 65). All the members of the family would be welcome at any time.

On May 27, 1918, he thanked Zaverio and his wife, Maria, for their gift of 250 *lire*, but sent it back: they can't afford it. More was still needed for kitchen equipment, so he borrowed again from the Piccolo Credito Bergamo, the local Catholic bank, and expected to repay his debts within two to three years. He was jauntily confident: he didn't mind the expenses because they were all 'one-off' (*Familiari*, I, p. 67).

While Don Roncalli was thinking about pots and pans and domesticity, Pope Benedict XV risked another rebuff by exploring the chances of a separate peace between Italy and Austria-Hungary (Seton-Watson, p. 492). Neutral Switzerland acted as intermediary. These efforts, however, were doomed to failure because Italy was now thoroughly locked in to the alliance with England and France.

The Italian government could not afford to end the war with so much of its territory still occupied by the enemy. It was in a bad bargaining posture. To have any influence at all in the postwar peace settlement and to implement the vague Treaty of London, it needed a victory. So on October 24, 1918, the first anniversary of Caporetto, the Italians attacked in numbers across the River Piave. After five days the town of Vittorio Veneto was taken (it gave its name to the battle) and the Austrians began to retreat. The retreat became a rout – Caporetto in reverse – as the Austrian army, made up of so many different nationalities now determined to go home and achieve independence, disintegrated. The Czechs, the Yugoslavs and the Hungarians revolted. The Italian government had its victory at the last gasp.

Italy could take its place at the conference table with some dignity. Benedict XV, however, was excluded from the peace conference (Seton-Watson, p. 493). On the Italian front, the armistice was signed on November 3, and the cease-fire came into force the next day at 3 p.m. (*ibid.*, p. 503). On the Western front the guns fell silent at 11 a.m. on November 11, the eleventh month. 1918. The Great War was over.

We have Don Roncalli's diary for these last, dramatic days:

November 4, 1918. The victory of our arms has been truly grandiose. We shouldn't boast about it because we are all sinners . . .

November 10, 1918. Great religioso-patriotic demonstrations. An incredible crowd, devout and orderly. I'm glad to see Catholics taking part in such demonstrations . . .

November 11, 1918. The latest news is that Kaiser William II has abdicated. There's someone who liked to say *Domine, domine* (Lord, Lord), and yet treated the Lord as though he were an equal. I remember seeing him in Rome in 1903 when he was frantically acclaimed by delirious crowds. What a difference between then and now (*Letture*, p. 407).

Roncalli was demobilised on December 10, 1918. He destroyed his army uniform, glad to be rid of it.

Chapter 6

Towards Propaganda and Fascism

And the flags. And the trumpets. And so many eagles.
How many? Count them. And such a press of people.
We hardly knew ourselves that day, or knew the City.
This is the way to the temple . . .

(T. S. Eliot, *Coriolan* (1920), from *Collected Poems 1909-1962*, p. 139)

For Don Roncalli, as for Italy as a whole, 1919 was a time of relief and hope, enthusiasm and new plans. There was a widespread yearning for change and a utopian desire for better things. The returning soldiers expected at least to find work if not 'homes fit for heroes'. Italy had ended on the winning side in the war; it hoped therefore for a share in the spoils and an important role at the conference table. Catholics, their contribution to the war now recognised, re-entered political life. The Vatican gave permission for Don Luigi Sturzo, a Sicilian priest, to found the Partito Popolare Italiano (henceforward PPI or Popolari). It presented its manifesto on January 18, 1919. Though Cardinal Pietro Gasparri, Secretary of State, had vetoed the use of 'Catholic' or 'Christian' in its title, and although it was not a 'confessional' party, it embodied the aspirations of the Catholic peasants and workers. Don Roncalli supported it enthusiastically from the outset. There was a sense – wholly deceptive, as it turned out – of a new age dawning. 'We are awakening as if to the light of a new day', Roncalli wrote (*Journal*, p. 208).

On the personal level, he had plenty of reasons for optimism. 'In four years of war, passed in the midst of a world in agony, how good the Lord has been to me' (*Journal*, p. 206). On May 9, 1919, his father was at last able to get a loan to buy La Colombera, the family home since 1892. It cost 57,000 *lire*. It was an exceptionally good year for silk-worms, and they were able to sell the whole lot and make a down payment of 11,000 *lire*. The Roncallis were still poor, but they were no longer dependent on Count Morlani. Since land reform was on the programme of the PPI, the Roncallis were among its 'natural' supporters.

Professionally, too, Don Angelo was happy. His work as warden of the new *Casa dello Studente* in the Palazzo Marenzi, via San Salvatore, in the upper city, was engrossing and satisfying. He had just over forty students. Education was the best way to prepare the future and fulfil his vows, now permanent, as a member of the Association of Priests of the Sacred Heart. He thought there could be no higher vocation than that of 'forming a new generation in the spirit of Jesus' (*ibid.*).

There were, of course, problems. Roncalli's notes for January 28, 1919, record a minor tragedy, a Bergamesque *Romeo and Juliet*. One of his students, M.S., fell in love with a girl glimpsed at a window opposite the Hostel. It was nobody's fault, Roncalli thought. It was

44

just that M.S. was 'dazzled by his first, unexpected, spontaneous feelings' (*Memorie*, p. 430). M.S. was expelled, as a warning to the others: falling in love was not part of the programme of the Student Hostel. It was already under attack from conservatives who were ready to pounce on the first sign of laxity or softness. Roncalli tried to mitigate the blow by fixing a place for M.S. at the Collegio Sant' Alessandro, where he would be removed from the window and temptation. The boy shed copious tears.

Roncalli, at 38, was rather out of his depth: his own adolescence and youth had not included the experience of human love, unless we count filial love. But he could feel the pain of it: 'How often the mystery of the youthful soul comes home to me with such suffering that I feel an ineffable tenderness' (*Memorie*, p. 431). Circumstances cast him in the role of defender of the institution and heavy-handed father. But he thought of himself rather as a mother, just as he had previously thought of God as Mother (cf. p. 36): 'I shall love my students as a mother her sons, but always in the Lord' (*Journal*, p. 208).

He was in demand as a preacher. In April he held three 'pulpit-dialogues' with Don Carozzi, his Roman seminary companion. One of them feigned ignorance and evoked crushing replies from the 'Catholic'. It was a diverting and popular form of apologetic entertainment.

Besides much preaching and his work at the hostel, Don Roncalli was also chaplain to the Union of Catholic Women. The title of its newsletter, *Gigli e Rose* (Lilies and Roses), did not suggest a very radical movement. He already knew a real Catholic feminist, Adelaide Coari, who had worked with Bishop Radini. She despised the lilies and roses world of sewing circles that so often passed for female Catholic Action, and held that women should learn their rights and engage in direct social action. She was now working in Milan. We will meet her again when she starts to correspond with Roncalli.

The Union of Catholic Women was going well in Bergamo, especially in the upper city: by June 1919 the youth group had over fifty dedicated members, and Don Roncalli was stirring up 'the more sluggish parishes' (*Memorie*, p. 450). He was no longer scared of women, but he still kept firmly to the rule he had given himself in 1910 when he was first appointed chaplain to the Union: 'The work I am doing requires great delicacy and prudence, as it frequently means dealing with women. I intend, therefore, that my behaviour shall always be kind, modest and dignified so as to divert attention away from myself and give a richer spiritual quality to my work' (*Journal*, p. 193).

He entertained private doubts about his bishop, Luigi Marella. He was kind and meant well but 'he doesn't understand certain situations and hasn't the courage to do the things that would bring him great honour; so he withdraws, bewildered, into his shell' (*Memorie*, p. 432). That was in February 1919. Two months later, Marella is said to be 'shy and terrified of everything that is new'. He responds to problems day by day, as they come up, instead of 'following a plan and carrying it out with energy' (*ibid.*, p. 444).

On June 8, 1919, he met Bishop Marella by chance on the funicular railway that links the upper and lower cities. 'Has the seminary rector said anything?' asked the bishop, cryptically. He hadn't, but next day Roncalli learned that he had been appointed spiritual director at the seminary from the start of the next academic year. It was a position of trust, but not of any great prestige. It meant that the absurd worries about his alleged 'modernism' had been put to rest.

When a conference of the newly founded National Union of Catholic Women (*Unione Femminile Italiana*), was announced for October 1919, he leaped at the chance to go to Rome and began to feel a certain nostalgia: 'To tell the truth I gladly welcome this opportunity to have a bath of *romanità*, and to offer my ministry among the students and seminarians to the tombs of the Roman saints' (*Memorie*, p. 464). But the journey began badly. At Milan railway station his wallet, containing 800 *lire*, was stolen. He tried to make light of the incident by thinking up an apt scripture comment ('You joyfully accepted the plundering of your property', Hebrews 10.34). He was tired out on arrival in Rome, and found the conference a bore. He went for long walks, admiring the modern art in the Galleria Borghese and discovering that Rome had changed much: new and expensive villas now covered the hill of Parioli. He sought out old friends, like his former rector, Mgr Bugarini. But his 1919 visit cured him of any lingering nostalgia: 'I must confess that the older I get, the less I like the Roman atmosphere. I'm like a pilgrim here; and even though there is a lot of good to be done, I wouldn't want to live here' (*Memorie*, p. 498).

Yet he couldn't leave, because he was still waiting for an audience with Pope Benedict XV. He spent a whole morning kicking his heels in the ante-chamber and began to feel impatient: 'This blessed audience is becoming a positive torture for me' (*Memorie*, p. 468). Finally, at noon on November 6, 1919, he saw the Pope. It went well:

> The Pope was so good. He asked me some questions about the workers' movement in
> Bergamo, and let slip a certain anxiety about it. He listened when I talked about my
> work with the students, and blessed it along with the work I am starting at the seminary.
> He made a most agreeable and affectionate impression. The blessing of the Pope is
> precious and will strengthen me (*Memorie*, p. 469).

Roncalli had audiences with all the popes of the twentieth century. He found Benedict XV the most sympathetic.

In September 1920 Roncalli suddenly became much more widely known. He was the second choice to address the sixth National Eucharistic Congress. Held in Bergamo, its theme was 'The Eucharist and Our Lady'. A contemporary account catches something of the atmosphere in which Don Roncalli delivered the most important speech of his life so far on the afternoon of September 9, 1920:

> The Rubini Theatre was more crowded even than the day before. Not a single corner
> was free. The stage itself was packed with bishops and notables. The scene cannot be
> described: hearts are full of joy; enthusiasm, restrained by reverence, shines out on all
> faces. The eucharistic hymn is sung, the president recites the prayers and sums up the
> work done during the morning. Then Professor Don Roncalli begins to speak ... His
> speech is many times interrupted by applause, and at the end the audience, deeply moved
> and enthusiastic, gave him a standing ovation (*Rosario*, p. 131, quoting the official *Acts* of
> the Congress).

Roncalli's Mariology is unremarkable and sound. He expounds the motto of Lourdes, *Ad Jesum per Mariam* ('To Jesus through Mary'), to show that Mary's role in salvation-history cannot be understood without reference to her Son. Thus she cannot be considered as a rival to Jesus or a threat to his role as 'the one mediator'. His exposition is solid rather than brilliant, buttressed by patristic quotations and vivified by poetry borrowed from the Song of Songs. The sermons of St Bernard guided him though these ambivalent regions. When the Song of Songs declares that 'as a lily among brambles, so is my love among maidens' (2,2), Don Roncalli enquired rhetorically, 'Who can fail to discern in the delicate image of the lily, Mary Immaculate, beautiful and resplendent?' (*Rosario*, p. 120). It would be churlish not to. Besides, the image had a long history. But when the lily is flanked by the apple-tree whose 'highly nutritious fruit' is said to be 'evidently' the Eucharist, it is tempting to think than allegorical exegesis, unchecked, obscures as much as it adorns.

But it was not the Mariology that won Roncalli a standing ovation. He earned it by his patriotic fervour and his cry, based on his wartime experience as chaplain, 'No, Christian Italy is not dead' (*Rosario*, p. 127). Anticlericals were saying that support for the *Popolari* had been drummed up by the clergy who were acting as its recruiting sergeants. But in Bergamo, he replied, Catholic Action is a *populist* cause and this 'vast and powerful organisation is merely the spontaneous emanation of the religious feeling of the people' (*ibid.*, p. 128). Its purpose was to bring to bear the principles of Catholic social doctrine, 'derived from the Gospels', on all the contemporary questions: unemployment, poverty, class-war, labour unrest, inflation.

Don Roncalli was not speaking in a vacuum. Only the previous month the Red Army had been driven back from the gates of Warsaw in a battle known as 'the miracle of the Vistula'. The victory was commonly attributed to Our Lady of Czestochowa. But now, Italy itself was being threatened:

> While we are gathered here for this Congress, our Italy is going through one of its blackest and most terrible hours. New barbarians are standing at the gates of our city. You have seen the red banners, symbols of violence, fluttering in sinister fashion above the factories where the people – sometimes gullible but always good at heart – are waiting for work. What is going to happen? Are we perhaps on the eve of a social revolution? (*Rosario*, p. 131)

They were not. But it was a reasonable enough question. The young Marxist theoretician, Antonio Gramsci, had been explaining at fervent factory meetings that Italy was in that terminal state known as 'prerevolutionary'. The bourgeoisie was alarmed, and looked to the right for protection.

Roncalli stayed calm. The peroration, which won him his standing ovation, was an invitation to hope. He told the story of the Polish Dominican St Hyacinth who had carried the Eucharist many miles to escape the Tartar hordes; but the statue of Our Lady proved too heavy for him, so he entrusted it to his parishioners and together they reached the safety of Kraków. The relevance was clear:

> Our spirits are not apprehensive. Our hearts are firm, even if the revolution should come. In the midst of universal ruin, salvation lies in our hands. Behold, we priests will raise aloft Christ in his sacrament, and will bless the swirling river of humanity. You laypeople will strap upon your backs the image of the Madonna, and will face with sure steps the abyss, the tempest, death itself. God will renew his miracles. We will bring to

safety the sacred pledges of civilisation, the Holy Eucharist and the Madonna, the
dearest objects of our faith and love, and after the agonising struggle, will lay them on
the altar of the *patria (Rosario*, p. 131).

It was not very clear. But crystal clarity cannot be demanded of a peroration. Don Roncalli was keeping his options open: without either advocating or damning the revolution,
he was trying to say that the Church should be present, somehow, in the very necessary
work of the reconstruction of society. His speech at the Eucharistic Congress established
him as a forceful orator and a potential leader. It won him a modest national reputation.
He was now, at 39, a distinctly 'promising' priest.

The first hint of a move from Bergamo came from Cardinal William Van Rossum, the
Dutch Prefect of Propaganda Fide. (After Dr Josef Goebbels had blackened the term 'propaganda', the department was rebaptised Congregation for the Evangelisation of Peoples,
an unwieldy mouthful that has not caught on.) Van Rossum said that he had his eye on Don
Roncalli for the post of national director of the Propagation of the Faith. Though many
dioceses, including Bergamo, had a flourishing organisation to support the work of the
missions, elsewhere in Italy the work was badly organised or totally unknown. Van Rossum
wanted an organiser, an animator and a fund-raiser.

Roncalli felt a pronounced aversion for the new post. He didn't want it at all. He protested that he did not have the organising ability he was being credited with, and that he
did not have the right temperament for the post. He is 'someone who doesn't get much
done; by nature lazy, I write very slowly and am easily distracted in my work' (*Natale,
1970*, p. 13). His self-description concludes: 'The active life of exterior movement to which
I have so far been condemned was never my ideal; I would have preferred a life of recollection and study in a monastic cell, with a taste for the direct ministry of souls but peacefully
and without fuss' (*ibid.*). Yet on one side is 'Thy will be done' and on the other 'self-love and
the reasons of the heart' (*Natale, 1970*, p. 18).

Roncalli was now a curialist, in the direct service of the Apostolic See. Propaganda Fide,
his particular branch of the Curia, was being expanded and re-organised as a direct result of
initiatives taken by Pope Benedict XV, whose encyclical *Maximum Illud* (November 30,
1919) was devoted to missionary activity in the much-changed post-war world. The encyclical stated three fundamental principles of missionary work. The first was that a local or
'native' clergy should be ordained as soon as possible; and from this indigenous clergy it was
expected that bishops would soon emerge. The second was that European missionaries –
there were at the time few others – should cast off every form of nationalism. This was
aimed particularly at the French. He was already looking forward to the end of the colonial
era which Roncalli was to hail as one of the 'signs of the times' in his encyclical *Pacem in Terris*.
The third principle was that everyone was to be involved in missionary work, by prayer,
sacrifice and financial involvement.

Roncalli directed this operation in Italy. He discovered an Italy that he hardly knew, and
as he moved round the country had to learn tact in dealing with apathy in the South and
existing missionary organisations in the North like the Missionary Union which felt threatened by the new centralism. The work also enabled him to travel round Europe to consult

other missionary bodies, so that he gained a more 'universalist' view of the Church than would ever have been possible in Bergamo.

But this did not happen all at once. Don Roncalli had arrived in Rome, but was in no hurry to set up house there. He returned to Bergamo to pack and on his way saw Cardinal Ferrari for the last time on January 21, 1921. Throat cancer made Ferrari speechless, but, as Roncalli put it, he 'continued to speak with eyes and pen'. On February 2, 1921, feast of the Purification of Our Lady, Ferrari died as the last notes of the evening Angelus rang out from the cathedral. It is Roncalli who records these details in an obituary he wrote at the time (*Dodicesimo anniversario*, p. 111 and following). Ferrari was, he said, a master of spirituality and the defender of the poor.

All Roncalli's spiritual guides were now departed. Radini Tedeschi had died in 1914 and now Ferrari in 1921. He was orphaned once more. Subsequently he would have many 'spiritual directors' but no more true father-figures or models of the episcopal ministry. From now on his memories of Radini Tedeschi and Ferrari would fuse with the accounts of great bishops in history to shape his concept of episcopacy.

As he set about his work at Propaganda, other, more minor, sub-episcopal dignities came his way. In March 1921 the cathedral chapter of Bergamo voted unanimously to make him an honorary canon (*Pastore*, p. 97). It was a way of saying 'thank-you' and an indication that they didn't expect to see him back: his Roman career was now properly launched. But he was Canon Roncalli for less than two months since on May 7, 1921, he was made a 'domestic prelate of his Holiness'. This allowed him to wear red piping on his soutane and to be addressed as *Monsignore*. He took it rather pompously in a letter home: 'This dignity is a great responsibility' (*Familiari*, I, p. 75).

Most of the time Roncalli was on the road, the itinerant pedlar of the importance of the missions. He chanced to be in Milan on September 8, 1921, when Achille Ratti, the future Pius XI, took possession of his see. Roncalli was keenly interested in the succession of Ferrari, and was surprised by the Ratti appointment. Here was someone who had spent his entire life among books, first as prefect of the prestigious Ambrosian Library in Milan and then as prefect of the Vatican Library. Roncalli had known him in Milan. Ratti had helped him by photocopying documents on St Charles Borromeo (at the time an expensive and elaborate process). But they had not been close. In 1918 Ratti had been thrown to the wolves as Vatican diplomatic representative (he was not yet Nuncio) in newly independent Poland. Roncalli wasn't quite sure what he thought of Ratti as Ferrari's successor. The man was aloof, reserved, enigmatic.

In Rome Roncalli turned down a seven-roomed apartment because it would have cost 15,600 *lire* a year (*Familiari*, I, p. 76, letter of August 3, 1921), but accepted a flat in Via Volturno 58, for 6,000 *lire* a year. Though not very close to Propaganda, it was handy for the railway station. He was able to offer hospitality to his old seminary rector, Mgr Vincenzo Bugarini, who had nowhere to go in retirement and felt unwanted, and he brought down his sisters Ancilla and Maria by one of the few trains that were still running - there was another strike - to become his housekeepers (*Familiari*, I, p. 78, letter of November 13, 1921). They found Rome very expensive compared with Sotto il Monte, but their cooking delighted Bugarini, and *Monsignore* their brother showed them the sights of Rome (*Familiari*, I, p. 79).

But then he was off over Christmastide, from December 17 to January 8, to see how missionary activity was funded and organised in France, Belgium, Germany and Holland. In Germany he saw the effects of runaway inflation and reported to his family: 'Think of the Germans and the Austrians whose money is worthless. They are far worse off than we are. But for the most part they are good people. And they will haul themselves up again before we do, because they work hard while we spend our time in strikes and revolutions' (*Familiari*, I, 81). This mythic contrast between the hard-working German and the indolent Italian had a long literary history.

No sooner was he back from his travels than on January 22, 1922, Pope Benedict XV died. For the first time since 1870 flags were flown at half-mast on government buildings. Yet his achievements, though considerable, were not widely appreciated. His pleas for peace had gone unheard. He had emptied the Vatican coffers, partly to provide 'humanitarian' aid to Soviet Russia. Though obviously unable to remove all inquisitors from key posts, he had put an end to the anti-Modernist campaign. He had witnessed the foundation of the PPI and seen the return of Italian Catholics to the mainstream of political life. And he had given new impetus to missionary activity. In the long-term, he proved to be one of the most enlightened popes of the century. The conclave had as usual to decide whether to continue or cancel out his policies. It needed fourteen ballots to reach a compromise conclusion, and was the most protracted and bloodiest conclave of the century.

Thanks to the diary of the cardinal of Vienna, Gustavo Piffl, it is possible to reconstruct what happened (*Quale Papa?* p. 138 and following). Roncalli's superior, Van Rossum, made the first move. He thought the time had come to elect a non-Italian. Unfortunately the foreigner he proposed, Merry del Val, was more Roman than the Romans, and his election would have meant a return to the rigours of Pius X, whose Secretary of State he had been. La Fontaine, patriarch of Venice, was another former inquisitor who could plausibly claim to inherit the mantle of Pius X, but was that what the fifty-three cardinals really wanted?

The alternative was Pietro Gasparri, author of the 1917 Code of Canon Law and Secretary of State under Benedict whose policies he would continue but without Benedict's imprudences. A vote for Gasparri would be a vote for sagacity. But since neither side would give way, the conclave was deadlocked. Thirty-six votes were needed to win. Merry del Val reached 17, La Fontaine peaked at 23 and Gasparri at 24. As they faded, Ratti, Archbishop of Milan for only five months, came through the middle. But it was a bruising contest. One witness, on oath during the beatification process for Merry del Val, reported that Gasparri had said that 'during the conclave Merry del Val's ambitions knew no bounds so much so that he incurred excommunication' (*Quale Papa?*, p. 142). Cardinal De Lai, whom we last met in 1914 deploring Duchesne, had acted as election agent for Merry del Val. When his candidate failed, he tried to impose on Ratti the condition that he would have Gasparri as his Secretary of State. But it is against conclave rules to make deals in advance. In theory, De Lai was excommunicated too. Ratti, unoriginally, took the name of Pius XI.

At least one person was overjoyed at Ratti's election. Duchesne, the venerable church historian, was now 79 and in the last year of his life. He had known Ratti as librarian in Milan and Rome. He felt his whole life's work was vindicated. With his Breton faith undimmed he had survived being put on the Index of Forbidden Books and he now looked forward to an era of flourishing scholarship in the Church. Enclosed in his vast black cape (the *pèlerine*) he followed the *sedia gestatoria* as it bore the new pope into St Peter's to the sound of silver trumpets.

Roncalli was more guarded in his judgement. The truth was that no one knew where Ratti stood on important questions. He had successfully avoided showing his hand in all the disputes that had raged with such passionate intensity over the last thirty years (see Tramontin, I, p. 146). Mgr Roncalli's first comment on Pius XI came in a letter to Don Antonio Guerinoni, a Bergamesque working in the nunciature in Madrid:

> The new Holy Father is well. I saw him again in a long audience a few days ago. He had the goodness to treat me with the trust that one might expect from an affectionate friend of Mgr Radini Tedeschi and the prefect of the Ambrosian Library. Yet I get between his feet as little as possible, and feel shivers run down my spine every time I have to go through those Vatican halls. Despite my constant and heart-felt attempt to serve the new pope as best I can, I don't envy – indeed I feel compassion – towards those who have to work in the Vatican. The Pope is truly good and wise; he shows that he has the Spirit with him (*Gran Sacerdote*, pp. 135–6. Letter dated July 21, 1922).

Roncalli moved house again in July 1922. The new flat was a charming roof-top eyrie cut into the facade of the church of Santa Maria in Via Lata. 'My crow's nest', he called it (*Gran Sacerdote*, p. 134). It was much more convenient for his office in Piazza di Spagna. Mgr Bugarini, now an established member of the household, moved along with them and pulled his weight. His knowledge of the Italian church proved invaluable. So many bishops had passed through his hands at the Roman seminary. But he had only another eighteen months to live.

By any criteria, Mgr Roncalli was a success at Propaganda Fide. He saw his work not in bureaucratic terms but as helping the pope, as the 'father of the family', to provide for the needs of all the missions (*Gran Sacerdote*, p. 139, letter to the vicar general of Parma, March 20, 1924). He more than doubled the collections for Propaganda, from 400,000 *lire* in 1920 to over a million in 1922 (Trevor, p. 123). But as he looked back later over his time at Propaganda, he saw it in a different light. Writing to his successor, Zanetti, he said: 'I am convinced that if there were any good fruits of my work, that was because I took up this ministry out of pure obedience. Then the Lord gave me the grace to love it, and I left with sorrow...' (*Gran Sacerdote* p. 152, letter of May 29, 1929). The pattern was becoming familiar: distaste, obedience, attachment and then the wrench.

It wasn't all hard work. In May 1923 he travelled throughout Sicily, a whole new enchanted world for a northerner like himself. The newspapers reported hail-storms near Bergamo, he wrote home, but Sicily 'is like a garden. Now that I've been all round the island, I can truly say that it's a semi-paradise' (*Familiari*, I, p. 78). Travel, he concluded, gave him 'an extraordinary appetite'. He had not yet joined the weight-watchers.

In his letters home Mgr Roncalli usually steered well clear of politics. But Mussolini was now in power and had apparently shed his anti-clericalism. The 'march on Rome', which was later hailed in Fascist mythology as an act of dashing heroism, was really the resolution of a fairly routine political muddle. Those Fascists who were not halted by driving rain arrived by train. Mussolini himself appeared in Rome on October 30, 1922, not in the uniform of the saviour of the nation but in the frock-coat and top-hat of the traditional politician. Only the irresolution of the army and King Victor Emmanuel III's sudden and unexpected change of mind let the Fascists into the city.

Mussolini played down his atheist and anti-clerical past. He knew that to hold and extend his power in Italy, he would have to woo the Church. His package of pro-clerical proposals included the introduction of religious education into primary schools, the appointment of official military chaplains, improved salaries for the clergy, and the return of the crucifix to public buildings. These were all measures no Liberal government had even contemplated. The Vatican was favourably impressed. Pietro Gasparri, Secretary of State, was able to have his first secret meeting with Mussolini on January 20, 1923 (Pollard, p. 28). Mussolini promised, among other things, to 'deal with the problem of Freemasonry', still dedicated, it was believed, to the final liquidation of the temporal power of the papacy. Gasparri promised in return to prepare a list of 'unreliable and mistaken men' in the Vatican service who were trying to build up the *Popolari* as an alternative to the Fascists. But nothing was known of this secret deal, which marked the beginning of the complicated minuet that would lead, eventually, to the Lateran Pacts of 1929.

Nothing was known about the deal, but its effects were soon felt. In July 1923 Don Luigi Sturzo was ordered to resign as secretary of the PPI, and he went into exile in London. He was succeeded by a young layman from Trentino, Alcide De Gasperi, whose first political experience had been gained in the Austrian parliament. But the writing was on the wall for the *Popolari*, and the only force that could conceivably have checked the Fascists was emasculated. Pius XI and Gasparri had decided that an apolitical Catholic Action was the best form of Christian 'presence' to the world. The doomed *Popolari* made their last stand under De Gasperi at the elections of April 6, 1924.

For the first (and last) time Mgr Roncalli had some advice for his family on an election. Using the typewriter bequeathed him by Mgr Bugarini, who had just died on February 14, 1924, he said:

> I recommend everyone not to get too excited about the elections. Vote when the time comes. Now it is better to let things be. Keep quiet and stay at home; think it out for yourselves, and let everyone do what they think is right. I, for example, remain faithful to the *Partito Popolare;* but because of the post I have with the Holy See I can't and mustn't make any public statements at all. For that reason I won't be coming to Bergamo to vote (*Familiari*, I, p. 96, letter of February 24, 1924).

So Roncalli had made up his mind early on what he would do. And he was going against *l'Osservatore Romano*, now edited by Giuseppe Dalla Torre, which had welcomed the march on Rome and Mussolini's pro-clerical package, and devoted more space to Catholic Action than to the *Popolari*. But Roncalli retained his independence of judgement. Two days before the election he wrote again to his family:

> I might have come to see you for the elections, but to tell the truth I preferred to stay here for reasons you will well understand. *In my conscience as a priest and a Christian, I don't feel I can vote for the Fascists.* Everyone has the right to think as they believe. In the end we'll see who was right; do what seems good to you. My advice is this: if there is freedom to vote, vote for the PPI list. If there is danger of trouble, stay at home and let the world go its

own way. Of one thing I am certain: *the salvation of Italy cannot come from Mussolini even though he may be a man of talent.* His goals may perhaps be good and correct, but the means he takes to realise them are wicked and contrary to the law of the Gospel (*Familiari*, I, p. 98, April 4, 1924. Italics added).

The warning to stay at home in case of violence was needed. The Fascists hung about the polling booths and intimidated the electors. The campaign headquarters of the PPI were attacked. Even so, the *Popolari* still won 40 out of 375 seats, compared with 42 for the Socialists and 17 for the Communists. But the Fascist landslide meant that the power of the *Popolari* was now broken. Its leaders would go into exile, prison or hiding.

The Vatican dropped the *Popolari*. This brought together in despondency those curialists who had pinned their hopes on the PPI. Roncalli now met for the first time Giovanni Battista Montini, the future Paul VI. Montini's father, Giorgio, was editor of *Il Cittadino di Brescia*, and a PPI member of parliament. But after the kidnap and murder of the Socialist deputy, Giacomo Matteotti, in June 1924, he never set foot in the chamber again, believing rightly that the Fascists would stop at nothing to secure their hold on power. His newspaper was suppressed.

Giovanni Battista, just back from a spell in Poland, was now at the Secretariat of State. He had to report to Giuseppe Pizzardo, head of the Italian section, on 'the spiritual and moral condition of the young' and to gather material he became student chaplain at the university. This whole milieu, more cultivated and sophisticated than anything Roncalli had previously known, was solidly anti-Fascist. Montini sensed a kindred spirit, sought him out, and invited him to address his students. This was their first documented contact (*Quinquagesimo anniversario*, pp. 57–8). Over the next three decades they became good friends.

Roncalli's sermon in Bergamo Cathedral on September 1, 1924, was a lament for the *Popolari*. According to the point of view adopted, it could be described as the most injudicious or the most courageous, the finest or the most foolhardy sermon he ever preached. The tenth anniversary of the death of Bishop Radini Tedeschi was the pretext. As his biographer and former secretary, Roncalli was the obvious choice as preacher. But the presence of the civic, political and military establishment turned it into a political event of some significance. The memory of 'My Bishop' moved Roncalli to an eloquence he had not displayed since the eucharistic congress of 1920. But the changed context made it even more dramatic. His listeners were concerned only with his answer to one question: what did he think of Fascism?

Roncalli's chosen theme was patriotism or 'true love of one's country'. Some of those present might be asking of Radini Tedeschi, whom they had not known: 'What did he do for his country? Was he so immersed in churchy affairs that he did nothing?' (*Pasqua 1976*, p. 30). As churchmen, said Roncalli, we have to be patriotic, because 'patriotism is a form of brotherly love'. But patriotism cannot be used as a protective cloak to cover everything a government does. The greatness of a country is not measured by 'military enterprises, diplomatic agreements or economic successes' about which the Fascists constantly orated, even if so far there was nothing much to show.

Patriotism, then, as he understood it, did not exclude a certain distance from the state, and this 'distance' was a condition of the Church's freedom. Roncalli cried:

O leave us the holy freedom of our peaceful and lofty ministry . . . Leave to us the guardianship of the fundamental laws of civilisation, which are the Ten Commandments and the Gospels; from this source derives the doctrine which enlightens and inspires every noble action, leading to sacrifice and heroism. Leave this to us. And *do not ask us for anything more (Pasqua, 1976*, p. 31: italics added).

It was a warning that there were limits to what could be asked of the Church. Roncalli plunged on, almost recklessly. Bergamo in the past had the reputation of being 'intransigent'. So it was. But this did not rule out good relations with the civil authorities. Radini Tedeschi had always behaved 'as a perfect gentleman' towards them. His contribution to the debate on education had been described by Giuseppe Toniolo as 'the most complete treatment of the question written in Italy or elsewhere' *(ibid.,* p. 32). Mention of Toniolo was dynamite for he had been the advocate of 'Christian democracy' and Catholic populism that were now regarded as enemies of the regime. After such effrontery, it was only a matter of time before the Fascist police caught up with Roncalli and - in the discreetest possible manner – invited the Vatican to remove him.

He had misjudged the mood in the Vatican. Just over a week after his Bergamo sermon, Pius XI denounced with some asperity any 'opening to the left' on the part of the *Popolari* (see Giacomo Martina in De Gasperi, *Lettere sul Concordato*, p. 123). In Germany and Belgium Catholic parties were already co-operating with non-Communist Socialists. Pius XI did not want that to happen in Italy. Thus any hope of an anti-Fascist alliance faded away. Mussolini was given a clear run. Roncalli opposed this policy for as long as he could not because he was of a rebellious nature – no one was less rebellious; he made his stand out of fidelity to the memory of Radini Tedeschi and the Christian democracy Toniolo had expounded. It made him look old-fashioned, naive perhaps, and unaware of the eddies of history. But at least he was more principled than the 'realists' in the Vatican who could come to terms with almost anyone.

His Bergamo sermon had no immediate consequences. And from November 1924, in addition to his work at Propaganda, he began to lecture in patristics at the Pontifical Lateran Athenaeum (his old *alma mater* in new dress). His lectures 'were popular and even applauded' (Trevor, p. 131). Yet it would soon all be over for him in Rome.

The high hopes he had entertained in the spring of 1919 when he destroyed his army uniform, said 'goodbye to all that' and supported the *Popolari*, had all vanished. The new uniform was a black shirt, and the sound of marching boots led away from the temple.

Chapter 7

Ten hard years in Bulgaria

'You will tell the truth — you will speak well of us. We Bulgarians like to be praised'. It is very easy to praise them: for their kindness, for their hospitality and friendliness.

(David Martin in *TheReligious and the Secular*, p. 131)

On the evening of February 17, 1925, Cardinal Pietro Gasparri, Secretary of State, summoned Mgr Roncalli and told him that he had been appointed apostolic visitor to Bulgaria. After this spell in 'purgatory' – he was assured that it would not last long – he would formally enter the Vatican diplomatic service and take up a congenial posting in Argentina where more than a tenth of the population was Italian. It sounded both enchanting and fishy.

Roncalli objected, with perfect truthfulness, that he had had no diplomatic training and knew nothing at all about Bulgaria. Surely there must be someone better prepared for this mission. Gasparri dismissed this by saying that his name had been put forward by Cardinal Giovanni Tacci, of the Congregation for the Oriental Churches, who presumably knew the field and had settled on him. Roncalli tried another objection: his sisters, Ancilla and Maria, would be very upset at him leaving Rome just when they were all properly installed. Shrugs from Gasparri. Roncalli had one final question, in his mind the most decisive: 'Was the mission to Bulgaria a matter of obedience?' It was indeed, and when Pope Pius XI heard his name mentioned he had said: 'Splendid, this is the man sent by Providence'. But even papal approval did not put his mind completely at rest, and he left saying he would think it over. All this Roncalli noted down the same evening (*Quindicesimo anniversario*, p. 27).

Later he used to recall that Gasparri did not seem to be very well-informed about Bulgaria and that his briefing was perfunctory. Gasparri had said to him:

> Listen, *monsignore*, I'm told the situation in Bulgaria is very confused. I can't tell you in detail what's going on. But everyone seems to be fighting with everyone else, the Moslems with the Orthodox, the Greek Catholics with the Latins, and the Latins with each other. Could you go there and find out what is really happening? (*Corriere della Sera*, March 29, 1959, Pope John in conversation with Indro Montanelli).

It did not take Mgr Roncalli very long to discover that to say 'the situation in Bulgaria is very confused' was a considerable under-statement.

Just as he had predicted, the news filled his sisters Ancilla and Maria with alarm and despondency. 'Groans, tears, endless lamentations' he noted in his diary. But they calmed

55

down a little after saying the rosary (*Quindicesimo anniversario*, p. 27). Roncalli felt responsible for them. They had built their world around him, and now it had come crashing down. In Rome as house-keepers to their priest-brother, they had a role and were appreciated. Back in Sotto il Monte they would be two maiden aunts with nothing to do. Roncalli assured them that whatever happened he would continue to look after them financially.

But it wasn't only the Roncalli sisters who wept at the prospect of Bulgaria. Roncalli himself confessed in a letter to Cardinal William Van Rossum, his superior at Propaganda, that after meeting Gasparri 'I shed many tears during the night, and even now – nearly a week later – when I think of it alone, especially in prayer, tears begin to well up in my eyes again' (*Quindicesimo anniversario*, p. 33). He had an audience with Pius XI on February 21, 1925. Pius was paternal but hardly more illuminating than his Secretary of State. Roncalli's diary records the Pope's words:

> Your name was suggested to me for this visitation. I was very happy about it. I was told that your title of monsignor would be enough, but I replied 'it is not a good thing when an apostolic prelate goes to a country and has to deal with bishops without being one himself'. I don't want a repeat performance of what happened to me in Poland. I was embarrassed at episcopal meetings when I had to take my place as the representative of the Holy Father, having precedence over the Polish bishops and archbishops. So I decided you should be consecrated archbishop (*Quindicesimo anniversario*, p.11).

So Roncalli became an archbishop because of humiliations undergone by Mgr Achille Ratti in post-war Poland. But if he knew nothing very helpful about Bulgaria, Pius XI could at least provide a parting gift, the *Scintillae Ignatianae*, a collection of maxims of St Ignatius arranged for day-by-day reading. Ignatius was not given to sparkling epigrams, so the gift may have been a recognition that in Sofia Roncalli would need all the spiritual consolation he could muster.

On March 3, 1925 *l'Osservatore Romano* announced that Angelo Roncalli would be ordained archbishop with the title of Areopolis, the ancient Roman city whose ruins still stand between the Dead Sea and the Red Sea. He made a retreat at the Villa Carpegna. He was consecrated on March 19, feast of St Joseph, in San Carlo al Corso, a church dedicated to St Charles Borromeo. His family were present, looking stiff and awkward, and the next morning he took them down to the crypt of St Peter's for his first episcopal Mass, and then presented them to Pius XI. Thus he repeated, in detail, the pattern of his priestly ordination twenty-one years previously.

But there was a difference. In 1904 he imagined he saw Our Lady smiling down at him. In 1925 there were no smiles, only intimations of crosses to be borne. This is how he remembered it five years later:

> The profound and lasting impression that I received during the whole ceremony of my consecration as bishop in Rome in San Carlo al Corso on March 19, 1925, and since then the difficulties and trials of my ministry in Bulgaria during these five years as Apostolic Visitor, without any consolation save that of a good conscience and a rather sombre prospect for the future, convince me that the Lord wants me all for himself along the royal road to the cross ... (*Journal*, p. 231).

The apprehensions he felt on the day of his episcopal ordination were well-founded.

Yet he was, in some fairly obvious sense, being promoted. His career was well and truly launched – even if towards unknown and possibly hazardous seas. During his retreat he pondered on the fact that 'I have not sought or desired this new ministry; the Lord has chosen me, making it so clear that it is his will that it would be a grave sin for me to refuse. So it will be for him to cover up my failings and inadequacies. This comforts me and brings tranquillity and confidence' (*Journal*, p. 218).

He was able to say exactly the same thing at every other change of direction in his life - including being elected Pope. His episcopal motto, borrowed from Cesare Baronius, summed up his attitude: *Obedientia et Pax*. The path to peace lay through obedience.

Yet this 'edifying' interpretation of his appointment cannot have banished entirely the suspicion that he was the victim of a plot or of some secret wheelerdealing. Dom Lambert Beauduin O.S.B., a good friend and then professor of fundamental theology at Sant' Anselmo in Rome, used to maintain that Roncalli 'was relieved of his teaching post at the Lateran on suspicion of Modernism' (see Trevor, p. 132). This theory has had wide currency. But at this date more attention was being paid to political than to theological unorthodoxy. Roncalli's sermon on Radini Tedeschi on September 1, 1924, which marked him out as an unrepentant supporter of the PPI (the *Popolari*), was enough to despatch him to Bulgaria where he could do no harm.

Beauduin had a great and permanent influence on Roncalli. He had vision. He was the founder of the 'liturgical movement' (Villain, p. 216), and was also a pioneer of social action and ecumenism. His knowledge and love of the Orthodox Churches had led him to take an interest in Bulgaria. On March 22, 1925, he introduced Roncalli to a fellow Benedictine, Dom Constantin Bosschaerts, who would go with him to Sofia as temporary secretary.

Other friends rallied round, notably Don Giovanni Battista Montini who dropped in for a long conversation the day before Roncalli left Rome for Bergamo (Fappani-Molinari, Letter of Montini, April 9, 1925). Between them, they managed to make some sense of his appointment. Its ecumenical importance was evident. St Cyril devised the Slav alphabet which is still called Cyrillic after him. He went to Rome to ask Pope Hadrian II to approve his newly created Slav liturgy and died there in 869. His disciples St Clement (Kliment) and St Naoum used this liturgy to evangelise Bulgaria. A thousand years later Bulgaria was an Orthodox country in a unique situation. Its hierarchy had been in schism from the ecumenical patriarch in Constantinople since 1872, and though it had traditionally looked to Moscow for leadership, the Moscow patriarchate was now powerless and persecuted. So Bulgarian Orthodoxy was adrift, and could go anywhere. It was beginning to take an interest in the burgeoning 'ecumenical movement' of Protestant inspiration.

Again, Roncalli and his friends were able to piece together the reasons why someone was needed in Bulgaria. Bulgaria had made the mistake of choosing the defeated side in the First World War. It had been punished by losing territory and its traditional friends. It was therefore isolated and biddable. As early as 1923, Kristov Kalkov, the future minister of cults, had an audience with Pius XI and meetings in the Secretariat of State. The possibility of a concordat was aired. That same year the Vatican librarian, the energetic French ex-cavalry officer Mgr Eugène Tisserant, had gone to Sofia in search of manuscripts and rare books. After the upheavals of war and the closing of many Russian monasteries, there were rich pickings.

It was Tisserant who had suggested that an envoy should be sent to discover the needs of the small minority of Catholics of Slav rite.

So it was possible to see Roncalli's mission to Bulgaria in a very positive way. It had three dimensions – ecumenical, diplomatic and pastoral. Though rather off the beaten track, it was no disgrace to be sent there. And it wasn't for very long.

One matter of great personal importance was resolved just before he left Bergamo. Baron Gianmaria Scotti agreed to rent Archbishop Roncalli part of Camaitino, the house of an earlier Roncalli. This meant that Ancilla and Maria could live there, look after the house and not be a burden on the parents. And Roncalli would have a place to stay during his summer holidays. Except when war made it impossible, he managed to spend about a month there every summer until 1958 when he was elected Pope. Camaitino became his great bond with Sotto Il Monte. He loved Camaitino. His letters to Ancilla and Maria over the years are filled with details about tiled floors and new curtains and furnishings. The books he couldn't transport were there too. On a clear day, he could see the spire of Milan Cathedral from his balcony. That helped him to concentrate on his work on St Charles Borromeo, which was now years behind schedule. But all that was for the future. On April 23, 1925, he said goodbye to all his family and his new acquisition and set off for Sofia.

It was the age of the train. He boarded the Simplon Orient Express, the world's most famous train, in Milan. It combined opulence, mystery, exoticism and scandal in about equal proportions, which is why novelists have loved it. The Orient Express was to play an important part in Roncalli's life. Until the outbreak of war he went back and forth along its route – Sofia, Constantinople, Paris, Venice, with Milan as the constant point of departure. He enjoyed his journeys. 'In the train', he tells his sisters, who had never been on such a luxurious journey, 'you can relax, read, pray, observe the beauties of nature and the variety of people' (*Familiari*, I, p. 205).

After two days on the Orient Express, Roncalli arrived at Sofia station. He was already rather portly, and was easily recognisable in his long black top-coat, soutane and soup-plate hat. He was greeted by Mgr Peev, a Bulgarian Capuchin friar who was Latin bishop for the south of Bulgaria. Sofia was still dazed, recovering from the shock of a terrorist bomb that had left more than a hundred dead and a thousand injured amid the ruins of the ancient church of Svata Nedela.

The foreign minister, forewarned of his arrival, did not want him to pass by the devastated church because it would give a bad impression of his country. So Roncalli went directly to the modest residence at Liuline Street 7, next door to the diminutive church of the Ascension. Over supper Bishop Peev and young Fr Stefan Kurtev began his initiation into Bulgarian complexities. First they dealt with the events of the last two weeks that had culminated in the Svata Nedela outrage. On April 13, 1925, King Boris III had narrowly escaped assassination while out hunting in the mountains. Nine suspects were arrested and summarily hanged. The next day the 'revolutionaries' killed General Constantin Gheorghiev, confident that the king would attend his funeral in the Svata Nedela church. A pillar at the base of the central cupola was stuffed with explosives. The king survived the blast, but the casualty lists made this the greatest man-made catastrophe since the war. All that had happened in the two weeks before Roncalli arrived.

The first and highly characteristic act of Archbishop Roncalli, the first papal representative in the country for over five centuries, was to ask King Boris to allow him to visit those wounded in the Svata Nedela attack. But immediately the Holy Synod, governing body of the Bulgarian Orthodox Church, criticised the apostolic visitor in its newspaper, *Tzarkoven Vestruk* (Dreyfus, p. 75). Roncalli's arrival meant, it suggested, that Latin 'imperialism' and 'proselytism' would be stepped up. Bulgarian Orthodoxy was the object of a devious Roman plot.

Yet the 62,000 Catholics of Bulgaria hardly posed a very serious threat. Moreover, they were divided among themselves. There were said to be about 48,000 Latins who were mostly urban and 14,000 Uniates of the Slav rite who lived in rural areas. Many of the Uniates were refugees from Macedonia and Thrace (as Roncalli noted in a lecture in 1954: *Natale, 1975*, p. 19). Their last bishop (or exarch) had died in 1924. The Latin Catholics were divided into two dioceses: the Dutch Bishop Jan Theelen C.P. ruled from Rustchuk in the north where all the clergy except three were Passionists like himself; Mgr Peev administered the southern diocese of Sofia–Plovdiv where all the priests except three were Bulgarian (*Irénikon*, 1928, p. 420). Tact was needed to get these disparate groups to work together. In addition, French sensibilities had to be attended to in Sofia where there were many French religious orders, chiefly Assumptionists, Vincentians, Christian Brothers, and Capuchin Franciscans. Roncalli's mission was to put some flesh on the bare bones of these statistics and give a first-hand report on the needs of the Bulgarian Catholics.

So he set about visiting the scattered mountain parishes of his 'Slav rite' Catholics. He knew hardly any Bulgarian, and used Fr Stefan Kurtev as interpreter. They travelled by mule, on horseback or in jolting carts. Cars were hardly ever seen in these poor areas, and roads were bad. Rivers were crossed on primitive-looking rafts. Everywhere he went he kept his soup-plate hat firmly fixed on his head. As he said in his 1954 lecture, 'I went to seek them out in the most distant villages, I entered their modest homes and became their neighbour' (*Natale, 1975*, p. 19).

He later thought that he was received 'with affection and joy' because he was the Pope's representative. Yet sometimes he was made sharply aware of the contrast between the pomp of Rome and the poverty of these Bulgarian villages. He wrote in a 1929 letter:

> My heart breaks when I think that you in Rome can devise no further ways of making the triumph of Jesus in the Eucharist, carried in the arms of his Vicar, more spectacular, while here we don't even have oil to light the lamps in the chicken-coops we use as chapels. But these poor lamps are a beginning (*Gran Sacerdote*, p. 153. Letter to his successor at Propaganda, from Jambol, May 29, 1929).

It does not occur to Roncalli that something of his success was due to his own personality. Yet soon he was known among the Catholic Bulgarians as *Diado*, the good father. Small boys out spying would rush home with the news that *Diado* was on his way. He brought concern to a forgotten people.

His round of visits over, Roncalli had – in theory – completed his work in Bulgaria. In October 1925 he led a party of Bulgarian pilgrims to Rome. They had an audience with Pius XI on October 14, 1925, which at least proved that they existed. His presence in Rome enabled him to present his report to the Congregation of the Oriental Churches in person. His main recommendation was that the Uniates of Slav rite needed a bishop. He favoured Fr Stefan Kurtev for this office, despite his youth: he was only thirty-five.

Kurtev was ordained bishop for the Bulgarians of the Byzantine Slav rite in San Clemente on December 5, 1926, in the presence of Archbishop Roncalli. San Clemente – entrusted to the Irish Dominicans – was chosen because it had the tomb of St Cyril, brother of St Methodius. Kurtev naturally took the name of Stefan Cyril. The only problem about Bishop Stefan Cyril was that he had been born into an Orthodox family, gone to school with the Assumptionists at Mustrackli, and then become a Catholic. To the Orthodox he was therefore a living illustration of Roman 'proselytism'.

With the appointment of Kurtev Roncalli had fulfilled the first part of his mission and worked himself out of a job: he no longer needed to make pastoral visits to the scattered Bulgarian Catholics. The next item on his agenda was to provide them with a seminary of their own. So long as all priests had to go abroad for their clerical studies, the Church would appear as irremediably 'foreign'. In December 1929 he acquired a site for a seminary, and paid a quarter of a million *lire* for 30,000 square metres (*Familiari*, I, p. 209). The seminary project was entrusted to the Jesuits. No one in the Vatican seemed to share his sense of the importance of the project. He was disappointed. Part of his difficulty with the Curia was that he had to deal with three departments – the Secretariat of State, Propaganda Fide and the Oriental Congregation – whose views did not always co-incide. Everyone seemed to have forgotten that he had been sent to Bulgaria on a temporary mission. No one mentioned Argentina any more. The provisional was beginning to look dangerously permanent.

Having done what he could for his flock, Roncalli had more time to devote to the second and more testing goal of his mission in Bulgaria: 'To make known and loved the Pope and the Catholic Church among the great mass of the Orthodox', as he put it in his 1954 lecture (*Natale, 1975*, p. 18). The Bulgarian Orthodox Church was a state Church. It had stiffened national morale and kept identity alive throughout the five centuries of Turkish rule. The bonds between language, culture, religion and nationalism were therefore very strong. By the same token, a suspicion of 'disloyalty' hung about the Catholics, simply because they were an anomaly. The Orthodox saw the monarch as the patron and protector of the Church. So although King Boris, a Saxe-Coburg, had been brought up a Catholic, he had to become Orthodox in order to succeed to the throne. *Raison d'état* demanded his conversion.

It was to this Church that Roncalli had to try to commend 'the Pope and the Catholic Church'. History made it uphill work. But Roncalli's attempts to dissipate prejudice and improve relations were an ecumenical apprenticeship that proved invaluable later on. Although 'ecumenism' was frowned upon in the Vatican at this date, Roncalli learned its ground rules from experience. The most basic rule of all was that one could not expect to begin a dialogue with condemnations. Friendliness in Christ was the starting-point, along with a capacity to listen and learn. What Roncalli found in his own experience was theologically confirmed by Dom Lambert Beauduin in his review *Irénikon*, of which Roncalli became a regular reader.

Roncalli's ecumenical apprenticeship consisted in getting to know Orthodox Church leaders who were merely a generalised abstraction to the Roman Curia – interchangeable bearded orientals with an incomprehensible history and an unknown language. One of his friends was Stepanosse Hovagnimian, archbishop of Nicomedia, Armenian patriarch in Bulgaria. When Roncalli met him in 1927 he was already eighty years old. He embodied living history. With about 50,000 of his Armenians he had escaped the Turkish massacres of 1896 and the even more terrible massacres of 1915. When Pope John addressed the Observers on October 13, 1962, just as the Council began, he recalled that he had given 'this venerable old prelate' a medal of Pius XI's pontificate: 'When a short time later he was dying, he asked that the medal should be placed upon his heart. I saw it there myself, and the memory moves me still' (DMC, vol IV, 1962, p. 607).

Roncalli's pastoral work and ecumenical meetings made him painfully aware of the problems of the Uniates, the term used to describe those Christians of Oriental rite who were in communion with Rome. Though relatively small in numbers (apart from the four million Ukrainians) they had great symbolic importance because they illustrated the truly Catholic nature of the Church. It was also hoped, rather more optimistically, that they would build a bridge between East and West.

Roncalli was in correspondence with Fr Cyril Korolevkij, professor at the Greek College in Rome, who had written a passionate plea for the Uniates called *Uniatismo* (it appeared, naturally, in *Irénikon* in 1927) and argued strongly against the excessive 'Latinisation' of the Uniate Churches – a complaint that has been heard as long as they have existed. Roncalli was more optimistic than Korolevkij about the chances of adapting some Latin devotions for the Uniate Churches but endorsed with enthusiasm Korolevkij's articles on the Uniates (*Gran Sacerdote*, p. 146. Letter from Sofia, July 13, 1927). Unity would not mean absorption.

One thing saddened him, however. The Uniate Churches were poor and understandably preoccupied with mere survival. They felt psychologically squeezed between the Orthodox who saw them as a 'Latin' bridgehead and Latin Catholics who, often enough, felt socially superior to them. So Roncalli makes a plea for 'paying attention to the real good they have done and their generous and energetic commitment' (*Gran Sacerdote*, p. 146).

While Roncalli was writing to Korolevkij in July 1927, he received a copy of *l'Osservatore Romano*. It contained the Holy Office decree forbidding Catholics to take part in the Lausanne Conference on Faith and Order (*Gran Sacerdote*, p. 147; for the Conference see Bell, pp. 29 and following). Roncalli accepted this decision without demur:

> The ban (on attending the Faith and Order Conference) seems a little harsh to the Orthodox; but it is perfectly logical for us. These conferences, over and above the good faith of some who take part in them, are the beginning of a new form of Protestantism. The decree of the Holy Office will undoubtedly help to clarify the situation (*ibid.*, p. 147).

It was relatively easy to accept exclusion from a particular meeting, even if the grounds – the fear of 'a new form of Protestantism' – seem with hindsight somewhat far-fetched.

In Bulgaria these theoretical debates were rendered otiose by a severe earthquake on April 14, 1928. The tremor was felt in Sofia, but its main epicentre was in the mountainous region of Plovdiv where most of the Uniate Catholics lived. Roncalli was on the spot the day after to assess the situation, returned to Sofia to cable the Vatican for aid, and three days later was organising food and blankets for the most needy. The shock had been terrible, and he was afraid for his life.

The Pope had sent half a million *leva* 'which created a very good impression in Bulgaria'. *L'Eco di Bergamo* had not forgotten its former correspondent, Roncalli, and got up a subscription for the victims. But the needs were endless. The earthquakes had been followed by heavy rain; the people refused to go back to their cracked and threatened houses; the wooden huts that had been promised them had not yet arrived; the mud was already deep and further floods were anticipated (*Familiari*, I, p. 164).

Roncalli did not regard the earthquake as an intellectual puzzle about the goodness of God; nor did he adopt Dr Pangloss' attitude that 'everything was for the best'. He saw it as imposing on him a practical task, a chance to exercise 'the corporal works of mercy'. Only a month before on March 6, 1928, he had urged Ancilla and Maria to 'spend yourselves in visiting the sick. That is a good thing that you can do. It is one of the most beautiful works of mercy... The Lord responds with mercy to those who are charitable' (*Familiari*, I, p. 155). Now he had to apply this lesson himself. He wrote about the earthquake to his sisters: 'As I've told you, not only am I well but I am happy to be here amid so much suffering provided I can bring help and comfort in the name of the Lord who made us all brothers' (*Familiari*, I, p. 164).

After these – literally – earth-shaking events, Archbishop Roncalli spent Christmas 1928 quietly in Constantinople. It had far richer historical memories and greater ecumenical importance than Sofia. He wrote to Simon Pietro Grassi, bishop of Tortona, on his priestly jubilee:

> I would be delighted to have you with me in this marvellous city of Constantinople that I am getting to know quite well. I wish you were here to discuss the great problems concerning the future of the Church – problems which are seen in a completely different and very interesting perspective from here, in this central but now almost spent heart of Orthodoxy, amid the imposing but desolate ruins of the Byzantine period, and on the threshold of the mysterious world of Islam in which there are new stirrings whose direction is in the hands of God (*Gran Sacerdote*, p. 151).

In 1928 the 'new stirrings' in Islam referred not to the oil-confident religious revival of fifty years later but on the contrary to the secularising policies of Atatürk who was determined to drag Turkey into the twentieth century. The judgement on the decline of the Phanar, home of the Ecumenical Patriarch, was harsh but accurate. Yet the Patriarch's symbolic importance remained. Living in the Balkans gave Roncalli insights into such problems that would not have been possible had he been limited to Bergamo or Rome.

But the price he paid was exile, and he began to feel its burden. As he approached the twenty-fifth anniversary of his ordination in 1929, he went through a crisis that had many elements. As he put it himself during his 1930 retreat at Rustchuk in the Passionist house that overlooked the Danube and the burning waste-gas of the Romanian oil-fields beyond:

> The trials, with which in recent months the Lord has tested my patience, have been many: anxieties concerning the arrangements for founding the Bulgarian Seminary;

the uncertainty which has now lasted five years about the exact purpose of my mission in this country; my frustrations and disappointments at not being able to do more, and the enforced restrictions of my life as a complete hermit, in contrast to my longing to work directly ministering to souls; my interior discontent with what is left of my natural human inclinations, even if so far until now I have succeeded in keeping them under control (*Journal*, p. 229).

This was Roncalli in his most sombre mood, though the retreat ends with him quoting the maxim of St Francis de Sales, 'I am like a bird singing in a thicket of thorns' (*ibid.*, p. 232).

How he resolved this crisis can be seen in his correspondence with Don Pietro Forno (1887–1938), the Bergamesque priest who was helping him with his edition of the *Atti* of St Charles Borromeo. But what brought them even closer together at this period was that they were both going through a time of trial. The nature of Forno's 'trial' is not made clear, but since Capovilla says that it was caused by 'the defects of his remarkable intellectual qualities and his frank and impetuous character' (*Dodicesimo anniversario*, p. 50) and since he wanted to migrate to another diocese, one may infer that he was having difficulties with his bishop. Like Roncalli he felt passed over, unappreciated.

In a letter from Sofia dated April 8, 1928, Roncalli makes use of a revealing historical parallel to their situation:

> Before going to sleep I've been reading Pastor's lives of the Popes. How many
> encouraging examples for you and me there are in these volumes. In the chapter on Paul
> IV, for example, we read how card. Morone – one of the greatest servants of the Church
> in the sixteenth century, a great diplomat, a man of exquisite courtesy, upright, pious,
> etc. – was held prisoner in Castel Sant'Angelo under this pope, no doubt a holy but an
> impetuous man, and there he (Morone) had to remain and put up with the most
> humiliating trials until the death of Paul who was, I repeat, a holy man who did a lot of
> good (*Dodicesimo anniversario*, p. 51).

This bed-time reading encouraged the fantasy that he himself, confined to Sofia for no good reason, resembled Cardinal Morone, locked up in the Castel Sant'Angelo on a whim of Pope Paul IV. Yet he still finds it difficult to criticise a tyrannical pope, even a long dead one.

An ironical post-script to this tale is that on October 11, 1962, the opening day of the Council, Pope John read out, as canon law prescribed, the profession of faith of Paul IV. Those observers who found its tone offensive and knew that Paul IV had been described as 'the most sinister pope in history' (Hans Kühner), would have been consoled to discover that Roncalli disapproved of his treatment of Cardinal Morone.

After this dodgy historical parallel, Roncalli tries to console his fellow-sufferer Forno with the thought that from time to time we all need a 'stroke of grace':

> You remember what I told you last year about the troubles I had with my ministry in
> Bulgaria? Well, when I was in Rome I had a stroke of grace which restored perfect peace
> to me. It is not that the reasons why I suffered last year have gone away. No, they are still
> there, or have perhaps diminished just a little. But I was granted a *raison d'être*, a reason for
> being and suffering; and so I love and suffer willingly... Since I was ordained bishop I

have recited every day one of the prayers of St Ignatius. I enclose a copy. It happened that one morning, when I was suffering the most, it seemed to me that this prayer had been very precisely answered. This reflection, too, brought me peace and contentment (*Dodicesimo anniversario*, pp. 51–2).

What was the 'Ignatian prayer' said daily by Archbishop Roncalli? He tells us in his retreat notes for 1930. It was the prayer, 'O eternal Lord of all things' which concludes the meditation on the Kingdom of Christ. 'To tell the truth', Roncalli confesses, 'I found it hard to say this prayer' (*Journal*, p. 230). It is indeed difficult for anyone with ambition to say that they want to 'imitate Christ in bearing all wrongs and all abuse and all poverty, both actual and spiritual' (*Exercises*, No. 98).

A letter written to his former secretary at Propaganda, Mgr Giovanni Dieci, on May 5, 1928, clearly refers to the same experience: 'Once you have renounced everything, really everything, then any bold enterprise becomes the simplest and most natural thing in the world' (Alberigo, p. 430). Nothing could make clearer the meaning of 'renunciation' as seen by Roncalli. It is an act of letting go in God in order to be with Jesus more intimately. It is renunciation for freedom. It was this attitude that permitted him to launch the 'bold enterprise' of the Council at the age of 77, when common sense would have said that it was folly.

The practical conclusion in the late 1920s was that he would not intrigue to get another posting. Whenever people in Rome said to him, 'But haven't you been in Bulgaria rather a long time?', he changed the subject (*Familiari*, I, p. 209). Unfortunately Forno received no comparable 'stroke of grace'. In February 1929 Roncalli writes to him less as a colleague than as a spiritual director who has to try a dozen different ways of saying the same thing:

> You say that you would like me to be given a big diocese in which there would be a job for you as well. Nothing doing. Bulgaria is my cross, and I'm sincerely ready to stay here until I die, if obedience wanted it. I let others waste their time dreaming about what might happen to me. You should do the same. The idea that one would be better off somewhere else is an illusion. Read the last pages of Manzoni's *I Promessi Sposi*. Simple words: but popular wisdom of the highest level (*Dodicesimo anniversario*, pp. 56–7).

In August 1929 he celebrated the twenty-fifth anniversary of his priestly ordination. He guessed (wrongly) that the second part of his life as a priest would be shorter (*Pastore*, p. 159). He wisely went on a diet. Most summers he was able to spend about two months in Italy. In the summer of 1929 he went to Prague, Czestochowa, Gniezno and Berlin where Mgr Eugenio Pacelli was nuncio. So he was not unaware of what was happening in Europe. The Fascist regime in Italy was now an outright dictatorship. The conventional view was that Pius XI was bravely standing up to the dictator Mussolini. The issues on which they monotonously clashed – Catholic Action, youth movements, education – revealed a deep and irreconcilable antagonism between a freedom-loving Church and an increasingly totalitarian state.

But then on February 11, 1929, came the startling news that the Pope and Mussolini had done a deal. Known as the Lateran Pacts, there were in fact three related agreements: a Treaty between the Holy See and Italy which acknowledged the sovereignty of the Vatican over its pocket-handkerchief territory in Rome; a financial convention which provided compensation for the loss of the Papal States in 1870; and a Concordat which would govern the future relations between the Holy See and Italy. Many Catholics were disappointed by these measures. The image of an heroic Pope courageously resisting the dictator gave way to that of a pragmatic Pope ready to come to terms with anyone. The ex-*Popolari* were particularly bitter.

One of the sharpest critics of the Lateran Pacts was Mgr Giovanni Battista Montini. He thought the agreement was merely a pseudo-reconciliation, a non-event from which Mussolini had gained a great deal of favourable publicity. 'Almost all thinking people', Montini wrote, 'are unhappy and full of reservations' (Fappani-Molinari, pp. 259 and following). He decided to spend still more time on FUCI, the Catholic Student Movement which, in time, would provide the link between the *Popolari* of the 1920s and the Christian Democrats after 1945.

But all this criticism of the Lateran Pacts was confined to private letters and conversations. The standard public response was one of great rejoicing. *L'Osservatore Romano*, in a notorious and never-to-be-forgotten phrase declared that 'Italy has been given back to God, and God to Italy' (February 12, 1929).

Away in Sofia Roncalli had no difficulty in following the official line. As a quasi-Vatican diplomat he had the task of explaining the Lateran Pacts to King Boris who – though Roncalli didn't know this – had a special interest in Italian events: he was thinking of marrying Princess Giovanna of the House of Savoy. Roncalli's enthusiasm for the Lateran Pacts was unfeigned. He accepted them at face-value. He did not have Montini's feeling for the long-term consequences. It was the fact of 'reconciliation' that impressed him, while *with whom* it was achieved was secondary. Roncalli wrote in a letter to Don Pietro Forno on February 18, 1929:

> You can imagine with what rejoicing for the cause of the Holy See and of Italy I
> followed the events of Rome. They seem more like a dream than a miracle of justice and
> God's goodness. Don't you find here a lesson and an encouragement for you as well? One
> protests in due form, waits and suffers; and then the Lord intervenes, bringing joy,
> liberation and salvation (*Dodicesimo anniversario*, p. 57).

So the signing of the Lateran treaties illustrated a universally applicable 'law' of the spiritual life: the papacy has lived patiently through its time of trial, and has now been rewarded.

Six days later he wrote to Ancilla and Maria with equal enthusiasm. He presents 'reconciliation' between the Pope and Italy as a Roncalli family tradition:

> You can imagine how I followed the rejoicing in all Italy over the *peace* arrived at
> between the Vatican and the Quirinal. Think what a joy that would have been for the
> deceased members of our family! Let us bless the Lord! Everything that free-masonry,
> that is, the devil, had done against the Church and the Pope in the last sixty years – all
> that has been over-turned . . . We should have the courage and the loyalty to recognise
> the miraculous aspect of these events (*Familiari*, I, p. 185. Letter dated February 24, 1929).

In 1929, gossip began to circulate suggesting Roncalli for the prestigious post of archbishop of Milan. Cardinal Eugenio Tosi, Ferrari's successor, had died on January 7, 1929, just a month before the Lateran Pacts. The new appointment would be made under the

Concordat rules, which gave the state a role. No sooner was Tosi in his tomb than gossip began to appoint Roncalli to Milan. On February 10, 1929, only three days after Tosi's death, he wrote to Ancilla and Maria: 'Rumours are going the rounds linking my name with Milan. Don't believe them. Pray the Lord that I may be preserved from dignities and responsibilities greater than those I already have. One should not waste time imagining things' (*Familiari*, I, p. 182). If they hear anyone talking about him going to Milan, they are to change the subject. This was the appropriate response from someone who had embraced 'the royal road of the cross'.

Yet it could not be denied that the appointment would have made sense. He came from Lombardy. At 48, he was the right age for a long and fruitful episcopal ministry. As the historian of St Charles Borromeo he had a thorough knowledge of the best traditions of the Milanese Church. He was in some sense the heir of Cardinal Ferrari, to whom he had been devoted. Add to these advantages the fact that he had been conveniently absent from Italy throughout the previous four years, and so had a clean political sheet.

In the event Cardinal Ildefonso Schuster O.S.B. was appointed cardinal archbishop of Milan in August 1929. The long delay between February and August suggests a battle royal behind the scenes. One of Mussolini's main concerns was to prevent any revival of the *Popolari* or any promotion for those associated with them. 'We will not permit', he said in June 1929, 'the resurrection of parties or organisations that we have destroyed once for all' (Pollard, p. 71). Schuster was politically reliable; Roncalli was not. On the first anniversary of the Lateran Pacts, Schuster was heard to declare that 'right from the start Catholic Italy and the Pope have blessed Fascism' – a statement so outrageous and false that *l'Osservatore Romano* issued a *démenti* in the form of a *Rettifica*, a term reserved for the gravest of blunders (Pollard, p. 167).

Soon Bulgaria was in the headlines again. Italy had long had ambitions in the Balkans, and a royal marriage seemed an excellent way of cementing relations with Bulgaria and extending Italian influence generally. King Boris III was an eligible bachelor of 35, while King Victor Emmanuel III's daughter, Princess Giovanna, was unattached and docile. Since Boris was an Orthodox Christian, a dispensation was arranged. The wedding took place amid great rejoicing according to the Catholic rite at Assisi on October 25, 1930. The royal couple had given written undertakings that their children would be brought up as Catholics. Naturally Roncalli, as apostolic visitor to Bulgaria, was present as a guest – though he had not negotiated the dispensation. Later that day he had an audience with Pius XI who presented him with a gold medal for King Boris. Italo-Bulgarian friendship and reconciliation all round had been sealed, as it were, with a kiss for the bride.

But the romantic idyll did not last long. Roncalli made his way back in leisurely fashion, arriving in Sofia on October 30. The next day King Boris and his bride, now Queen Giovanna, had a splendid Orthodox marriage ceremony in the cathedral of Alexander Nevski in Sofia. This 'second marriage' made Pius XI furious. On Christmas Eve he denounced the royal couple who had given the most solemn undertakings and then gone back on their word. A choleric man, he felt betrayed. And quite unfairly the apostolic visitor in Sofia, Roncalli, had to shoulder part of the blame for what had happened.

The fuss over the Bulgarian marriage showed that Pius XI and Roncalli had completely contrasting temperaments. While the Pope waxed indignant and dramatised the situation, his apostolic visitor stayed cool, looked for a diplomatic solution, and played down the force-ful papal statements. He wrote to Bishop Jan Theelen on December 27, 1930:

> More painful for me is the sense of the uselessness of my attempts to persuade the King
> to make a simple declaration that would have explained the significance of the October
> 31 marriage, a declaration that would have averted the solemn words of the Pope that
> cannot have been very pleasant for his Majesty. But for everyone else, and perhaps for the
> King himself, the incident could be providential in that it makes it clear that the Pope
> does not trifle with the Lord and sacred things. In any case, as you will notice, the Holy
> Father's language could not have been more balanced and kind (*Familiari*, I, p. 243).

But Pius XI thundered on. On the last day of 1930 he published his encyclical *Casti Con-nubii* which defended the sanctity of Catholic marriage against all those who dared to break its rules. Of course he had other targets besides the Bulgarian royal family. He also de-nounced (though not by name) the Lambeth Conference, the Anglican assembly, which had rather tentatively approved of birth-control.

Pius XI renewed his tirade against royal promise-breakers in March 1933. Boris and Gio-vanna had their first child, Princess Maria Luisa, in January and she was baptised by Metro-politan Stefan Georghiev. The apostolic delegate – the office had been raised to this diplomatic dignity on September 26, 1931 – wrote an official letter of protest to King Boris: 'I think of the pain of the Holy Father and of all good Catholics around the world; and then I myself grieve that no real advantage can accrue either to your royal family or to the Bul-garian people from these continued outrages to the human conscience ... (*Familiari*, I, pp. 285–6. Letter dated January 15, 1933). Capovilla calls this letter 'an energetic protest'. It seems rather to be written under orders from Rome and to have a touch of more-in-sorrow-than-in-anger. The consequence, however, was that Roncalli was banned from court for a year.

He did what he could to soften the blow for the youthful exile Queen Giovanna. That the natural rejoicing over her first-born should have been marred by an ecclesiastico-political dispute was hard to bear. Roncalli invited her to go to Mass privately at the Apostolic De-legation (rather than in a public church). On March 19, 1933, feast of St Joseph, the very day on which Pius XI was denouncing yet again those who violated the sanctity of Catholic marriage, he gave her a handsome missal as a sign that she was not included in the Pope's displeasure (Trevor, p. 157). A more experienced Italian exile than she, he treated Giovanna with kindness and thoughtful chivalry.

It was difficult to extend the same indulgence to King Boris. But Boris was capable of defending himself. A few days after Roncalli's protest, he explained his position:

> You know perfectly well, your excellency, that by family and baptism I was a Catholic. If
> I have acted as I have twice over, it was solely out of concern for the interests of my
> country. The Holy Synod was beginning to doubt my loyalty towards the Orthodox
> Church. The Communists seize upon anything that can turn the people against me. I
> have to do all I can for this torn and divided country (Dreyfus, p. 83).

Once the initial *raison d'état* argument for King Boris's conversion to Orthodoxy had been accepted, the rest followed. It was difficult to refute his case. He could continue to rule in

Bulgaria only as a loyal and faithful Orthodox Christian. In any case, Roncalli, as a keen student of *Irénikon*, would have been perfectly aware of the validity of the Orthodox sacraments from the point of view of Catholic theology.

Pius XI was not the easiest of popes to work for. He was impatient and easily carried away by his immediate emotions. Ludwig von Pastor, Austrian ambassador to the Holy See and the historian whom Roncalli used as bedside reading, said in an official memo that 'he almost always went against the advice that was given him' (Stehle, p. 81). One source has a story which confirms this picture: 'After the Orthodox baptism of Prince Simeon, heir to the Bulgarian throne, Pius XI kept Roncalli kneeling before him for forty-five minutes as a penance . . . But some years later, Pius XI put this right. He explained that although as Pope Pius XI he could not apologise, as plain Achille Ratti he could' (Bergerre, p. 75).

It was time for Roncalli to think of leaving. The same thought had finally penetrated the Vatican. In 1933 there was gossip about him moving down the line of the Orient Express to Constantinople, where the apostolic delegate, Mgr Carlo Margotti, had been something of a disaster. By 1934 Constantinople was no longer the attractive proposition it had seemed six years earlier. Atatürk imposed tight police restrictions on all Christian activities. Roncalli wrote to Andrea Cesarano who had been his first guide to Constantinople and, since 1931, archbishop of Manfredonia:

> Recently I was asked by Rome if I were prepared to go to Constantinople as the eventual successor of Mgr Margotti. I replied that I was always ready to go where obedience demanded, even if that meant doing a provisional stint in hell; but as to whether I liked the idea or not, I had no illusions about the place. I believe that Constantinople is a good post for someone content to hold together what remains of the beleaguered Catholic flock, while waiting patiently for the doors to be opened for an apostolate among the Turks (*Quindicesimo anniversario*, p. 72).

The last remark suggests that Roncalli had been hoping for something rather more adventurous than a patient holding operation. Yet the transfer from Sofia to Constantinople was a promotion and made sense: he was becoming an expert on the Balkans. It was the only move in his life that he knew about well in advance. On November 17, 1934, he was officially informed of his transfer to Constantinople by the *sostituto*, Mgr Giuseppe Pizzardo.

So his Christmas homily in Sofia in 1934 became his farewell to Bulgaria. He was leaving Sofia for Constantinople. His historical imagination took wing and he recalled that the fourth-century Emperor Constantine had at first thought of establishing his imperial capital, the 'second Rome', in Sofia (*'Roma mea est Sardica'*), until in the end strategic considerations led him to Constantinople. So in some sense Roncalli was following in the footsteps of Constantine who had great plans for Bulgaria. He concluded his sermon with the 'Irish custom' of leaving a lighted candle in the window at Christmas to show Jesus and Mary that the family was waiting for them:

> Dear brothers, nobody knows the paths of the future. Wherever I may go, if a Bulgarian passes by my door, whether it's night-time or whether he's poor, he will find that candle lighted at my window. Knock, knock. You won't be asked whether you're a Catholic or

not; the title of Bulgarian brother is enough. Come in. Two fraternal arms will welcome you, and the warm heart of a friend will make it a feast-day. Such is the charity of the Lord whose graces have made life sweet during my ten year stay in Bulgaria (*Natale*, 1975, p. 11).

He was given a great send-off from Sofia on January 4, 1935. Representatives of the king and the archbishop were present. It made a striking contrast with the way he had slipped in anonymously ten years earlier. Judged by that criterion, his mission to Bulgaria was success-ful. In his private *Journal* he used more rigorous standards. He wrote in August 1934: 'What has Mgr Roncalli been doing during these monotonous years at the Apostolic Delegation? Trying to make himself holy and with simplicity, kindness and joy opening a source of blessings and graces for all Bulgaria, whether he lives to see it or not . . . The rest does not matter' (*Journal*, p. 239).

Chapter 8

The innocent suspect

*Let me remind you of the old maxim: people under suspicion are better
moving than at rest, since at rest they may be sitting in the balance without
knowing it, being weighed together with their sins.*

(Franz Kafka, *The Castle*, chapter 5)

Archbishop Roncalli arrived in Istanbul - revived name for the city, imposed by Atatürk —
on January 5, 1935. He was met at the station by Mgr Angelo Dell'Acqua, his new secretary, a
Milanese. His first duty was to report to the police. From now on he had the Kafka-like
experience of being a suspect wherever he went. But he brought a human touch to his arrival by paying an unscheduled courtesy call on Vali Muhidden Ustundag, the city governor.
Ustundag, who had known Roncalli's predecessor, the austere and unbending Margotti,
was at first icy cool; but he succumbed to the new man's charm and they ended up drinking
raki together on the terrace overlooking the Bosphorus. It was a good start to what was a
daunting assignment: how to be Vatican representative in an Islamic country that was busily
rejecting Islam and all religion as retrograde.

The next day, the feast of the Epiphany, he formally 'took possession' of his cathedral of
the Holy Spirit. It is a modest, barrel-vaulted church in basilica style, built in 1846. In its
courtyard stands a rare statue of Benedict XV, revered in Istanbul as the 'protector of the
East' during the First World War. Roncalli's next significant act was to bring to a close the
Octave of Prayer for Christian Unity on January 25, 1935, feast of the Conversion of St Paul.
He preached a sermon in French that he had evidently prepared with great care. In it he
announced his policy for Constantinople – he still preferred the old name.

He now had direct pastoral responsibility for the 35,000 Catholics who lived in and
around Istanbul. They included 'Latins' of various nationalities – in order of importance
French, Italian, German and Austrian – as well as a rich variety of 'Uniates': Armenians,
Chaldeans, Syrians, Maronites, Melkites, Bulgarians and Greeks. The 'Uniates', if not ex-
actly at home, were at least near enough to their places of origin to feel nostalgic. The list of
Churches sounds rather like the peoples present in Jerusalem on the day of Pentecost; and
Roncalli knew that it would need a comparable miracle to unite them. But that was his
ambition.

Quite evidently Roncalli had gone to Istanbul with a very clear idea of what his task was:
first to unify his own mixed bag of a flock, and then to seek good relations with the 100,000
or so Orthodox Christians who still clustered around the ecumenical patriarch, Photius II,
in the Phanar. From the start he established his authority by the reasonableness of what he

said. He succeeded because of the simple contrast between his approach and the prickly high-handedness of his predecessor.

It was less easy to establish good relations with the Turkish authorities. This was not because he was ill-disposed towards them, but because they were in the process of creating a thoroughly secular state. The heirs of the 'Young Turks' had broken the power of the caliph and the mullahs; they saw no reason why the power of the Christian priests should survive. Within a month of Roncalli's arrival, *La Vita Cattolica*, the diocesan weekly, was suppressed, along with every other kind of publication that could conceivably be construed as 'religious propaganda'. He wrote, not without humour, to coadjutor Bishop Andrea Bernareggi of Bergamo on February 3, 1935:

> I don't know what I'm going to say in my Lenten pastoral letter or whether it will be published. All that's left for me to talk about is prayer and liturgy. Even the theological virtues are banned. I hope that at least it will still be possible to talk about charity. But to have any dealings at all with the Turks, as the recent earthquake in the island of Marmara showed, can be dangerous (Alberigo, p. 440).

This was to become a familiar pattern in the post-war Communist countries: the Church would be allowed to exist provided it was confined to the sacristy.

Mustafa Kemal, who gave himself the name of Atatürk, 'father of the Turks', should not be thought of as a benevolent Fabian reformer. He dealt most savagely with all opposition. His biographers, who are not unsympathetic to him, open one chapter with this chilling sentence: 'Having hanged every prominent man in the country known to be opposed to his policies, and imprisoned lesser rivals, Mustafa Kemal could now take stock' (Orga, p. 272). Taking stock in 1935, Atatürk decided to launch an attack on Christian religious dress. This was entirely logical. Atatürk's policy was 'Westernising' at least in outward forms. Since Moslems had to sacrifice the fez in the name of modernity, it followed that Christians should abandon their soutanes and habits. The fez, after all, being brimless, was very suitable for Moslem prayer; and the very phrase 'to put on a hat' meant to apostasise from Islam. So Atatürk made his Westernising intentions plain by appearing one day in a panama hat (Orga, pp. 260–3).

Christians had to follow this secularising example. Religious habits were abolished by a law which came into force on June 13, 1935. Roncalli did not take this measure too tragically. He wrote to the retired bishop of Bergamo, Marelli, on April 13, 1935:

> As you know from June all the priests and monks and friars here will have to go about in secular dress. It's a great trial for everyone. We'll be happy enough if it stops there. Let's hope there's no imitation of what is happening in Mexico (*Quindicesimo anniversario*, p. 78).

In Mexico priests were being hunted down and shot: Atatürk's anti-clericalism did not go so far. In the end, the loss of religious dress was the least of Roncalli's worries. 'What does it matter', he remarked to Dell'Acqua, 'whether we wear the soutane or trousers as long as we proclaim the word of God' (Dreyfus, p. 93). The main result was to provide posterity with memorable photographs of Archbishop Roncalli in bowler hat and sober suit, looking for all the world like a Lombardy businessman who found it difficult to cut down on the *pasta*.

A much more serious problem was the government pressure on Christian schools. The Christian Brothers closed down four of their eight schools in his first year. The Sisters of Our Lady of Sion were forced to close two schools, but managed to expand the one nearest the cathedral. There was not much that Roncalli could do. He had no official diplomatic status, and nowhere to deliver his protests.

These difficulties, however, drove Roncalli back upon the pastoral work that he preferred. Compared with Bulgaria, he was now in his element 'blessing, consecrating, preaching' as he told Marelli (*Quindicesimo anniversario*, p. 77). The Apostolic Delegation at 87 Olçek Sokak Street also needed attention. He began work on the chapel, redecorated his study, reordered the archives and the library. He tried to give the Delegation the atmosphere of a religious family. His faithful servant, Luigi Bresciani, who had followed him from Sofia, looked after his material needs. There were readings at meals from Fr Faber's *Spiritual Conferences*. He saw himself as the father of his little family. 'The exercise of pastoral and fatherly kindness', he noted, 'such as befits a shepherd and a father, must express the whole purpose of my life as Bishop' (*Journal*, pp. 246–7).

Roncalli was always a well-organised and methodical worker. But the only time he had for personal work was between the hours of ten o'clock and midnight (*Journal*, p. 246). On one side of his desk was the Philips radio; on the other the Siemens telephone. Photographs of his family, numerous in his bedroom, were excluded from his study on the grounds that a Vatican representative should be 'like Melchizedek, without father or mother' (Righi, p. 21).

Yet it was there in July 1935 that he received the news that his father was dying. He tried to console his mother with the thought that 'when someone is gravely ill in the house, it is as though Jesus himself becomes visibly our guest, and that he sits there bringing comfort, blessings and holiness' (*Familiari*, I, p. 353. Letter dated July 25, 1935). But before this letter arrived in Sotto il Monte, Giovanni Battista Roncalli had died at the age of 81 – exactly the age his son would reach. Angelo – he became a little boy once again – went alone to the chapel 'to weep like a child'. That was on the day the telegram came. 'Now', he wrote, 'I am a little better, but tears keep welling up in my eyes' (*ibid.*, p. 353).

But there was no question of returning for the funeral. There wasn't time, and in any case he was needed in Turkey at this particularly tense moment in the life of the Church. He insists so much on the pressure of work that one suspects his mother had reproached him for his absence. Yet his only thought was to console her. But did he choose the right approach? In his letter home he says:

> As soon as the news of the death was made known people began to phone the
> Delegation. Tomorrow four Istanbul papers and *l'Osservatore Romano* will carry the news.
> Hundreds of Masses will be offered for the repose of his soul, and thousands of
> communions. A solemn requiem Mass is being prepared for Thursday in the cathedral. I
> think it will be a most imposing ceremony. In all this you can find some compensation
> for my inability to be present at Sotto il Monte in person (*Familiari*, I, p. 357).

Roncalli drew consolation from the fact that if his parents had not made the sacrifice of their son to the Church, no one would ever have heard of 'our poor, dear father, and who would have prayed for him?' (*ibid.*). He treated his mother with great gentleness thereafter, installed her with Ancilla and Maria at Camaitino, and wrote to her directly more often than before.

On October 2, 1935, Italy invaded Abyssinia. It was a coldly calculated and long-prepared move against the last sovereign state of Africa. According to Mussolini, its purpose was to win Italy 'a place in the sun', to provide an outlet for emigration from the *Mezzogiorno*, to display the martial virtues that were part of the ideology of Fascism, and to demonstrate that Italy was now a 'world power'. It was a popular war, even rallying to the government some previously dissident intellectuals like Benedetto Croce. The Vatican was embarrassed. *L'Osservatore Romano* pretended that nothing was happening.

However, on the very day the League of Nations discussed sanctions against Italy, Pius XI declared that 'the hopes, the demands, the needs of a great and good people should be recognised and satisfied' (Ragionieri 2, p. 2250). This piece of Vaticanese was taken to mean that Italy had a right to a colonial empire. It was a shocking remark because it totally ignored the hopes and the needs of the people of Abyssinia who, incidentally, had a long Christian tradition. The people of Abyssinia were now to be massacred, bombed and (it was later learned) gassed into submission. Though the Vatican abstained as far as possible from the conflict, the Italian clergy did not always show such restraint. There was a new form of *union sacrée*. Bishops blessed the departing troops: On November 18, 1935, all the mothers of Italy, from Queen Elena herself to the humblest peasant, were invited to donate their wedding rings for the war effort. This melodramatic and largely symbolic gesture would have been unimaginable, wrote one historian, 'without the help of the Church's network of contacts and powers of persuasion' (Ragioneri, 2, p. 2250).

Archbishop Roncalli's only comment on the war came in a letter to Ancilla and Maria who – it was sometimes a sore point – did not have wedding rings:

> We have to pray for this agitated world, and especially for our Italy. These are big questions: reason about them too much, and there's a danger of getting them wrong. But it's clear that the old fairy-tales are making a come-back. The big fish wants to eat the little fish. The little fish says the sea is big enough for everyone. Enough: let's hope and pray the war will soon be over because it is, after all, a war (*Familiari*, I, p. 366).

For this cartoonist's-eye-view of the situation, Roncalli needed to be far away and able to stand back from events. In Italy they were being bombarded with propaganda about how the benefits of civilization were being brought to a benighted African people. In the process the ancient Ethiopian Church was systematically destroyed.

Roncalli's problems in Turkey were of a different order. He decided at the start of 1936 to introduce a few words of Turkish into worship. From January 12, 1936, the 'Divine Praises' ('Blessed be God, blessed be his holy name . . .') had to be recited in Turkish in his cathedral, a practice he recommended elsewhere. It was a small change, indicative of his desire that the Church should make its home among the Turkish people; but as his pontificate showed, any change of principle can have an importance far beyond its immediate effect. The 'changes' were not appreciated by everyone. In his diary he records:

> When the *Tanre Mubarek olsun* [Blessed be God] was recited, many people left the church

displeased . . . [But] I am happy. On Sunday the Gospel in Turkish before the French
Ambassador; today the Litany in Turkish before the Italian Ambassador . . . the Catholic
Church respects everyone. The Apostolic Delegate is a bishop for all and intends to
honour the Gospel which does not admit national monopolies, is not fossilised, and
looks to the future (Trevor, p. 169).

Roncalli saw his linguistic innovations as a way of making the Church more genuinely
'Catholic'. He was denounced to Rome. In his October 1936 retreat he remarks that 'the
difference between my way of seeing situations on the spot and certain ways of judging
the same things in Rome hurts me considerably; it is my only real cross' (*Journal*, p. 244).

On other fronts he was moving cautiously forwards. Though not regarded by the government as an accredited diplomat, he made regular journeys to Ankara when he could – he
needed police permission – and made himself known to sympathetic ambassadors. His diplomatic style was original, owing more to the Gospels than to Machiavelli. In his 1936 retreat at Ranica, Bergamo (where the strike had been in 1911) he stated his method: 'Above all
I wish to render good for evil, and in all things try to prefer the Gospel truth to the cunning
of human politics' (*Journal*, p. 244). Without realising it, he was, however, laying solid foundations for his diplomatic activity during the war when Turkey's neutrality made it a
meeting-ground for all the contending parties, and Istanbul ceased to be a backwater.

Maxims about returning good for evil were handy in his dealings with the Greek government. Greece was his responsibility just as much as Turkey, and it was his headache. He
was even more 'suspect' in Orthodox Greece than in post-Islamic Turkey. But he knew that
the Greek mistrust of the 'Latins' whom they still called 'Franks' was founded in the terrible
experience of the crusades. In scholarly correspondence about the likely whereabouts of the
remains of St Demetrius of Salonika, he concedes that almost anything was possible in the
thirteenth century 'when the Venetians and the crusaders were stealing everything they
could lay hands on' (*Quindicesimo anniversario*, p. 82). In the folk-memory the 'Franks' had
robbed, raped and pillaged. Mussolini's aggressive Mediterranean policy reopened the old
wounds. In 1923 Italy had briefly occupied the island of Corfu after a bombardment that
killed many Greek refugees. Roncalli told Davide Cugini: 'In Athens we don't ride about
in a carriage. The bombardment of Corfu is still echoing in Greek ears. No doubt my predecessor was a very acute man, but he was also too optimistic' (Cugini, p. 54). For all these
reasons, the Greeks found it difficult to distinguish between the Vatican and the Italian government.

To add to the complications there were the Latin-rite religious, mostly French, who after
Greek Independence in 1832 had flocked in to run schools and hospitals. The last straw was a
handful – some 2,000 – of Greek 'Uniates' who had been repatriated from Turkey by the
Treaty of Lausanne in 1923. Since they challenged the national consensus by their very ex-
istence, they were regarded as – so to speak – a Trojan horse. The identification of 'being
Greek' and 'being Orthodox' was almost complete.

Apart from encouraging the local Catholics to hold firm, the main purpose of Roncalli's
mission to Greece was to discover what form of Vatican representation the Greeks would be
prepared to accept. The short answer was none. The monarchy had been restored with the

aid of the military in 1935, and Roncalli hoped that general elections of January 1936 would enable him to clarify his position with the new government.

But the elections resolved nothing either for Roncalli or Greece. General Metaxas became prime minister even though he had only six followers in parliament. Greece was under economic pressure from Germany and political pressure from Italy. Mussolini, irritated by Greek opposition to the Abyssinian war in the League of Nations, revived his claim to Albania. On the pretext of forestalling a *coup d'état*, from April 1936 Metaxas abolished parliament, began to govern by decree, declared a state of emergency, and used the army to put down a general strike (Woodhouse, pp. 230-1). It was not the most propitious moment for the arrival of a Vatican envoy who happened to be an Italian and was based on Istanbul. It would have been difficult to devise a more daunting set of obstacles.

So Roncalli was understating things when he wrote to his family on June 19, 1937:

> You know how I stand with the Turks. But the difficulties with the Greeks are greater. These splendid people give me fine words; but as you know the Orthodox are afraid of the Pope. So I need a lot of patience. (*Familiari*, I, p. 408).

He always seemed to stay in Greece longer than he had planned. He used the delays to indulge in spiritual tourism. He got to know about Greek monasticism by going round the monasteries. Here is how he describes to his mother a visit to Mount Athos:

> Up there are more than twenty huge monasteries and as many small ones: it is unique in the world. Women are not allowed, and since the mountain rises abruptly from the sea, it would be difficult for them to land anyway. . . One has to take the most difficult paths on horseback, and this made me entrust myself to St Joseph and my ancestors – as I always do – so as not to fall off. I didn't fall off once. I was there for three days and it takes at least five hours by horse or mule to get to the top; so one's bones get shaken up, and then there was the bad food and sleeping on hard beds etc . . . But this diversion did me good. I returned to Athens fitter than ever (*Familiari*, I, p. 379. The visit to Mount Athos was May 17–20, 1936).

But he had overestimated his fitness. In December 1936 he fell ill in Athens with nephritis. Back in Istanbul he was soon cured thanks to what Capovilla calls 'the energetic interventions' of Dr Lorando who also gave him a complete medical check-up. But the illness had been a scare or what he called 'a grave warning'. He saw 'signs of old age in my thinning hair' when they met for what turned out to be the last time on October 7, 1937:

Sister death was busy just about then. Don Pietro Forno, co-editor of the *Acta* of St Charles Borromeo, died in November 1938 while saying Mass. He had been one of Roncalli's best friends. Kemal Atatürk died on November 10, 1938 – Roncalli regretted that he was unavoidably absent in Greece – and few thought that Pope Pius XI could last much longer. First he was seen to be 'limping badly' (*Familiari*, I, p. 408), and then he began to doze off during audiences, and often missed what was said to him. Pius was 80, but he was not finished yet. Irish historian D. A. Binchy noted at this time that there was 'some mighty force in him, some spiritual dynamo charging the feeble battery' (Binchy, p. 71). Twice in March 1937 Pius XI roused himself with two forceful encyclicals, *Mit Brennender Sorge* (March 14,

1937) and *Divini Redemptoris* (March 19, 1937). The sub-titles explained their purpose: 'On the situation of the Catholic Church in Germany' and 'Against Atheistic Communism'.

With these encyclicals Pius XI dealt a blow to the two collectivist systems, Nazism and Communism. Though usually placed at opposite ends of the 'left' and 'right' spectrum, they both resulted in repressive dictatorships in which the rule of law was suspended and the individual human person was subordinated to the omnipotent state. Moreover, both their leaders, Adolf Hitler and Joseph Stalin, presented themselves as heroic saviours of the nation and encouraged a preposterous 'personality cult'. But despite these similarities, Pius XI did not quite put both dictatorships in the same bag. The emphasis in *Divini Redemptoris* fell on the 'intrinsically evil' nature of atheistic Communism, with which no Catholic could collaborate. *Mit Brennender Sorge* eloquently denounced those who 'idolatrously divinize race or the People or the State or a particular form of State', complained that the Church's rights were being violated, but that might be remedied if the Concordat were properly applied. There was no Concordat with the Communists, anywhere.

Roncalli's letters at this time are full of references to the need for the Church to be adaptable and able to respond to new needs. He wrote to Mgr Luigi Drago on February 21, 1938, that he was happy to be in Istanbul because 'I can work in my own style, that is in the style of a Church that is both teacher of all and always modern according to the demands of the times and the places' (*'chiesa maestra a tutti e sempre moderna secondo le esigenze dei tempi e delle località'*) (Alberigo, p. 448). That simple phrase provides a bridge between the Roncalli who in 1908 sympathised with the aspirations of 'Modernism' and the reforming Pope John of 1958. And the bridge was constructed not out of speculative theories but out of pastoral concern.

These reflections went on against an increasingly gloomy international background. It looked as though history would repeat itself and that a Pope would die on the outbreak of a European conflict. Italy's growing *rapprochement* with Germany made war more than ever likely. Despite their common emphasis on 'charismatic' leadership – the *Führer* and the *Duce* – there were differences between the two right-wing ideologies, and it was not inevitable that they should have become allies. The most significant sign of their new friendship was Hitler's visit to Rome in May 1938. The swastika, a twisted and perverted version of the cross, was seen for the first time in the streets of Rome, a sinister portent. Pius XI roused himself for another bout of indignation: 'It is not found out of place or out of season to raise up in Rome, on this feast of the Exaltation of the Holy Cross, the symbol of another cross which is not that of Christ' (Holmes, pp. 73–4). Preferring not even to be in the same city as Hitler, he then departed to Castelgandolfo.

L'Osservatore Romano studiously ignored the visit, and the Vatican museums were shut for its duration. But despite papal displeasure, Hitler's visit to Rome was a great success, and henceforward Italian domestic and foreign policies were more closely aligned with those of the Germans. In particular Mussolini began to persecute, not very efficiently, Italy's 40–70,000 Jews. Cardinal Schuster of Milan who had welcomed the Fascists had his eyes opened. If the hope had been to 'Christianise' Fascism, now it was on the contrary being 'nazified'.

For this reason the strengthening of the alliance between Germany and Italy led to increasing tensions between the Church and the Fascists. The anti-clerical strand in Fascism was revived. Roncalli had personal experience of this when he went home to Bergamo in mid-August 1938. The episcopal palace of Bishop Andrea Bernareggi, who had taken over from Bishop Marelli in 1936, was daubed at night with insulting slogans. The offices of Catholic Action, the last national organisation not incorporated into the Fascist state, were attacked. The bishop was not able to communicate freely with his clergy. Roncalli was the chief guest preacher at the regional Eucharistic Congress held at Ardesio from August 29 to September 4, 1938. But it was not a moment for escapist piety. It was one of the few occasions when the priests of Bergamo had been able to gather freely round Bernareggi. They entrusted Roncalli, as an outsider and an archbishop, with the task of expressing their solidarity with the bishop. It took the form of a letter addressed to Bernareggi. Since he was in the midst, that might have seemed rather redundant; but it was designed to reassure him that he was not alone.

The letter is an important piece of evidence about the Church-state clash at the time, but it was not a ringing clarion-call to action of any sort (text in *Dodicesimo anniversario*, pp. 72–4). More in sorrow than in anger, Roncalli deplores the outrages heaped upon this good man, and claims that successive bishops of Bergamo have always known how to 'render nobly to Caesar what is Caesar's and to God what is God's'. Local pride prompted him to find the attack on Catholic Action particularly unfortunate, since 'Catholic Action already existed in Bergamo while the rest of Italy slept' (*ibid.*, p. 73). But there was no suggestion that the Church should become a focus of opposition to a regime to which the clergy of Bergamo, at the time, could not imagine an alternative. Roncalli was no doubt additionally cautious in that as a Vatican diplomat 'he ought not to have involved himself in such grave events of a local nature' (to borrow Capovilla's phrase).

The Munich crisis came within a month. Roncalli's final meeting with Pius XI was devoted to the impending conflict. In his panegyric of Pius, he reports the Pope as saying: 'I am not afraid for the future of the Church. She only wants to be free. I know well what fate may well await her – sorrow and persecutions; but she will always have the last word, because she embodies the divine promises. But, on the other hand, I tremble for the nations . . .' (Dreyfus, p. 94).

Pius XI died on February 10, 1939. It is difficult to know what Roncalli really felt on his death, for his response was complicated by the fact that his mother was also dying at the same time. Despite the urgent pleas of his family, he could not return for the end. He was 'like a soldier, under orders' (*Familiari*, I, p. 459). He had to stay in Istanbul because the death of a pope and the election of a new one meant a round of formal condolences and official visits. It must have seemed incomprehensibly self-important in Sotto il Monte, where the diplomatic minuet was another world. All they knew was that Angelo, having missed the death of his father, was now going to miss the death of his mother. Ancilla and Maria – for once we have their side of the correspondence – give a touching picture of Marianna Roncalli in her last months, as she lay bedridden;

> Frequently she would recall her children, and especially you who are so far away; and you should have seen how, poor thing, she came to life again when she got a letter from you. She wouldn't entrust it to anyone else; she wanted to take it in her hands and read it for herself. But then thinking she might make mistakes, she would have it read by

Enrica, and murmur: It's understandable that he can't come, but let's hope that he might. But if the Lord abandons me here, and I know how to do his will, we'll meet together in Paradise (*Familiari*, I, pp. 459–60).

So Marianna Roncalli died, of 'flu, at the age of 85, on February 20, 1939, during the *novemdiales* or nine days of mourning for the deceased pope. Angelo paid for her to have a splendid funeral, explaining that after all 'she is the mother of a Bishop' (*Familiari*, I, p. 460).

Roncalli had few comments on the conclave – the shortest of the century. Eugenio Pacelli, the Secretary of State, was elected, predictably enough. 'Being pope today', Roncalli remarks, 'is enough to turn your hair as white as your soutane' (*Familiari*, I, p. 465). He declares himself 'most happy' with the outcome and is convinced that 'the Lord had a hand in this election' (*ibid.*, p. 467). He had no thought that he would be present at the next conclave, still less that he would be elected. In March 1939 he followed Pius' Coronation Mass on Vatican radio, and continued to marvel at this modern device.

The election of Pius XII indirectly enabled him to secure an historic 'first'. A representative of the Ecumenical Patriarch, Benjamin I, was present at the *Te Deum* for the new pope. On May 27, 1938, Roncalli went along to the Phanar to thank Benjamin who embraced him warmly. Roncalli had met an earlier patriarch in 1927, but that visit had been private and unofficial. After an enmity lasting so long the 'kiss of peace' between Benjamin and the Pope's representative, Roncalli, prefigured the embrace between the brother patriarchs, Athenagoras and Paul VI, in Jerusalem in January 1964. The Christian East and the Christian West, Constantinople and Rome, were finally able to meet in the land of their common origin.

That happy outcome was a good illustration of Roncalli's ecumenical method, as he outlined it to the Reverend Austin Oakley, personal representative of the archbishop of Canterbury to the ecumenical patriarch and the first Anglican he came to know. He thought in the long-term. One could not expect to batter down the walls of Christian divisions, but, said Roncalli, 'I try to pull out a brick here and there'.

Roncalli's meeting with the ecumenical patriarch was one of the few pieces of good news in 1939. On Good Friday – April 8 – Italy invaded Albania. It took about a week to overcome the army of King Zog. Yet Roncalli's next letter home – from Istanbul on April 22, 1939 – ignores these events and shows him in his most 'patriotic vein:

I'm feeling happier now because the skies are clearing. I don't believe that we will have a war. For our part we try to be at peace with everyone, not speaking ill of anyone and not getting mixed up in political matters.

It's true that there are some who like to speak ill of Italy, but they are wrong. There are arrogant people among us, and there is no lack of exaggeration; but as a country Italy is organised and respectful of religion and still the best place to be. There is no need to bother about what third and fourth parties are doing. As you know, I stay out of politics, but I cannot deny what I think and feel (*Familiari*, I, pp. 470-1).

Roncalli was not exactly beating the Fascist drum, but he was giving them, as *Italians*, the benefit of whatever doubt was going. It would be anachronistic to blame Roncalli for holding such views; it would be dishonest not to mention that he held them.

'I don't believe that we will have a war', Roncalli wrote optimistically in April 1939. On May 22, 1939, Hitler and Mussolini signed the 'Pact of Steel', a remarkably nonchalant document in which the *Duce* accepted the German terms 'without fixing their purpose or their limits' (Ragionieri, 2, p. 2272). War was now inevitable; the only question concerned its timing and occasion.

Pius XII had become pope just in time to utter vain exhortations to peace. His last-minute appeal, broadcast on August 24, 1939, was brushed aside as irrelevant, setting a pattern that would recur frequently in the next five years: 'Empires which are not founded on justice are not blessed by God. Statesmanship emancipated from morality betrays those very ones who would have it so. The danger is imminent, but there is yet time. Nothing is lost by peace; everything may be lost by war' (Holmes, p. 122). The last epigrammatic sentence was attributed in curial circles to Giovanni Battista Montini.

As the war machines clicked into gear, Roncalli had a meeting on August 2 with the new German ambassador to Turkey, Franz von Papen. They got on well. If the concept is not too absurd, von Papen represented the smiling, Catholic face of Hitler's Germany. We will meet him again. Then Roncalli flew to Rome via Athens and Brindisi to report to Cardinal Maglione, the new Secretary of State, and the substitute under-Secretary, his old friend, Giovanni Battista Montini. So he was in Italy on 'the day war broke out', and saw Pius XII on September 5. But Italy was not yet in the war.

On his return to Turkey he organised a committee to aid Polish refugees on the day Warsaw fell – September 28, 1939. What tradition called 'the corporal works of mercy' would be from now on at the top of his agenda. Yet the war seemed very far away when he made his retreat November 12–18, 1939. The beauty of the scene enchanted him, and for once in a while he records some visual impressions:

> Every evening from the window of my room here in the Jesuit residence, I see a cluster of boats on the Bosphorus; they come round from the Golden Horn in tens and hundreds; they gather at a given spot and then they light up, some more brilliantly than others, offering a most impressive spectacle of light and colour. I thought it was a sea festival for Bairam (one of the two great annual Moslem feasts) which occurs about now. But it was simply the fleet organised to fish for *bonito*, the large fish which is said to come from far away in the Black Sea (*Journal*, pp. 251–2).

Then, as though to off-set any aesthetic self-indulgence that would be inappropriate in wartime, he moralises the scene and reminds himself that as a 'fisher of men' he should show no less zeal and courage than these Turkish fishermen (*ibid.*).

But the thought of the war, however remote, kept on breaking in. In the East, Germany and the Soviet Union, accomplices at last, had cynically carved up Poland, and began to destroy its elite of priests and intellectuals. In the West it seemed that nothing much was happening. It was the period known as the *'drôle de guerre'* or the phoney war, the *Sitzkrieg* (stationary war) that preceded the *Blitzkrieg* (war of rapid movement). The main consolation for Roncalli, as he sat down to write his letter home on Christmas Day, 1939, was that Italy had not yet been drawn into the conflict:

> Think of all the unfortunate people who are at war, the Poles and those poor Finns and

the Germans themselves and the Russians. What do the troops know about all this? They suffer and die, causing grief to countless families. It is the leaders who are responsible. It is they who are obstinate, and they're all the same.

We're blessed in Italy. This time we really must admit that *Il Duce* is guided to act for the good of Italy (*Familiari*, I, pp. 489–90).

In 1940 the Vatican ordered Roncalli to devote more time to Greece. He paid three visits there between January and May. There were times, indeed, when he wished someone else would take over from him: 'I confess I would not mind if it were entrusted to someone else, but while it is mine, I want to honour the obligation at all costs. "Those who sow in tears shall reap in joy". It little matters to me that others will reap' (*ibid.*). But the deteriorating political situation made his mission more difficult than ever. Metaxas was still in power. As a Greek patriot, he was deeply distrustful of German and Italian intentions in the Mediterranean. The Italian occupation of Albania was virtually complete, which meant that Greece had Italian troops along its northern border. It was not a time when Roncalli's protestations of neutrality and universal love were likely to carry much weight. He was more than ever the 'suspect'.

The British government also began to take an interest in him. Later, after Italy's entry into the war, Vatican diplomats of Italian nationality – that is, the majority of them – were treated as 'enemy aliens' (*Actes et documents*, 4, Introduction). In neutral Turkey, Roncalli was spared this indignity. But in a city where everyone was carefully watching everyone else, it would not have escaped notice that he met von Papen again on January 26, 1940. Roncalli saw in him the Catholic aristocrat with a pious wife who did the flower arrangements in the Delegation chapel and sometimes swept the floor.

The Vatican knew rather more about von Papen's past and was not so easily taken in. He had been one of the 'government of barons' who accepted the end of the Weimar Republic in the foolish belief that they could 'control Hitler'. Not remarkable for his courage, von Papen had shown a certain bravery in 1934 when he made a speech critical of the Nazis. But the murder of the aide who helped him draft the speech brought him back to his senses. He was sent to Austria to prepare the *Anschluss* or union of Austria and Germany. This was not a particularly 'Nazi' cause, and many German and Austrian Catholics welcomed the idea of a 'Greater Germany'. It was of a different order from later territorial claims. Having dealt satisfactorily with Austria, von Papen was despatched as ambassador to Turkey early in 1939. It was not a top post, but neither was it an irrelevant side-show: Turkey guarded the Dardanelles with an efficient army of two million men, and would form the German right flank in any eventual conflict with the Soviet Union. In April 1940 von Papen was proposed as German ambassador to the Holy See. Pius XII consulted Konrad von Preysing, bishop of Berlin, who said no. Von Papen was thought to be too shifty. Pius refused his *agrément*. Von Papen remained in Turkey.

Roncalli had to follow the instructions of the Secretariat of State. They were simple. The Vatican was neutral, even if that meant being equidistant between the two contending parties and making no moral discrimination between them. There was certainly no belief that the 'English' were morally superior or more idealistic. Here, for example, is how Roncalli's superior, Mgr Domenico Tardini, minuted a request from Lord Halifax in 1940 that the Vatican should publicly dissociate itself from the Axis powers:

> A curious fellow, Lord Halifax, a scolding lecturer. The mysticism of the Foreign Office comes down to the interests of Britain (Utilitarianism). He professes to be defending religious interests, but in fact seeks political goals. He tries to get the Holy See to say that Nazism is as bad as Communism, forgetting that only yesterday the British government was courting the Communists. His purpose is evident: to provoke the Holy See into a statement useful to England and damaging to the Axis (*Actes et documents*, 4, No. 166).

This mistrustful attitude towards British intentions would have been picked up by the British Embassy in Ankara, despite Austin Oakley's assurances that Roncalli was a man of peace and genuinely neutral.

On May 10 1940 the Germans invaded neutral Holland, Luxembourg and Belgium, thus circumventing the Maginot Line. They swept all before them. Roncalli did not think he was breaking with neutrality in presenting his condolences at the Netherlands Legation on May 15. The French Army was routed, much of the British Expeditionary Force escaped via the beaches of Dunkirk, and Paris fell on June 14.

For Roncalli personally, the decisive date in this critical month of June 1940 was not the 22nd, when the Franco-German armistice was signed in the famous railway carriage at Compiègne, but the 10th, the day Italy entered the war. Only six months before he had thanked God for Mussolini and believed that his protestations of non-belligerency were sincere; now that card-house of hope collapsed. It was a blow partly because he had always loved France – even though largely from a distance and through the eyes of Radini Tedeschi – but even more because Mussolini had not kept his word.

Next day, June 11, 1940, he received Mgr Joseph Guillois, a Frenchman and his episcopal chancellor, solemnly gave him the kiss of peace, and because he did not trust himself to improvise, read out the following text written the night before:

> A day of sadness. Italy has declared war on France and England . . . War is a terrible *periculum*, danger. For the Christian who believes in Jesus and his Gospel it is an iniquity and a contradiction. 'Deliver us, O Lord, from famine and war'. I think that today my duties of wisdom, moderation and charity have become more grave than ever. I must be the bishop of all, that is the *consul Dei*, God's consul, father, light, encouragement for all. Nature makes me want the success of my dear country; grace fills me more than ever with the desire to seek and work for peace (*Letture*, p. 286).

This was when Roncalli's war really began. How he tried to be a man of peace in time of war will be the subject of the next chapter.

Chapter 9

God's consul

Mussolini speaks from the balcony of the Palazzo Venezia. The news of the
war does not surprise anyone and does not arouse very much enthusiasm. I
am sad, very sad. The adventure begins. May God help Italy!

(Count Galeazzo Ciano, Mussolini's foreign minister and son-in-law, *Diaries*, p. 264,
June 10, 1940)

Italy's entry into the war was a bitter blow for Archbishop Roncalli. It made his tightrope
walk of neutrality considerably more difficult, especially in Greece. The war was unpopular
with the Italian people who had not been consulted about it. Many Italians expected that an
isolated Britain would soon seek a negotiated peace. Roncalli half-shared this widespread
view. On June 21, 1940, he wrote home:

> Let's hope that the war with England will soon be over. Otherwise it will be a very bad
> look-out for our cousin in the navy [Peppino Roncalli]. All of you should remember
> what Bishop Bernareggi wrote on the outbreak of war. His were golden words. At a time
> like this one should speak little, pray a lot, and impose some sacrifices on oneself.
> General Pétain put it very well yesterday. One of the causes of the French defeat was
> their unbridled enjoyment of material pleasures after the Great War. The Germans on the
> other hand began to impose limitations and sacrifices on themselves, and so were
> prepared and strong. It's another form of the parable of the wise and foolish virgins
> (*Familiari*, I, pp. 508–9).

Roncalli must have been one of the few people in Europe capable of presenting the German rearmament policy ('Guns before butter') as an illustration of how to be an evangelical
wise virgin.

Roncalli had a long conversation with von Papen on August 12, 1940. He reported on it
the next day (*Actes et documents*, 4, pp. 105–11). It was his most important diplomatic despatch
to date, and he knew it. Von Papen had just returned from Berlin where he found Hitler's
position was this:

> He repeated that it had never been his intention to annihilate England, but rather to
> make it behave more reasonably towards Germany... He would deeply regret having to
> pass over to an all-out attack; but the attack would surely come, and he would be happy
> if, after the first blows, England decided to negotiate an agreement.
> The way the English and the French are completely deceived about German war
> resources – von Papen went on – is painful to behold. They have a spirit of hatred and

detestation of Germany that we Germans have never had towards them. We have tried and will continue to try to treat them with respect, and not with the contempt they habitually display towards us.

Von Papen was engaging in diplomatic propaganda, stressing for the benefit of the Holy See the contrast between the 'reasonable' Germans and the obsessed, hate-inspired English. Roncalli noted that von Papen made the next remarks 'in a more lively tone'. Not surprisingly. He had reached the heart of the matter:

Despite the various estimates that may be made of Hitler's character . . . there are still so many open possibilities, and the future could be rich in surprises. One of them could be that after the war Catholicism would become the 'formative principle' of the new German social order, rather in the way Mussolini had wisely endowed Italy with the concordat and social legislation inspired on some points by the great teaching of Leo XIII.

Von Papen was overplaying his hand here. The notion that Mussolini was inspired by the social teaching of the Church was a pleasant fantasy; and the picture of a Hitler domesticated into Catholicism was even more fantastic.

But it was all part of von Papen's diplomatic propaganda. To pursue his military aims. Hitler needed docile Catholics, and in 1940 he had begun to relax his anti-Church policy with that in view (see Helmreich, p. 348). The whole shimmering prospect that von Papen dangled before Roncalli depended on German Catholics being involved ever more closely in 'the cares, the sufferings and the joys of this great and noble nation'. Von Papen expected the war to be over by November 1940 (they were in August). Then there would be something for Italy too. In the redrawn German map of Europe, Italy would replace France as 'the major responsible power' in the Middle East, be conceded the island of Corsica and some territory around Nice, and the 'Tunisian' problem would be solved in favour of Italy.

Though Roncalli gives it as his opinion that von Papen was 'a sincere and a good Catholic', he was not listening altogether uncritically. He pressed von Papen on two points. First, was he distinguishing clearly between Hitler's views and his own? What von Papen was saying made some sense as the wish-fulfilment of a German Catholic who still hoped that Hitler could be 'controlled'. But could he really speak for Hitler? The other crucial question was about Hitler's sincerity. Von Papen tried to reassure him on both points.

Roncalli added one last detail, of great importance for the future. While he was closeted with von Papen, his secretary, Righi, was out walking in the embassy garden with Baron Kurt von Lersner, who was supposed to be von Papen's cultural attaché. As a Lutheran, he was an admirable foil to the Catholic von Papen. Roncalli came to like him and trust him. When the two Vatican diplomats got back home to the Delegation, they compared notes and reported:

Together we were allowed to glimpse an outline of the reconstructed Europe of tomorrow: for example, Alsace-Lorraine and Luxembourg would be absorbed into Germany; Belgium and Holland with their independence restored but demilitarised. The same to be said of the new Poland and the protectorate of Bohemia and Moravia. Finally the cost of the war for the two Axis powers would be borne by the colonial

possessions of Belgium and Holland in the form of raw materials . . . France would
restore the former German colonies and pay war indemnities. Both von Papen and
Baron Lersner foresee the end of the war by this autumn.

It was Roncalli's duty to transmit accurately what he had heard, not to comment on it.
But at the same time, there is something sinister in this calm recital of the consequences of
Hitler's *Neue Ordnung* or New Order. He fully expected to have to live with it. When Roncalli's report arrived in the Secretariat of State, Tardini minuted it: 'This fellow has understood nothing' (*'Questo non ha capito niente'*). The good-natured Roncalli had been too
gullible, and had been taken for a diplomatic ride.

Matters of high politics were strictly excluded from his letters home. He told his sisters,
instead, how he was rebuilding, at his own expense, the Apostolic Delegation. 'The nasty
little entrance you used to know', he wrote, 'has been replaced by a large atrium with four
columns' (*Familiari*, I, pp. 514–15). It looked out over the garden which was ablaze with roses
and magnolias. He had icons in the chapel and the text *Ad Jesum per Mariam* was inscribed
above its door. What he does not tell his sisters, however, is that on the very day he was
writing to them, September 5, 1940, he had met a party of Polish Jews who brought grim
news from Nazi-occupied Poland. He helped them on their way to the Holy Land. Von
Papen's assurances about the 'independence' of Poland were already exposed as nonsense.

A month later – according to von Papen, the war ought to have been over – he began the
most sombre retreat of his life at the villa house of the Sisters of Our Lady of Sion. It was at
Terapia and overlooked the Bosphorus. But this time there were no twinkling lights of fishing boats out at sea. Following a suggestion of Pius XII, he took Psalm 51, the *Miserere*, as the
basis of his meditations. So he was praying this Jewish prayer, in the midst of a community
dedicated to ministering to Jews, at a time when the first inkling of the terrible fate that
awaited them had begun to emerge. Some things became clearer to him.

The first was simply that no nation can claim to have God on its side. This 'murderous war
that is being waged on land and sea and in the air' was certainly no crusade: 'It has been
asserted, and is still being asserted, that God is bound to preserve this or that country or
grant it invulnerability and final victory, because of the righteous people who live there
and the good they do. We forget that although God has made the nations, he has left the
constitution of states to the free decisions of men' (*Journal*, p. 257). Men go to war because
they want to: 'War is desired by men, deliberately, in defiance of the most sacred laws. That
is what makes it so evil. He who instigates war and foments it is always the "Prince of this
world" who has nothing to do with Christ, the "Prince of peace"' (*ibid.*).

There was something rather forced in the cheerfulness of his next letter to Ancilla and
Maria. He rattles on about what it feels like to reach sixty and reports his latest attempts to
keep his weight down. In the evening he has only soup and fruit, with no bread or wine. For
breakfast nothing but coffee and fruit. At lunch, however, he 'eats like a good Christian'. He
claims that this regime is working well. He is in the best of health, has slimmed a little, and
retains 'the freshness and agility of youth' (*Familiari*, I, p. 525). The war breaks in as he wishes
them a happy Christmas. For the first time since he arrived in Turkey he will not be singing
Midnight Mass. Though Turkey is not at war, a black-out has been imposed on Istanbul as a
precaution against air-raids.

As part of his keep fit at sixty campaign Roncalli started to go for afternoon walks around the strangely deserted city. Most of the men of military age were away in the army. The removal of the capital to Ankara – Atatürk had been pursuing some atavistic memory of a Hittite capital 4000 years before – had deprived Istanbul's European quarter, Pera Beyoglu, of its vitality. The city seemed moribund. It was like a museum. This had its compensations for those who stayed behind. Roncalli's afternoon walks became archaeological excursions. He particularly loved the Studion, near the Golden Gate, once a centre of monastic arts and sciences, and used to say the rosary among its ruins. He found plenty of traces of Byzantium in Istanbul, and became something of an expert on Greek inscriptions.

Turkey was just the place for someone with historical imagination. The first great Councils – Ephesus, Chalcedon, Constantinople – had all been held there. Roncalli kept beside him on his desk a list of the 856 (*sic*) episcopal sees which had once flourished in 'Asia Minor' (Righi, p. 94). He thought it would be a good joke to send to his old friend Borgongini Duca, Nuncio to Italy, a post-card from Eraclea of Europe of which he was titular bishop. 'We are here under your jurisdiction', Roncalli wrote from the straggling village, Eregli, that was all that remained.

Then there was Antioch, once the cultural rival of Rome, and equally the city of St Peter, where the followers of Christ were first given the nickname 'Christian'. Roncalli also became familiar with the Greek fathers, especially St John Chrysostom, priest of Antioch, who was press-ganged into becoming bishop of Constantinople and died in exile. Roncalli preached on him at the conclusion of the Octave of Prayer for Church Unity in 1941 (text in Alberigo, pp. 458–63). Living in Turkey gave him a sense of Christian origins and a knowledge of the Oriental tradition. He was delivered from the narrowness of Roman theology.

But his plunge into the past, though it could be used to divert – in both senses – ambassadors of scholarly leanings, could not provide an escape from the present. Early in 1941 von Papen was back with news that the understanding between the Axis powers (Germany and Italy) and the Soviet Union was complete. Since he had just seen Hitler, Molotov, the Russian Foreign Minister, and King Boris of Bulgaria, this seemed like authoritative inside information, and Roncalli hastened to transmit it:

> The Triple Pact grows ever stronger, and the basis of a *new order* in Europe is already laid down. Some nations have already joined the Pact; others are on their way. The door is open for all those who want to join, also for Turkey . . . I got the impression [Roncalli is now speaking in his own name] that once England is liquidated, the Axis and Russia will not give excessive importance to Turkey and that its independence could be guaranteed in the future redrawing of the map of Europe (*Actes et documents*, 4, pp. 273–4).

Once again the new order and its consequences are accepted with what looks like equanimity. The use of the typically totalitarian word 'liquidated' is chilling. And there was a lack of political perceptiveness in swallowing uncritically von Papen's assurances about the solid friendship that bound Germany and the Soviet Union together. Within six months Operation Barbarossa, the Nazi attack on Russia, was launched to prove the hollowness of that claim.

But Roncalli was now in deep water, caught up in plots and counter-plots. The Baron von Lersner was up to something, and Roncalli begins to do favours for him and report his conversations. Von Lersner was an anti-Nazi who secretly wanted the removal of Hitler so that a deal could be done in the West (see *Actes et documents*, 4, pp. 367–8). But the removal of Hitler could only be achieved on the hypothesis that there existed 'good' Germans who were prepared to take the risks involved. This was precisely what the allied doctrine of 'unconditional surrender' – already applied in practice – excluded. Though the United States was not yet in the war, President Franklin D. Roosevelt's moral and economic support for Britain strengthened British resolve to fight on to the bitter end. On January 6, 1941, Roosevelt declared that he would not deal with the Nazi regime and that 'no one can tame a tiger or turn it into a charming kitten' (Dreyfus, p. 97).

This robbed the anti-Nazi Germans of hope. It made von Lersner very angry indeed. Roncalli reports him saying: 'No one loves peace any more. Roosevelt has now torn off the mask. His first statements suggested sincerity. But he was play-acting to secure re-election. Once he won, he behaved like everyone else' (*Actes et documents*, 4, p. 382). Now that Roosevelt had joined the baying pack, Lersner was forced to look elsewhere for moral leadership and peace initiatives. He attributed the following remark to 'an important Turk', but it was clear that these were his own views: 'Today, the greatest man in the world, much greater than Hitler or Churchill or Mussolini, would be the one who had enough moral influence to bring governments to consider concrete peace proposals' (*ibid.*, p. 380). But there was only one candidate for this historic role: Pope Pius XII.

Roncalli's report remains as detached as usual. But it would be surprising if he did not feel a certain *frisson* of excitement. For here was a German Lutheran proposing papal mediation to end the war. What Benedict XV had been rebuffed for attempting in August 1917 was now being offered to his successor. Moreover, to demonstrate his sincerity, von Lersner casually revealed details of German plans for the Balkans. The next month, March, German troops 'peacefully' entered Bulgaria and in April twenty-one divisions fell upon Yugoslavia and Greece, to help out the Italians who were being held. This was impressive, but it was not impressive enough. It was known in the Secretariat of State that the allies would not depart from their policy of 'unconditional surrender', and that the language of 'peace' was regarded as treasonable in Nazi Germany. So nothing could be done.

There was a division of opinion within the Secretariat of State. Tardini continued to denounce 'unconditional surrender' as barbarous and iniquitous. Montini, on the other hand, had a better understanding of why it was insisted upon. That Roncalli was aware of this difference in broad terms is shown by the fact that he wrote a *private* letter to Montini recommending von Lersner to him (*Saggio*, p. 32. Letter dated April 23, 1942). Presumably Roncalli wrote – unusually – to Montini because he had already had enough abuse from Tardini about his naiveté. He was prepared to be naïve for peace.

But what he did not know was that Montini had already concluded that the insistence on 'unconditional surrender' meant that Italy could only achieve a separate peace by switching sides. Italy's only alternative to continuing the war on the German side was to dump Mussolini, abandon the Axis, and wager on an Allied victory (see *La Repubblica*, September 7, 1983: interview with ex-Queen Maria José of Savoy). But since such a scheme was perilous, treacherous even, it is unlikely that anyone would risk talking about it to a Vatican diplomat in such a nest of spies as Istanbul. In any event, Roncalli was completely taken by surprise when it actually happened.

He was also taken by surprise by the German attack on Russia on June 22, 1941. Only three days earlier he reported that Germany had signed a non-aggression pact with Turkey. Roncalli saw it merely as a feather in von Papen's cap and not as a necessary securing of the right flank before the attack on Russia: 'It crowns the tenacious and fortunate endeavours of von Papen . . . It is a step towards peace, and it demanded an act of courage on the part of Turkey in view of its commitments to Great Britain' (*Actes et documents*, 4, p. 560). Roncalli shared in von Papen's success with some enthusiasm. The same day – June 19, 1941 – he wrote to his sisters: 'This very day a treaty was signed between Germany and Turkey who will not grab each other by the throat. What more can one ask? I believe that Italy will now do the same. Now try to say that your brother was not a prophet!' (*Familiari*, I, p. 543). But his prophetic gifts were strictly limited. Not only had he failed to foresee the long-planned Operation Barbarossa, but on the word of von Papen had frequently informed the Vatican that the relationship between Germany and Russia was in good shape.

Von Papen and von Lersner flattered Roncalli by taking him into their confidence. But they did not tell him everything. The weakness of his one-sided reliance on German sources became apparent. It was not that Roncalli got on badly with the British ambassador, Sir Hughe Knatchbull-Hugessen. It was simply that when they met, they met for tea. They never discussed strategic or political matters; their talk was confined to technical questions about – for example – the transmission of Vatican correspondence, aid for starving Greece or Italian refugees in the Middle East. Unlike von Papen, Sir Hughe did not think it was any part of his mission to win over the apostolic delegate to his country's cause (Righi, pp. 202–3).

It would have required superhuman powers of detachment – or consummate acting skill – to hide all signs of partisanship in such a complicated situation. Roncalli claimed to be on good terms with all the belligerents by being *nec procul, nec prope* (neither too distant nor too close): 'I read in the Old Testament that Jacob also had sons who disagreed among themselves. But he, the father, *rem tacitus considerabat* – pondered the matter in silence' (Trevor, p. 186). It was a text he would make use of as Pope, by which time he was old enough to play the patriarchal role more successfully.

Just when he thought he had found a method for dealing with the problems of Istanbul, he was ordered to Greece. This time he was told to stay as long as was necessary finally to resolve the question of Vatican diplomatic representation. His dependence on the Germans was such that he needed a visa from von Papen to travel to Greece, and used German air transport for most of the journey. Greece was in chaos. He was told he would have to go via Sofia. What had been a mere stop-over became an important diplomatic mission. He met King Boris, Queen Giovanna, leading politicians, and the Orthodox metropolitan, Stefan. These were all old acquaintances. His patient work during ten years in Bulgaria now paid off.

King Boris revealed that the Russians had been putting pressure on him to attack Turkey, the traditional Bulgarian enemy. He resisted their blandishments and threats. This inevitably brought him closer to the Germans. But Boris would say very little about the Germans. He preferred to steer the conversation towards Italy, 'in which he has complete confidence', and to reminisce about King Victor Emmanuel III, his father-in-law. When Boris told him that last time he was in Rome he had gone incognito into St Peter's, said his prayers at

God's consul

various altars and kissed the foot of St Peter's statue, Victor Emmanuel said: '*Bravo*, you did well' (*Actes et documents*, 5, pp. 91 and following).

King Boris then recounted the story of the Serbian Orthodox patriarch, Gavrilo Dozić, who had allegedly fled to some rocky mountain refuge 'with a stock of ham to keep him from hunger and a vast collection of records, especially those of Josephine Baker, the famous black dancer, to keep him from melancholy'. But this tale of the pusillanimous patriarch was a calumny, a product of the German propaganda machine. The truth was that Patriarch Gavrilo was arrested in a monastery, brutally beaten up, and eventually sent to Dachau for refusing to collaborate with the Nazis (Alexander, pp. 10-11). That Roncalli should have repeated the calumny without raising any critical questions about it is scandalous. Contained in an official report, it would have reinforced the Vatican prejudice against the Serbian Orthodox.

The most astonishing feature of this interview was the way King Boris asked the papal diplomat to help him deal with the anglophile leanings of the Orthodox metropolitan, Stefan: '*Monsignore*, do try and see him'. Roncalli sought out the metropolitan and reported to Rome on his meeting:

> He showed himself still somewhat under the spell of the Anglo-American organisations which on the pretext of charity pursue the illusion of world peace through the union of Christians (*ibid.*).

This embarrassing text was not published until 1969. It shows that, at sixty, Roncalli still had a lot to learn about ecumenism.

He was on surer ground when he urged the Vatican to support Bulgaria's border claim against Yugoslavia. The Bulgarians wanted Ochrida, site of the monasteries of Sts Clement and Naoum, disciples of St Cyril and Methodius. 'Poor as they are', King Boris explained, 'they represent the Jerusalem of the Bulgarian nation'. Roncalli comments: 'It is the highest wisdom not to upset or offend against the psychological characteristics of different peoples'. The truth was that Bulgaria, so far, had done rather well out of the war. All Bulgaria's gains depended on its alliance with Germany and the acceptance of Hitler's 'New Order'.

Roncalli's work was now in devastated Greece. Travel by road was difficult: so many bridges had been blown up in a desperate attempt to slow down the German advance. So whenever possible, Roncalli travelled by air, and he found hunger as well as destruction, for the British had imposed a food blockade. Roncalli summarised his impressions in an early report to the Vatican:

> At Salonika they are still not too badly off compared with Athens; and it also seems that life is tolerable in the country and on the islands. But here we are in a situation where *parvuli petunt panem*, children beg for bread, and there is not enough bread. Strict rationing has been imposed on the city, quite inadequate for the ordinary nutrition of a young person, a robust man or a mother with children (*Actes et documents*, 5, pp. 99–100).

Roncalli's sympathy with the defeated Greeks comes through very clearly in this passage; and he soon translated it into practical help. But his very presence was ambivalent: he was in Greece only by favour of the Germans and the Italians. When he discovered that there were Bergamesque troops in Athens. On July 28, 1941, he wrote home: 'There are many good soldiers here from Bergamo. Their chaplains speak highly of them. They are part of the occupying forces, and naturally prefer that to being at the front. But they are good soldiers who have already been at the front and won honour for themselves' (*Familiari*, I, p. 546).

To adjust the balance, Roncalli also visited the German wounded and the British prisoners of war. But the hungry, defeated Greeks were his main concern. He explained how he saw his role in a despatch to the Vatican dated August 4, 1941, as one of 'God's Consuls', that is, as 'a bishop who has the holy freedom to present himself to the conqueror in the name of a spiritual authority, and in the name of the interests of the conquered people' (*Actes et documents*, 5, p. 125). On September 9, 1941, a group of Greek laymen approached Roncalli and asked him to get the Holy See to intervene, to allow through a shipment of 360,000 tons of grain, already paid for, from Haifa in Palestine. He made a quick dash to Rome and saw Pius XII. But the needs outstripped the resources, and Roncalli was under no illusion that the trickle of Vatican aid could 'solve' the problem of famine in Greece.

An important engagement was on May 17, 1942, Whitsunday. Roncalli always liked to celebrate Pentecost in his cathedral, dedicated to the Holy Spirit; there was pomp and clouds of incense and afterwards forty guests were entertained to lunch at the Delegation. But on this Pentecost Sunday he also had the duty of celebrating the twenty-fifth anniversary of the episcopal ordination of Eugenio Pacelli, Pope Pius XII, then uneasily reigning. It was an anniversary that no papal diplomat could possibly miss. Roncalli reminded his congregation that Pacelli had been ordained bishop in 1917, at the very time when the three peasant children at Fatima had their first vision of Our Lady. But that was not really what he wanted to say. If the episcopacy must be seen against the background of the whole people of God, showered with the gifts of the Spirit, then the papacy itself must be seen against the background of the whole episcopal college. Only in this way would the papacy become intelligible to those Orthodox or Protestant Christians who rejected its claims as extravagant, unfounded or even blasphemous.

Roncalli went on: 'All the Apostles received an *equal mandate* from Jesus, but Jesus entrusted to Peter a pre-eminent place as pastor and father' (Righi, p. 255). Carefully avoiding any 'Vicar of Christ' terminology (a thirteenth-century innovation), he calls the pope repeatedly 'the Bishop of Rome' and speaks of his 'seat' (*sedes*) and 'chair' (*cathedra*) (see Tillard, p. 92 and following, for the importance of this usage). This was a return to an earlier tradition, *before* the division of East and West. It was another instance of going back in order to go forwards. Long before he became pope himself, he had already thought much about the office, and clarified his vision of an essentially *pastoral* papacy. He concluded his Pentecost sermon:

> Whatever concerns the Bishop of Rome makes the hearts of believers in Christ beat faster, wherever they may be, scattered throughout the world, without distinction of language or race or nationality: for he is the *sign of union* amid so many passions and conflicts of interest, and represents an *invitation* to order, gentleness and reconciliation (Righi, p. 255).

He was speaking, of course, of Pius XII, but it is legitimate to see the passage as prophetic. The papal ministry is for service, not power.

The same is true of the episcopal ministry. In July 1942, Roncalli was back in Greece to confirm those Italian soldiers who had somehow slipped through the parish net. There were moving incidents. When he visited the headquarters of the Italian Eighth Army, a corporal broke ranks, approached Roncalli, knelt and kissed his ring. 'What is it, my son?' asked Roncalli. The corporal replied: '*Monsignore*, may I embrace you in the name of all of us?' He did so, to applause from the men (Righi, *ibid.*). This very 'Italian'event on a remote hillside in a devastated country says as much about Roncalli as the most elaborate treatise on his idea of episcopacy. He managed to create an atmosphere in which such things could happen and seem natural.

In late 1942 Roncalli, in his role as God's consul, had the experience of failure. In December he made repeated appeals to Field Marshal Wilhelm von List, the German commander in Greece, to spare the lives of a group of Greek partisans. But the orders could not be changed. The executions went ahead as planned.

Though no one knew it, the turning-point of the war had been reached. Early in 1943 the Germans, surrounded at Stalingrad, suffered their first serious defeat – cynically sacrificing the Italian expeditionary force. By the end of February German and Italian resistance in North Africa was practically over. The number of prisoners held by either side was now about the same. Tracing prisoners of war became Roncalli's main work during this period. Along with the Red Cross, the Vatican acted as a clearing house for information about prisoners of war on all sides. The Russians, however, did not join in this scheme, for the chilling reason given by Ernst von Weizsäcker, German Ambassador to the Holy See: 'The Soviet regime is not interested in the fate of its own prisoners of war because it considers them traitors' (*Actes et documents*, 9, p. 238). So one could not bargain information about them in exchange for news of the German and Italian prisoners in Russia. But Roncalli was ordered by Tardini to do what he could on March 18, 1943. He thought that if anyone could pull it off, it would be Roncalli.

Rather than risk a rebuff by going to the top and speaking with the ambassador in Ankara, he preferred to start with the consul general in Istanbul, Nicholas Ivanov. They had a fascinating discussion on the Soviet Union's attitude to religion, but on the substantive issue of the prisoners of war held in the Soviet Union, Roncalli got nowhere, either with Ivanov or the ambassador. He surmised, correctly, that they were acting under orders from Moscow. A note of disappointment, almost of despair, creeps into his report to the Vatican: 'I will continue to keep you informed, though I feel a wrench in my heart at the gloomy prospect of persistent refusal by the Russians, unless the Lord, having listened to so many prayers, grants a miracle' (*Actes et documents*, 9, p. 238). He was now working closely with Raymond Courvoisier, director of the Red Cross in Ankara, who was able to confirm Moscow's unremitting hostility. So there was nothing he could do. He had spent three months banging his head against a diplomatic brick wall. It was another failure on the part of God's consul to modify the harshness of war.

He needed Raymond Courvoisier and the Red Cross (known as the Red Crescent in Turkey so as not to upset Islamic susceptibilities) in the other task which now engrossed him: aiding Jews. Von Papen, speaking on oath to the postulator of Pope John's beatification cause, claimed that he 'helped 24,000 Jews with clothes, money and documents' (see Zizola, in *Oggi*, April 13, 1963). It is difficult to translate charity into statistics. It would be better in this context to follow the Talmudic verse which says, 'He who saves a single life, saves the world entire' (Keneally, p. 371). Roncalli had been made aware of the problem at a relatively early stage of the war, through refugees from Poland. He was haunted by the fate of the *Struma*, which left the Romanian port of Constanza in December 1941 carrying a human cargo of 769 Jewish refugees. It was mysteriously blown up by a mine, and there was only one survivor. Roncalli wrote to Mother Marie Casilda, a Sister of Our Lady of Sion, 'Poor children of Israel. Daily I hear their groans around me. They are relatives and fellow-countrymen of Jesus.' (*Actes et documents*, 9, p. 310: Letter dated April 14, 1943).

Istanbul played a key-role. Turkey was still neutral, and the last escape-route out of Nazi-occupied Europe led through the Balkans and via Istanbul. It also led to Palestine, then under British mandate. But the British argument against accepting more than a limited number of refugees in Palestine was that 'there might be spies among them', and that Jewish expansion ought to depend upon Arab consent that was unlikely to be forthcoming (see Wasserstein, Bernard, *Britain and the Jews of Europe, 1939–1945*). Istanbul was at the crossroads of information if not of immigration. Roncalli was better informed than his superiors in the Vatican. The Jewish organisation had offices in Istanbul and was desperate for help. Chaim Barlas of the Jerusalem Jewish Agency met him on January 22, 1943. It was the first of many meetings that culminated a year later in a visit from the Grand Rabbi of Jerusalem, Isaac Herzog.

In January 1943 Chaim Barlas asked Roncalli to transmit three very modest but basic requests to the Vatican. Would the Vatican sound out neutrals like Portugal and Sweden to see if they would grant temporary asylum to Jews who managed to escape? This would involve no financial liability. American Jewry would look after them. Second, would the Vatican inform the German government that the Palestine Jewish Agency had 5000 immigration certificates available? Finally Barlas wanted Vatican Radio to declare loud and clear that 'rendering help to persecuted Jews is considered by the Church to be a good deed' (*Actes et documents*, 9, pp. 87–8). That such a statement was thought necessary was a measure of how deep the roots of Christian anti-Semitism were. Though Roncalli's task here was simply to transmit, not to explain or justify, there is no reason to believe that he regarded these requests as anything other than reasonable and fulfillable.

The Vatican thought otherwise. Its reply came in the form of a letter from the Secretary of State, Cardinal Maglione, to Fr Arthur Hughes, the *chargé d'affaires* in Cairo, who worked closely with Roncalli. They conferred in Istanbul on January 12, 1943. Maglione's answer was disappointing, pompous and disconcerting. The Holy See had helped Jewish emigration in the past by taking soundings and providing subsidies, but 'unfortunately this help has increasingly encountered no slight difficulties which, for the time being, are insurmountable'. Since no 'subsidies' had been requested, it was impossible to understand why 'taking soundings' should run into such insurmountable difficulties. Maglione said nothing about what Vatican Radio might do, and was distinctly cool about 'the transfer of Jews to Palestine, because one cannot prescind from the strict connection between this problem and that of the Holy Places, for whose liberty the Holy See is deeply concerned' (*Actes et documents*, 9, p. 137).

Maglione's words were worse than any of Pius XII's 'silences'. Yet they represented the firm and considered position of the Vatican. On May 4, 1943, Maglione wrote to Mgr William Godfrey, apostolic delegate in London, to say that 'the religious feelings of Catholics throughout the world would be offended and they would fear for their rights if ever Palestine came to belong exclusively to the Jews' (*Actes et documents*, 9, p. 272).

Roncalli was not a party to such callous indifference. He did what he could. He managed to give some practical help to the Jews of Slovakia. Capovilla sums it up:

'Through his intervention, and with the help of King Boris of Bulgaria, thousands of Jews from Slovakia who had first been sent to Hungary and then to Bulgaria and who were in danger of being sent to concentration camps, obtained transit visas for Palestine, signed by him' (*Cronologia*, p. 578). That he did succeed, and rapidly, in this affair is proved by the fact that on May 22, 1943, Chaim Barlas thanked Roncalli for his intervention (*Actes et documents*, 9, p. 307). Two months later, Roncalli tried to use the same channels again. He wrote to King Boris on June 30, 1943, in an ambiguous style designed to flatter his prejudices and yet lure him into compassionate action:

> I know that it is only too true – according to what I read coming out of Bulgaria – that some of the sons of Judah are not without reproach. But alongside the guilty, there are also many that are innocent; and there are many cases where some sign of clemency, over and above the great honour it would bring to a Christian sovereign, would be a pledge of blessings in time of trial (*Actes et documents*, 9, p. 371).

Boris replied that he would do his best, but pointed out that his own position was threatened. On August 28, 1943, King Boris died mysteriously during a return flight from Germany after seeing Hitler. It was assumed that he was killed as an unreliable ally. His six-year old son, Simeon, succeeded him. With Boris's death went Roncalli's last slim chance of influencing events in the Balkans.

In the midst of these dramatic events, on July 26, 1943, Roncalli acquired a new Secretary. The pint-sized Mgr Righi departed to be replaced by the giant (or so he seemed) Irishman, 30 year old Mgr Thomas Ryan. 'He comes from good farming stock like ourselves', Roncalli told his family, 'and he speaks Italian just like us' (*Familiari*, I, pp. 629–30). The Secretariat of State may have believed that Ryan, as an Irishman, ought to get on better with the Allies. However that may have been, he spoke English and began to teach Roncalli the rudiments of the language.

Throughout this time there were dramatic events in Italy. The war in North Africa was over by May 13, 1943. 'Everyone knew' that the invasion of Italy was next on the Allied agenda. On the night of July 9–10 the Allies landed in Sicily and met with little resistance, some Italian regiments joyfully surrendering while others simply melted away. It was the end of the road for Mussolini. He was arrested, having forgotten to shave. It was July 25, 1943. 'By midnight, the news had spread through Rome and the whole complex fabric of fascism, which people had taken to be so strong and durable, disintegrated in minutes' (Mack Smith, p. 347). There began the curious inter-regnum of the aged Marshal Badoglio, who introduced himself to the nation on this same July 25 with the inauspicious slogan, 'The war goes on' (*La Guerra continua*), but soon began to negotiate with the Americans through neutral Lisbon while swearing to the Germans that he was doing nothing of the kind. It could not last.

On September 8, feast of the Birthday of Our Lady, Italy signed the armistice which took it out of the war. Confusion reigned. As King Victor Emmanuel fled southwards with as much loot as he could carry, a Committee of National Liberation was founded. It was an alliance of Communists, Christian Democrats (including many of Montini's former students), Liberals and Socialists. Its aim was to oppose the Nazis who overnight had become the occupiers instead of the allies of Italy. There was a hiatus of power. The Germans swiftly poured in eight divisions to hold the line in the south. The Badoglio government played for time, and then submitted to the inevitable. Italy declared war on Germany on October 13, 1943.

This was a startling reversal. What did they think of it in Sotto il Monte? On October 16, 1943, when the reversal of alliances was completed, Roncalli has little to say to his family except that they should keep their heads down:

> The war, a great punishment of the Lord, has been brought down on the heads of Italians. This is not the moment to be apportioning blame. We have to suffer, be silent, and do our own duty in the painful circumstances of the present. But above all and always we should remain at the disposition of the duly constituted government, and behave like ants who continue to work away even when the temporal order is about to burst into flames. Each one of us should be intent on the duties of his own household or milieu, letting the soldier be a soldier, and leaving politics to those who want to be politicians; your business is to pray, suffer, obey, and be silent, silent, silent. This sacrifice will bring down on you a blessing in time (*Familiari*, I, pp. 6334).

One cannot say that Roncalli's imagination was fired by the prospect of the Italian resistance movement. He did not see it as a second *Risorgimento*, in which Italians could purge their guilt and contribute towards their own liberation. 'Letting the soldier be a soldier and the politician a politician' was a prudent, unheroic recipe for a quiet life. But Roncalli's refusal of partisanship can be read more positively as a commitment to peace. He genuinely believed that there would have to be reconciliation in the end. So on October 16, three days before Italy's declaration of war on Germany, he goes out of his way to remark that 'my relations with the Germans, in Greece and in Turkey, were always good and remain good now' (*Familiari*, I, p. 633).

The immediate consequence of Italy switching sides was that the country including Rome became in effect German-occupied. It was urgent therefore to get the remaining Italian Jews out of the country as soon as possible. Many were put on ships heading for Palestine. Roncalli *protested* to Cardinal Maglione, not at the fact that they were helped to escape, but at their destination. Since this was the only instance of Roncalli questioning the wisdom of a Vatican decision, his feelings must have been very strong. On September 4, 1943, he wrote to the Cardinal Secretary of State:

> I confess that this convoy of Jews to Palestine, aided specifically by the Holy See, looks like the reconstruction of the Hebrew Kingdom, and so arouses certain doubts in my mind . . . That their fellow Jews and political friends should want them to go there makes perfect sense. But it does not seem to me that the simple and elevated charity of the Holy See should lend itself to the suspicion that by this co-operation, at least an initial and indirect contribution is being made to the realisation of the messianic dream. Perhaps

this is no more than a personal scruple that only has to be admitted to be dissolved, so clear it is that the reconstruction of the Kingdom of Judaea and Israel is no more than a utopia (*Actes et documents*, 9, p. 469).

After this outburst, Roncalli never referred to the matter again. But his scruple was rather disconcerting, because in 1943 the problem was to find any country at all that would take those who had escaped the extermination camps.

Roncalli's practice was better than his theology. He continued to help Jews on their way to Palestine, and earned the following testimonial from Isaac Herzog, grand rabbi of Jerusalem:

> I want to express my deepest gratitude for the energetic steps that you have taken and will undertake to save our unfortunate people, innocent victims of unheard of horrors from a cruel power which totally ignores the principles of religion that are the basis of humanity. You follow in the tradition, so profoundly humanitarian, of the Holy See, and you follow the noble feelings of your own heart. The people of Israel will never forget the help brought to its unfortunate brothers and sisters by the Holy See and its highest representatives at this the saddest moment of our history (*Actes et documents*, 10, p. 161: letter dated February 28, 1944).

But the situation on the ground was getting more and more desperate, as the last escape routes were systematically sealed off. On March 23, 1944, the Germans entered Hungary and began deporting Jews to Auschwitz. The limits on Roncalli's ability to help Jews were now cruelly apparent. There was very little room left for manoeuvre. On April 25, 1944, Mgr Dell'Acqua, Roncalli's former Secretary now in the Secretariat of State, wrote a despairing memo which probably referred to the attempt to find a ship for 7000 Jews whom the Romanians wanted to let go, if transport to Palestine could be found:

> I do not think that Mgr Roncalli can do anything in this matter. His position vis-à-vis the Turkish government is very delicate. The government considers the Apostolic Delegate to be a 'distinguished guest', and no more. Further, I think that if the refugees boarded a Turkish ship, that would mean the Turkish government had given its permission. One could think about an approach towards the German Ambassador in Ankara, von Papen, in view of the good relations which exist between him and Mons. Roncalli; but it does not seem to me to be opportune (*Actes et documents*, 10, p. 243, fn. 4).

But the friendship with von Papen was now of no avail. Von Papen got his orders from Berlin on April 6, 1944. They were clear. The German view was that Palestine is an Arab country, and so Jewish emigration there was not to be encouraged, and such a concession would 'upset our counter-espionage and our sea strategy' (ADAP, doc. 320). Yet one or two ships still managed to get through. The most useful thing Roncalli could do was to forward to the Vatican diplomats in Hungary and Romania the 'Immigration Certificates' issued by the Palestine Jewish Agency. They conferred no real rights, but they sometimes worked and were better than nothing. It was these 'Immigration Certificates' that gave rise to the myth that Roncalli issued 'baptismal certificates' to Jews. This story was popularised by Ira Hirshman in his book *Caution to the Winds* (New York, 1962).

Von Papen – it was his redeeming feature – had certainly helped Roncalli in his work for Jews. As nuncio to France Roncalli wrote an unsolicited letter to the President of the International Tribunal on Nazi war crimes at Nuremberg. It probably saved von Papen's life. Roncalli wrote: 'I do not wish to interfere with any political judgement on Franz von Papen; I can only say one thing: he gave me the chance to save the lives of 24,000 Jews' (Zizola, *Oggi*, April 13, 1983). Von Papen reported this on oath to the Pope John beatification tribunal. He also described their last meeting in Turkey:

> When I had to leave – recalled by Berlin – he came to greet me at the first stop after the main station. For ten minutes we paced up and down on the platform like old friends. In the end, I knelt down and asked for his blessing. I did this because I thought it would be the last time I would see him, since the Allies would certainly hang me. Then the Apostolic Delegate put a letter in my hands. Now it is in the American Archives. I read it in the train. A brother could not have written with greater cordiality (*ibid.*).

One event stands out like a beacon in the otherwise grim year of 1944. Roncalli's Pentecost sermon gleams with the conviction that the war is drawing to a close, that it is time to think of post-war 'reconstruction', and that the Holy Spirit is still at work in the world, mysteriously but powerfully. Only the Spirit can break down the barriers set up by races and nations, he said, surveying his mixed congregation. Catholics in particular liked to mark themselves off from the 'others' – 'our Orthodox brothers, Protestants, Jews, Moslems, believers or non-believers in other religions'. The list was comprehensive enough for Istanbul. However:

> My dear brothers and children, I have to tell you that in the light of the Gospel and the Catholic principle, this logic of division does not hold. Jesus came to break down all these barriers; he died to proclaim universal brotherhood; the central point of his teaching is charity, that is the love which binds all men to him as the elder brother, and binds us all with him to the Father (Righi, p. 259).

'Catholic' should be a unifying, inclusive term – not a mark of exclusive distinction. So he prayed for 'an explosion of charity' to realise this vision. It was the most 'visionary' or 'utopian' homily delivered by Roncalli in Istanbul. Yet it came from a darkened and grieving world.

On December 6, 1944, out of the blue, Roncalli received a telegram from Tardini announcing that he had been appointed nuncio to France. Mgr Joseph Guillois, who had been with him the day Italy declared war on France, congratulated him on this happier occasion. But Roncalli's feelings were more mixed, as his diary recalls:

> Late at night Tardini's coded telegram arrived, like a thunderbolt. I was astonished and dismayed. I went to the chapel to ask Jesus whether I should elude the burden and the cross, or just accept it; but as calm returned I decided to accept according to the principle *non recuso laborem* [I do not refuse work] (*Lettere*, p. 287).

His amazement and apprehensions were justified. Forgotten in the East for nearly twenty years, he was moving from what, but for the war, would have been a minor diplomatic post to the most prestigious Nunciature in the Pope's gift.

Chapter 10

Difficult mission to France

They order, said I, this matter better in France.

(Laurence Sterne, *A Sentimental Journey*, 1768)

Frenchmen are just like Italians, minus their good humour.

(André Frossard, 1983)

The train of events which led Archbishop Roncalli unexpectedly to Paris began at 9 a.m. on June 30, 1944, when General Charles de Gaulle had an audience with Pope Pius XII. Familiar with *grandeur*, de Gaulle was impressed: 'Pius XII judges everything from a point of view that transcends human beings, their enterprises, and their quarrels'. Pius XII feared that liberated France would relapse once more into its age-old feuding, and grieved over the sufferings about to befall the German people, but, de Gaulle adds, 'it was the action of the Soviets in Poland today and in the whole of Eastern Europe tomorrow that filled the Holy Father with most anxiety' (*Mémoires de Guerre*, 2, pp. 233–4).

But France and the Holy See did not see eye to eye on everything. For the next five months a symbolic battle raged around the nuncio to France, the bearded, ascetic and uncommunicative Mgr Valerio Valeri. De Gaulle demanded his removal on the grounds that he had been close to the Vichy regime of Marshal Philippe Pétain (see *Actes et documents*, 11, p. 38 and following). Pius refused. He defended the strict juridical position: his nuncios were appointed to *states*, not to particular governments or heads of state. Valeri, he pointed out, was already nuncio to France at the time of the Popular Front in 1936. He had outlasted two very different regimes. He could cope with another.

Though technically correct, this approach ignored the passionate feelings that were running high as France was gradually liberated. For de Gaulle a new and better France was coming to birth in which anything that smacked of 'collaboration' with the Nazis had to be ruthlessly purged. Valeri had to go. Pius would not budge. An *impasse* was reached.

Paris was liberated in August, after a messy insurrection and very little destruction. The next day, August 26, 1944, de Gaulle led his forces down the Champs-Elysées and into the cathedral of Notre Dame for a *Magnificat* in thanksgiving for the liberation of Paris. God had indeed toppled the mighty from their thrones. But it was a far from untroubled celebration. Shots rattled round the nave. One looked in vain for Cardinal Emmanuel Célestin Suhard, archbishop of Paris. He was held prisoner in his own palace, suspected of 'collaboration'. Like most French bishops he had welcomed Pétain in the confusion and despair of defeat, and supported his 'national revolution' until its subjection to Germany and antisemitic element became clear. The resistance movement had divided French Catholics, and Roncalli would have to deal with these divisions within the French Church.

September, October and November passed by, and the Vatican had still not officially re-cognised the new regime in France or named a new nuncio. To Pius' mortification, the Rus-sians stole a march on him. They were the first to recognise de Gaulle, and so were able to have their ambassador to Vichy confirmed in office. This forced Pius' hand. The end of the year was approaching and tradition had it that the papal nuncio, as dean of the diplomatic corps, should present the New Year greetings to the head of state. In the absence of a nuncio, the task would fall to the most senior man present, who chanced to be the Russian ambas-sador. To avert such a *contretemps*, Pius decided to give way and appoint a nuncio quickly.

His first choice was Archbishop Joseph Fietta, since 1936 nuncio to Argentina, who was telegraphed on December 2, 1944. He replied the next day, declining Paris on health grounds. Tardini despatched the fateful telegram to Roncalli on December 5 (*Actes et docu-ments*, 11, p. 633, p. 637 and p. 639). It had all been done at great speed, and Roncalli was the second choice for France. He was the stopgap. Not much was known about him in Rome. One reporter asked a curial prelate what he knew about Roncalli and was told: 'He's an old fogey' (Bergerre, p. 45).

The 'old fogey' so suddenly catapulted to the Vatican's most prestigious diplomatic post was now sixty-three, and perfectly well aware that he did not come out of the top drawer of Vatican diplomats. He had not been at the Ecclesiastical Academy where they were trained. To his friend Giacomo Testa, he quoted the maxim of Teofilo Folengo (1496–1544): 'Where horses are lacking, the donkeys trot along' (Alberigo, p. 470).

On his way through Rome he asked Tardini, confidentially, 'who had picked out my name from the vast sea of the Vatican diplomatic service'. Tardini gruffly replied that it was all the Pope's doing, and hinted that he did not approve (Alberigo, p. 472). Tardini's biogra-pher confirms this suspicion: 'When Roncalli arrived in Rome in haste and anxious to be on the banks of the Seine, Tardini, his immediate superior, did not waste time on compli-ments, nor would he accept any thanks. He said that he had no part in the appointment which was the result of the direct intervention of the Pope' (Nicolini, p. 183). Later the story was put about that Roncalli, a second-rater, had been chosen to snub de Gaulle. Pius said: 'I want to make it clear that I was the one who acted in this nomination, thought of it and arranged it all. For that reason you may be sure that the will of God could not be more manifest or encouraging' (Alberigo, p. 472, letter to Giacomo Testa, February 7, 1945). But while encouraging him, it also bound him to Pius by an extra tie of loyalty.

If little was known about Roncalli in Rome, he was almost totally unknown in Paris. Cardinal Suhard awaited the arrival of the new nuncio with some apprehension. His own position was far from secure. He knew that his name was on a government list of bishops to be removed. The Pope had given way on the matter of the nuncio: would he hold out on the bishops? There was much ugly baying for blood. Suhard also knew that Rome was watch-ing attentively the experiment, begun the previous year, of sending priests to work in the factories and dockyards of France. Pius XII supported the idea in general, but on condition that Suhard personally supervised the experiment and was answerable for it. Where would the nuncio stand on the priest-workers?

Suhard was relieved to get a letter commending Roncalli from Mgr Giovanni Battista Montini, the substitute or second in command at the Secretariat of State. Montini was widely and correctly believed to be Francophile. He wrote on December 23, 1944:

In announcing officially this nomination to your eminence, I am quite sure that you will be delighted to learn of it for you know, at least by reputation, the excellent qualities of the new Representative of the Holy See in France. He has distinguished himself not only in his earlier missions in Turkey and Greece, but also in the pastoral ministry, as assistant to a great Bishop, Mgr Radini Tedeschi, whose well-deserved fame has spread beyond the boundaries of the diocese of Bergamo (*Mission*, p. 3).

It was far from evident that the mention of Radini Tedeschi would mean very much to Suhard. The fact that he had been in Paris in 1893 as a legate was not fresh in everyone's memory. However, Montini's blessing on the new man was important because it suggested that Roncalli was closer to him than to Mgr Alfredo Ottaviani who reigned at the Holy Office (see Guitton, p. 26). And that further meant that he would not be systematically hostile to the kind of pastoral experiments that Suhard wanted to encourage.

Once the decision had been taken, events moved swiftly. Roncalli left Ankara on December 27, 1944, was bundled in and out of aeroplanes and transported 'like Habakkuk' as he put it (*Dodicesimo anniversario*, p. 81) on a series of short-haul flights that took him to Beirut, Lydda, Cairo, Benghazi, Naples and finally Rome on the afternoon of December 28. Without pausing to rest he had meetings that same day with Tardini and Montini who now formed a dyarchy in the Vatican, Pius XII having dispensed with a Secretary of State. Next day he had an audience with Pius and a meeting with the ousted Valerio Valeri who, though now officially out of favour in France, had drafted Roncalli's New Year speech for him. Roncalli always felt that his predecessor Valeri had been unjustly treated and voted for him in the 1958 conclave as a mark of respect. Then he had lunch at the Palazzo Taverno with Guérin, de Gaulle's man in Rome.

He left Rome at 10 a.m. the next day in a plane specially provided by the French government, could see nothing of Paris except the Eiffel Tower shrouded by the mist, and landed at the Villa Coublet military airport at two in the afternoon. He installed himself in the Nunciature at 10 avenue Wilson, and that same evening presented his respects to Georges Bidault, foreign minister, at the Quai d'Orsay. December 31 was a Sunday. He rested most of the day, but had his first meeting with Suhard in the evening. Next morning he presented his credentials to de Gaulle, provisional president of the Republic, at the Elysée Palace and thus was in position, by eleven o'clock, to the right of the Russian ambassador, Bogomilov, who, in a sense, was the cause of all this frenzied agitation throughout the last four days.

He had a pleasant surprise. There was a familiar face in the crush. Menemencioglu, the Turkish ambassador, had been telling everyone what a splendid fellow Roncalli was and basked in the glory of having helped to prepare him for his present mission. Since the Turks had paid no attention to him while he was in Turkey, here was a paradox that needed some explanation. Menemencioglu later elegantly declared: 'I would like you to inform the Holy Father that the Turkish government would like to pay the Nuncio in Paris the honours it was unable to confer on the Apostolic Delegate in Istanbul' (Alberigo, p. 471 – letter to Giacomo Testa). Roncalli murmured an apology to Bogomilov, and arranged that his first exchange of diplomatic courtesies would be with the Russian embassy. He then launched into his Valeri-prepared greetings. Conventional and second-hand though the speech was, it constituted the first formal act of recognition of the new French government by the Holy See. *Monsieur le Président*, Roncalli began,

> . . . Thanks to your political sagacity, this beloved country has recovered her liberty and at the same time her faith in her own destiny. We do not doubt that the New Year will see further progress and fresh triumphs. So once again, France resumes her place among the nations. With her clearsightedness, her zest for work, her love of freedom and her spiritual ardour, of which I was an admiring witness during my long years in the Middle East, she will be able to indicate the way which, in union of hearts and justice, will at last lead our human society towards a time of tranquillity and lasting peace (*Mission*, p. 6).

Uttered on January 1, 1945, these words were not banal. They meant that in the eyes of the Vatican the Vichy regime had been an aberration in which France had lost her liberty and her place among the nations. The quarrel about legitimacy was over: full and ungrudging recognition was given to the provisional government. At the same time there was a hint ('union of hearts and justice') that the work of purging should be carried out with restraint and without splitting the nation irrevocably.

Roncalli's first appearance in France was a minor triumph. He had mollified de Gaulle and shown consideration for the Russian ambassador. But it was a *diplomatic* triumph, largely unnoticed outside a narrow circle of professionals. This was to be Roncalli's fate throughout his difficult mission to France. As nuncio he was responsible for relations with the French state which remained separate from the Church. Though all his instincts were pastoral and apostolic, he had to learn to keep them in check. He could not act as 'principal bishop' as he had in Istanbul. It was not his role, and the French Church would have resented it. If he travelled in France, it was by episcopal invitation.

But he naturally tried to introduce himself to the French Church on his arrival in Paris. On the feast of the Epiphany, January 6, 1945, he wrote what he called, 'a humble and simple letter' to all the bishops of France. He gently praised Valeri, treated the bishops with respect, and let them understand that he was not going to act as a ferocious new broom. It worked. 'About a hundred bishops' replied to his letter. While appreciating that he had to tread cautiously with the government, those whose heads were likely to roll felt that the new nuncio was on their side.

He introduced himself to a wider public on January 21, 1945, with an address at St Joseph des Carmes, the church of the Institut Catholique. It was the Octave of Prayer for Christian Unity, and he tried to link his last words in Constantinople with his first in Paris: 'These shining points, Constantinople and Paris, which stand for two worlds and two civilisations, are spanned, as it were, by a brilliant rainbow upon which glow the last words of Jesus' farewell prayer, "That they may all be one" ' (John 17.21: *Mission*, p. 8).

Roncalli's French was always a little haphazard, and his poetic efforts sometimes caused merriment. A candid account of Roncalli's early efforts to preach in French is given by Denise Aimé-Azam. He liked to frequent his 'parish church', St Pierre de Chaillot. He preached there during some solemn ceremony, but the microphone was defective and nothing but loud shrieks and wails emerged from it. Roncalli descended from the pulpit and spoke from the centre aisle: 'Dear children, you have heard nothing of what I was saying.

That doesn't matter. It wasn't very interesting. I don't speak French very well. My saintly old mother, who was a peasant, didn't make me learn it early enough' (Aimé-Azam, p. 27). There was general hilarity. The truth was, and Roncalli admitted it, that whatever knowledge of France he had was due to Bishop Radini Tedeschi who 'spoke French elegantly, knew her history perfectly and well understood her genius' (*Mission*, p. 179).

His letters home were reassuring and vague. On February 20, 1945, he wrote from Paris for the first time:

> I sleep better in Paris than in Istanbul. Not that I need much sleep here, and am content with little. There are important questions to be dealt with on which depends the good of the Catholic Church in France. I do my best, knowing that I am here at the explicit and personal desire of the Holy Father. And so I feel alert and serene in everything I do (*Familiari*, II, pp. 9–10).

He offers few clues about his work. He lives in 'a princely palace with everything one might need, two secretaries, three nuns, three staff, five servants and a splendid car' (*ibid.*, p. 14). The car was a black Cadillac. In this privileged world, he kept himself humble by remembering La Colombera and Sotto il Monte.

He was well aware of the delicacy of his mission. He felt he was 'walking on live coals' (to Cardinal Alfredo Ildefonso Schuster of Milan, *Mission*, p. 25). For his family he varied the metaphor and spoke of 'thorns amid the roses (*Familiari*, II, p. 14). His most difficult immediate problem was how to deal with the government's request for the removal of allegedly 'collaborationist' bishops. How he resolved it can be studied in the work of André Latreille, who was 'director of cults at the Interior Ministry' during the relevant period from July, 1944 to August 1945 (*De Gaulle, la Libération et l'Eglise Catholique*, Cerf, Paris, 1978). The story has often been mythologised. It can now be told plainly.

As early as July 26, 1944, the Interior Ministry had drawn up a list of prelates 'who had caused the greatest scandal during the occupation'. The list had twenty-five names, included three cardinals – Suhard (Paris), Gerlier (Lyons) and Liénart (Lille) – and among the bishops were Beaussart, auxiliary of Paris and Courbe, head of Catholic Action. So as to appear constructive, the Interior Ministry thoughtfully produced another list of six bishops worthy to become archbishops, and twenty-two priests who were good bishop material. It was a well-meaning but clumsy gesture: it looked as though the new regime was attacking the freedom of the Church to make its own appointments.

By the time Roncalli arrived in Paris the harshness and sweeping nature of these charges was realised. So the word 'collaborationist' was dropped, and the accusation was that the bishops had preached submission to Vichy – which was undeniable – and that 'a fair number of prelates had publicly taken positions favourable to German propaganda'. But the charges remained vague, were often based on unfounded local denunciations, and they ignored subsequent behaviour. One of the incriminated bishops, Gabriel Pinguet of Clermont was actually in Dachau. Cardinal Gerlier of Lyons was never allowed to forget that he had once said: 'Today France is Pétain, and Pétain is France'. But later he had written a vigorous pastoral letter against the treatment of the Jews and protested to the *Wehrmacht* against the massacre of hostages. Gerlier in short had redeemed himself. Others had done the same.

Thus by January, 1945 the original list of twenty-five had been whittled down to a dozen or so. 'Find me ten or twelve', Georges Bidault urged Latreille on January 28, and he was particularly insistent that the head of Beaussart should roll. But the Vichy regime had been 'legitimate' and so obeying it was no crime, even retrospectively. It would be against justice to treat the bishops as scapegoats. Then there was the Church-state problem: was the new French government trying to appoint bishops on political grounds?

What Roncalli thought about these questions can be gathered from Latreille's account of their first meeting on February 17, 1945:

> He welcomed me with amusement and cordiality. A very lively talker, stout, friendly, words tumble forth from him so that it is hard to get a word in edgeways. Yet he says he really does want to be well-informed. He tells me the likely way the Vatican is interpreting the events: the bishops have committed no fault, and though they might have made some mistakes, are they not the victims of a handful of wild men?
>
> I explained to him not so much the attitude of the government as that of the Catholics in the Resistance movement. The Bishops bore a heavy responsibility. The silence of the majority and the declarations of some had given the impression that they had failed to apply the principles of papal doctrine to the time we live in. So there was a crisis of conscience for the French, especially for those who had been in the Resistance.
>
> And today there is a natural reaction. It is not hostile to the Church, but it cannot be ignored without exposing the Church to 1) serious internal divisions, 2) a revival of anti-clericalism, and 3) the scornful indifference of part of the people.
>
> I managed to make myself understood. The Nuncio admitted that public peace had to be secured and that being hated by the people could be an argument against an offending prelate. But we have to say exactly what we want, and we have to produce evidence. And we mustn't expect the new nuncio to become the Torquemada of the French Bishops (Latreille, p. 60).

They met again a week later. on February 26, 1945. Now that he had discovered that La-treille had ten children, Roncalli was more forthcoming and showed him photographs of his own family. There was still no documentary evidence on the bishops. The nuncio was more concerned about another matter. De Gaulle wanted to appoint the philosopher Jacques Maritain as his ambassador to the Holy See. It was a shrewd move, for neither his Catholic nor his Gaullist credentials could be questioned.

It is a sign of the tenseness of Franco-Vatican relations that Mgr Tardini managed to make an issue out of Maritain's appointment. It seemed an innocent enough proposal. But in 1944 Maritain had travelled through Latin America on a lecture tour in which he spoke of human rights and Allied war aims. His lectures were gathered in a volume called *Derechos Humanos (Human Rights)*. To speak of 'human rights' in certain Latin American countries was to tread on egg-shells: the nuncios of Chile and Argentina reported that Maritain had left a wash of controversy in his wake. So even when Tardini eventually granted Maritain's accreditation, he could not resist adding in his blunt Roman Borgo way that 'the Holy See would have preferred someone not involved in public party political controversies' (*ibid.*, p. 679).

This was to inflate the Maritain affair out of all proportion. On January 23, 1945 Roncalli had a 'long conversation' with de Gaulle and, on orders from Tardini, presented the acceptance of Maritain as ambassador to the Holy See as yet another 'concession' to France – the first 'concession' being the removal of Valeri. De Gaulle somewhat wearily repeated that the removal of Valeri implied no hostility towards him as an individual, and that he had indeed been honoured on his departure with the *Légion d'Honneur (Actes et documents*, 11, p. 686). As for Maritain, de Gaulle confided, 'vigorous and incisive as he is with pen in hand, in practical matters he is humble, shy and clumsy'. Accordingly, he added confidentially, but Roncalli passed it on, Maritain's stay in Rome would be brief and he would soon be replaced by 'someone better qualified and formed in the best traditions of the French diplomatic service' (*ibid.*, p. 687). Despite de Gaulle's disparagement, Maritain, back in Paris by April 11, 1945, remained at his post in Rome for three years. There his friendship with Mgr Montini ripened.

Germany was over-run and finally capitulated unconditionally on May 8, 1945, V-E day. Roncalli did what he could to ensure that all prisoners returned home as soon as possible. He visited the Germans still held at Douai. He worked with three French priests, Mgr Rhodain and abbé Le Meur of *Secours Catholique* and the remarkable abbé Desgranges who founded, or rather refounded, the *Fraternité de la Merci* for the redemption of all captives, including political prisoners (Aimé-Azam, p. 77). This was controversial. But the three of them had already grasped that the basis of the new Europe they could see emerging would be Franco-German reconciliation. Roncalli agreed.

Meanwhile the question of the 'collaborationist' bishops had been largely taken out of his hands. Ironically, this was partly the result of his success in getting Maritain accepted as French ambassador to the Holy See. De Gaulle and Bidault negotiated through Maritain directly with the Holy See – in practice Tardini – to such good effect that by June 1945 the Vatican had accepted that 'some' bishops would have to go. A long conversation with the justice minister, Pierre-Henri Teitgen, also convinced Roncalli that the sacrifice of a few bishops would improve relations with the government. Further talks with M. de Saint-Hardouin, of the Quai d'Orsay, whom he had known in Istanbul, suggested that since the questions of subsidies for Catholic schools would soon have to be faced, it was prudent not to fight hopeless battles. So on July 27, 1945, seven prelates 'of France and the Empire' were discreetly removed. They went out with neither a whimper nor a bang. They were spared humiliation, given pension rights in their former dioceses, and the reasons for their departure were not made public.

There was an embarrassing instance in the summer of 1945. No cardinals had been created since the start of Pius XII's pontificate in 1939; war-time difficulties, it was said, made a consistory impossible. Now that the war was over, de Gaulle and Bidault wanted the Pope to reward with a cardinal's hat the three archbishops who had most clearly dissociated themselves from Vichy, Jules Saliège of Toulouse, Petit de Juleville of Rouen, and Clément Roques of Rennes. Their promotion would clearly be seen as a political event. Roncalli was opposed to it. He explained why to Jacques Dumaine, then head of protocol at the Quai d'Orsay:

> Their names were put forward by the government, and they are fine men . . . But there
> are difficulties. For instance Mgr Saliège, the Archbishop of Toulouse, has been
> paralysed for six years and cannot utter a word, while Mgr Petit de Juleville, the
> Archbishop of Rouen, suffers from agoraphobia. Only Mgr Roques is active and able to

speak, so the situation is not very promising. Your ministers tell me that a priest should be judged by his intelligence, his priestly virtues and his courage. I tell them that physical presence is also important, even within the church – and especially at a Consistory (*Quai d'Orsay 1945-1951*, quoted Johnson, p. 64).

On December 31, 1946, Roncalli was back again at the Elysée Palace to present the good wishes of the diplomatic corps to the President. These speeches punctuated his stay in France. This time he devised another burst of poetry which confirmed his reputation as a 'character': 'In a few days time the door of your home will be adorned with a fine bouquet of orange blossom', by which the Nuncio simply meant that de Gaulle's daughter, Elizabeth, was getting married (*Mission*, p. 48). He was not to know that, within a month, de Gaulle would huffily resign. On January 26, 1946, he withdrew to Colombey-les-deux-Eglises to await his recall. He felt himself as the leader of the nation, not of a party. A series of coalition governments succeeded in excluding both the Gaullists and the Communists who, with five million votes, were the largest single party. Pius XII was not unhappy about this.

An indication of Roncalli's detachment from immediate political concerns is that on September 27, 1946, after his audience with Pius XII, he nonchalantly went off to the Vatican Library to see what material there was on Gerolamo Ragazzoni, bishop of Bergamo from 1577 to 1592, who had also served as nuncio to the French court (*Letture*, p. 594). That Roncalli should be interested in such a figure, linking Bergamo and Paris and living in the historical period he had made his own, was natural enough. But it showed a capacity to distance himself from the problems of de Gaulle and the MRP.

Of course Roncalli did have contacts with Christian Democrat leaders from the MRP (*Mouvement Républicain Populaire*) and other political figures during his early years in France: that was his job. Aimé-Azam recalls that apart from Robert Schuman, the MRP leaders regarded Roncalli as a *polichinelle* or puppet, someone manipulated by the Roman Curia or, in Balzac's vocabulary, a man 'lacking in principle and character'. In his September 27 audience with the Pope, Pius had recalled the old saw about the nuncio being 'the hand, the eye and the heart' of the Pope in France. The maxim could be given a charitable interpretation, as Roncalli did in 1949 (*Mission*, p. 106). But to some it sounded ominous and sinister, as though the nuncio were merely a papal spy in France.

Those who bothered to meet him found a different Roncalli. He was friendly, unassuming, loquacious and inclined to go on and on about Bergamo. Anyone who mentioned a 'red hat' got slapped down. 'Hats', he said to someone who wondered when he would become a cardinal, 'hats – I prefer to look at ladies' hats' (Aimé-Azam, p. 42). He felt most at home in his corner room with its bay window from which, as in tourist pictures of Paris, the Eiffel Tower could be seen. His huge desk was in the darkest corner of the room. He sat his visitors in the light. From time to time, he would emerge from his lair and pace up and down, hands in his belly-band, talking volubly. Denise Aimé-Azam, to whom we owe this description, relates how one day Roncalli wanted to find a book by John Henry Newman which he knew was on the bottom shelf. Down went the portly nuncio on hands and knees, all dignity gone. He didn't find the Newman, but fished out instead an English translation of Dom Guéranger's *Année Liturgique* and explained, somewhat bizarrely, 'I use this to brush up my English' (Aimé-Azam, p. 61). He became a well-known figure in his *quartier*. He picked up the daily gossip in conversation with Yvette Morn who ran the newspaper kiosk on the corner of avenue Moreau and avenue Pierre I de Serbie. He knew her story. She was Jewish and her mother had been at Ravensbrück. Later Pius XII told him that it was undignified for a nuncio to walk the streets of Paris.

As in Istanbul, Roncalli did what he could to improve the plant that he had inherited. He describes 10 avenue Wilson in a letter to Montini:

> The Nunciature of Paris, bought from the Prince of Monaco in 1921 in the time of Mgr Cerretti, is certainly decorous; it is no better than the principal residences of diplomats in Paris, in fact far more modest, but that is as it should be. On the whole it is a worthy and noble residence. What surprised me, however, as soon as I saw it, was the unsatisfactory nature of the dining room used for great occasions. Mgr Valeri tried to improve it, giving it a cement roof with a terrace on top which allows one to take a few steps in the open air in the summer, to say one's office or to meditate in solitude. But the dull white walls remained, not much relieved by a large picture of St Peter's Square, certainly painted with good intentions . . . but more suitable as the drop-curtain of a small country theatre than a room to be used by diplomats (*Mission*, p. 115: letter dated March 10, 1950).

He remedied the bareness of the dining room by acquiring, thanks to a legacy, two tapestries woven in the Vatican workshops in the seventeenth century. One depicted 'Pope Urban VIII in the middle of the thirty years war praying with members of his court' and the other 'Pope Urban examining a plan of fortification for the Leonine City or some other town' (*ibid.*). Roncalli assured Montini that the tapestries were a good investment. Cheaply bought, they were now worth millions. Cardinal Nicola Canali, top financial man at the Vatican, had approved. Later, Roncalli had a Bergamesque painter, Pietro Servalli, execute Roman scenes on the panelling.

But in post-war France this preoccupation with interior decoration appeared irrelevant, risible and even blasphemous in a man of God. Priests working in the industrial suburbs despised those who lived in the *beaux quartiers* and wondered how they could possibly understand the workers' problems. As nuncio Roncalli was limited by what he saw from his bay window. Whatever tourists might think, Paris was not summed up in the Eiffel Tower. True, Roncalli knew that there were 'unbelievers' somewhere way out there. In an early letter to his family he explains that 'Paris is a city of five million inhabitants, and many of them lead a life that is completely cut off from the Church'.

Those Parisians 'completely cut off from the Church' were largely the workers. Despite the efforts of the Young Christian Workers (known as *Jocistes* in France), it was estimated that only one per cent of working-class males went to Mass. Cardinal Suhard had discovered the 'dechristianisation' of France when he became bishop of Bayeux and Lisieux in 1928. As early as 1929 he told a seminarian: 'There is a whole region around Caen, containing all our great factories where Christ is unknown; this is our true mission territory. Day and night this thought haunts me: I long for missionaries' (*Chronicle*, p. 17). As archbishop of Paris, he could do something about this longing. In 1941 he founded the *mission de France*, a new style seminary whose aim was to prepare hand-picked young priests to work effectively in a working-class milieu. He chose Lisieux for its base because St Theresa was the patron of the missions. In 1943 he started another seminary along the same lines for the capital, the *mission de Paris*.

But something unforeseen and unwelcome changed everything. In the course of 1942 800,000 young Frenchmen were marched off to forced labour in Germany (*Service de Travail Obligatoire* – STO). The Germans refused to allow chaplains to accompany them. Suhard took advice from, among others, the young Jesuit Jean-Marie Leblond who assured him that 'there is nothing in the Church's tradition to prevent priests working with their hands and earning their living'. So Suhard secretly assigned twenty-five priests to join the *déportés*. Most of them were soon discovered and two perished in concentration camps (*Chronicle*, p. 18). They were the first priest-workers.

Other priests had comparable experiences in prison camps or the resistance movement. They discovered that an immense cultural gap yawned between the Church and the workers. The Latin language and the ancient rites did not speak to the workers. The priests returning from the prison camps had learned fraternity and solidarity and were unwilling to be mere props of an unjust social order. They wanted to be identified with, not separated from, the workers. They wanted to use everyday language to relate the aspirations of the workers to Gospel values. There was a good deal of romantic *ouvrièrisme* in these attitudes.

But on a deeper level, it was their understanding of Christianity itself that had changed. In work and prison camps priests and Catholic Action militants discovered a faith that was 'heroic' – leading to prison or death; 'total' – for faith had to cope with all the problems of daily living; and 'anomic' – because they had to improvise liturgies in strange places. This description comes from Emile Poulat who adds that 'when the prisoners returned from Germany, whether they were priests or laymen, believers or unbelievers, they brought with them an incommunicable experience'. So on their return, there was a problem of reinsertion. They were unable to settle down into the old pre-war routine. Inevitably, they shocked the bourgeoisie.

As nuncio Roncalli had to listen to the complaints of middle-class Catholics who believed that the priest-workers were Communists in all but name. They supplied him with stories of a shock/horror nature. Fr X has said Mass in a boiler-suit. Instead of saying *Dominus vobiscum*, Fr Y greets the congregation with '*Salut, les copains*' ('Hi, pals'). Fr Z translated *Ite Missa est* as 'Go, the Mass of the world is beginning'. The habit of denunciation to Rome was a French tradition. Mgr Montini once quoted the remark: 'Out of any two French Catholics one is sure to be packing his bag to go to Rome to denounce the other' (Guitton, p. 26). In the nature of the case, it was the alarmed bourgeoisie who called on the nuncio. Those complained about wrote him off and declared that he was 'in the pocket of the conservatives'.

As was his duty, Roncalli forwarded to Rome the reports he thought were serious. But the Vatican did not reply with one voice. Mgr Alfredo Ottaviani at the Holy Office was hostile to the priest-workers and eagerly accepted the denunciations. In 1947 he addressed the following set of questions to Cardinal Suhard:

> Do the priest-workers fulfil the obligations of the priesthood (saying the divine office, keeping the promise of chastity)? Was evening Mass really necessary? Why this new form of apostolate? Did it not harm the traditional ministry of the priest? Were there not other ways of reaching the masses? (*Chronicle*, p. 51).

The French felt that such questions came from a bureaucrat who had never seen the inside of a factory. Moreover, they had a nastily inquisitorial flavour of 'guilty until proved innocent'. The other voice in the Vatican was that of Mgr Montini. He had been heard to say: 'When so much is at stake, risks must be taken, lest one should be guilty of failing to do all that is possible for the salvation of the world' (*Chronicle*, p. 51).

Where did Roncalli really stand on this question which dogged him throughout his eight years in France? The French would dearly have liked to have known. A letter written as pope permits one to reconstruct his position. His natural inclination was to agree with Ottaviani that the two states of life, priest and worker, were in the end incompatible. On the other hand, like Montini he understood the generosity, self-sacrifice and zeal which led priests to want to do factory work. So his letter to Cardinal Maurice Feltin, dated October 8, 1959, is mildness itself. It contained '*suggestions* made in the Lord' and hoped that 'the desire to preserve in all circumstances the fervour, piety and sacred character of the priesthood' should not exclude 'coming close to the workers and bringing them the breath of light and grace' (*Lettere*, p. 171). In 1964 Montini, by then Pope Paul VI, approved a modified form of 'priests at work'.

In the late 1940s, however, the priest-worker debate was only a particular form of a much wider question. How much pastoral initiative could be left to the local Church? Had the French Church, thanks to its intellectual endeavours, earned the right to offer leadership to the rest of the Church? And how well informed was Roncalli, as nuncio, about what was going on?

It was a time of great intellectual effervescence in the French Church. The Jesuits at Fourvière and the Dominicans at Le Saulchoir were renewing theological studies through a return to scripture and the fathers. Henri de Lubac's *Catholicism* dazzlingly showed the social dimension of salvation as a counter-blast to the distorted collectivisms of Nazism and Communism. Yves-Marie Congar defined the nature of 'reform' (*Vraie et fausse réforme dans l'Eglise*), and laid the foundations for the ecumenical theology the Council would find indispensable (the collection *Una Sancta*). Etienne Gilson on St Thomas Aquinas and Henri Marrou on St Augustine proved that at last Christian themes could be at home in secular universities. At the review *Esprit* Emmanuel Mounier and his friends were already denouncing French colonialism.

Moreover, there was talk of a 'Catholic renaissance' in literature, of which the poet Paul Claudel and the novelists Georges Bernanos, François Mauriac and the half-American Julien Green were the best-known representatives. Catholicism was intellectually respectable. It was all the more influential in that the Parisian vogue at the time was for the despairing nihilism dubbed 'existentialism' typified by Albert Camus' Sisyphus, absurdly pushing his boulder up the hill, and Jean-Paul Sartre's Roquentin experiencing nausea as he contemplated the roots of a tree trunk. But Sartre had been in prison-camp with Jean-Marie Leblond S.J. and in 1948 Camus addressed the Paris Dominicans and urged them to seek Christ 'in the blood-stained face of history in our own age'. It was an exciting time to be in Paris.

There is no evidence that Roncalli shared in any of this excitement. When Bernanos, who had claimed part of the prophetic inheritance of Péguy, heard that the nuncio had attended a lecture on his novels, he assumed that they were about to be put on the Index of Forbidden Books (*Combat pour la Liberté*, II, p. 646). He was exaggerating their importance in Roman eyes. But when André Gide was placed on the Index shortly after his death in 1951, Mauriac protested vociferously. It seemed that the only interest of the Vatican and its representative in literature was as material for burning.

As for Pierre Teilhard de Chardin S.J. who was by now living in New York but whose visits to Paris were always the signal for intellectual coteries to gather, Roncalli felt out of his depth. One day Roncalli remarked to Robert Rouquette S.J.: 'This Teilhard fellow . . ., why can't he be content with the catechism and the social doctrine of the Church, instead of bringing up all these problems?' When Rouquette replied that the Church could do without another Galileo affair, the Nuncio grew angry (Rouquette, I, p. 315).

Roncalli's lack of real involvement in French intellectual life was partly due to ignorance. Aimé-Azam guesses that his picture of France and the French was derived from St Francis de Sales which, by 1949, was rather misleading (Aimé-Azam, p. 54). The fact is that he simply did not have the background of French culture that was needed to keep pace with the rapidly spinning turntable of wit, allusion and knowingness that makes up 'conversation' in Paris. Besides, he was in his late sixties, and was overwhelmed by the mass of paper-work he had to do.

But Roncalli's historical curiosity never flagged, and France offered him a rich store of memories. It was natural that he should be drawn to Avignon where the Palace of the Popes still stands as a gaunt and impressive ruin. In Avignon he astonished the archivists with his knowledge of the papacy in exile and even more by his interest in John XXII, the last 'legitimate' Pope John. Without having 'if-I were-pope-fantasies', he was already persuaded that it would be a good idea to rescue the name John – both Baptist and Evangelist – for the papacy. After his election he told Cardinal Feltin that he had chosen the name 'in memory of France and in memory of John XXII who continued the history of the papacy in France' (Bergerre, p. 70). In short, Roncalli preferred his historical studies to contemporary works. One reason may simply have been that, as nuncio, he was uncomfortable with so much modern writing on the Church.

So, for example, Cardinal Suhard's great pastoral letter, *Essor ou déclin de l'Eglise* (Progress or Decline of the Church), published on February 11, 1947, seemed to sum up the swaggeringly confident mood of French-Catholicism. It was known that Suhard had consulted Dominican and Jesuit theologians in its drafting. It appeared as the manifesto of the 'new Church' that was emerging. (In Oxford, a decade later, a club of Catholic intellectuals gave itself the name 'the Suhard Society'.) But behind the scenes there was a furious row. Pius XII was very angry.

He was annoyed because the sweep and scope of Suhard's pastoral were so wide-ranging that, in Vatican eyes, he seemed to be setting up a rival *magisterium*. It was up to the Pope, not the Archbishop of Paris, to decide whether the Church was advancing or declining. In every pontificate there is a Church that Rome likes to suspect. Under Paul VI in the late 1960s this was the Church in the Netherlands. In the 1940s the French Church was the fall-guy. Moreover, Suhard's pastoral led to demands for the adaptation of Church life to contemporary needs. It led to a call for new forms of apostolate. But since Pius XII did not believe that the Church was in need of radical reform, such language was *anathema* to him.

Where did Roncalli stand? Or, more appropriately, on which fence did he uncomfortably sit? He was loyal to Pius XII, and rationalised his loyalty by denouncing – in private – French arrogance. He wrote during his December, 1947 retreat:

> I am delighted to praise these dear, good Catholics of France, but I feel it part of my mission not to conceal, through a desire not to be uncomplimentary and unpleasant, a certain disquiet concerning the real state of this 'eldest daughter of the Church' and some of her obvious failings. I am concerned about the practice of religion, the unresolved question of the schools, the lack of clergy, and the spread of secularism and communism. My plain duty in these matters may come down to a matter of how much and how far. But the Nuncio is unworthy to be considered the ear and the eye of Holy Church if he simply praises all he sees, including what is troublesome and wrong (*Journal* p. 291: December 1947).

This is Roncalli at his most severe and censorious. He is the 'eye and ear' of the Holy See. Something has happened to its 'heart and hand'. No *bonhomie*, no diplomatic bluff, no amount of engaging chatter about Bergamo could disguise the fact that he did not like much of what was happening in France. This gave rise to what Rouquette called 'the Roncalli mystery': how was it that a man who appeared so conventional and conservative in France could turn out to be a pope that astonished the world?

A key incident concerned the enthusiastic abbe Boulier, a man who chafed under the restriction of being a parish priest in Monaco. He had gone to a Communist-inspired 'peace meeting' in Poland in November, 1948. He made the inevitable meal-ticket speech. In his peroration he declared: 'If we, who are engaged upon the struggle for peace, are asked "Who are the Communists among us?", we will reply, "All of us" '(*Chronicle*, p. 52). This remark brought the roof down in Warsaw. It nearly brought the roof down over Suhard in Paris as well.

On February 5, 1949, Cardinal Suhard issued a solemn statement in which he denounced 'habitual and close collaboration with Communism' (*Chronicle*, p. 53). On March 5, 1949, *l'Osservatore Romano* pointed out that 'it is not just "habitual and close collaboration" that is to be avoided. The greatest vigilance is needed even in small actions where there is any risk of error' (*ibid.*). This was regarded in France as an offensive remark. It was believed to be (though it was not) a rebuke without precedent to a cardinal.

On March 17, 1949, Roncalli invited all the French cardinals and archbishops to the Nunciature to discuss the *affaire* Boulier. He warned them that Ottaviani at the Holy Office was very fierce on Communism and could quote on his side *Divini Redemptoris* (1937). It had declared that 'Communism is intrinsically evil, and no collaboration can be allowed with it'. The French prelates knew that, and were upset at the presumption that they were in some way 'pro-Communist'. Roncalli worked through Montini to such good effect that *l'Osservatore Romano* of March 31, 1949, carried an article which praised the *mission de Paris* and in particular Cardinal Suhard 'who has full responsibility for it'. Even though this changed the subject, it could be considered a kind of apology. 'Placing' articles in *l'Osservatore Romano* was the way inner-curial battles were waged.

At this point Montini was successful in trying to explain 'from the inside' what the priest-workers were trying to do, and showing that their primary motivation was not to engage in politics but to be with Christ in poverty: 'But only one thing is necessary for these men, who are seeking God in poverty, for themselves and for others: and that is to know that they are following in the footsteps of Christ, the Lord of the humble and the poor' (*Chronicle*, p. 53). In this instance Roncalli had 'made known' the views of the French episcopacy, yet the mystery of his own intentions remained. After a good lunch at *Etudes*, cigar in hand, he cheerfully described to the Jesuits the Vatican attitude towards France as 'a half-turn to the left followed by a half-turn to the right' (Rouquette, I, p. 315). They laughed dutifully, wondering where his real convictions lay.

If there was any disagreement between Roncalli and Suhard, both men took pains to cover it up. Nuncio and Cardinal came together on December 29, 1948 to protest against the imprisonment of Cardinal József Mindszenty in Budapest – proof, if any were still needed, of their resolute anti-Communism. They continued to work in tandem up to Suhard's death on May 30, 1949. The most bizarre joint function they attended was a lunch on April 3 with 'three thousand people over seventy years of age, gathered from the city parishes' to celebrate the fiftieth anniversary of Pius XII's priestly ordination. Roncalli hastened to write to the Pope about it:

> Once the Pope was hailed as *salus Italiae*, the salvation of Italy, and there were some who refused to acknowledge this title. This is no longer the case. It is now magnified, and arouses echoes in the whole world. It is no longer the Pope, the 'salvation of Italy' but the Pope 'the salvation of the whole world' . . . The Catholic poet of France, Paul Claudel, coins a happy phrase in a recent book: 'The parish priest of the world'. This very day I met the aged poet at the poor people's dinner in honour of your Holiness. I reminded him of his words. He was delighted (*Mission*, p. 101).

One can take this as a piece of court-flattery or as a prophetic statement about how he, Roncalli, would transform the papacy. It is a fact that Italy took second place in his pontificate. Suhard did not think in such terms. His final pastoral letter appeared in mid-April. Its title was 'The Priest in the City' (*Le Prêtre dans la Cité*) and it showed that Suhard was to be optimistic, tenacious and defiant to the last.

On May 29, 1949, Roncalli visited Suhard on his death-bed and saw that he was fading fast. He attended the funeral in Notre Dame on June 8, 1949, and no doubt remembered the day, nearly five years earlier, when Suhard had been kept out of his own cathedral. To Bishop Pierre Brot, Suhard's auxiliary and literary executor, Roncalli wrote: 'Almost five years of spiritual contacts had set the seal on a brotherly love that not even the slightest shadow has disturbed: we understood each other so well' (*Mission*, p. 104). No one is on oath in a letter of condolence, and much of this one is written in mortuary slab prose – 'this illustrious pastor', 'the incomparable prelate' and so on.

Suhard bequeathed Roncalli a surplice. What else had Roncalli inherited? Suhard summed up the mood of French Catholicism at the time. He was open to the modern world and ready to learn from it. He believed that there should be a dialogue with Communists and other men of good will and that it could not begin with fulminations. He wanted a renewal of the Church on all levels, a reanimated, active laity and a priesthood adapted to modern industrial life. These were all factors which influenced Roncalli in the long run, even if his first reaction and duty as nuncio was to be suspicious of their novelty. But there is a lot of Suhard in Pope John's pontificate. The 'French' or 'Suhardian' ideas lay fallow in his mind, waiting the time when they would be seen as pastorally necessary, evangelically based, and justified as a response to history.

Roncalli wore Suhard's surplice for the first time on June 29, 1949, when he ordained forty-nine priests in Notre Dame. Once again, he was acting as stopgap. These were all 'Suhard priests' who had mostly been through prison or labour camps. Had Suhard lived, he would have ordained them himself. For Roncalli, this ordination Mass in Notre Dame was the high point of his mission to France. He confided in his diary:

> In the story of my life this feast of St Peter will remain a solemn memory... Several times I was nearly overcome by emotion, but I managed to control myself. Everything was enchanting. At the end I gave the solemn papal benediction; and in the sacristy I said a few words to the newly ordained, whose attitude edified me so much. I commented upon my archiepiscopal motto, *Obedientia et Pax* [Obedience and Peace] and on Yves de Chartres' remark to Pope Urban II: *Cum Petro pugnare et cum Petro regnare* ['To fight with Peter and to reign with Peter']... For the first time I wore Cardinal Suhard's surplice (*Cronologia*, p. 614).

However, there was more to this episode than meets the eye. Roncalli was edified by the new priests, because it was feared that some would disapprove of him replacing their beloved Suhard. There could have been a demonstration. His private appeal in the sacristy for them to 'fight with Peter' was made in the knowledge that the Holy Office was about to publish a decree which would cause consternation in France and seem like the repudiation of Suhard's entire mission. Pius XII signed the decree the next day, June 30, 1949, and it came out, with unconscious humour, on July 14, anniversary of the storming of the Bastille. It excommunicated all those who 'knowingly and with full consent defend the materialistic doctrines of Communism'. No surprise there. But the decree also included in the ban those who collaborated 'in any way' in actions that would lead to a Communist regime (see *Documentation Catholique*, No. 1048, July 31, 1949). Though apologists argued, probably correctly, that the decree was 'really' aimed at Eastern Europe or Italy, the French saw it as an attack on themselves and a rejection of Suhard's attempt to come to terms with the modern world. The Vatican had cynically waited for his death to reveal itself as a politically conservative and essentially anti-Communist institution.

As Nuncio, Roncalli was guilty by association. Pope John's own 'social' encyclicals, *Mater et Magistra* (1961) and *Pacem in Terris* (1963) would be an attempt to redefine the Church's position on socialism and communism. But as Nuncio he had no comment.

Roncalli found a successor for Cardinal Suhard. The translation of Maurice Feltin, archbishop of Bordeaux, to Paris was announced on August 15, 1949. Two years younger than Roncalli, Feltin came from the northern slopes of the Alps, from the village of Delle. Roncalli called on his relatives there on August 20 on his way home to Italy. They had something in common: they were both mountain village boys from opposite sides of the Alps, and shared a certain rugged spiritual commonsense and a weight problem. They were made cardinals together in 1953, continued to correspond, and Feltin, as president of Pax Christi, the Catholic peace movement, initiated him into the critical thinking about nuclear weaponry that is found in *Pacem in Terris*.

Roncalli had an audience with Pius XII at Castelgandolfo on September 6, 1949. One might have expected some discussion of the impact of the Holy Office decree, but that does not figure in Roncalli's diary:

> In the name of France I thanked his Holiness for the welcome he had given to Frenchmen of both high and humble condition who were so edified when they visited him. With what spiritual joy I heard him say: 'But that is my great concern and consolation – to welcome these men of the world, even if they think differently. Isn't this the way the pastor should live? Am I not here for sinners, for those who have gone astray? They are all equally sons' (*Letture*, p. 437).

This paternalistic version of the pastoral office – let the sinners come to me – was in complete contrast with the 'identification with the oppressed' that was the basis of pastoral work in France. It was also in complete contrast with Pope John's habit of declaring to visitors to the Vatican, 'I am your brother Joseph'. But ten years earlier he treated the Pope as an oracle.

The appointment of Feltin began the second phase of Roncalli's difficult mission to France. They got on well, though Feltin did not claim a close friendship with the Nuncio. Feltin's portrait of Roncalli is more nuanced and perceptive than any we have so far seen:

> He was always friendly, understanding and sought to smooth out difficult problems; but when action was needed, he did not lack decisiveness and firmness of character. His goodness was not soggy but strong. Furthermore, he could be subtle, perspicacious and far-sighted; and I could give plenty of examples of the way he slipped through the grasp of those who sought to exploit him (Bergerre, p. 69).

In 1950, Feltin's first year of office, 'those who sought to exploit' the nuncio were the conservatives or *intégristes* as they were locally known. It was a Holy Year, and crowds of pilgrims flocked to Rome. Pius XII with his upturned gaze, his rimless spectacles, his arms extended to embrace the world, seemed to embody the very essence of the papacy as it was then conceived. The *intégristes* were delighted. But others in France were disenchanted. Almost every decision taken by Pius XII in 1950 appeared to be aimed at the French Church.

The first blow was the apostolic exhortation, *Menti Nostrae*, on the sanctification of priestly life. Pius XII expressed his sadness at 'the alarming spread of revolutionary ideas' among some priests who, he averred, 'were not highly distinguished for learning or austerity of life' (Holmes, p. 185). This was evidently an allusion to the priest-workers, but its mandarin aloofness caused much irreverent merriment by the time it reached them. Anyone who thought that life in a modern factory was insufficiently 'austere' was not really in touch. As for 'lack of learning', the priest-workers accepted the charge, adding however that book learning cut them off from the workers and that there were other equally valuable forms of knowledge. But *Menti Nostrae*, though it exhibited deep disapproval of the priest-workers, did not put an end to them: they remained the responsibility of the French bishops. The axe did not finally fall until 1953 by which time Roncalli was gone.

But *Menti Nostrae* was mere skirmishing compared with the mighty encyclical letter *Humani Generis* which appeared on August 12, 1950 at a time when most of the theologians it incriminated were away on lecture tours or on holiday. Its impact may fairly be described with the over-worked phrase, 'theological bombshell'. The fall-out was considerable. It had much the same effect as *Pascendi* forty-three years before. And as in 1907 the fact that the encyclical mentioned no names meant that suspicion knew no bounds. Who will be next? was the question theologians asked themselves as they returned from their summer holidays.

In order to determine 'against whom' *Humani Generis* was written, the only course was to consider which theologians lost their jobs. Using this criterion, the attack seemed to be directed principally against the Jesuits at Fourvière, Lyons, where the three Henris — de Lubac, Rondet and Bouillard — were all forbidden to teach. And there were many others who were 'guilty by association'. Henri de Lubac (made a Cardinal in February, 1983) suffered the cruellest fate: not only was he banned from teaching, but he was forbidden to live in a house where there were students, lest they be corrupted by his pernicious influence. In practice it meant that he was deprived of the life-blood of a proper library. De Lubac was held to be the leader of *la théologie nouvelle* ('the new theology'). Its principal novelty was a meticulous return to the patristic sources.

Another group banned from teaching was made up of those, again mostly Jesuits, who were believed to have fallen under the spell of Teilhard de Chardin. Though he had been forbidden to publish, since 1924, except on strictly scientific matters, his lecture notes and speculations were circulating in *samizdat* form and copies hastily duplicated in evil-smelling purple ink were eagerly passed from hand to hand. Like the theologians mentioned in the previous paragraph, Teilhard was deemed to have fallen into 'immanentism'; but he was also guilty of what *Humani Generis* called 'the conjecture of polygenism', that is the idea that the original human beings were a group rather than a single couple (D–S, 3897).

The Dominicans at Le Saulchoir were just as severely hit as the Jesuits of Fourvière. Marie-Dominique Chenu had a book put on the Index in 1942: he had maintained that the study of St Thomas Aquinas could only gain if attention were paid to his historical background. This inoffensive truism was anathema to those scholastic theologians who claimed to 'prescind' from the dimension of time and utter only 'eternal verities'. Chenu was also rumoured to be theological adviser to priest-workers in the Paris region. He was the first to develop systematically the idea of 'signs of the times' (see his article in *La Nouvelle Revue Théologique*, 'Les Signes du temps', January, 1965, pp. 29–39) that Pope John was to make his own. But Chenu had been talking about the need to detect the Holy Spirit at work in secular history from the 1940s. A passage in *Humani Generis* seemed to be aimed directly at Chenu. The encyclical is ironic about those who imagine that 'theology should constantly exchange old concepts for new ones, in accordance with various philosophies that it uses as instruments in the course of time' (D–S, 3822). Chenu had said nothing of the kind, but the cap fitted approximately.

Yves-Marie Congar, another Dominican who believed in historical theology, was also sacked but he was told by his Master-General that it was for 'false irenicism'. He was in Greece when *Humani Generis* appeared. He was sent into miserable exile in Cambridge, and not allowed to talk with Anglicans or even his brother Dominicans at Blackfriars, Oxford. The director of the Editions du Cerf, the Dominican publishing house, was fired. The Dominican review, *Jeunesse d'Eglise*, was suppressed. Fr Jérôme Hamer OP was brought down from Belgium to become regent of studies at Le Saulchoir. (In 1984 he became prefect of the Congregation of Religious.)

It is difficult to know what Roncalli thought about this wave of repression. On the scholasticism versus history issue his sympathies were with Congar and Chenu, as his opening address to the Council makes clear: 'The substance of the ancient deposit of faith is one thing, the way in which it is presented is another' (Abbott, p. 715). But that future event was of no consolation to either theologian in 1950. Roncalli was not directly involved in the purge. On August 21, ten days after *Humani Generis*, he left for Italy and did not return until mid-October. Back in Paris, he was unaccountably silent: his memoirs have a six-months gap between July and December, 1950. In any case, Roncalli was let off the hook in another way. Since most of the ousted theologians were religious, the task of disciplining them could be safely left to their major superiors.

Pius XII chose this moment to define the bodily Assumption into heaven of the Virgin Mary in a solemn ceremony in St Peter's Square. It was November 1, 1950 the feast of All Saints. The definition was controversial for a number of reasons. It raised the question of the relationship between the *magisterium* and history, and of tradition and scripture. It was the first (and possibly last) exercise of infallibility as defined by Vatican I, and even then did not meet that Council's implicit conditions: whereas Vatican I thought that a definition could be used to put an end to controversy and crisis in the church, in this instance bishops from all over the world were said to be 'almost unanimous' (D–S, 3902), which made the definition redundant. It set up an additional barrier to ecumenism. It was an act of defiance of the world. This last aspect was well brought out by Cardinal Giuseppe Siri, who was close enough to Pius XII to be considered his dauphin. Siri explained that the definition of the Assumption 'was an act of courage because Pius XII challenged directly with an infallible definition a world that did not like teachers' (Siri, on 25th anniversary of Pius XII's death, October 8, 1983, p. 4). This made it sound like an act of ecclesiastical *machismo*. French theologians, still reeling from *Humani Generis*, saw it as a loyalty test.

Roncalli had no problem in accepting the definition of the Assumption. He had celebrated the feast since childhood. Ten years after the definition he wrote: 'As Nuncio to France, I was one of those fortunate enough to be present at the ceremony in St Peter's Square. I felt no anxiety about this doctrine, having always believed it; during my years in Eastern Europe my eyes were constantly drawn to images of the "falling asleep of the Blessed Virgin Mary" in churches of both Greek and Slav rite' (*Journal*, p. 337). He concludes his meditation: 'The mystery of the Assumption brings home the thought of death, of our death, and it diffuses within us a mood of peaceful abandonment; it familiarises us with and reconciles us to the idea that the Lord will be present at our death agony, to gather up into his hands our immortal soul' (*Rosario*, p. 56).

In the last phase of his mission to France, 1951–2, finding French Catholics quarrelsome and argumentative, Roncalli devoted more time to those 'outside' the Church. While most French Catholics saw the nuncio's role in terms of the inner life of the Church, the traditionally anti-clerical socialists and radicals understood just how much he had contributed to the good relations between France and the Holy See in this post-war period. The protracted debates on Catholic schools (*écoles libres*) were never allowed to degenerate into bitterness. The 1951 legislation solved the problem amicably (though not finally): Catholic schools received some public funds on the grounds that, with the birth-rate booming, the state system could not otherwise cope (see Jackson, J. Hampden in *A Short History of France,*

Cambridge, 1959, p. 208). For Roncalli 'the maintenance of peaceful relations between Church and State' was 'the primary *object* of the Apostolic Nunciature' (*Mission*, p. 180). Judged by this criterion, his mission to France was a success. The virulent Church-state quarrel was over. Moreover, he had learned that he could get on with other than Christian Democratic politicians, a lesson he took home to Italy where it was a novelty.

Roncalli reached out even further in 1951 when he was appointed official Vatican observer to UNESCO. He addressed its General Conference on July 11, 1951. Though a young organisation ('hardly disengaged from the swaddling bands of its infancy' as he put it), it was acquiring a definite shape. At a special Mass in Saint Pierre de Chaillot, he gave the Catholics working in UNESCO the ground rules for dialogue with unbelievers and other believers. The starting-point was the altar inscription in the Athens market-place: 'To the unknown God' (*Ignoto Deo*). There is an anonymous search for God, and wherever there is justice and truth, grace is also present. As usual, Roncalli had a maxim to express the attitudes which followed: 'To look at each other without mistrust; to come close to each other without fear; to help each other without surrender' (*Mission*, p. 146, where the words are attributed to Cardinal Lecot at the Elysee Palace in 1893). It was in France and at UNESCO that he learned that it was possible to set aside ideological barriers and address 'all men of good will'.

One particular race had a special claim on his attention: the Jews. His wartime memories were still vivid. In Algiers cathedral in March, 1950 he spoke of the Jews as 'the children of promise' (Romans 9.8). He became very interested in Simone Weil, and in 1952 wrote to her father, Dr Bernard Weil, with the idea of visiting the austere room – it had a sleeping bag but no bed – where she used to work (*ibid.*, p. 114). He read *La Connaissance Surnaturelle* and greatly admired it. He was moved by her final note which begins, 'I believe in God, the Trinity, the Incarnation, Redemption, the Eucharist and the Gospel . . .', but then explains why she must remain 'on the threshold' of the Church. Roncalli treasured this text, and gave a copy of it to Cardinal Augustin Bea before it was published in 1962 (in *Pensées sans ordre concernant l'amour de Dieu*).

Roncalli's departure from Paris was as unexpected as his appointment there. On November 14, 1952, he received a letter from Montini marked 'private and confidential'. It was rather puzzling. In the name of Pius XII Montini asked whether he would be prepared to succeed the patriarch of Venice, Carlo Agostini, in the event of his death which was imminent. No one at all was to be told or consulted. So Roncalli had to confide in his diary: 'I prayed, thought about it, and answered *Obedientia et Pax* [Obedience and Peace]' (*Pasqua, 1978*, p. 28). He wrote to Montini the same day: 'I pray that the Lord may cure the Patriarch of Venice, and grant him many years to come. But if I should succeed him, may I be granted the grace to merit the ancient saying about St Mark as the disciple and interpreter of Peter' (*Saggio*, p. 57). For the pastorally-minded Roncalli Venice would be a marvellous fulfilment of a dream of youth. The four hundred years of shared history between Venice and Bergamo meant that it would be like going home.

On November 29, 1952, he received a telegram from Montini to say that the Holy Father had decided to 'elevate him to the sacred purple' at the Consistory on the coming January 12, 1953. Feltin of Paris and Grente of Le Mans were also to be created cardinals (*Saggio*, pp. 57–8). He reacted calmly to this not unexpected news. It meant that it was now certain he would be leaving Paris, if not for Venice, then for the Roman Curia – a prospect that did not fill him with unmitigated joy. Moreover, he was worried by the news received the same day that Ancilla, 'who has always been the most precious treasure of my household' (*ibid.*, p. 59) was dying of cancer. He made a quick journey to Sotto il Monte to see her, and by December 12 he was at Ancilla's bedside. Though the doctors had given her only a few weeks to live, she lingered on for another year until November 11, 1953.

Back in Paris the news that he was to become a cardinal – but not that he might be going to Venice – had become public knowledge. The round of official congratulations began with the prime minister, Antoine Pinay, and President Auriol, who said it would make a sad leave-taking. When Feltin, shortly to be his brother cardinal, called to congratulate him, he found Roncalli uncharacteristically 'sad, gloomy and troubled'. Feltin asked, 'All the same, aren't you really glad about it?' Roncalli replied: 'No, I'm not at all happy because I wanted to stay in France. I love France and I love Paris, and I hoped to stay a little longer. I can't really see myself in Rome, going along day after day to meeting after meeting and concerned with administration. That's not what I'm good at. I'm really a pastor' (Bergerre, p. 69). What he couldn't tell even Feltin was that he would escape this curial fate only if Agostini died. On December 29 he opened his copy of *Le Figaro* at breakfast and learned that Agostini had died. Roncalli had narrowly escaped the Roman Curia.

Becoming a cardinal and patriarch of Venice did not go to his head. He reminded himself that 'there have been rogues and saints among the cardinals' (*Pasqua*, 1978, p. 29) and that being a cardinal was an honour, not another sacrament. He found it helpful to return to Book III, chapter 23, of *The Imitation of Christ*, Its subject is 'the four things that bring great inward peace' and its maxims, so evangelical in spirit, are essential for understanding Roncalli:

Choose always to have less rather than more.
Seek always the lowest place and to be beneath everyone.
Seek always and pray that the will of God may be wholly fulfilled in you.
Behold, such a man enters within the borders of peace and rest
(*Pasqua, 1978*, p. 45: letter to Mgr Gustavo Testa, then nuncio in Berne, dated December 2, 1952).

He had arrived in France in December, 1944 in haste and without fuss. He left nine years later with all the leisurely and elaborate rituals of official leave-taking. On January 15, 1953, President Vincent Auriol, making use of a special privilege that used to belong to 'Catholic' heads of state, handed over his red biretta. He then decorated Roncalli with the *Légion d'Honneur*. Meanwhile in Rome his appointment as patriarch of Venice was finally announced. Some French people were offended that 'their' cardinal, instead of going to an influential post in the Curia where he could defend the French Church, was heading for Venice. The 'image' of Venice was of a toy-town city with canals and lagoons, of unearthly beauty but fairy-tale irrelevance to the modern world. On February 5, 1953, Roncalli organised a farewell dinner at the Nunciature to which he invited the eight men who had been prime minister during his time in France: Georges Bidault, Félix Gouin, René Pleven, Edgar Faure, André Marie, Robert Schuman and Antoine Pinay (Dreyfus, pp. 118–19). They all came. Capovilla quotes a remark that went the rounds: 'Only under the nuncio's roof could French politicians of such diverse views meet each other in a friendly way' (*Mission*, p. 185).

General Georges Vanier, Canadian ambassador, paid tribute to Roncalli in the name of the diplomatic corps on February 19, 1953. The nuncio, he suggested, summed up in his person the three characteristic products of Bergamo: wine, silk and steel. The wine evoked 'the warmth of your heart and the vivacity of your spirit'. Silk hinted at 'a sense of nuances' and made clear that he would never be 'one of those severe, Goya-type cardinals'. Finally the steel stood for 'the firmness of character which makes no compromise where truth is concerned' (*Mission*, p. 186). One is left wondering why the French Church did not see Roncalli the way the diplomats did. Four days later, on February 23, 1953, he left France. His diary records:

> Left France for good. Got up at 4.30 a.m. after a good night's sleep. Sorrow at departure, but sweetness in union with God and a sense of 'goodness turned into love'. Holy Mass at 6 a.m. A silent, emotional farewell at 7.30, with a few tears here and there . . . I bless the Lord and thank him for all his kindness to me (*Pasqua, 1978*, p. 31).

At last he was going home to be the pastor he had always wanted to be. He was seventy-one. It seemed likely to be his last posting.

Chapter 11

The seasons of Venice

Venice is a seasonal city, dependent more than most on weather and
temperature. She lives for the summer when her great tourist industry leaps
into action, and in winter she is a curiously simple, homely place, instinct
with melancholy, her piazzas deserted, her canals choppy and dismal.

(James Morris, *Venice*, p. 203)

The consistory of January 12, 1953, was the second and, as it turned out, the last of the pontificate of Pope Pius XII. Though no one realised it at the time, it completed the college which would elect his successor, and therefore the next pope was somewhere among their number. Roncalli was pleased to see Valerio Valeri made a cardinal. Of the new intake of twenty-four, ten were Italian. At the time this was widely hailed as a move towards 'internationalization': *only* ten were Italian. Eight of them were destined to spend the rest of their lives in the Roman Curia. The exceptions were Roncalli and Giuseppe Siri, archbishop of Genoa since 1946. Still only forty-seven, a man of some brilliance, he was considered not only to have the ear of Pius XII but to be his secretly designated successor. He would be one of Roncalli's rivals in the conclave of 1958. Political significance was read into the nomination of 'Iron Curtain' cardinals, Alojzije Stepinac of Zagreb, Yugoslavia, and Stefan Wyszyński of Gniezno-Warsaw, Poland. Both were under house arrest and unable to come.

Even before he left Paris, Roncalli was beginning to build up his team for Venice. The vicar capitular, Mgr Erminio Macacek, came to see him on February 3, 1953, bringing with him Don Loris Capovilla. Born in 1915 in a small mainland town near Padua, Capovilla lost his father and knew poverty before entering the Patriarchal seminary in Venice. Small, vivacious and energetic, he had 'done a bit of everything' since his ordination. He had been army chaplain, broadcaster, journalist, editor of the diocesan paper, *La Voce di San Marco*. He was not Roman-trained. Roncalli took to him at once and made him his secretary. They were not parted until his death. In Capovilla Roncalli got much more than a secretary: he got a spiritual son, a literary executor, a *confidant* and a Boswell.

He took possession of his diocese in the grand style on March 15, 1953. He did not disdain pageantry or find it tiresome. Young Albino Luciani, whom he ordained bishop of Vittorio Veneto on December 27, 1958, eventually became patriarch of Venice on February 8, 1970. He abolished the procession of gondolas which had been the traditional accompaniment to the entry of the patriarch. Roncalli toyed with the same idea, but gave it up because Venetians enjoyed processions. Gondoliers and others had specially repainted their boats. Roncalli introduced himself that same afternoon to the people of Venice with characteristic directness:

I come from a modest family and was brought up in contented and blessed poverty –
a poverty that has few needs, builds up the highest virtues and prepares one for the great
adventure of life.

Providence took me away from my native village and led me along the roads of
East and West. It allowed me to come close to people of different religions and
ideologies, and to study grave and menacing social problems. Yet Providence also
allowed me to maintain a balanced and calm judgement. I have always been more
concerned with what unites than with what separates and causes differences.

I dare not apply to myself what Petrarch, a lover of Venice, used to say of himself. Nor
have I tales to tell like Marco Polo when he returned here among his own. But strong
bonds bind me to Venice. I come from Bergamo, land of St Mark, the land where
Bartolomeo Colleoni was born. Behind the hills of my youth lies Somasca and the cave
of St Jerome Emilian.

No doubt the great position entrusted to me exceeds all my capacities. But above all I
commend to your kindness someone who simply wants to be your brother, kind
approachable and understanding . . .

Such is the man, such is the new citizen whom Venice has been good enough to
welcome today with such festive demonstrations (Alberigo, pp. 207–10).

Roncalli at seventy-one had a charisma that was not merely explained as the sum of his
goodness, sincerity and charm. It was difficult to dislike him. Meeting the painter, Giuseppe
Cherubini, a tiny figure with, however, a long flowing beard, Roncalli shook hands instead
of having his ring kissed and explained: 'We're both patriarchs – you by your magnificent
beard, I *ad literam*, literally' (Cugini, p. 58).

Venice took to the patriarch, and the patriarch took to Venice. He loved its traditions and
the links with Byzantium. Familiar with the history of the city, Roncalli knew that it had
fallen from its former glory. Now it had crumbling palaces and pockets of poverty. It came
to life during its festivals – of cinema, painting and music – when it provided a picturesque
décor for international jet-setters. In the summer it was crowded out with tourists, artists
and *nouveaux riches*. But the population of the historic city was declining as the young
looked for work in Marghera and Mestre, by now large industrial towns. Roncalli made
his first visit to Porto Marghera within a few days of arriving. He said Mass for the victims
of industrial accidents. He recorded in his diary: 'Made a deep impression on me, and was
well received' (*Pasqua, 1978*, p. 34 – March 27, 1953). As patriarch he saw another Venice that
the tourist posters preferred to ignore.

The contrast between magnificence and poverty continued to strike him. He told his
sister Ancilla on May 15, 1953: 'The Venetians are indeed very good, courteous and affectionate towards their Patriarch. But there is also great poverty here' (*Familiari*, II, p. 333).
Later, as Christmas approached, and the piazzas were full of returning 'migrant workers',
he wrote to Maria: 'In Paris I had plenty of work, but it was as nothing compared with here
. . . I'm like the mother of a poor family who is entrusted with so many children' (*ibid.*, p.
344).

As usual in a new place, he liked to get his domestic arrangements sorted out as soon as
possible. His palace, a plain, unheated building on the left of St Mark's Basilica, gave onto

the piazzetta dei Leoncini, so called because of the two rusty lions who guarded it. It was, he told Mgr Bruno Heim who was now in Vienna, 'a modest but welcoming place' and guests could always be squeezed in somehow (*Pasqua, 1978*, p. 79). But the guest rooms were cold and draughty in winter (*Familiari*, II, p. 344). Heim, an heraldic expert, advised on how to set out the traditional coat of arms: a lion of St Mark on a white ground. He preferred not to live in the rooms on the first floor, once occupied by his predecessor, Blessed Pius X, and installed himself on the second floor. He knocked down a wall and had a new partition built so that his bedroom opened onto his study. He looked out onto the inner courtyard. Except for caterwauling cats, it was very tranquil, especially at night when he worked on the history of Venice and his introduction to the fifth and final volume of the *Atti* of St Charles Borromeo's visitations. 'With this work', he told David Cugini, 'which has gone on for forty years, I hope to leave to our grand nephews and nieces a little sign of affection for Bergamo and win respect for my humble name' (Cugini, p. 56). He meant that he would be remembered for these five volumes. He could not have been more wrong.

Over the door to his study he placed the words *'Pastor et Pater'* (Shepherd and Father) as a reminder of how his authority should be exercised (Alberigo, p. 249). He persuaded Pius XII to give him a new auxiliary, and was pleased when Cardinal Adeodato Piazza, prefect of the Consistorial Congregation, to give him an auxiliary bishop, and was pleased with Mgr Augusto Gianfranceschi who had been a parish priest in the inner city (*Pasqua, 1978*, p. 8: letter to Piazza, June 19, 1953). In Guido Gusso, a twenty-two-year-old from the nearby fishing village of Caorle, he found the perfect batman who eventually accompanied him to Rome. Guido was frustrated because he was not often called upon to drive the Fiat 1400 that the Catholic Bank of Venice had presented to the patriarch. It wasn't much help in the city of canals. And Roncalli preferred to take the *vaporetto*, the water bus. House-keeping, finally, was looked after by discreet nuns from the Istituto delle Poverelle in Bergamo. He would dearly have liked to have had his two sisters, Ancilla and Maria, as his housekeepers now that he was at last back in Italy. But his first two years in Venice were overshadowed by a secret distress: both Ancilla and Maria were dying of stomach cancer.

On October 19, 1953, he was appointed to three Roman Congregations – Oriental Churches, Propaganda Fide, and Religious. Though not expected to attend their sessions, he went to Rome and met twelve cardinals in three days (*Cronologia*, p. 654). He neither envied nor wanted to change places with them. To Heim he had quoted the remark of Sarto, the future Pius X: 'I prefer to be a cardinal in the forest rather than a cardinal in a cage' (*Pasqua, 1978*, p. 79).

He also met three French Cardinals, Feltin, Gerlier and Liénart, who were in Rome to save what they could of the priest-worker experiment. Roncalli's successor, Mgr Paolo Marella, had arrived in Paris on June 1, 1953, with orders to suppress the priest-workers altogether (*Chronicle*, pp. 63 and 77). Now that Roncalli was himself on the receiving end of curial instructions, he felt more sympathetic towards the French. He continued to keep his friendships in good repair. But his thoughts kept coming back to Ancilla.

His last letter to her is dated November 8, 1953, just three days after the French Cardinals and their fateful audience with Pius XII and three days before her death. He wrote very simply:

Dear Ancilla, Today I took possession of my titular church of Santa Prisca, so I'm now a fully-fledged cardinal. But my heart carries around a wound – the thought of my dear sister. I say to the Lord, *Fiat voluntas tua* [Thy will be done], but saying it costs me a lot; how much more costing it must be for you who are so tried and suffering . . . I'll come and see you on Friday or Saturday next, the 13th or the 14th, but I can't say exactly when. Affectionately (*Familiari*, II, pp. 340–1).

But he was not able to keep his promise. On November 11, 1953, while he was inaugurating the new junior seminary at Fietta, Ancilla died. He did see her on November 13 as she lay in an unadorned coffin in his house at Camaitino. The patriarch bowed low among the peasant women gabbling their *Ave Marias* and prayed for his sister whose life had been one long round of domestic drudgery, relieved only by the recurrent feasts of the Church. Before the coffin was finally sealed, he kissed her on the brow.

He watched them as they trooped off to the village graveyard and laid Ancilla to rest alongside their parents, Giovanni and Marianna. A vicious wind lashed the cypress trees and scattered the autumn leaves. Roncalli would not be buried here. He had already revised his will and arranged to be buried, along with earlier patriarchs, in the crypt of St Mark's. The other members of his family would all come to rest here in the Sotto Il Monte cemetery, Teresa in 1954, Maria in 1955. But there was no time to linger. They had to hurry back by train to Venice. It was already dark, and Roncalli was in a pensive mood. Capovilla heard him murmur, *'Guai a noi se fosse tutta un illusione'.* With the rhythm of the train and the rain beating down on the windows, the mysterious remark, 'Woe to us if it's all an illusion', was imprinted on Capovilla's memory because 'it revealed a disconcerting aspect of genuine humanity in my patriarch, who was normally always so strong and self-controlled' (*IME*, p. 53). Whether Roncalli was thinking of the pomp of Venice, Ancilla's wasted years or eternal life itself, his doubt brought him closer to common humanity.

But he did not repine, and was soon writing two letters in three days to Mgr Giovanni Battista Montini about a plan he had at heart. The Giorgio Cini Foundation had recently completed the restoration of the Benedictine Abbey on the island of San Giorgio, just across from the Doge's palace and the basilica.. Roncalli was glad to be chairman of the Cini Foundation Committee. It was just the sort of project to appeal to him. It involved the rescue of a neglected island and the conservation of a historic church of great beauty designed by Andrea Palladio. But San Giorgio was far from being merely a museum. It was now a cultural centre with concerts and symposia and an open-air theatre. It had a technical school run by the Salesians and the Marina orphanage. Roncalli assured Montini that this was the kind of work – cultural and conservationist but at the same time charitable and socially useful – that was once the pride of Italy.

Count Vittorio Cini also contributed to the restoration work in the patriarchate (*Saggio*, p. 65). So Roncalli was already well in with the Venetian 'establishment'. Like all Italian bishops, alongside his ecclesial role, he had an indirect 'civic' function. He met prefects and mayors, city and provincial councils, chiefs of the police and the fire-brigade. He organised a Mass for journalists on the feast of St Francis de Sales. He welcomed the rugby team 'Faema' at the Patriarchate and blessed the oil-tanker 'Marilen' at Porto Marghera. He was becoming a well-known personage, a civic asset, a Venetian landmark.

He was also involved, willy-nilly, with politicians and especially the dominant Christian Democrats. In the pontificate of Pius XII bishops were expected to support the Christian Democrats as a way of keeping the Communists permanently out of power. Elections were fought on a simple 'Rome or Moscow' ticket. Roncalli had been in Rome shortly before the April 18, 1948 election and attended a youth rally in St Peter's Square, when he was disconcerted to hear Carlo Carretto, a young Catholic Action leader, denounce the politicians present – including the Christian Democratic party secretary, Alcide De Gasperi – as too timid and feeble in their opposition to Communism. Roncalli saw this as an abuse of Catholic Action:

> That's not what the Lord wants. The Christian steers clear of clash and rhetoric . . .
> There's a whole web of relationships with the entire political class that demands delicate
> respect and a sense of duty. As witnesses to Christ, our first task is not struggle but
> sowing the good grain, not victory but suffering (*Letture*, p. 351).

But by the time Roncalli arrived in Venice the 'system' was firmly in place and well-oiled. Dr Luigi Gedda, head of Catholic Action and the Pope's man, had set up 'civic committees' which in effect turned every parish into a recruiting and propaganda office for the Christian Democrats. Cardinal Alfredo Ottaviani, of the Holy Office, used to boast that 'you can say what you like about the divinity of Christ but if, in the remotest village of Sicily, you vote Communist, your excommunication will arrive the next day' (Magister, p. 52). In private, Montini and his friends were critical of this systematic anti-Communism. It appeared to dispense the Christian Democrats from any concern for the social justice they had been founded to defend; and it pushed them to the right. But if Montini thought in terms of political strategy, Roncalli saw the problem in more spiritual and human fashion: his mission was one of reconciliation.

In the run up to the elections of June, 1953, Roncalli was not altogether a free agent. He had to harmonise what he said with the bishops of his province not to mention the known desires of Pius XII. His eve-of-poll declaration, when it eventually came out on May 30, 1953, was full of studied understatements: 'Above all, we must vote, we must all vote, and we must not throw our votes away. As Christians and Catholics you cannot and should not campaign on behalf of those who profess anti-Christian doctrines which the Catholic Church has condemned and condemns' (Alberigo, p. 211). Roncalli recalled that the experience of fifty years of 'trying to create social justice without Christ's Gospel' had not been very successful. Only die-hard Communists would dispute that truism. It was interesting that a bishop should recognise that the Soviet Union had been 'trying to create social justice' at all. Roncalli's pre-electoral statement was milder than that of most Italian bishops. He uttered no dire threats of excommunication and tried to write as a pastor offering elucidation rather than as a prince-bishop imposing his will.

No doubt it was vain to imagine that elections could ever lead to reconciliation. But on February 11, 1954, there was an anniversary that spoke explicitly of 'reconciliation': it was twenty-five years since the signature of the Lateran Pacts. Roncalli preached on this theme at 6.30 p.m. in St Mark's, and became overnight a national figure. His life-long meditation on the meaning of history led him to tackle two questions: what should Italian Catholics, in

1953, think of Mussolini? how does the Church come to change its policy on important issues?

The problem posed by the Lateran Pacts, especially the manner in which they were secretly negotiated and suddenly announced, was that the Church had quite simply changed its mind. It gave up its age-old claim to the restoration of the Papal States. Roncalli patiently explains 'It was natural that the Popes should feel it their duty to defend themselves, whatever the cost, until the day when there was a new sign from heaven, which would find a response in the papal conscience and so put an end to its otherwise justified claims and assertions' (Bertoli, p. 19).

But then there was a difficulty. It looked as though Mussolini himself was being presented as the 'new sign from heaven'. That was hard to swallow. How could such a man be a 'sign from heaven' still less 'the man of Providence' as Pius XI was alleged to have called him? Roncalli's commentary on Pius' remark was listened to in intense silence. He knew how to keep an audience in suspense:

> Consider: the man whom Providence put in the path of Pius XI, the one who, because of his freedom from outmoded ideas, was able to grasp more clearly and with greater intuitive penetration the problem of Reconciliation, this same man later became a cause of great sorrow to the Italian people. It would be inhuman and unChristian to deprive him of this title of honour despite the immense calamity he brought upon us. He was firm and decisive in drawing up and ratifying the Lateran Pacts. So we have to entrust this humbled soul to the mystery of divine mercy which sometimes chooses vessels of clay for the realisation of its plans, and then breaks them, as though they had been made for this purpose alone (Bertoli, pp. 18–20).

The Lateran Pacts, in other words, were Mussolini's 'redeeming feature', and remained so despite the subsequent tragedy. Predictably the left-wing press read Roncalli's sermon as an attempt to rehabilitate the hated dictator. But it was something much more profound – more like a healing of the Italian national psyche. This was recognised by Montini, whose anti-Fascist credentials were never in doubt, who wrote to congratulate and thank Roncalli for his address (*Saggio*, p. 66: letter of March 5, 1954). Montini was increasingly his Roman *confidant*. They wrote to each other frequently.

Pius XII was now said to be gravely ill. Not too ill, however, to announce the date for the canonisation of Blessed Pius X, May 29, and to make an important statement on atomic weapons, on Easter Sunday, April 18, 1954. He called them:

> new, destructive weapons of unheard-of violence, arms likely to bring down a dangerous catastrophe upon the whole planet, to encompass the total extermination of all animal and vegetable life and all the works of man over even vaster areas, arms that are capable, with their long-lasting radio-active isotopes of polluting for a long time the atmosphere, the earth, the very oceans, even though they may be very far from the zones directly affected and contaminated by nuclear explosions (*Saggio*, p. 69).

Roncalli took the Pope's statement seriously. He refers to 'these memorable and awesome words directed against the abuse of nuclear energy, which is the terror of all who live in this tragic and mysterious age'. It was Roncalli's first documented mention of the nuclear threat (*Saggio*, p. 69). It suggests that one can recognise the originality of *Pacem in Terris*, while conceding that it owes more to Pius XII than is commonly supposed.

Despite this burst of activity at Eastertime, Pius XII's illness continued to cause anxiety. It was believed – and he certainly believed – that he was mortally ill. He had already vouchsafed his 'dying words' to Cardinal Giuseppe Siri: *'Depositum custodi, depositum custodi'* ('I have kept the deposit of faith') (Siri, address to Synod, October 9, 1983). A conclave was therefore imminent. Roncalli would have to think about it. It occurred to others, if not also to himself, that he was a candidate and *papabile*.

Roncalli's first mention of the Pope's precarious state of health came in a letter to his whole family dated March 3, 1954:

> I owe the Holy Father infinite gratitude for having named me Patriarch of Venice and still more cardinal. Join with me in praying that the Lord may long preserve this great Pope.
>
> To tell you the truth, his death would cause me great bother: I would have to interrupt for at least a month the splendid work that I have begun with my pastoral visitation. I don't want to change my programme for this year (*Familiari*, II, p. 353).

A conclave would be a nuisance because it would interfere with his pastoral plan: visitation of all the parishes to be followed by a Synod of the whole diocese.

The illness of Pius XII hung sombrely over 1954, overshadowing the more predictable events: it had been declared a 'Marian year' – it was the 100th anniversary of the definition of the Immaculate Conception of the Virgin Mary; and Blessed Pius X was due to be canonised on May 29. Roncalli threw himself into the preparations for the canonisation with a will. The chapel and study of Sarto on the first floor, once occupied by Pius X, were restored to their 1903 state as a memorial. There were still surviving relatives about, and on May 16, 1954, Roncalli gave first communion to some of Pius X's grand-nephews and nieces. He told Montini that he preached almost every day, and rarely failed to mention Pius X, even if briefly (*Saggio*, p. 70). He presided over the inter-diocesan committee which pleaded that the mortal remains of the new saint should 'go on pilgrimage' to the cities where he had once been known. Roncalli's energy pulled this off, despite difficulties about security (*Saggio*, p. 75). All in all the canonisation brought, in the time-honoured phrase, 'great honour to the Church of Venice'. And throughout this period Roncalli was increasingly dependent on Montini as his friend in high places.

They were in correspondence again over the Marian year. Roncalli had no problem about celebrating the 100th anniversary of the definition of the Immaculate Conception; in 1904 he had helped Radini Tedeschi celebrate the half century of the definition. However, he did not hold the view, common among mariologists in the pontificate of Pius XII, that one could not have too much of a good thing. There was a search for new and more extravagant titles. Invited to sign a petition in favour of a new feast, the Queenship of Mary, Roncalli politely declined:

> I beg you to forgive my silence so far which is evidence of my uncertainty and the fear that such a feast could prejudice the great action already undertaken towards the

refashioning of the unity of the Catholic Church in the world . . . For many, however
well disposed towards the Catholic Church, it would be merely irritating and – as the
modern phrase is – counterproductive . . . Meanwhile, I am happy to say *Salve Regina,
Mater misericordiae* [Hail holy Queen, Mother of mercy] (Alberigo, p. 489: letter dated
April 22, 1954).

He prudently added, however, that should 'the supreme authority of the Church' decide
to set up such a feast, he would be among the first to celebrate it. This was just as well since
six months later the encyclical *Ad Coeli Reginam* established the feast of the Queenship of
Mary and directed that it be kept on May 31. Yet Roncalli's objection of principle remained
on the record. It was most unusual for an Italian prelate to oppose a new Marian feast on
ecumenical grounds. The ground was being prepared for the sound and sober mariology of
the Council.

Despite this misjudgement, he was invited by a letter of Montini to go to Beirut, in the
Lebanon, as papal legate at the National Marian Congress (*Saggio*, p. 73: letter dated June 15,
1954). It was a great honour and a mark of trust. It meant that Pius XII, or just possibly
Montini, had not forgotten Roncalli's diplomatic past and still cast him in a modest international role. But before he could set off for Beirut, he was preoccupied with a more personal celebration.

The 50th anniversary of his ordination fell on August 10, 1954. He regarded the anniversary
as a private event to be marked by extra prayer and recollection at Sotto il Monte. He thought
he was entitled to some peace and had been feted enough in Venice and Bergamo when he
became a cardinal. He did not want another fuss. In a letter to the Venetians he gave explicit
orders that 'there should be no celebration, either liturgical or cultural, of this anniversary'
(*Pastore*, p. 339: letter dated August 10, 1953). Naturally enough, his orders were ignored.

This caused him to write one of the most incensed letters of his life. It was addressed to his
nephew, Don Battista, son of his brother Giovanni, who was still on the long road to ordination. Battista had already tried his uncle's patience by shilly-shallying about his vocation
and fussing about the difficulties of study (see Alberigo, p. 482: letter to G. Battaglia dated
September 28, 1951). But now there was a sudden change of gear. Don Battista, who had
certainly meant well, received this thunder-bolt from his uncle patriarch on August 2,
1954. It is revealing as an instance of what could make Roncalli really angry:

> Dear Don Battista, When I got back to Venice I heard from Mgr Loris (Capovilla) that
> celebrations are being planned for my priestly jubilee. I *have told you many times that there
> are to be no festivities for me.* I intend to take part in the ordinary celebration of the
> Assumption at Sotto il Monte: I will celebrate a low Mass at 7 or 8, and will be present at
> the High Mass and take part in the procession later in the afternoon. But I do not want, I
> do not desire that *anything more should be done than in previous years.* So: no guests from
> Bergamo or anywhere else, whether clergy or laity, friends or relations: I want to be
> *alone, alone,* with my family and the dear parishioners of Sotto il Monte. Have you got
> that? Tell also dear Don Mario (Minola) that he has no need to put himself out for me.
> Why do you have to offend me and make me suffer? Are you trying to stop me from
> coming at all?
> (*Familiari*, II, pp. 357–8; italics in the original).

After this avuncular wigging, Don Battista did what he was told. He was soon to find that the advantages of having his Uncle Angelo in high places were not unmixed. Roncalli hated nepotism.

So Roncalli celebrated the fiftieth anniversary of his ordination, in the place where he was born and grew up, in comparative peace. Here is how he described the day:

A wonderfully bright sky after merciful night showers. The sound of the *Angelus* from San Giovanni roused me at once with a *Laus tibi, Domine* [Praise to you, O Lord]. There followed an hour of prayer in the chapel with the breviary lessons about St Laurence in my hand, on my lips, in my heart: pages that are a poem. What is my poor life of fifty years of priesthood? A faint reflection of this poem: 'My merit – God's mercy' (*Journal*, p. 307).

Another note, written the same day, shows how he used his Breviary as a prayer of intercession for all those he had known: 'Every day as I say my Breviary, I think of all the places I have been in: at Prime I pray for France; at Terce, Turkey; at Sext, Greece; at Nones for my beloved Bulgaria. And I pray for all, the living and the dead' (Righi, p. 103).

One reason he wanted to lie low for his golden jubilee celebration was that gossip and speculation continued to present him as eminently *papabile*. His tranquillity at Sotto il Monte was disturbed by a French would-be prophet, Gaston Bardet, who not only predicted that he would become pope but guessed the name he would choose when elected. Bardet sent him the proofs of a book he had written, with a request for a preface. Roncalli replied from Sotto il Monte on August 26, 1954, in pained tones:

My Dear Friend, I received your letter with the page proofs for which you invite me to write a preface. For some weeks I have been very worried about this, so much so that I haven't been able to think about anything else (Capovilla, Archives).

After that introduction, Roncalli told Bardet bluntly that he was 'the victim of a serious and dangerous hallucination', and that the words of Jesus applied: 'Get thou behind me, Satan'. He thinks it better that they should not meet.

But Bardet was not so easily brushed aside. He went to Venice, had a meeting with Roncalli, repeated his predictions and said, in Capovilla's hearing, that his pontificate would be marked by 'doctrinal interventions and disciplinary reforms'. Roncalli was still worried by Bardet as late as January 1955. He referred to him in a letter to his sister, Maria:

Some mad Frenchman, who has revelations and second sight, has even given the name I will take when they make me pope. Mad, mad, the whole lot of them (*Familiari*, II, p. 368).

But a disturbing flicker of doubt remained.

It was all perfectly ridiculous. He had the Lebanon to think about. He flew out on October 19, 1954 and returned in leisurely fashion by ship a week later. As papal legate, he made two important speeches. He listened *on his knees* to the radio message of Pius XII (*Cronologia*, p. 672). He enjoyed the trip, as did Guido Gusso, now firmly established as his driver and factotum. He met the Melkite patriarch, Maximos IV Saigh, who would play an important part in the Council, and the 92-year-old Maronite patriarch, Anthony Arida, who made him feel distinctly youthful (*Familiari*, II, p. 360). With a conclave looming, such innocent remarks about his own physical fitness at seventy-three could seem loaded. The speculation would not go away.

On November 10, 1954, he wrote to Maria and asked, pointedly, 'Who wants to be more than a cardinal?' He went on: 'I have become insensible to everything, and if the Lord called me swiftly, I would not want to complain. His will is enough for me. Obedience and peace' (*Familiari*, II, p. 361). His contemporaries had been dying one after another. He had preached five funeral orations in as many months. But the one person who seemed loath to die was Pius XII. Even cardinals had no inside information about the Pope's state of health. Roncalli was only repeating press gossip when he told Maria that 'the Pope seemed to be about to die, and then he got better, only for a relapse to follow'. There were rumours of some expensive new treatment. Roncalli was not sure whether it was worth it:

> I have little confidence that the Holy Father will be cured; despite so many doctors and medicines and so much expense. His life is a miracle, but miracles, as you know, only last a very short time. And perhaps we are all wrong, my dear Maria, to complain. At our age, to be alive at all is a bonus (*Familiari*, II, p. 366: letter dated January 8, 1955).

So he still expects a conclave shortly. And he is fit: 'Among the old people here the Patriarch is the most vigorous and is regarded with wonder by the good people of Venice' (*ibid.*, p. 368). That was for his sister Maria only.

But there was to be no conclave for another four years. The expensive new treatment from the Swiss specialist appeared to work. Pius XII recovered or, more accurately, survived. How far he was in charge was much debated. Then, in November 1954, something happened that left Roncalli utterly disconcerted: his friend Giovanni Battista Montini was abruptly removed from his post at the Secretariat of State and sent off into exile as archbishop of Milan. This was, of course 'a great honour'. But in plainer language it meant that Montini had been sacked from the Roman Curia after nearly thirty years. Nor could he be said to be 'acquiring the pastoral experience needed to equip him for the papacy', since there was never any intention of making him a cardinal, though this was the tradition of the ancient and prestigious see of Milan. It was a daunting task for someone whose health was frail, and who had never managed a diocese, still less one so huge and complicated. Why had Pius XII done this? What did it all mean?

Roncalli first heard the news at noon on November 3, 1954, while at Pompeii for a meeting of Italian cardinals and archbishops. It was announced later that same day, aptly enough, for it was the feast of St Charles Borromeo. Capovilla describes Roncalli's reaction: 'He was dumbfounded. It was all very well to say that the Curia's loss was Milan's gain, but what puzzled Roncalli was that Pius XII in extreme old age should deprive himself of his most efficient aide. As he remarked to Capovilla: 'Where else will we find someone capable of writing a letter or drafting a document in the way he can?' (*Saggio*, p. 15). Was there some shady intrigue in the background?

On his way back to Venice Roncalli stopped in Rome and called on Montini. He was struck, Capovilla noted, 'by the air of departure, tinged with sadness, that already hung about the apartment'(*ibid.*). Capovilla had noted that the relationship between these 'two courteous men' 'went beyond the bounds of protocol', and that they had 'lived out their friendship with prudence and discretion' (*Saggio*, p. 14).

Roncalli invited Montini to come to Venice and preach on the feast of the Ascension. Montini was able to plead a multitude of tasks in his new diocese and he could not come just yet.

Two anecdotes from 1955 reveal that Roncalli had Montini in mind as successor to Pius XII. Answering a question put to him at a meeting of academics on the Isola San Giorgio he said: 'If Montini were a cardinal, I would have no hesitation in voting for him at the conclave' (*Lettere*, p. 40). Later two cousins, Giovanni and Candida Roncalli from Milan, came to stay with him at the Patriarchate. He said: 'Look what happened to little Angelo, the son of Battista Roncalli, a farm-worker: he became Patriarch of Venice and a cardinal of the Holy Roman Church. The only thing left now is for him to become pope, but that won't happen, because the next pope will be your Archbishop' [i.e. Montini] (*ibid.*). This was a common opinion among pundits. The only thing wrong with it was that Montini was not yet a cardinal, and therefore would be excluded from the next conclave.

Montini's banishment was a mystery at the time. Many fanciful explanations have been offered for it. The true story is worth setting down because of its bearing on the conclaves of 1958 and 1963. The illness of Pius XII in 1954 put the question of his succession on the agenda. It also meant that effective control of the Roman Curia passed into the hands of the five influential cardinals – Pizzardo, Piazza, Ottaviani, Canali and Micara – who were known as 'the Pentagon' (Falconi, p. 243). They did not like Montini who was, they believed, 'too liberal'. He was opposed to Luigi Gedda and the 'civic committees'. He was favourable to the 'opening to the left'. He had tried to get the scandalous Catholic novelist Graham Greene to write in *l'Osservatore Romano*. He had defended the catastrophic priest-worker movement. He had been intimate with Alcide De Gasperi, the Christian Democratic leader, who died on August 19, 1954, out of favour with Pius XII. (Roncalli was unable to go to De Gasperi's funeral at Trent, but he sent along his auxiliary Gianfranceschi and Capovilla.) Thus in the small world of the Roman Curia Montini's enemies gathered their evidence and awaited their opportunity.

Yet so far he had avoided preparing any rope by which he might be hanged. But then he made a false move, prompted, characteristically, by his desire to stay in touch with the young. He attended a secret meeting of the Catholic Youth Movement (GIAC) at the Villa Carpegna in Rome. Its purpose was to scupper Gedda's alliance with the Neo-Fascists which was having – they believed – the most harmful effect on the Church. But Gedda was the favourite of Pius XII. There being no other way to protest, Mario Rossi, president of GIAC, resigned. This was unheard of. Leaders of Catholic Action were nominated by the Pope and not supposed to resign (*Quale Papa?*, p. 153).

Rossi's letter of resignation was delivered to Montini, as was right and proper: he dealt with Italian affairs while Tardini covered the rest of the world. Rossi explained why he thought the reactionary and Fascist tendencies of Luigi Gedda were a grave danger for the Church. Montini kept the letter on his desk, wondering what to do about it. But when the news of Rossi's resignation was leaked, Montini was accused of 'concealing information from the Holy Father'. His motive had been to protect Rossi from his own impetuousness.

But in Curial eyes he had behaved unforgiveably. His removal in November 1954 followed inevitably.

But Roncalli never dwelt on disappointment for long. In Lent 1955 he was more concerned with the 'Mission to Venice'. This enterprise was made possible by 'the peaceful resolution of the Roman question' (Alberigo, p. 219). Fifty years before it would simply not have been possible to have thirty-five young laypeople addressing the Venetians on the streets, bridges and squares of the city (*Familiari*, II, p. 375). The laity were backed up by twenty-five priests who preached more conventionally in churches. This symbolic division of labour expressed the then current theory of Catholic Action: the clergy acted on the faithful while the laity dealt with the world. Roncalli judged that the Lent 1955 Mission had been a success. His criterion was that there were clear signs of 'spiritual renewal'.

Roncalli reached out towards those who were considered opponents if not enemies. The thirty-second Congress of the Italian Socialist party was due to meet in Venice on February 1, 1957. In a Candlemasday exhortation Roncalli, speaking as Venetian and patriarch, welcomed the Congress. The city had a tradition of hospitality, and St Paul recommended a bishop to be *hospitalis et benignus* – hospitable and kind (*Letture*, p. 45). He hoped the Venetians would appreciate as he did 'the exceptional importance of this event, which is of great moment for the immediate future direction of our country'. In the definitive edition of his Venetian writings, *Scritti e discorsi*, this banal sentiment was dropped. It did not do for an influential Italian prelate to suggest that a Socialist Party Congress might matter for the country's future.

But Roncalli had gone much further than that. He deplored the 'gap' that had opened up between Christian and secular culture, and prayed that the Congress might help to bridge it: 'It is certainly inspired – I am willing to believe – by the desire to bring about the mutual understanding that is needed to improve living conditions and social prosperity' (*ibid.*). These innocent welcoming remarks caused a furious row. Roncalli had perpetrated another *gaffe*. He was publicly praised by *L'Unità*, the Communist paper, for providing the basis for co-operation between Catholics and the left, and privately though courteously rebuked by Dell'Acqua (*Utopia*, Eng., p. 221). There was once more talk of his naïveté. He was too easily exploited. He was too good to be trusted in a cruel and wicked world. But Roncalli's judgement was confirmed by Count Giuseppe Dalla Torre, editor of *l'Osservatore Romano*, who wrote *privately* to congratulate him on 'disarming sectarianism' (*Utopia*, Eng., p. 222). It was by no means, as the right-wing critics charged, an 'opening to the left', but it was a prior condition of any such opening. Many Italians were grateful.

Roncalli's concern for ecumenism had already been shown in 1954 when he gave three lectures during the Octave of Prayer for 'Christian Unity on 'The Church in the Slav World', 'The Church and Separated Oriental Christians', and 'The Church and Protestant Confessions'. Now, on September 18, 1957, he was invited to speak at the 7th Week of Study of the Christian East. He saw what he called 'the modern renaissance of patristic studies' as opening the way to reconciliation. In the patristic era the differences between East and West did not lead to schism. But he still assumed that the aim of the Catholic ecumenical movement was to encompass the 'return' to the one true fold of those who had strayed from it. In any case he was merely echoing current Catholic orthodoxy. He described Leo XIII's 1896 apostolic letter 'to princes and peoples' as 'a touching appeal for a return to unity' and Pius XII's encyclical *Mystici Corporis* of 1943 (which identified the 'Mystical Body of Christ' and the Roman Catholic Church) as 'a most wonderful document' (Alberigo, p. 241). These were the parameters within which Catholic ecumenists had to work at that date. But an ecumenism of 'return' had little hope of making any progress.

There were other strands in Roncalli's thinking, however, that pointed beyond it. Roncalli quoted the impassioned words of Cardinal Bessarione to the Council of Florence:

> What defence will we make before God for being separated from our brothers, when it was to unite us and gather us into one flock that Christ came down from heaven, became flesh and was crucified? What defence do we have before posterity? Venerable Fathers, we will not suffer such shame, we will remain far from such counsels, we will not provide so badly for those who come after us (SD, III, pp. 234–43).

Roncalli continues: 'Is the reponsibility for the split all on the side of our separated brothers? It is partly theirs, but it is also ours to a great extent' (*ibid.*, p. 243).

Roncalli wanted 'this splendid movement towards Christian unity' to have a regular place in Catholic teaching, preaching and catechesis. To this end he revived an idea first put to him by Dom Lambert Beauduin in 1926. Beauduin proposed an organised ecumenical movement in the Church on the analogy of Propaganda Fide, the missionary Congregation. That implied working on two levels: a broadly-based movement in the local churches to sensitise Catholics to the problems; and a Rome office within the Curia to co-ordinate and keep the ecumenical cause on the Roman agenda. It was the germ of the idea of the Secretariat for Christian Unity.

Back in Venice Roncalli was immersed in the final preparations for the diocesan Synod. It took place in St Mark's Basilica from November 25 to 27, 1957. It was the culmination of his pastoral plan for Venice. It 'crowned', as he put it, the pastoral visits he had been making to parishes since he arrived. It was prepared for in depth by study commissions and courses at the Seminary in which 'all were able to speak their mind' (Alberigo, p. 247). But it was not a democratic assembly and there was no debate. Roncalli was following the recommendations of canon law and the example of Radini Tedeschi who held a Synod in Bergamo in 1910 (see above, pp. 64–5). He also had St Charles Borromeo in mind and presented the Synod as a typically Tridentine institution which still had life in it and met 'the demands of the modern age'. This ability to pour new wine into old bottles constantly baffled those hasty commentators who wanted to know whether Roncalli was a 'conservative' or a 'liberal'.

It was in the context of the Synod that he first used the term *aggiornamento* which became his slogan and trade-mark. In his October 8 letter to the people of Venice he wrote:

> You've probably heard the word *aggiornamento* repeated so many times. Well, Holy Church who is ever youthful wants to be in a position to understand the diverse circumstances of life so that she can adapt, correct, improve and be filled with fervour. That in brief is the nature of the Synod, that is its goal (SD, III, 263–5).

He would use the same language, adding the notion of 'reform', to describe the purpose of the Council. He saw synods and councils as the 'constitutional' way of renewing the Church's youth.

Roncalli addressed the Venice Synod on each of its three days. His most important contribution was his account of 'episcopal authority'. The bishop is described in the liturgy, he said, as *dominus et pater* (Lord and father). But he had enough experience of ecclesiastical life to know that the language of spiritual paternity could mask the reality of tyranny and oppression. It was the problem he had thought about often before, notably in Istanbul: as bishop he must be neither bully nor doormat. Roncalli reflected on the pitfalls:

> *Authoritarianism* stifles life and leads to a rigid, external discipline and to complicated, harmful over-organisation. It represses legitimate initiatives, is unable to listen, confuses harshness with firmness, inflexibility with dignity. *Paternalism* is also a caricature of paternity. It keeps people immature in order to maintain its own superior position, behaves liberally towards some, but fails to respect the rights of its subordinates. It speaks protectively, and does not accept true collaboration (SD, III, pp. 342–56).

By now, Pius XII was 81. He was kept alive by his Swiss gerontologist, Dr Paul Niehans, who had devised what he called 'living cell' therapy – the regular injection of finely ground tissues taken from freshly slaughtered lambs (see Hoffmann, p. 24). It would have seemed very remiss of Curial cardinals not to have thought about the succession in advance. Roncalli would make a welcome contrast with Pius XII's way of exercising authority. Not only that, but historical analogy worked in his favour. Two generations before, so ran the legend, a simple and holy Patriarch of Venice, Sarto, had become Pope Pius X, now St Pius X. What had happened before could happen again. But the resemblance between Sarto and Roncalli was very superficial, based on the fact that both were of humble origins, fat and patriarchs of Venice. But while Sarto, who had never travelled outside Italy, was nervous, anxious and fanatical, the much-travelled Roncalli remained serene and used to weary people in Venice, as he admits, with the exhortation of St John the Evangelist in old age – 'Love one another – that is enough – it is the Lord's command, the Lord's command' (Alberigo, p. 255).

Roncalli theorised about authority to the Venice Synod. It remains to ask how far he managed to live up to his own ideal. Did he achieve 'spiritual paternity' in which he did not 'lord it over his flock, but loved them as sons and brothers' (Alberigo p. 250)? Was he perceived as one who, in his own words, combined 'trust with prudence, firmness with mercy, patience with decisiveness' (*ibid.*, p. 252)? These are impossible questions. Since they describe an ideal, they belong rather with the postulator of his cause than with a biographer. One cannot say that there was never a disgruntled cleric in the diocese of Venice. All one can say is that his clergy were sorry to see him go but glad that it was to become pope.

In his Ascension Day sermon of 1958 he preached on the meaning of the Paschal Candle which is greeted with the threefold acclamation, *Lumen Christi, Deo Gratias*. It was a simple exposition in three points. *Christ is Light* for individuals, for the Church, for society (or the 'world'). Behind that simple scheme can be discerned the outline of the Council and the title of its most important document: *Lumen Gentium*.

Tommaso Gallarati Scotti records an enigmatic conversation with the Patriarch in June, 1958, about a month after the Ascension Day sermon. Gallarati Scotti discussed what might happen in the 'not very far distant conclave' and piously deplored the way it was already being set up in the press as though it would be a straightforward political choice between left and right. Gallarati Scotti concludes his report: 'The Patriarch heard me out, but seemed far above such vain concerns, and in the end he said to me with his usual simplicity, "The ways of God are manifold" ' (*Utopia*, Ital., p. 461). In other words, he was not ruling himself out. But the longer the delay, the less his chances were. He felt he was getting old. In September, 1958, only a month before the conclave, he complains of fading memory and says he 'must be chary of accepting engagements to preach outside my diocese, because I have to write down everything first' (*Journal*, p. 316).

With hindsight the Venice years have inevitably been seen as an apprenticeship for the papacy. The truth is that they were probably the best preparation he could have had. He was dealing with people all the time, of all conditions and cultures. In his waiting room you could meet the art historian Bernard Berenson or Cardinal Stefan Wyszyński or the boys from the Marghera football team. He had played an important and sometimes controversial role in national affairs. He had continued to travel abroad – to the Lebanon, Portugal and France – on Marian business. He had kept his friendships in good repair and made new ones. He had come home after thirty years of exile and shown that he could run an Italian diocese with skill, tact and a style of authority that enabled people to grow. He had worked towards a systematic pastoral plan for his diocese. He had shown a remarkable capacity for work and meeting deadlines.

One of his secrets was that he was orderly. 'Most long-lived people', writes Desmond Morris, 'have a sense of self-discipline'. This does not mean driving the self despotically but 'imposing a pattern on the ordinary events of the day'. Roncalli had his Breviary and his afternoon nap in a chair. He also had the other qualities needed to age well: 'a twinkle in the eye', a sense of humour and impishness, and something to live for (*The Sunday Times Magazine*, November 20, 1983, p. 79).

At seventy-six he did not have the mind-cast of an old man. The prospect of a conclave has been known to rejuvenate cardinals who were otherwise heading for the grave. When Roncalli heard the news of the death of the Pope he noted in his diary: 'Sister death came quickly and swiftly fulfilled her office. Three days were enough. On Sunday, October 9 at 3.52 a.m. Pius XII was in paradise' (*Lettere*, p. 481). But having got Pius safely into heaven he did not look backwards. Instead he looked to the future good of the Church and expressed his hope in a typical image: 'One of my favourite phrases brings me great comfort: we are not on earth as museum-keepers, but to cultivate a flourishing garden of life and to prepare a glorious future. The Pope is dead, long live the Pope!' (*ibid.*). He left Venice for ever by the 9.40 train on October 12, 1958, seen off by the mayor and other notables.

Chapter 12

1958: the wide-open conclave

In a world filled with frightening violence, it would not be totally strange if
the Lord were pleased to give his Church a poor and humble pontiff,
concerned only with protecting the helpless and dissipating darkness from
people's minds and terror from their hearts. We are weary of too much
learning, too much power, we are weary of greatness, prestige . . . words.

(Don Primo Mazzolari in *Adesso*, November 1, 1958, on hearing of the death of
Pius XII)

On Saturday, October 11, 1958, his last full day in Venice, Cardinal Roncalli watched on live
television as the mortal remains of Pope Pius XII were transported from Castelgandolfo to
the Vatican. In his diary he wondered whether any Roman emperor, on his way to the Campidoglio, had enjoyed such a triumph. The crowds were paying tribute, he thought, not to
evanescent military might but to 'spiritual majesty and religious dignity'.

No doubt that was true enough. But careful editing spared the viewers the more horren-
dous incidents along the route. When the cortege arrived at St John Lateran, it paused for a
last tribute to the late pope in his cathedral church. Those close enough heard a startling
noise like a fire-cracker from within the coffin. In the Roman heat a process of fermentation
had begun which burst it open (see Hoffmann, p. 25). That was bad enough, but then the
man responsible for embalming the body, the papal doctor Riccardo Galeazzi Lisi (he was
really an oculist) worked throughout the night to re-embalm the much abused corpse. He
assured worried Vatican officials next morning that Pius XII could safely be exhibited in St
Peter's. He was wrong. Throughout the day the mourners filed past the bier on which Pius
XII lay in state: gradually his face turned green, then ashen-coloured, and a foul stench was
emitted. Roncalli heard what had happened when he arrived in Rome that afternoon.

His diary on Monday, October 13, was mostly concerned with what had gone wrong at
the funeral that same day. He could not see why the public needed to be present when the
body was placed in its triple coffin – it was now blotchy and disfigured. The most vivid and
precious memory of the day was his 'last look at the cadaverous face of the Holy Father. Oh,
the great lesson of death!' (*ibid.*). Another observer remarked that it was only in death that
Pius XII was seen without his glasses. The result was that he looked 'more human, more
friendly, more defenceless'.

Yet the exploding corpse and disastrous incompetence of Galeazzi Lisi were symbolic of
the unhealthy atmosphere that prevailed in Rome during the last years of Pius XII. The
moment he died, court favourites departed and old scores were settled. The once-powerful
Sister Pasqualina Lehnert, known as *Virgo Potens* because she controlled access to the Pope,

left the Vatican to write her memoirs. Galeazzi Lisi tried to hawk pictures of the papal corpse to the international press. He gave a press conference at which he described in great detail his own specially devised method of taking out the inner organs and embalming the body. The press found it nauseating (Lai, p. 280). Without waiting for the conclave, the cardinals dismissed Galeazzi Lisi from the Vatican service on October 20. Roncalli was well aware of the mood in Rome. The papal nephews had been so important in the pontificate just ended that Roncalli found it necessary to warn his own nephew, Don Battista Roncalli, not to dare come anywhere near Rome. He wrote to his bishop, Giuseppe Battaglia of Faenza, on October 24 in the strongest terms: 'I have already written to him (Don Battista) to say that on no account should he move until he has my approval. The atmosphere here is so foul with verbal malice and the press that the weary old remark is bound to be heard: "Here's the nephew, here come the relatives" '(Alberigo, p. 490). Though he did not hold Pius XII personally responsible for the unsavoury atmosphere, he recognised that from 1954, date of Pius' grave illness, the pontificate had been dominated by intrigue, nepotism and gossip. He welcomed the conclave as a chance to make a fresh start.

On the day of the funeral Roncalli installed himself along with Don Loris Capovilla and Guido Gusso, at Domus Mariae, a large conference centre on Via Aurelia 481. He later remarked that it would have been a better venue for a conclave than the Vatican where the rooms were either too cramped or too grandiose. Strictly speaking a conclave does not begin until all the cardinals and their assistants are sealed up inside the Vatican, which in this case did not happen until Saturday October 25, 1958. So there were two working weeks devoted to preparing the conclave and celebrating the *novemdiales* or nine days of mourning. Cardinal Luigi Masella was elected *camerlengo* or chamberlain (Pius having neglected to fill the post). He presided over the daily meetings of cardinals known as 'general congregations'. Their purpose was not to 'fix' the conclave or to preempt its decision. It was rather to provide a job-description of the sort of pope the Church needed in 1958. Names were not supposed to be discussed at this stage.

The problem facing the cardinals was one which always occurs after a long pontificate: continuity or change? The atmosphere already evoked after the death of Pius suggested that there would have to be 'change' of some sort. This did not imply any discredit to his memory. There was a consensus for change both on the part of those who regarded the late pope as an unrivalled genius, the like of whom could not be expected to recur, and also by those who felt that the pontificate just ended, despite its splendid facade and the enthusiastic audiences the Pope had gathered, had not altogether met the needs of the contemporary Church.

One of those unmet needs could be grasped simply by looking round the table in the Consistorial Hall where the cardinals met. The full complement of the college of cardinals was seventy. But when Pius died, there were only fifty-five cardinals: two (Mindzenty and Stepinac) were unavoidably absent, while two more died before the conclave began. So they were reduced to fifty-one electors. For unfathomed reasons, Pius had held only two consistories in his long reign, in 1946 and in 1953. The result was not only that the college was undermanned and restricted in its choice; it was also an immensely aged body. Twenty-four of them, nearly a half, were actually older than Roncalli. Why Pius neglected his succession is something of a mystery. *'Après moi, le déluge'* he is supposed to have said to the French ambassador. In this geriatric group, it was not surprising that some of the eighty-year olds should have regarded Roncalli as a sprightly youngster.

Though names were not to be mentioned in the general congregations the ban could not be applied to informal meetings and consultations. Lobbying was intense but discreet. There were invitations to lunch, and many phone calls. The lobbying was all, of course, on behalf of someone else. It was not done to push oneself forward, but some cardinals played the role of king-makers. Roncalli was not a king-maker, and he was surprised to find after the first general congregation on October 13 that some of his brother cardinals considered him a serious candidate. Cardinal Maurilio Fossati, archbishop of Turin, told him plainly 'We want you'. Gaetano Cicognani, prefect of the Congregation of Rites and brother of the apostolic delegate in Washington, said 'I could imagine kneeling at his feet'. A few days later Cardinal Elia Dalla Costa, archbishop of Florence, remarked to Roncalli, 'You'd make a good Pope'. 'But I'm seventy-six', he objected. 'That's ten years younger than me', replied the ancient (*Quale Papa?* pp. 151–2).

But it would be wrong to conclude from these early hints that Roncalli was already home and dry. He was *papabile*, one candidate among others. Much later Roncalli was able to claim that he had accepted the burden of the pontificate 'with the joy of being able to say that I did nothing to obtain it, absolutely nothing'. 'Indeed', he added, 'I was most careful and conscientious to avoid anything that might direct attention to myself' (*Journal*, pp. 348–9). There is no need to impugn Pope John's truthfulness. But his remarks should be applied, as he intended them, only to the conclave itself. In the pre-conclave period he was as active as anyone.

The Italians led the intrigues and the plotting. Some of them had been preparing for years for this moment. At eighteen out of fifty-one, they formed the largest national block by far. They knew each other and they knew the field. The non-Italian cardinals had scarcely met at all; Pius XII never brought them together for consultation. Cardinal Maurice Feltin, archbishop of Paris, said 'Each one of us knew perhaps about three or four of his colleagues or at most about a dozen (Bergerre, p. 199). What Feltin omitted to say was that all six French cardinals undoubtedly knew Roncalli, and some of them became cardinals on his recommendation. The French and Italians together made up about half the college. They held the key to the conclave. But there was no guarantee, or even likelihood, that they would vote together.

Yet after the second general congregation on Tuesday October 14, Roncalli was a worried man. His candidature was already looking solid enough to make him fear that he might be elected. He prayed, 'on bended knees, that the conclave should not be a disaster for the universal Church'. It is worth giving his diary for the day, discreet though it is:

Second day in Rome. At 10.30 the Congregation of Cardinals in the Consistorial Hall. Everything went well, but it's all confidential. After leaving I visited the substitute, Mgr Dell'Acqua, who is always very kind. His account of the last hours of Pius XII was pretty miserable but also very edifying. He confirmed the continued good will of the Pope for me personally and for what I was doing. The welcome he gave me in March on my return from Lourdes, and the letter he wrote to congratulate me on my September 18 homily at Castelfranco, brought me great consolation. To lunch today I had dear

Augusto Gianfrancheschi, Bishop of Cesena, and in the evening a most delightful and valuable conversation with Count Dalla Torre, editor of *l'Osservatore Romano (Vent'Anni,* p. 40).

His September 18 homily had been a tribute in Latin on the hundredth anniversary of St Pius X's ordination. Gianfrancheschi had been his auxiliary in Venice and had nothing to do with the conclave. Dell'Acqua and Dalla Torre were not inside the conclave either. But they could give him a good breakdown on the state of opinion within the Roman Curia. As editor of *l'Osservatore Romano* for nearly thirty years, Dalla Torre knew the scene, but he didn't know who was going to be elected. His paper prepared twenty-five biographies of *papabili.* In 1939 ten had been considered sufficient, and even that was unnecessary because 'everyone knew' that Pacelli would be elected.

No such predictions could be confidently made in 1958. It was a genuinely open conclave. Lists of contenders appeared from time to time, but they sprang from nowhere and had not the slightest authority. Roncalli, contrary to some reports, was on almost everyone's list, even if not highly placed. Capovilla recalls that Giacomo Lercaro (Bologna), Ernesto Ruffini (Palermo), and Alfredo Ottaviani (Holy Office) appeared as the leading contenders, closely followed by Luigi Masella *(camerlengo),* Valerio Valeri (Religious) – Roncalli's predecessor in France – and only then the patriarch of Venice. Capovilla also admits that Roncalli, though by no means unknown, was not regarded by the Roman Curia as a 'first class man' and that even his fellow Bergamesques, though they loved and appreciated him, thought of him as an old buffer in carpet slippers who was unlikely to transform the Church or indeed do anything at all (*Vent'Anni,* p. 14).

Nevertheless his candidature continued to gain ground. On Wednesday October 15 he was up early to celebrate Mass for the domestic staff at Domus Mariae and preached on Martha and Mary. His diary hints at what was happening: 'Great butterfly flutterings around my poor self. The odd fleeting encounter which, however, did not disturb my calm' (*Vent'Anni,* p. 41). In other words he was being sounded out. Ottaviani began to support him, arguing for a 'transitional pope' (*Quale Papa?* p. 151). What this meant was well put by a French abbot, who was 'close to' Cardinal Achille Liénart, archbishop of Lille. He was countering the candidature of Cardinal Giuseppe Siri, archbishop of Genoa, who was fifty-two. If elected, he could be pope for forty years. 'What we need', said the abbot, 'is an old man, a transitional pope. He won't introduce any great innovations, and will give us time to pause and reorganise. In that way the real choices that cannot be made now will be postponed'. Of course the consensus that was building up about a caretaker pope did not point inevitably or only to Roncalli. There were other suitable candidates for a do-nothing papacy.

Even though he was not a member of the conclave, Mgr Domenico Tardini was influential from his privileged position in the Secretariat of State. He knew its workings intimately, better than anyone except his old rival, Archbishop Giovanni Battista Montini. Roncalli met Tardini for an hour before lunch on October 15. He found the gruff old bear 'friendly and good' and somewhat pathetically anxious to be invited to lunch at Domus Mariae where he would find more cardinals gathered under one roof than anywhere else (*Vent'Anni,* p. 41). A few days later Roncalli visited Tardini's *elite* orphanage at Villa Nazareth, where working-class boys were given a first-class education, and was delighted by it. So during this pre-conclave period the two men cleared up what ever misunderstandings may have lingered on. This was common prudence on both sides. It was obvious that a future pope, whoever he was, would have to make use of Tardini in some capacity.

However he was not yet won over to supporting Roncalli's candidacy. He was said to be working on behalf of Cardinal Luigi Masella. But the real threat to Roncalli came not from Masella but from Cardinal Gregory Peter Agagianian. He became aware of this when he visited his friend Cardinal Celso Costantini, formerly secretary of Propaganda and an old China hand, who was awaiting an operation in the Margherita Clinic, via Massimo. Roncalli feared for his life, rightly, for Costantini died the next day, October 16. But with his dying breath he told Roncalli that he thought the time had come for a non-Italian pope and that he would be supporting Agagianian.

Roncalli did not think Agagianian really qualified as a 'non-Italian'. Born in Akhaltzikhe in 1895 he had received the nominal title of 'Patriarch of Cilicia of the Armenians' in 1937. But he had become 'more Roman than the Romans', and was now pro-prefect of Propaganda Fide, sometimes known as the 'red pope' because of his supposed influence. On the eve of the conclave, Roncalli said to Giulio Andreotti, the Christian Democrat politician:

> The other day I went to see Cardinal Costantini just before he died. He said to me: 'This time, at long last, we'll have an Oriental Pope'. I was amazed that any well-informed man could say such a thing. The 'East' doesn't exist except as a category created by Westerners. Ask a Chinese whether he has anything in common with an Indian or a Turk. It's much easier for an Italian to reconcile the Lebanese and the Egyptians than for a so-called 'Oriental' pope (Andreotti, pp. 72–3).

If Roncalli was prepared to make this point so openly to a layman, it is a fair bet that he argued in the same way with his fellow-cardinals. But of course to oppose Agagianian's candidature did not mean that he was pushing his own.

But he was taking some initiatives, and the notion that he merely waited on events with arms folded can be refuted by inspecting his diary. On October 16 he sought out Cardinal Giuseppe Pizzardo, who rather fancied himself as a *grande elettore*, at his apartment. Pizzardo brought up the matter of Montini. Those who had secured his exile from Rome in 1954 did not want to see him return in 1958 as Secretary of State, the only conceivable post for someone with his background. Had Montini been a cardinal, he would himself have been a strong runner. Even in absence, he hovered over the conclave. Pizzardo sounded Roncalli out about whether he would bring back his friend Montini. According to Zizola, 'the Patriarch calmly replied that he did not and would not seek to be elected pope, and so the question did not arise' (*Quale Papa?* p. 154). So no deal was struck. But Roncalli remembered such conversations after his election, and though he honoured Montini in every way he could think of, there was never any question of him returning to Rome. Later, there was the further consideration that Montini was more useful to the Council outside than inside the Vatican.

A bitterly cold wind, harbinger of winter, blew over Rome on October 16, the day Costantini died. Next day Roncalli dashed off a letter to Mgr Valentino Vecchi, rector of the

Patriarchal seminary in Venice. Was he saying farewell? The letter allows us to glimpse part of the case he was putting in the general congregations:

> As for the Pope now dead and taken up into glory, it only remains to continue the acclamation, Long live the Pope! and to pray that his successor, whoever he may be, may not represent a new departure but rather progress in living out the perennial youthfulness of the Church, whose mission is always to lead souls towards the divine heights where the Gospel sanctification of human life is realised . . . (*Utopia*, Italian, p. 459).

So there was to be no formal repudiation of Pius XII, on the contrary: Roncalli did not think that the Church progressed by turning somersaults. But that the 'continuity' he argued for would be 'continuity with a difference' was hinted at by the use of his favourite image: the Church's perennial youthfulness. But how was it to be expressed by these fifty-one elderly men gathered in Rome?

The second week of general congregations began on Monday, October 20. It was one of Roncalli's busiest days so far. He was assiduous in meeting all the right people. His diary records 'a long conversation with Cardinal Ottaviani at the Holy Office, followed by a visit to Cardinal Masella, *camerlengo*' (*Vent'Anni*, p. 41). The same day Tardini achieved his ambition of lunch at Domus Mariae, and it was after lunch that Roncalli visited his orphanage. That evening a Bergamesque prelate, Mgr Pietro Sigismondi, was invited to dinner. The purpose of their meeting was not to swap stories about Bergamo. Sigismondi was a close collaborator of Agagianian at Propaganda Fide, so he may have come along to mediate between the two candidates who were now beginning to outstrip the rest of the field.

As if this were not enough for one day, Roncalli also went to confession to Mgr Alfredo Cavagna, national chaplain to the Young Catholic Women, and records 'I was very happy with it' (*Vent'Anni*, p. 51). Perhaps we should probe no further. But the text Roncalli quotes immediately afterwards, 'Those who are guided by the Spirit are sons of God' (Romans 8.14), seems to echo a conversation in which Cavagna settled a scruple by assuring him that he would have to follow wherever the Spirit led. That is a guess. But it is not a guess that as soon as Roncalli became pope, he chose Cavagna as his regular confessor.

On Tuesday, October 21, the cardinals attended the funeral of Cardinal Costantini at San Giovanni dei Fiorentini and drew lots for their 'cells' in the conclave. They also entrusted Cardinal Antonio Bacci, a celebrated Latinist, with the task of writing the speech *De eligendo pontifice* to express their common mind about what kind of pope they were searching for. It seemed to point unambiguously to Roncalli.

This would explain why the following day, Wednesday, October 22, it looked almost as though he had resigned himself to becoming pope. He went down into the crypt of St Peter's where he had said his first Mass in 1904. He prayed that Peter 'would be the true protector of Christ's Church' in the 'great impending event of the conclave'. He entrusted himself to the great popes of the past, dwelling especially on the memory of Pius XII. He said a *De profundis* ('Out of the depths have I cried to thee, O Lord') not for the deceased popes but to beg for their intercession. He was crying to them 'out of the depths' for help (*Vent'Anni*, p. 42). In 1904 he had imagined 'the marble and bronze popes . . . giving me courage and confidence' (*Journal*, p. 171). Now in 1958 he felt they would soon become his 'venerable predecessors'. This was also the first time he was able to inspect the excavations under the crypt, and he pronounced himself well pleased. Later, however, the leading archaeologist complained that he was ignorant of the excavations and that, whenever she tried to talk about the bones of St Peter, he turned the conversation to St Charles Borromeo (Guarducca, p. 74). He simply did not share Pius XII's passionate interest in the supposed apologetic value of the finds.

Meanwhile, he was working quietly on the French connection. Cardinal Maurice Feltin came to see him at Domus Mariae on October 21, and on Thursday October 23 he went to the French College, via di Santa Chiara, where he met the agoraphobic Roques of Rennes and Grente of le Mans who was 'in good shape despite his age'. 'Both of them', he confided in his diary, 'were very friendly towards me' (*Vent'Anni*, p. 23).

October 23 was the day when the inescapability of what was going to happen began to come home to him. Three pieces of evidence all point in the same direction. He had a conversation with Mgr Dell'Acqua who later reported:

> Cardinal Roncalli, with that simplicity that always marked him, said to me, pensive and confused, 'As you've seen, Don Angelo, my name has been appearing as *papabile*. What should I do?' I answered, your eminence, leave it in the hands of the Lord, and if such is his will, do not refuse. Let him guide you and help you to face up to the sacrifice involved. You won't lack good aides (ANSA, July 3, 1973).

Yet a letter written the same day to Giuseppe Piazzi suggests that he had a fairly shrewd idea what God's will was going to be. He had seen Piazzi, bishop of Bergamo, only ten days before, on the day of Pius' funeral. So the letter was designed to let him know how things had moved on since then:

> Just a word as I enter the conclave. Treat it as a request for prayers from the Bishop and the diocese that as a good Bergamesque I hold most dear. Thinking of all the lovely images of Mary dotted around the diocese, calling to mind our patron saints, bishops, famous and holy priests, religious men and women of outstanding virtue, my soul finds comfort in the confidence that a new Pentecost can blow through the Church, renewing its head, leading to a new ordering of the ecclesiastical body and bringing fresh vigour in progress towards the victory of truth, goodness and peace. It little matters whether the next pope is from Bergamo or not. Our common prayers will ensure that he will be a prudent and gentle administrator, a saint and a sanctifier. You follow me, your excellency? (*Vent'Anni*, p. 47).

His excellency would have understood perfectly well. Roncalli was paying tribute to the spiritual traditions of the Bergamo diocese that had formed him. Though it didn't strictly matter where the next pope came from, it now seemed likely that he would come from Bergamo, Capovilla heads this letter 'presentiment'. One could just as easily call it 'foreboding'. Roncalli ended the day by going to pray in two of his favourite Roman churches, Sant' Andrea della Valle and the Gesù (*Cronologia*, p. 746). This was what he had always done when he had a problem. He had a problem now.

Friday, October 24 was the eve of the conclave. Roncalli wrote his last letter before becoming pope to Giuseppe Battaglia, bishop of Faenza, to say that he was 'rather worried'. It was the letter already quoted in which he forbade his nephew, Don Battista, to come to Rome for the time being. But this ban only made sense if he expected to become pope; otherwise he would have no patronage to dispense. Once again he turned to the Psalms, his daily prayer for a lifetime, and invited Battaglia to say with him Psalms 77 ('I cry aloud to the Lord') and 86 ('Incline thine ear, O Lord . . . for I am poor and needy'). Towards the end of the letter, Roncalli becomes quite explicit. It is no longer a question of perhaps or maybe:

> When you have heard that I had to surrender to the darts of the Holy Spirit, expressed
> through the common will of those gathered here, you can let Don Battista come to
> Rome with your blessing. And then between us you and I can decide what is the best
> thing to do for him 'in the Lord'. As for me, would to heaven that this chalice might pass
> away from me! Do me the kindness to pray for and with me. I have reached the point at
> which if the words of Daniel apply to me − 'You have been weighed in the balance and
> found wanting' (Daniel, 5.27), I would inwardly rejoice and bless the Lord for it.
> Naturally, not a word to anyone. Affectionately (*Vent'Anni*, p. 49).

He had no illusions about what becoming pope would mean. The 'flourishing garden' he had talked about on the death of Pius XII had now become Gethsemani. To a Venetian visitor he remarked: 'Venice is a bed of roses compared with Rome. Rome will be a bed of thorns' (*Quale Papa?* p. 155). After the letter to Battaglia, even Capovilla, a most cautious witness, conceded that Roncalli now had 'the clear and unambiguous awareness of the probability that he would be elected Pope' (*Letture*, p. 412).

On the evening of October 24 Roncalli summoned Giulio Andreotti to Domus Mariae. It may seem strange that the patriarch should want to see a layman and Christian Democrat politician − he had already been Minister of Defence − at this eleventh hour. But there were both personal and public reasons for a meeting. Andreotti was the nephew by marriage of Mgr Giulio Belvedere, an old Roman seminary friend of Roncalli, who had fought for justice within the Roman Curia and been shabbily treated as a result (Andreotti, pp. 49–51). Again, in 1956 Andreotti had been instrumental in persuading the government to allow the Venice junior seminary, then some distance away at Bassano on the mainland, to return to a listed building next door to the Patriarchal seminary. So Roncalli now wanted to thank him for this good work and make sure that he left 'without any debts'. He trusted his Roman friends to conclude the affair of the junior seminary. From this Andreotti concluded that Roncalli was saying '*addio*' to Venice. He did not expect to return.

Their Venetian business over, Roncalli launched with cheerful indiscretion into the tabu topic of the conclave: 'You haven't mentioned the gossip that's been going the rounds in the last few days. It's true we're all saying "Not me, Lord, not me", but the Holy Spirit's tongues of fire have to fall on one of us. In these weeks I've twice meditated on the *Spiritual Exercises* of St Ignatius because one has to keep one's feet on the ground' (Andreotti, p. 72). This was most probably an allusion to the 'three degrees of humility' with its preference for 'insults with Christ rather than honours' (see p. 130). Why should Roncalli feel the need to keep his feet on the ground unless he were in imminent danger of being swept off them?

Then he said: 'I received a message of good wishes from General Charles de Gaulle, but that doesn't mean the French cardinals will vote the way he wants them to. I know they would like to elect Montini, and he would certainly be good; but I don't think the tradition of choosing from among the cardinals can be set aside' (Andreotti, p. 72). So Roncalli's cultivation of the French cardinals had not guaranteed him their automatic support. Indeed one of them had set off for the conclave declaring openly: 'The only certain thing is that it won't be Roncalli' (Dreyfus, pp. 139–40). However, one witness, Cardinal Eugène Tisserant, says in his posthumous memoirs that 'the French cardinals were the great electors of Roncalli – he had assured them that he would solve the priest-worker question' (*Quale Papa?* p. 155). But this is not incompatible with Roncalli's eve-of-conclave doubts. The French cardinals – or some of them –might have preferred to vote for the absent Montini. Quite a lot of energy was being expended in scotching the idea that a non-cardinal (i.e. Montini) could be a serious candidate. Benny Lai met Cardinal Siri who had thumped the table with so much vigour at the absurd notion of electing an outsider that he had smashed the ruby in his ring. No one thought of Tardini.

Roncalli's concluding remarks have already been quoted. He noted the objections to Agagianian who was only spuriously 'non-Italian'. Andreotti deduced from this remarkable interview – Capovilla vouches for its substantial accuracy – that he had been talking to the next pope. The uncertainty was over. So sure was he that he rang *Concretezza*, a magazine he edited, and directed them to prepare just one photograph: that of Angelo Roncalli.

The next day Mgr Antonio Bacci delivered the speech *De eligendo pontifice*. It was the last public act before the conclave's veil of secrecy descended. Bacci's task was to turn into decent Latin the job-description thrown up by the general congregations. A shy and retiring man, he was rather astonished to be suddenly taken notice of. He explained why in a book entitled *With Latin at the Service of Four Popes:* 'I remember that my address was well received by the press. Some wrote that I had clearly and precisely drawn the portrait of John XXIII. In fact I had simply presented to the cardinals the ideal figure of a pope that the present age demanded. So the merit was not mine' (Bacci, p. 89). Bacci was too modest. Whether by luck or inspiration, he was prophetic:

> We need a pope gifted with great spiritual strength and ardent charity. . . He will need to embrace the Eastern and the Western Church. He will belong to all peoples, and his heart must beat especially for those oppressed by totalitarian persecution and those in great poverty. . . May the new Vicar of Christ form a bridge between all levels of society, between all nations – even those that reject and persecute the Christian religion. Rather than someone who has explored and experienced the subtle principles belonging to the art and discipline of diplomacy, we need a pope who is above all holy, so that he may obtain from God what lies beyond natural gifts . . . He will freely receive and welcome the bishops 'whom the Holy Spirit has chosen to rule over the Church of God' (Acts 20.28). He will be prepared to give them counsel in their doubts, to listen and comfort them in their anxieties, and to encourage their plans.

The whole address was deeply 'revisionist'. It was a point by point description of what Pius XII was not. Bacci voiced the cardinals' desire to have a pope who was accessible to bishops. They wanted someone less aloof, autocratic and remote. Pius was magnificently endowed with 'natural gifts', and his outlook had been shaped (some said deformed) by a lifetime in diplomacy. Bacci said clearly that they wanted someone different. The most remarkable piece of prophecy concerned the hope that the new pope would 'form a bridge . . . even towards those who reject and persecute the Christian religion'. Pius XII had been content to denounce them. When Hungary was invaded in 1956 he expressed his sense of outrage (and impotence) with three encyclicals in as many days. If Bacci were heeded, the conclave would elect a different sort of man with a different style.

Bacci's address was at 2 p.m. on Saturday October 25. By four o'clock the conclave was cut off from the world. The shutters on the windows looking out over the city were sealed (to prevent communication by flash-light or mirror). There was enough food in the kitchens to withstand a minor siege. The good weather had returned. It was sticky and uncomfortable inside the Vatican, especially in the apartments of the Noble Guard where Roncalli was quartered. Eight cardinals, their secretaries and servants (known as *conclavistas*) lived rather on top of each other. But they formed a sympathetic little group – what Capovilla called 'a splendid family' (*'una bella famiglia', Letture*, p. 9). Besides Roncalli, there were four other Italians, all old friends and well-disposed towards him: Ernesto Ruffini (Palermo), Maurilio Fossati (Turin), Gaetano Cicognani (Rites) and Valerio Valeri (Religious). Finally there were Benjamin Arriba y Castro of Tarragona, Spain, and two Latin Americans, Giacomo Luigi Copello of Buenos Aires, Argentina, and Carlos Maria de la Torre of Quito, Ecuador. Congenial though these companions were, they did not form a pressure group within the conclave; but there is plenty of evidence that they talked things over between ballots. Capovilla had never seen Roncalli 'so engrossed and moved'.

The secret of the 1958 conclave was well kept. But Roncalli himself set us on the way towards understanding what happened. The very last entry in his *Journal of a Soul* reads: 'As the voting in the Conclave wavered to and fro I rejoiced when I saw the chances of my being elected diminishing and the likelihood of others, in my opinion truly most venerable and worthy persons, being chosen' (*Journal*, p. 349). So the conclave was by no means a foregone conclusion. There was a contest, and a relatively tough one, for Roncalli did not receive the two thirds plus one he needed until the eleventh ballot. There were four inconclusive ballots on Sunday October 26, feast of Christ the King. By the end of the day, according to Zizola, Roncalli had twenty votes and Agagianian eighteen. Lercaro of Bologna, considered the most 'progressive' candidate, had four votes, as had Valeri. Two votes, believed to be French, had gone to Montini as a protest against his absence (*Quale Papa?* p. 157). At the Armenian College three months later, Pope John revealed that the names of Roncalli and Agagianian 'went up and down like two chickpeas in boiling water' (*Vent'Anni*, p. 25). But by lunchtime next day, two ballots later, the conclave was deadlocked. Agagianian was making no progress. The attempt to present him as someone who, in Bacci's words, could 'embrace the Eastern and the Western Church' failed: he had become remote even from his fellow Orientals. Tisserant therefore abandoned Agagianian and fell back on Masella as an alternative. Tisserant, a massive bearded figure, was immensely learned. He thought Roncalli didn't know enough to become pope. At this point, Roncalli may have lost some votes and slumped to about fifteen ('wavering to and fro'). Two more ballots and still the smoke was black. Nothing was resolved.

Two fragments of conversation are recorded from the evening of October 17, second day of the conclave. The first came from Cardinal Fossati. In his preface to Leone Algisi's biography of Pope John he wrote:

> Everyone knows that the cardinals drew lots for the cells. Cardinal Roncalli drew number 15, and I drew 16, next door to him in the apartment of the Noble Guard. So we were neighbours. I'm sure the Holy Father will forgive me if I break the secrecy and say that at a certain moment the friend felt the need to go along to the cell of the other friend, to encourage him (Algisi, p. 6).

The context makes it clear that Fossati was comforting him because he was gaining ground, not because he was losing it.

The second conversation that can be assigned to this same evening is less banal. Cardinal Alfredo Ottaviani gave an interview in 1968 in which he said:

> In the last days of the conclave I went to visit the Patriarch in his cell and said: 'Your eminence, we have to think about a council'. Cardinal Ruffini, who was also present, was of the same opinion. Cardinal Roncalli made this idea his own, and was later heard to say, 'I was thinking about a council from the moment I became Pope' (*Epoca*, December 8, 1968).

Ottaviani, the pro-prefect of the Holy Office, was here claiming credit for having been the first to propose the summoning of a Council. In February 1975, the ageing and half-blind cardinal repeated the claim in conversation with Bernard R. Bonnot, an American graduate student. He said that on the night of October 27, 'many cardinals', including himself and Ruffini, visited Roncalli in his cell because they already knew that he was going to be elected. Among the topics they discussed was 'what a beautiful thing it would be to call a Council' (Bonnot, p. 13). So in the minds of such shrewd operators as Cardinal Ottaviani and Ruffini, the contest was already over. Their minds raced ahead to Roncalli's pontificate. Roncalli's own votes, by now thrown away, went to Valerio Valeri, as a somewhat belated consolation for his humiliation in France. Roncalli stated this publicly, many times (*Dodicesimo anniversario*, p. 62, fn. 2).

But he was still just short of the thirty-five votes he needed. Zizola assigns him thirty-two, as Agagianian's support crumbled and Ottaviani, now firmly on his side, brought over the 'packet' of votes from Masella (*Quale Papa?* p. 159). It took three more ballots on October 28 for him to reach the haven of thirty-eight. He began the day with Mass at 6 a.m. in the Mathilde Chapel. He then served Capovilla's Mass, bringing up the cruets at the offertory and ringing the bell at the *Sanctus* and consecration – a throwback to his time as altar-boy in Sotto il Monte. Cardinal Wyszyński was also present. The Introit Psalm took on a special resonance for Roncalli, 'O Lord, thou hast searched me and known me . . . thou discernest my thoughts from afar' (Psalm 139.1–2). In the Gospel Jesus told his disciples to 'love one another' (John 15.17). After a speedy continental breakfast in the Sala Regia, the cardinals conferred in subdued tones and glided silently about visiting each other singly or in small groups until at 9 a.m. the bell summoned them to the Sistine Chapel for Mass and the *Veni Creator* (*Vent'Anni*, p. 6, for this whole paragraph).

Once more the voting slips were tipped into the waiting chalice for the ninth and tenth ballots. To the intense disappointment of the crowd, at 11.10 a.m. black smoke emerged once more from the Sistine flue. But within the Conclave, there was a growing sense that the *dénouement* was not far off. 'Certain looks and certain allusions' convinced Capovilla that there would be a pope before the day was out. Roncalli went straight from the Sistine Chapel to his cell, sat down on the divan and said he wanted to be alone. Towards one o'clock Capovilla returned to accompany him down to the Sala Regia for lunch. But Roncalli said: 'I'm not coming down. I'll have a bite here. Have something brought. We'll eat together' (*Vent'Anni*, p. 7). The resourceful Guido Gusso had made friends with the sisters in the kitchen. He returned at 1.20 with a meal that Roncalli and Capovilla ate facing each other across rather a rickety table: soup, a slice of meat, a glass of wine, an apple. But neither found it easy to eat or talk. Perhaps a dozen words were exchanged in quarter of an hour. Roncalli dozed for about twenty minutes and then settled down at his desk to jot down some notes towards his acceptance speech: he already knew its majestic and striking opening chord – '*Vocabor Joannes*, I will be called John'. At four o'clock the bell rang to call him back to the Sistine Chapel for the decisive eleventh ballot. At 4.50 p.m. he was elected pope with thirty-eight votes.

Even on this day, of all days, Roncalli remained self-possessed enough to make a few notes for his diary. Becoming pope was not going to alter the methodical habit of a lifetime. What had happened to him had not yet had time to sink in, but his spontaneous response was, 'I'm ready':

> Third day of the conclave. Feast of the Holy Apostles Sts Simon and Jude. Holy Mass in the Mathilde Chapel, with much devotion on my part. Invoked with special tenderness my saintly protectors: St Joseph, St Mark, St Lawrence Justinian and St Pius X, asking them to give me calmness and courage. I thought it wiser not to eat with the cardinals. I ate in my room. At the eleventh ballot I was elected pope. O Jesus, I too can say what Pius XII said when he was elected: 'Have mercy on me, Lord, according to thy great mercy' (Psalm 51). One would say that it is like a dream and yet, until I die, it is the most solemn reality of all my life. So I'm ready, Lord, 'to live and die with you' (2 Corinthians 7.3). About three hundred thousand people applauded me on St Peter's balcony. The arc-lights stopped me from seeing anything other than a shapeless, heaving mass (*Vent'Anni*, p. 12).

This text is unique in papal history: a diary entry for 'the day I became Pope'.

Chapter 13

The first ninety days

If anyone expected Roncalli to be a mere caretaker Pope, providing a
transition to the next reign, he destroyed the notion within minutes of his
election . . . He stomped in boldly like the owner of the place, throwing open
windows and moving the furniture around.

(*Time Magazine*, November 17, 1958)

The doors to the Sistine Chapel remained firmly locked, but the secretaries and attendants already knew that a pope had been elected and guessed who he was. By about five o'clock, most of them had gathered on the so-called Ladies' Balcony overlooking St Peter's Square: this was the first sign to the waiting crowd and the television crews that there would soon be 'white smoke'. Don Loris Capovilla and Guido Gusso were waiting in the deserted Sala Ducale. Tradition had it that the new Pope's secretary should be the first outsider to enter the Sistine Chapel. After half an hour or so a door was opened and out came Cardinal Thomas Tienchensin, Archbishop of Peking, in a wheelchair because of a car accident. Capovilla looked in and saw Roncalli's empty throne, the third from the end of the right-hand side. All the canopies except his were folded down (*Letture*, pp. 10–11). So he *was* pope. But where was he? Smiling cardinals told Capovilla, now catapulted into prominence, that his Holiness was already vesting in the sacristy.

Another *conclavista*, Mgr Jean-François Arrighi, a Corsican who was in the conclave as Cardinal Tisserant's secretary, described the transformation that had come over Roncalli during the conclave: 'Before the final vote, the Pope looked overcome, but when the result was announced, he was completely calm. I said to myself, "That man has faith"' (Lawrence, p. 19).

It was Tisserant, as dean of the college of cardinals, who had asked the ritual question, 'Do you accept?' Until he answered this question, Roncalli was still the patriarch of Venice. He replied:

> Listening to your voice, 'I tremble and am seized by fear'. What I know of my poverty
> and smallness is enough to cover me with confusion. But seeing the sign of God's
> will in the votes of my brother cardinals of the Holy Roman Church, I accept the
> decision they have made; I bow my head before the cup of bitterness and my shoulders
> before the yoke of the cross. On the feast of Christ the King, we all sang: 'The Lord is our
> judge, the Lord is our lawgiver, the Lord is our king: he will save us' (Isaiah 33.22)
> (*Vent'Anni*, p. 50).

With these words he became pope.

Tisserant's next ritual question was: 'By what name do you wish to be known?' The Pope's answer was the first of his many surprises: 'I will be called John'. Not another Pius, or even a Leo or a Benedict whom he greatly admired: John. Some explanation was called for. Pope John gave it, prompted by the notes he had jotted down earlier that afternoon: 'The name John is dear to me because it was the name of my father, because it is the dedication of the humble parish church where we were baptised, and because it is the name of innumerable cathedrals throughout the world, and first of all of the blessed and holy Lateran Basilica, our own cathedral' (*Vent'Anni*, p. 51). That confident and affectionate mention of 'our own cathedral' was a first hint that he would take his duties as 'Bishop of Rome' seriously.

As the cardinals racked their brains trying to remember what they could about the long and mostly ignominious line of Johns, the new Pope helped them out and allowed himself – could it be? – a wry historian's joke: 'It is the name which has been most used in the long series of Roman Pontiffs. Indeed there have been twenty-two unquestionably legitimate supreme pontiffs named John. Nearly all had a brief pontificate' (*ibid.*). Just the name for a 'transitional pope'. Pope John did not reveal that for years he had been studying Pope John XXII, last legitimate pope of the name, who reigned from 1317 to 1334. But more profoundly, it was the deliberate retrieval of an *evangelical* name from the rapscallions who had dishonoured it and the anti-Pope John XXIII who had, so it was believed, made it unusable: Baldassare Cossa, the last claimant to the name, was an ex-pirate who had massacred, cheated and perjured his way to the papacy.

Pope John explained very simply that he loved the name John because it had been borne by the two men in the Gospels who were closest to Jesus: John the Baptist and John the Evangelist. But it was his conclusion that moved even the hard-bitten college of cardinals. He had called himself John in order to renew the exhortation of the Apostle John: 'My children, love one another' (*ibid.*, pp. 51–2). The message was love.

The next hour was aimiably chaotic. Before leaving the Sistine Chapel, Pope John revived an old custom by placing his now redundant red skull cap on the head of Mgr Alberto di Jorio, secretary of the conclave, thus creating him a cardinal. In the sacristy, prelates fussed and pressed around him, congratulating him and asking for a blessing. Capovilla pushed his way through and asked that the first blessing should be for Venice, Bergamo and all the family at Sotto il Monte. 'Yes, gladly' he replied, 'first for those related according to the Spirit and then the relatives according to blood; we'll talk about it later, later'.

According to *Time*, a reliable source on such matters, the new Pope weighed 205 lbs (Fox, p. 335). His girth was not stated, but it was enough to embarrass Annibale Gammarelli, the pontifical tailor, for whom popes came in two sizes: thin and fat. The larger of the two white cassocks failed to meet round the front. Gammarelli had to fix it with safety pins, and a surplice concealed his improvisation from the television cameras. At 6.08 p.m., exactly an hour after the 'white smoke', Cardinal Nicola Canali announced to the world the 'great joy' that we had a pope, and at the name of Roncalli, and still more that of John, what Capovilla called 'a wave of enthusiasm' swept over the square (*Letture*, p. 9). Anthony Burgess put it more vividly: 'The crowd gaudiated magnally: old ladies in black wept, teeth gleamed in stubbled faces, strangers shook hands with each other, children jumped as though Mickey Mouse were soon to come, the horns of Roman cars rejoiced plaintively' (*Earthly Powers*, p. 550). At 6.20 Pope John appeared on the central *loggia* of St Peter's and gave his first blessing

urbi et orbi, on the city and on the world. He did not make a speech: that 'custom' was introduced only later.

Pope John afterwards tried to describe his feelings as he stood up there before the noisy,
invisible crowd:

> I remembered Jesus' warning: 'Learn of me, for I am meek and humble of heart'. Dazzled
> by the television lights, I could see nothing but an amorphous, swaying mass. I blessed
> Rome and the world as though I were a blind man. As I came away I thought of all the
> cameras and lights that from now on, at every moment, would be directed on me. And I
> said to myself: if you don't remain a disciple of the gentle and humble Master, you'll
> understand nothing even of temporal realities. Then you'll be really blind (*Vent'Anni*, p.
> 21).

Meanwhile, back in the sacristy, there were more scenes of cheerful chaos. Tardini and his
staff from the Secretariat of State had come to present their homage. Cardinal Tisserant,
now in charge as dean of the sacred college since the office of *camerlengo* lapsed on the election of a pope, thundered that they were all excommunicated. They had broken in before
the conclave had been officially declared over. There followed half an hour of comic confusion during which Tisserant strode around with upset dignity, his beard wagging as he alternately excommunicated or cried, 'Don't kill him now you've made him Pope' (*Vent'Anni*, p.
22). The cause of all this uproar gently enquired, 'Where do we go now?'

It was up to him to decide where to spend the night. He preferred not to go back to cell
number fifteen, and headed for the almost deserted apartment of the Secretary of State. It
had not been lived in for years. The vivas continued to echo round the square below, but
since the shutters were still sealed, nothing could be seen. Pope John certainly did not literally 'fling open the windows of the Vatican' on his first night. The telephone was dead.
There was no radio. Pope John was completely alone.

At 7.30 p.m. Mgr Dell'Acqua arrived with a Latinist to help draft his radio message for the
next day. He dined alone at 9 o'clock in a badly-lit corner of the vast apartment. Capovilla,
unsure of the protocol, had already eaten, but he stayed long enough to see an aged man-
servant, Pio Manzia, totter in with a bottle of champagne. 'Holy Father', he explained, 'it is a
tradition that the head of the household should open a bottle of champagne, offer it to his
Holiness, and take away what's left for himself' (*Vent'Anni*, p. 23). Pope John took a glass,
and let Manzia have most of it. He was not going to deny anyone his perks.

Then he paced up and down in the gallery, saying his rosary. He broke off to say, 'Before
lying down I want to see Tardini'. Capovilla objected: 'But you've seen him with all the
others in the vesting-room'. 'I know', said Pope John, 'but hasty compliments are not enough. He's the most important person around here. Get him along' (*Vent'Anni*, p. 23). He
wrote in his diary:

> Today the entire world writes and talks of nothing except me: the name and the person.
> O my dear parents, O mother, O my father and grandfather Angelo, O Uncle Zaverio,
> where are you? What brought this honour upon you? continue to pray for me (*ibid.*, p.
> 43).

Giulio Nicolini, Tardini's biographer, says that this late-night meeting was merely to fix an appointment for the following morning. Pope John lifted the absurd excommunication and said, 'The first audience will be for you' (Nicolini, p. 176). Next morning, Pope John surprised him by inviting him to sit down – in Pius' time subordinates knelt before the Pope – and asked him to become his Secretary of State. In Tardini's own account (as reported by his former pupil, archbishop, later cardinal, Sebastiano Baggio):

> He didn't give me any choice. I told the Holy Father that I wouldn't serve under him, because new policies would need new people; and I reminded him that I had frequently disagreed with him in the past; I reminded him that I was tired, whacked out, and that my health was getting worse; I told him about my long-cherished ambition of at last giving myself entirely to the orphan boys of Villa Nazareth. It made no difference. The Pope listened to me with kindness and interest, but to every point he replied: 'I understand, but I want you to be my Secretary of State'. Finally I knelt down and offered him my obedience. Such is life (Nicolini, pp. 177–8).

Why should Pope John have to be so determined to appoint as his closest collaborator someone with whom he had disagreed in the past and who was so reluctant to accept the office? The hypothesis of a deal struck during the conclave – votes for Roncalli on condition that Tardini was his Secretary of State – has already been excluded. A two-man ticket was against the spirit and the letter of the conclave rules. But that does not mean that Pope John was insensitive to the feeling in the conclave that a pope inexperienced in the ways of the Curia should be flanked by someone who knew its workings intimately.

Since Pope John's relationship with the Curia is crucial for understanding his pontificate, it will be as well to give here the witness of Mgr Igino Cardinale, soon to become his chief of protocol:

> Pope John was not a curial man. He didn't know too much about the Curia, and *what he knew he didn't like*. His relationship when in Bulgaria, Istanbul and elsewhere had not always been very good. So he remained the outsider. He never intentionally over-ruled the Curia, but he felt free to make up his own mind. His attitude was that he would always be respectful towards the Curia, but would not be bound or limited by it (Cardinale, conversation with the author, Brussels, March 30, 1980).

This was common knowledge in the inner circles of the Vatican. Consequently, the immediate appointment of Tardini was a clear signal to the whole Curia. Pope John began his pontificate with a gesture of reconciliation towards the Curia he had inherited. There would be no sackings or abrupt dismissals. He would not employ a new broom. Later Pope John would pay a painful price for this kid-gloved handling of the Curia; but as an opening move it was tactically shrewd.

Having secured Tardini's consent, Pope John discussed with him another appointment which in his own eyes, if not those of the world, was almost as important. He wanted a confessor and spiritual director. Tardini explained that the official confessor of the papal household was by tradition a friar. But he was free to choose anyone. Pius XII had a learned Jesuit, Fr Augustin Bea, rector of the Biblical Institute. Pope John's diary records: 'I prayed and reflected about this. I chose without hesitation Mgr Alfredo Cavagna; he is holy, good, learned, prudent; he knows the Roman scene well, and will be able to help me with discretion on many matters' (*Pastore*, p. 11). Cavagna was two years older than Pope John and had a similar background. He had been secretary to a bishop and helped organise a diocesan Synod. He had organised national clergy weeks to bring clergy and laity closer together. He served Pope John in many other roles, as we shall see. But his most important role was as confessor. Throughout his pontificate, unless prevented by some urgent business, Pope John made his confession to Cavagna at 3 o'clock on Friday afternoon, the day and the hour of Jesus' death.

On this first crowded day of his pontificate, Pope John was driven up the hill to Vatican Radio to broadcast his first message to the world, *Hac trepida hora* (In this moment of trepidation). It began as a conventional enough discourse taking the form of greetings and thanks to all and sundry in the Church. It was strongly anti-Communist. But he went on to announce the two major themes that would mark his pontificate: *unity* in the life of the Church and *peace* in the secular order. His good wishes embraced the Orthodox Churches and 'All those who are separated from this Apostolic See'. He quoted Jesus' prayer 'that all may be one' (John 17.11); it became the linking thread of his pontificate. He deplored the way the wealth of nations was squandered on the arms race and devoted to preparing 'pernicious instruments of death and destruction', instead of being used 'for all classes of society, especially the least favoured' (*Vent'Anni*, pp. 53–4). This contained the germ of his great social encyclicals.

The elderly Don Luigi Sturzo, once leader of the Popular Party, commented on the radio message: 'Peace, justice, liberty, mutual understanding of rights and duties – all in the accents of love' (*Avvenire d'Italia*, November 1, 1958). Pope John meanwhile, his first day as pope over, moved into the papal apartments and noted in his diary, mysteriously, 'emotion and sadness' (*Vent'Anni*, p. 43.)

By next day he was feeling more cheerful. His diary records:

> October 30, Thursday. The first nominations arouse general approval, especially that of the secretary of state. Begin with him the most urgent business and appointments.
> Above all the consistory and the nomination of new cardinals. I give him the names beginning with Mgr Montini, Archbishop of Milan, and Mgr Tardini, who headed a litany on which we were in perfect agreement. When we reached the total of seventy, old and new, we paused for a moment but then, reflecting that at the time of Sixtus V the Catholic Church occupied only about a third of its present territory, we went on and arrived at a list of 23 new cardinals (*Vent'Anni*, pp. 43–4).

Sixtus V (1585–90) had founded the Curia in its modern form and decreed that the number of cardinals should not exceed seventy. Pope John departed from precedent because, in the changed situation, it seemed common sense to do so. He also put right, at a stroke, Pius' neglect of the college of cardinals and began to realise his predecessor's largely unfulfilled ambition of 'internationalising' it. Pope John's consistory included 'first ever' cardinals from the Philippines, Japan, Mexico and Africa. He was particularly pleased with his appointment of the first black cardinal, Laurean Rugambwa, archbishop of Dar-es-Salaam, Tanzania. But with Tardini's approval, he placed Giovanni Battista Montini at the top of his list as a consolation for past injustice and a presage for the future.

However, this did not mean that he intended that his pontificate should be merely 'keeping the chair of Peter warm' for Montini whose eventual return as pope was regarded by the Roman Curia, not without apprehension, as inevitable. He knew that many would continue to think of him as a stop-gap pope whose reign would be characterised by placid inactivity. One 'old prelate' took Capovilla aside and exhorted him: 'Beg the Pope not to dream of writing encyclicals or making too many speeches or canonising too many saints or inventing new festivities for St Peter's Square. Let's have a period of calm' (*Vent'Anni*, pp. 17–18).

The undemanding old prelate would have been delighted that Pope John seemed more interested in reviving lost traditions than starting new ones. He restored the fur bonnet seen in portraits of Renaissance popes, and preferred it to the white skull cap, which kept slipping off. He fussed over his coat of arms. Mgr Bruno Heim, the heraldry expert who had been a colleague in Paris, instructed to include a lion of St Mark's, Venice, depicted the beast rampant, with claws extended. 'Don't you think' asked the Pope, 'that he's too fierce, a little too – er –Germanic?' (Trevor, p. 268). He wanted his lion to be 'more human'.

Pope John's love of tradition came out in the preparations for his coronation, fixed for November 4, feast of St Charles Borromeo, the man to whom he had devoted so much midnight oil. He would have the full ceremonial, complete with the Franciscans burning smoking flax to remind him of mortality, (*'Sic transit gloria mundi'* – 'Thus does the world's glory pass away'), the fans of ostrich plumes, the *sedia gestatoria* or portable chair, and the tiara. Albino Luciani, whom Pope John named bishop of Vittorio Veneto a few weeks later and who would succeed him as John Paul I in 1978, swept away all these traditions. Pope John liked them. Nevertheless, the tiara, symbolising regal power and the temporal claims of the papacy that he was happy to abandon, always seemed incongruous on his head. But he enjoyed pomp. His diary for November 4, 1958 reads simply: 'Wednesday. Grand coronation in St Peter's. The event communicated to the whole world' (*Vent'Anni*, p. 44).

There was, however, one simple innovation which turned out to have crucial importance: Pope John decided to preach a homily at his Coronation Mass. This had never been done before. The ceremony was already immensely long, but Pope John insisted. He went over his prepared text with Mgr Cardinale, who winced over what he thought were certain linguistic 'modernisms'. Formed in the school of Pius XII, Cardinale was accustomed to the curial practice of taking Palazzi's *Dizionario* as the standard authority on usage. He explained this to the Pope, who peered over the top of his spectacles and said: 'Well, if need be, we shall reform *even* Palazzi' (Cardinale). Pope John aimed for a literary style that was simple, direct, unpompous. He had already summoned the evergreen editor of *l'Osservatore Romano*, Count Giuseppe Dalla Torre, now onto his fourth pope, and told him to cease referring to 'the illuminated Holy Father' or 'the most Supreme Pontiff'; and he was to drop phrases like 'as we gathered from the august lips' (Elliott, p. 256). If he meant 'the Pope said' he was to write 'the Pope said'. I shall follow this precept from now on and call him 'the Pope', 'Pope John' or simply 'John'.

As Coronation Day approached, John's worries went beyond questions of style. He felt that since he became pope, he had been neglecting his family. His nephew Don Battista had turned up on his first day as pope, and been gently returned home to Fusigiano (*Vent'Anni*, p. 43). The others mattered more. So on the eve of his Coronation more than thirty brothers and sisters, nephews and nieces, disembarked at Stazione Termini. In sober Sunday suits and black dresses, they fidgeted with their hats as they tried to make conversation with the Vatican officials sent to greet them. They were whisked by bus to Domus Mariae. Then they had their audience. Some of them wept openly. John said: 'Come on now, no crying. After all, what they've done to me is not *so* bad'. He wanted to know how everyone was. Yes, Don Battista had been to see him, had trouble explaining himself to the Swiss Guards, and had got lost. No, he would not be having a job in the Vatican. No, his niece, Sr Angela, would not become his housekeeper. *Sotto voce:* 'One Sr Pasqualina was enough'. So, the mayor of Bergamo wanted to honour his brothers with the title of *Cavalieri della Repubblica Italiana* (Knights of the Italian Republic). It would be better to decline. They were to remain the Pope's brothers, the Pope's family. That should be enough. And after the Coronation they went back to their fields.

The Coronation Mass began at 8 a.m. and lasted for five hours. Mgr Enrico Dante, master of ceremonies, saw to it that everything went according to the rubrics. This was no mean feat considering that the last Coronation had been in 1939. But there was something different about *this* coronation. The forms were the same, but John's homily gave them a different meaning.

Cardinal Nicola Canali had placed the tiara on his head with the age-old formula: 'Know that thou art the father of princes and kings, pontiff of the whole world and Vicar of Christ on earth'. But in his homily John had carefully explained that he wanted to be a good shepherd of the flock, after the pattern of Christ. Because it was so simple, it was revolutionary. Moreover, as John developed his thoughts, he seemed to be contrasting his pontificate, just begun, with that of his predecessor: 'There are those who expect the pontiff to be a statesman, a diplomat, a scholar, the organiser of the collective life of society, or someone whose mind is attuned to every form of modern knowledge' (*Vent'Anni*, p. 56). These expectations had been created by Pius XII, who was often discovered late at night mugging up some new technical subject so that next day he might dazzle his hearers. John would not try to emulate him, partly because he could not but even more because it involved a mistaken idea of the papacy (or in John's orotund Vaticanese, 'betrayed a concept of the Supreme Pontiff that was not fully in conformity with its true ideal'). But what was the alternative? John went on: 'The new Pope, through the events and circumstances of his life, is like the son of Jacob who, meeting with his brothers, burst into tears and said, "I am Joseph, your brother" ' (Genesis 45.4) (*Vent'Anni*, p. 57). Joseph (Giuseppe) was John's second baptismal name. Here he was, as it were, descending from his throne and putting himself on the same level as his brothers. It was a long time since a pope had used such language. It had certainly not been used, and could not be imagined, on the 'august lips' of Pius XII.

Pope John's words would inevitably be interpreted as a repudiation of his predecessor. This was not his intention; but it was the effect. He was trying to say that he would not compete with Pius and that Pius should not be admired for the wrong reasons: his true greatness was to be sought not in his genius but rather in the way he had acted as Good Shepherd. But it didn't come out quite like that. He seemed to be emphasising that his pontificate would be very different, for 'every pontificate takes on its character, its face as it were, from the supreme pontiff who embodies it and gives it its special features' (*ibid.*). The effect of this November 4, 1958 homily was practical as well as theoretical: the idea that a pope should be above all 'pastoral' was used as a yardstick in the 1978 conclaves.

Two days after his Coronation, Pope John met the Roman and international press. This was another 'first'. John had the press eating out of his hand. Some tough-minded journalists admitted, afterwards and in private, to tears. It was not so much what he had to say as his evident friendliness and warmth that won them over. He had been reading the papers a lot, he told them, 'not out of vanity but because it gives me great pleasure to see the interest which the world had in the papacy and also' – with a broad smile – 'to learn the secrets of the conclave' (Negro, Silvio, in *Corriere della Sera*, November 7, 1958). But his remarks had a sting in the tail: 'It seems that though the efforts of the journalists have been remarkable, the silence of the cardinals has been even more remarkable'. The subtle Silvio Negro, then the reigning prince of Vaticanologists, pointed out that the Pope spoke only of the silence of the *cardinals*, and did not mention the *conclavistas* or attendants who were also inside the conclave.

Negro noted that Pope John looked younger than his seventy-six years – he would be seventy-seven within the month, that his gestures were vigorous, his eyes twinkling and that, far from being overwhelmed by his awesome office, he seemed to relish being pope. He had a quality that can only be called gusto, which was also seen in his liturgical style: he incensed the altar *allegro con bria*. What most struck Negro, however, was the fact that the Pope was improvising and did not have a prepared text. This was a great contrast with Pius XII who always wrote out his speeches in full, and once confessed: 'When I speak, I see only the pages in front of me'. John, when not blinded by television lights, evidently saw the people who were there, not the pages he did not have.

He told the journalists his favourite story about Joseph meeting his brothers and said: 'I am your brother, too, even if before God I am the first of brothers and as pastor have to guide my brothers'. Negro concluded his article: 'His face is constantly illumined by a confident and humorous smile. The listener feels that he is gradually caught up in a family atmosphere and that he is taking part in a conversation' (*Corriere della Sera*, November 7, 1958).

This first favourable impression remained and grew. It is the reason why Pope John had such a good press, especially in the 'honeymoon' period of his pontificate. (Later, the right-wing press would declare him to be politically naïve.) But once again, contrast heightened the effect. After the gravely hieratic and austere Pius XII, a fat and genial 'brother Pope' was astonishing. Moreover, the spontaneity of his approach meant that he was constantly unpredictable, and therefore 'newsworthy'. That the Pope should walk in the Vatican gardens and actually chat with the gardeners – they had been instructed to vanish on the rare occasions that Pius XII went for a walk – seemed like a major event: the papacy had been reclaimed by humanity.

The Roman Curia was less easily impressed than the journalists. Its members read the enthusiastic stories in the press about the 'peasant Pope' who was so poor that he had to carry his shoes to school. They were well aware that a process of mythologisation starts as soon as someone is elected Pope: talent becomes genius, and ordinariness is proof of humanity. Their ingrained professionalism made them sceptical of such romancing, and the 'revisionist' remarks at the Coronation Mass had startled some.

Then Pope John took an initiative to get the Curia on his side. The key department, the Secretariat of State, was summoned for an audience on November 17. Some of them, Tardini above all, had given him orders when he was in Turkey and France. John confirmed them all in their posts, said he needed them, emphasised that a 'pastoral' pontificate needed a 'pastoral' Curia, and let them into a secret: he had decided that Tardini and Montini would be made cardinals along with twenty-one others on the following December 18 (*Vent'Anni*, p. 103). He told them this well ahead of the official announcement in *l'Osservatore Romano*. So they enjoyed the pleasure of being in the know. He didn't have to tell the Curia in advance. It was a simple ploy, but it worked.

On Sunday, November 23, Pope John 'took possession' of his cathedral, the Basilica of St John Lateran. In his mind, it was an event almost equal in importance to his Coronation; and it lasted just as long. He describes the day in his diary:

> November 23, Sunday. One of the most wonderful days of my life. Took possession of my cathedral of St John Lateran. Everything beautiful and solemn . . .
>
> The return from the Lateran to the Vatican: simply triumphal. The homage of the Roman people, all along the route, to their new Bishop of Rome, was moving and unexpected, and therefore all the more precious. On the way there and back arranged to be accompanied by cardinals Tisserant, the dean, and Pizzardo. They wept with emotion. All I could do was remain in a state of humiliation, a sacrificial offering for my people; in abandonment, but with great and confident simplicity (*Vent'Anni*, p. 44).

John had been brought up at a time when Popes could not even leave the Vatican to test the public response. Rome was not just an indifferent backcloth for him. It was alive with memories. The new relationship with the Italian Republic, now firmly wedded to democracy, allowed Pope John finally to relinquish all temporal claims and present himself as *pastor*. In practice it would mean a disengagement from national politics. That theme will be explored in a later chapter. But withdrawal from the political arena did not imply either silence or abdication. The essential tasks of every priest and bishop in the Church was to teach. 'Go and teach all nations' was the mandate given by Christ.

But there are many forms of teaching. Pius XII had been a great didactic Pope, who had exalted his own *magisterium* more than any pope since Pio Nono. Pope John, however, was more concerned with catechesis than with *magisterium*. Roman liturgy was often no more than a baroque spectacle. But he wanted the liturgy to teach. Inert and passive presence were not enough. This was to be the basis of the Council's liturgical reform. Those who say Pope John would not have approved of it do not know their man: he always linked together liturgy and catechesis, worship and teaching, the Word proclaimed in the Gospel and the Word shared out in Communion, or, in his language, the *book* and the *chalice*.

This emphasis on catechesis rather than *magisterium* was novel. The difference in the two approaches can be put this way: while *magisterium* lectures the world from the outside, catechesis takes people where they are and seeks to ground the Gospel in the thick of human life. Pope John was more concerned with communicability than with orthodoxy.

His visitors noticed the difference in papal style. He didn't impose on people. If an audience with Pius XII was, as Mgr (later Cardinal) Antonio Samorè admitted, 'rather like undergoing a particularly stiff oral examination', meeting John was more like chatting with one's favourite grandfather. There was little concern for protocol. Cardinal Joseph Martin, archbishop of Rouen, told the following story from this early period: 'I apologised for calling him "your eminence" instead of "your holiness". But he said there was nothing to apologise for, all the more since he'd changed his title so many times in the course of his life: don Angelo, monsignore, your grace, excellency, eminence, holiness. "But now", he said with a smile, "I'm through with changing titles"' (*Letture*, p. 390).

He brought the same informality to his meetings with political leaders. His first audience with a head of state was with the ill-fated Shah of Iran, Mohammed Reza Pahlavi Aryamehr, then still on the way to the zenith of his power. John said to Capovilla: 'We'll see how the conversation goes. I can tell him about the time I saw his father in the Piazza Quirinale when I was in my twenties . . . After all, he's going to be far more worried about making a good impression than I am. Making a good impression is none of my business; but he probably cares about it' (IME, p. 67). His diary was now crammed. He hardly had time to notice his seventy-seventh birthday on November 25. He received Paul Henri Spaak, Secretary-General of NATO, in the afternoon. Next day it was the turn of Igor Stravinsky, the exiled Russian composer. He had been in office for just over a month. He felt the need to retire to Castelgandolfo to pray for an hour in the room where Pius XII died.

But before that there was one event that added some more brush strokes to the portrait that was gradually being filled out. He went along to the Lateran Athenaeum, the modern equivalent of the old Roman seminary where he had studied more than fifty years before. It was another informal 'conversation', slightly rambling, full of joky stories about eccentric professors of his day. *L'Osservatore Romano* provided only an inadequate paraphrase. Capovilla preserved John's own version, and sent it as an end-of-year present to *Sursum Corda*, the Roman seminary magazine (*Lettere*, pp. 85–7):

> In the last month, since October 28, when my name and official title were changed, I've had this experience: I hear people talking about the Pope, in indirect or direct speech. For example, 'The Pope should be told this' or 'This will have to be dealt with by the Pope'. When I hear this I still think of the holy father Pope Pius XII, whom I venerated and loved so much, forgetting that the person they are talking about is *me*, who chose to be called John.
>
> Very slowly I'm getting used to the new forms of speech involved in my new ministry. Yes, I am, most unworthily, 'the servant of the servants of God', because the Lord willed it; the Lord, not I. But every time I hear someone address me as 'Your Holiness' or 'Holy Father' you can't imagine how embarrassed and thoughtful it makes me (*Lettere*, p. 87).

This 'conversation' at the Lateran Athenaeum was widely if selectively reported. But the next day, Friday November 28, there was a private conversation that remained undisclosed until well after his death. John was walking in the Vatican Gardens towards sunset, as 'the dome of St Peter's took on fairy-tale hues' in Capovilla's phrase (*Letture*, p. 352). He said to his secretary:

> A month has gone by and everything has happened with great naturalness . . . I feel in my heart the problems of the whole world. But my soul is at peace. If a commission of cardinals came to tell me that, all things considered, I should return to Venice, it would not cost me anything to retire (*Letture*, p. 252).

Capovilla interrupted to object rather pedantically that since he had already appointed

Giovanni Urbani as patriarch of Venice, he could not return there. 'Very well', said John, 'I'd happily retire to Sotto il Monte'. But he was not really thinking of resignation. He continued, more gravely: 'I'm not afraid of opposition and do not refuse suffering. I think of myself as the last of all, but I have in mind a programme of work and I'm not fussing about it any more. In fact, I am pretty well decided' (*ibid.*). He was talking about the Council, but so far very few knew about his project. This decision, the most important of his pontificate, was based on a realistic appraisal of the likely opposition, and was partly a way of overcoming or circumventing it. The notion that a group of cardinals might recommend his abdication was fanciful, but it had just enough truth to be uncomfortable. He needed to be assured not so much that he had God on his side, but that he was on God's side.

On Christmas Day he went to the Bambin Gesù children's hospital and the next day to the Regina Coeli prison down by the Tiber. This was where his reputation took off and soared. In the otherwise dull Christmas period the world media saw the visits as another manifestation of the approachably human Pope who confessed (though this was censored by *l'Osservatore Romano*) that one of his brothers had been caught poaching, and embraced a murderer who had asked, 'Can there be forgiveness for me?'

John's diary expresses his genuine surprise at the remarkable effect of his visits:

> Friday 26. My visit to the Regina Coeli prison. Much calm on my side, but great astonishment in the Roman, Italian and international press. I was hemmed in on all sides: authorities, photographers, prisoners, warders – but the Lord was close. These are the consolations of the Pope: the exercise of the fourteen works of mercy. . . .
>
> The press, Italian and international, continues to exalt my gesture in visiting the prison yesterday. And for me it was such a simple and natural thing (*Vent'Anni*, pp. 45–6).

The long-term importance of these visits was that they illustrated what he meant by saying that he would be first and foremost a 'pastor'. In such matters, example counts for more than laborious explanations. He had found a lived parable of goodness. And the world responded.

Some saw a still deeper meaning in his spontaneous actions. An unnamed 'writer' copied out a text from *Il Santo (The Saint)*, the novel by Antonio Fogazzaro that had been placed on the Index of Forbidden Books by St Pius X. He sent it to Pope John as a thank-you offering. It read:

> Vicar of Christ, there is something else that I beg of you. I am a sinner unworthy to be compared with the saints, but the Spirit can speak even through the most tainted lips. If a woman (St Catherine of Siena) could beseech a pope to return to Rome (from Avignon), so I can beseech your holiness to go out of the Vatican. Go out, Holy Father. But the first time, at least the first time, go out for one of the works of your ministry. Daily Lazarus suffers and dies, so go out and meet Lazarus. In every poor suffering creature Christ cries out for help (*Transizione*, p. 17).

So Pope John ended 1958, a year like any other year except that in it he chanced to become pope. He was astonished by the world's response to his simple gestures and deeply grateful to God. In his first ninety days he had, in famous phrase, 'flung open the windows of the Vatican'. Capovilla, this time behaving like a wet blanket, declares that he never heard Pope

John use this expression and that he did not like draughts (*Transizione*, p. 69). Another myth exploded. But Capovilla concedes that it was spiritually true. The 'world' was suddenly interested in the papacy again. Simply by being faithful to himself and the spiritual tradition in which he had been brought up, he began to transform the papal office and the way in which it was perceived.

But he had not yet unveiled how he proposed to carry the universal Church along with him in the process of transformation. The means chosen was the summoning of an ecumenical Council. John had been thinking about it in his first three months in office. It was the hidden, unspoken agenda, the inner face of his life as he struggled to discern what the Holy Spirit wanted for his Church.

Chapter 14

The inspiration of the Council

Pius is not the last of the Popes . . . Let us have faith, and a new pope and a reassembled council may trim the boat.

(John Henry Newman, writing to Alfred Plummer, April 3, 1871, quoted in *Infallibility in the Church*, Darton, Longman and Todd, London, 1968, p. 77)

After the Christmas visits to hospitals and the Regina Coeli prison, the 'image' of Roncalli as 'good Pope John' was firmly established in the public mind. In the more discriminating world of the Roman Curia he was seen as accessible, unpompous and willing to learn. He restored the audiences a *tabella* – abolished by Pius XII – in which heads of Congregations saw him at regular intervals to discuss routine business. Wherever he could, he delegated authority. The result was that the Curia became more efficient, a fact which the British Minister to the Holy See, Sir Marcus Cheke, grudgingly acknowledged: 'Under Pius XII the Vatican was chaotic; John XXIII made the organisation work' (Lawrence, p. 8). But all this was compatible with the placid, 'transitional' Pope envisaged by some of his cardinal electors. What hardly anyone realised was that Pope John had the idea of summoning a Council right from the start of his pontificate.

We have already seen that Cardinals Ernesto Ruffini and Alfredo Ottaviani claimed to have put the idea to him even earlier. They raised it during the conclave. This is not at all unlikely. In 1939 Ruffini, then secretary of the Congregation for Seminaries and Universities, urged the newly elected Pius XII to summon a Council. The problems to be resolved, he averred, 'were as abundant as they were at the Council of Trent' (see Weber, Francis J., 'Pope Pius XII and the Vatican Council', in *The American Benedictine Review*, September, 1970, p. 421). A Council was Ruffini's favourite nostrum for putting the Church to rights. He and Ottaviani were also associated with the 1948 project for a Council. It was not surprising that they should return to the idea ten years later. It was in the air.

Capovilla, however, states quite clearly: 'I do not find it hard to believe that Cardinal Ruffini had talked about a council to Pope John, either directly or indirectly. But the fact remains that Pope John always said he made his decision in perfect freedom, and "without anyone having previously talked to him about the matter"' (Capovilla, letter to the author, April 15, 1981).

John's own subsequent accounts of when and how the idea of the Council came to him have muddled and misled everyone. But Capovilla is emphatic in saying that he first mentioned 'the necessity of holding a council' on October 30, 1958, just two days after his election (*Lettere*, p. 746). This was obviously not yet anything so firm as a 'decision', but neither was it merely a vague idea casually thrown out to test the wind. By November 2, we have

156

the first *documented* mention of the idea: in a memo after an audience with Cardinal Ruffini, John noted that they had discussed the possibility of calling a Council (*Lettere*, p. 267). So even before his Coronation on November 4, the idea of calling a Council was already beginning to possess him.

It grew naturally out of his conversations with the non-Roman cardinals, his electors, as one by one they came to say farewell. In his diary he said that these conversations taught him about 'the expectations of the world and the good impression that the new Pope could make. I listened, noted everything down, and continued to wonder what to do – concretely and immediately' (*Utopia*, Italian, p. 313). There were endless variations on the same theme: in pastoral, ecumenical, juridical and Church-state matters, he realised, the Roman Curia and the local Churches were poles apart. As he faced this panorama of problems, Pope John began to think about a Council. Becoming pope had not magically endowed him with instant solutions for the universal Church. The best course would be to get all the bishops thinking about these problems together.

Thus the idea of summoning a Council is pushed right back to the first days after Pope John's election. This changes our perspective on both the pontificate and the Council. The Council was not 'accidental' to the pontificate or a kind of afterthought; it was co-terminous with the pontificate as a whole, and acted as its goal, policy, programme and content.

But not everyone consulted at this early stage approved of the idea. Capovilla was initially opposed to it, and argued very sensibly that for a man of John's age a Council would be a hazardous project entailing a lot of hard work. The more prudent course would be to build the pontificate on his strengths, in particular 'the talent or charism of paternity that you undoubtedly possess' (*Utopia*, Italian, p. 314). John went away to think about this in prayer. A few days later after evening rosary with the papal household, he answered Capovilla's objection: 'The trouble is, Don Loris, that you're still not detached enough from self– you're still concerned with having a good reputation. Only when the *ego* has been trampled underfoot can one be fully and truly free. You're not yet free, Don Loris' (*ibid.*). Capovilla's alternative suggestion about 'the charism of paternity' smacked too much of the 'personality cult'.

Once Pope John had fixed his sights on the project, he moved swiftly towards the fateful decision. On November 21 he went to Castelgandolfo accompanied only by his secretary and confessor for a week's rest and retreat. The subject of the Council was discussed again in the car. By November 28, John's mind was almost made up, and he had counted the cost. But still the project remained top secret. It was restricted to a few trusted friends.

But could the Council be made to work? How would it be organised? Vatican I had been interrupted by war in 1870. Now there were three times as many bishops, and that would create logistical problems. Pope John already had a good knowledge of conciliar history, but further studies were done in December, 1958 and January, 1959 to see what could be learned from 'the last time'. He soon became convinced of one thing: six years had elapsed between the announcement of Vatican I and its actual celebration. At seventy-seven, he was too old to contemplate such a leisurely time-scale, and, anyway, modern methods of communication and travel made it unnecessary. A way would have to be found of speeding up the process of consultation and drafting.

The reference to Vatican I also raised the question of the subject-matter of the proposed

Council. Vatican I was a truncated Council. It had dealt with the relation of faith and reason and defined the primacy and infallibility of Peter and his successors (whom it nowhere calls 'popes'). It had not had time to consider the role of bishops and how they related to the primacy. This resulted in a lop-sided view of the Church. The balance would have to be adjusted. However, while this was the starting-point, the Church and the world had changed so much in the intervening period that Vatican II would also be a council in its own right, and not simply an appendix to the unfinished Vatican I.

Further research among the archives brought to light two facts that had been unknown outside a small circle of adepts: the idea of calling a Council had already been considered twice in the twentieth century. In 1923 Pius XI asked to see the files on Vatican I – like Roncalli, he was an archivist. But to everyone's embarrassment they could not be found. They were eventually discovered stuffed in an old cupboard under a disused staircase (Negro, Silvio, *Corriere della Sera*, January 26, 1959). Pius XI's notion was that after the holocaust of the Great War, in which Catholics found themselves on opposite sides, a Council would powerfully display and reinforce Catholic unity. But he dropped the idea pending the resolution of 'the Roman Question' (*Letture*, p. 262).

Pius XII's project was much more developed. It began at the initiative of Ruffini, since 1945 archbishop of Palermo, Sicily, and Ottaviani, now assessor at the Holy Office. In February, 1948 they wrote a memo setting out the reasons for calling a council:

1) To clarify and define a number of doctrinal points, since a mass of errors are abroad on philosophy, theology and moral and social questions.

2) Then there are the great problems posed by Communism and caused by the recent war, not to mention questions that could be raised about the methods and means that could be morally used in any future war.

3) The Code of Canon Law needs *aggiornamento* [*sic*] and reform.

4) Directives are needed in other areas of ecclesiastical discipline such as culture and Catholic Action etc . . .

5) The Assumption could be defined (Caprile, I, 1, pp. 15–16. Numbering added).

Pius XII was interested. He wanted to define the Assumption anyhow. And in 1948 as in 1923 there were the same reasons for displaying the unity of Catholics after a murderous war had driven them apart. But he hesitated because of the difficulty of lodging so many bishops and the harmful effects of their absence from their dioceses. However, he was sufficiently committed to instruct the Holy Office to set up five secret commissions to make preparatory studies.

Pope John brooded over this material, treasure trove for the archivist. But now it had far more than a mere historical interest for him. It threw light on how his own plan was likely to be received. For Ruffini, the instigator, and Ottaviani, the organiser of the 1948 project, were still very much alive and influential in 1959. Their views carried weight in the Curia. But as he read on, Pope John became despondent as he realised that their idea of a Council was not at all what he had in mind. This can be seen simply by looking at what the two most important commissions wanted to put on the agenda.

Among the topics proposed by the 'Speculative Theology' commission had been false philosophies (idealism, existentialism, new gnosticisms), the methods of dissidents (dogmatic minimalism; convergence of doctrines; treating Catholic and heterodox doctrines as equal) and errors on the Mystical Body. The 'Practical theology' commission offered to study (among other topics) onanism, periodic continence, artificial fecundation, sterilisation, psychoanalysis; and the validity of baptism administered by a non-Catholic minister who is in error on the nature of the sacrament (Caprile, I, 1, p. 17).

In Pius XII's time, one group argued that a very short Council, say three to four weeks, would be enough to demonstrate Catholic unity and cohesion, and that its main business would be to condemn contemporary errors and define, by acclamation, the Assumption. Their opponents replied that a Council organised in this fashion would be 'untraditional' and could hardly be taken seriously. Meanwhile the sixty-five selected bishops who had already been consulted responded with some enthusiasm and proposed all manner of confusing new topics for inclusion on the agenda. Pius XII began to weary of the whole affair. He decided that a Council was unnecessary. Anything a Council could do he could do better – and more economically. So in 1950 he defined the Assumption and condemned contemporary errors in his encyclical *Humani Generis*. The work done in the 'Speculative Theology' commission had not been entirely wasted: the errors they had gathered found their way into *Humani Generis*.

This Council-that-never-was contained important lessons for Pope John as he thought about his own project. The whole approach was wrong. It betrayed an obsession with continuing the battle against 'Modernism'. From the start John determined that his council would be open to wider aspirations and would not just be negative. He expressed this by saying that its purpose was 'pastoral'. This meant it would not be primarily concerned with doctrinal questions but with the new needs of the Church and the world. One feature of this documentation convinced him that he was right: the replies of the sixty-five bishops showed that there was in the Church a genuine hunger for a Council. If a handful of bishops felt that way in 1949, then it was likely that a consultation with all the world's bishops a decade later would evoke an even more enthusiastic response. Thus what led Pius to reject the idea of a Council confirmed John's judgement that it was more than ever necessary.

Pope John's decision to hold a Council crystallised in December 1958 as he discerned the spirits and browsed among the archives. On January 9, he met Don Giovanni Rossi who had been secretary to his hero, Cardinal Ferrari, forty years before. John said: 'I want to tell you something marvellous, but you must promise to keep it secret. Last night I had the great idea of holding a council'. Rossi murmured his approval. What can one say in such circumstances? But John's next remark took him by surprise: 'You know, it's not true to say that the Spirit assists the Pope'. Rossi thought he had misheard, but John put his mind at rest when he went on: 'The Holy Spirit doesn't help the Pope. I'm simply his helper. He did everything. The council is his idea' (Rossi, in *Utopia*, Italian, p. 315).

There was one other matter to be dealt with. On January 25, 1959, John announced not only the convening of the Council but also a synod for the diocese of Rome and the *aggiornamento* of canon law. Many commentators thought it was incongruous to yoke the three items together; they were so clearly disproportionate in importance. Where did the other two ideas come from? Pericle Felici reported:

The other two undertakings were suggested to him by others after he had begun talking about the Council. 'They told me', he said, 'that a Synod for the diocese of Rome would be a good preparation for the Council. Fine, I replied, let's hold a Synod. Someone else said to me that it would be a good time to think about revising the Code of Canon Law because it is rather out of date. I said, that's good, let's think about the Code. But in any case, let's make the Council our main concern' (*l'Osservatore Romano*, June 3, 1973, '*Il Primo Incontro con Papa Giovanni*': the conversation took place on February 10, 1960).

From this we may conclude that the two other projects, though far from trivial, were strictly subordinated in Pope John's mind to the council.

The next step, which was far from easy, was to inform Cardinal Domenico Tardini, his Secretary of State, which he did on January 20. Tardini's office memo, written that same evening, is couched in his customary laconic style:

Audience with the Holy Father who told me that yesterday afternoon had been for him a period of meditation and recollection. As the programme of his pontificate, he has thought of three things:

Roman Synod, Ecumenical Council, *Aggiornamento* of the Code of Canon Law.

He will announce these three things to the cardinals after the ceremony at St Paul's next Sunday. I said:

1. that these were three splendid initiatives

2. that the idea of making the first announcement to the cardinals was very opportune because it is new but it links up with ancient papal traditions and will no doubt be most pleasing to the Sacred College (Nicolini, p. 187).

Pope John's diary, likewise written that same evening, substantially confirms the Tardini memo:

His immediate response was the most gratifying surprise that I could have expected: 'Oh, that really is an idea, an enlightening and holy idea. It comes straight from heaven, Holy Father. You will have to work on it, develop it and publicise it. It will be a great blessing for the whole world'. I didn't need anything more. I was happy. I thanked the Lord for my idea which now received its first seal of approval here below – a pledge of that divine blessing which I was humbly confident would not be lacking (*Utopia*, Italian, p. 316).

What Tardini privately thought, we do not yet know. His biographer drops a tantalising hint that there is more to be said about the January 20 meeting than has been recorded. He quotes Tardini's diary account, given above, and then mysteriously goes on: 'This does not mean that his pen stopped here. There is reason to believe that he filled several more pages which await their moment to emerge from the silence of the archives' (Nicolini, p. 188, fn. 3). The Vatican Archives have a seventy-five year rule. All will be revealed in the year 2034.

The trouble with this outline of what happened on January 20, 1959, is that it is flatly contradicted by what Pope John said in 1962. And since these 1962 accounts were the first to be publicly known – the same-day extract from Pope John's diary was not published until 1973 – they have become the authorised version. Yet they are thoroughly misleading.

Pope John was more likely to have got it right on the day itself than three years later. John misremembered, certainly, and his unconscious editing of his memories throws light on what he wanted to believe about the Council – that the idea was an inspiration – than on what exactly happened on January 20, 1959.

The contradiction emerges in an address to Venetian pilgrims on May 8, 1962, when he told them how the Council came about:

> Where did the idea of the Ecumenical Council come from? How did it develop? The truth is that the idea and even more its realisation were so unforeseen as to seem unlikely.
>
> A question was raised in a meeting I had with the Secretary of State, Cardinal Tardini, which led on to a discussion about the way the world was plunged into so many grave anxieties and troubles. One thing we noted was that though everyone said they wanted peace and harmony, unfortunately conflicts grew more acute and threats multiplied. What should the Church do? Should Christ's mystical barque simply drift along, tossed this way and that by the ebb and flow of the tides? Instead of issuing new warnings, shouldn't she stand out as a beacon of light? What could that exemplary light be?
>
> My interlocutor listened with reverence and attention. Suddenly my soul was illumined by a great idea which came precisely at that moment and which I welcomed with ineffable confidence in the divine Teacher. And there sprang to my lips a word that was solemn and committing. My voice uttered it for the first time: a Council (DMC, IV, p. 258 and *Letture*, pp. 264–5).

Again on September 15, 1962, just three weeks before the Council was due to start, he wrote in his *Journal*:

> Without having thought of it before, I put forward, in one of my first talks with my Secretary of State, on January 20, 1959, the idea of an ecumenical council, a diocesan synod and the revision of the code of canon law, all this being quite contrary to any previous supposition or idea of my own on this subject. I was the first to be surprised by my proposal, which was entirely my own idea (*Journal*, p. 349).

These passages have embarrassed commentators. 'John's 1962 descriptions', says Bonnot tartly, 'are ingenuous but seem incompatible with the facts' (Bonnot, p. 59). Capovilla resorts to casuistry and explains that in the phrase, 'without having thought of it before', the 'before' refers to the time before he became Pope (*Letture*, p. 266).

John had told Tardini on Tuesday of the Octave of Prayer for Christian Unity. He still had to tell the world. But he was now bubbling over with enthusiasm and could no longer contain his secret. On Thursday, January 22, 1959, he gave an audience to Giulio Andreotti. In a vain attempt to avoid political interpretations being placed upon the visit, the whole Andreotti family was invited. The two younger children, aged five and seven, bounced about on the gold and damask chairs, while the thirteen- and nine-year-olds looked on with mature scorn. John asked, 'Have you noticed any changes?' Andreotti confessed that he had not. John pointed out that he had had all the doors of the cupboards around the walls removed; whenever he had been in this room as nuncio or patriarch it reminded him of a hat-shop. But this light-hearted opening was only the prelude to more serious matters (Andreotti pp. 77–8). While the younger children were still cavorting about, Pope John revealed his plan: a

Council of the universal Church. He said that he thought two years should be enough to prepare it, but Tardini disagreed, quoting the example of Vatican I that needed six years' preparation. At his age, he could not accept such a long time. The Andreotti family – those who had been listening – were sworn to secrecy for another three days.

Meanwhile the Mass at St Paul's-without-the-walls had already been announced without the slightest hint that anything of significance would take place. Readers of the Saturday, January 24 edition of *l'Osservatore Romano* learned that the Pope would proceed to the Basilica of St Paul's and there recite a prayer he had specially composed for 'the Church of Silence'. The phrase referred to the persecuted Churches of Eastern Europe and China.

When the day came, John was up before dawn, as usual. He said Mass and attended Capovilla's Mass in his private chapel, remaining there in prayer until 9.30. During breakfast he cast an eye over the newspapers and the reports from the Secretariat of State but said nothing. At 10 o'clock he went down by lift. A car was waiting to take him to St Paul's. On the way he was uncharacteristically silent. The photographs of his arrival at St Paul's show him anxious and tense. He was genuinely apprehensive about how the cardinals would react. Some of them already knew – Tardini had been authorised to inform them – but others would have to wait until after the ceremony in the Basilica. It took longer than anticipated and was not over till 1 o'clock.

Then the seventeen cardinals made their way to the chapter-room of the abbey on the first floor. Pope John's address began at 1.10 and lasted half an hour. Pope John tried hard to speak in his usual intimate tone. He wanted to open his heart, trusting in their goodness and understanding, and said he would confine himself to a few points. He went on about how the city of Rome had changed since their student days. All this was listened to with impassivity.

He moved on from the city to the world, and painted an uncharacteristically gloomy picture of the 'world' using lurid and dualistic colours. He was saddened by those who 'abuse and endanger human freedom, reject faith in Christ the Son of God, redeemer of the world and founder of the Church, devoting themselves entirely to so-called terrestrial goods under the inspiration of the one whom the Gospels call the prince of darkness' (Alberigo, p. 276). He was here faithfully echoing the Manichaean interpretation of Communism that was routine under Pius XII. He still seemed to be using borrowed language when he went on to deplore 'the lack of discipline and the loss of the old moral order' which had, he claimed, reduced the Church's capacity to deal with error (*ibid.*, pp. 276–7). This pessimism about the present state of the world – sunk in error and in the grip of Satan – so contradicts Pope John's usual attitudes that some explanation is called for. The simplest is that this address had one precise goal: to win over the cardinals to his project of a Council. To assist this process he reflected the views he knew they held.

Pope John maintained the suspense almost until the end of his address. He told them he had reached a decision. It was based on tradition. There were periods of renewal (*rinnovamento*) when the Church sought greater clarity in its thinking' (he did not say 'doctrine'), 'a strengthening of the bond of unity, and greater spiritual fervour' (Alberigo, p. 277). Having defined the three aims of the Council, the moment had at last come to use the word:

Venerable brothers and our beloved sons! Trembling with emotion, and yet with humble resolution, we put before you the proposal of a double celebration: a diocesan synod for Rome and an ecumenical council for the universal Church (*ibid.*).

Pope John added just one thing more. He asked everyone to pray for

a good start, a successful implementation and a happy outcome for those projects that will involve hard work for the enlightenment, the edification and the joy of the Christian people, and *a friendly and renewed invitation to our brothers of the separated Christian Churches to share with us in this banquet of grace and brotherhood,* to which so many souls in every corner of the world aspire (*Utopia*, Italian, p. 322, italics added).

That was what the Cardinals heard Pope John say. But that is not what appeared in the authorised version of the speech. The clause italicised above became 'a renewed invitation to the faithful of separated communities likewise to follow Us, in good will, in this search for unity and grace' (see Hales, p. 98). These are allowed to belong to communities (which is undeniable) but not to *Churches* (which carries a theological load). And instead of 'sharing in the banquet of grace and brotherhood' they are exhorted to *search for* unity and grace as though they had no inkling of them. Though the overall meaning was just about maintained, the edited version was much less friendly in tone and left other Christians perplexed about whether they were being taken seriously and to what they were being invited. The edge of Pope John's ecumenical commitment was blunted by timorous censors. Not for the last time.

The seventeen cardinals were unresponsive to his dramatic announcement. For all they appeared to care, he might have been reading out his laundry list. He was bitterly disappointed. He said so plainly: 'Humanly speaking, we would have expected that the cardinals, after listening to our address, might have crowded round to express their approval and good wishes' (Caprile, I, 1, p. 51). But they did nothing of the kind. John later charitably tried to explain that they had been stunned into silence and needed time to gather their wits. Later still, he contrived to rewrite the whole scene. By the time he addressed the opening session of the Council on October 11, 1962, he believed that the simple words, 'an ecumenical council', had worked a kind of miracle: 'It (the announcement) was completely unexpected and like a flash of heavenly light, shedding sweetness in eyes and hearts. At the same time it gave rise to great fervour throughout the world in the expectation of holding the Council' (Abbott, pp. 711–12). That may have been true of the world-wide response to the Council. But among the cardinals who were actually present on January 25, 1959, as John noted at the time, 'there was a devout and impressive silence' (Rynne, p. 2).

In this impressive and yet disappointing silence Pope John gave his blessing, left the chapter house, descended the staircase, got into his car, registration number SCV 1, and was greeted with applause all the way back to the Vatican. But that happened every time he went out. Capovilla asked him how he felt. He replied: 'It's not a matter of my personal feelings. We are embarked on the will of the Lord . . . Now I need silence and recollection. I feel tired of everyone, of everything'.

Despite Pope John's insistence that the cardinals should be the first to know, the news was out even before he began to speak. At 10 o'clock that morning, just as John was getting into his lift, the Vatican Press Office received a statement from the Secretariat of State which was to be released at 12.30. It was assumed that by this time the Pope would at least have started his address. But, as we have seen, he did not begin speaking until 1.10. But the journalists who haunted the Vatican had to read the laconic communiqué very carefully to discover its significance. The key passage read:

> The Holy Father, inspired by the age-old traditions of the Church, announced three events of the greatest importance: a diocesan Synod for Rome, an ecumenical Council for the Universal Church, and the *aggiornamento* of the Code of Canon Law, to be preceded by the promulgation of the Oriental Code (Caprile, I, 1, p. 51).

The press hand-out was given in *l'Osservatore Romano* the next day. While the page one lead story was about Pope John's anti-Communist speech in the Basilica, the news about the Council was relegated to an inside page. Thus the process of cutting the Council down to size began on the very day it was announced. It was so successful that in New York Cardinal Francis J. Spellman was not even sure that his old buddy the Pope really wanted a Council. He said: 'I do not believe that the Pope wanted to convoke a Council, but he was pushed into it by people who misconstrued what he said' (Elliott, p. 290).

Spellman was very far away, but no such excuses applied to Cardinal Giacomo Lercaro, archbishop of Bologna, usually regarded as the most 'progressive' of the Italian bishops. He was sceptical and withering:

> How dare he summon a council after one hundred years, and only three months after his election? Pope John has been rash and impulsive. His inexperience and lack of culture brought him to this pass, to this paradox. An event like this will ruin his already shaky health, and make the whole edifice of his supposed moral and theological virtues come tumbling down (Gorresio, quoted by Dreyfus, p. 205).

It was just as well that these remarks were not made public until nine years later. By then Lercaro had made handsome amends. He became the architect of the Council's liturgical reforms and the principal target of right-wing attacks. ('After Martin Luther', wrote Tito Cassani in 1967, 'the most formidable menace to the Church's unity and integrity is Cardinal Lercaro'.) In 1959 Lercaro was not alone in thinking that Pope John was making a grievous mistake in calling a Council. It was the standard opinion in the Roman Curia.

It was also the immediate judgement of Giovanni Battista Montini in Milan. On the evening of the day Pope John announced the Council, Montini called his old mentor, the Oratorian Fr Giulio Bevilacqua, and said: 'This holy old boy doesn't seem to realise what a hornets' nest he's stirring up'. 'Don't worry, Don Battista', replied Bevilacqua, 'let it be, the Holy Spirit is still awake in the Church' (Fappani–Molinari, p. 171). At least someone had understood what Pope John was trying to do.

Chapter 15

The struggle for the Council

'Where shall I begin, please your majesty', he asked. 'Begin at the beginning',
the King said gravely, 'and go on till you come to the end: then stop.

(Lewis Carroll, *Alice in Wonderland*)

The far-sighted Cardinal Giovanni Battista Montini soon overcame his hesitations about the hornets' nest that was being stirred up, and became an enthusiastic and tireless defender of the Council. But he warned that it could give rise to 'expectations, dreams, curiosity, utopias, velleities of every kind and countless fantasies'. This comment seems cold-waterish. But in this same pastoral letter to the diocese of Milan, Montini put his finger on the essential truth about Pope John's initiative: 'It seems that he had divined a hidden expectation not only on the part of the episcopal college but of the entire Catholic world as well. A flame of enthusiasm swept over the whole Church. He understood immediately, perhaps by inspiration, that by calling a Council he would release unparalleled vital forces in the Church' (*Church*, p. 156).

But the enthusiasm and energies generated by the announcement of the Council still had to be harnessed to the drudgery of preparing it. Yet very little seemed to be happening between January 25, 1959, and Whitsunday of that year when John announced that Domenico Tardini would be president of the Ante-preparatory Commission. Behind the scenes, however, there was an epic struggle that concerned the very nature of the Council. Was it to be a Council of renewal and reform, as Pope John wanted, or would it be a defensive Council concerned above all to ward off contemporary errors, like the failed project of 1948-9? The Curia was prepared to humour the old man's whim and accept a Council, provided it could keep a firm grip on the preparations. Age-old curial wisdom declared: he who controls the agenda controls the meeting.

It was difficult to escape the feeling that while Pope John was charming the crowds with his droll audiences and keeping the press busy with his *bons mots*, the Curia was getting on with the serious business of running the Church. Cardinals Ottaviani and Pizzardo, for example, continued to behave as they had in the previous pontificate, and even intensified their repressive activities. While Pope John was opening some windows, they were firmly closing others. In December 1958 Pizzardo stopped the Catholic university of the Sacred Heart in Milan from awarding an honorary degree to Jacques Maritain. The distinguished neo-Thomist, who had also served as French ambassador to the Holy See, was deemed 'unsound'. Not to be outdone by the Prefect of the Congregation for Universities and Seminaries, Ottaviani at the Holy Office banned Don Lorenzo Milani's book, *Esperienze Pastorali (Pastoral Experiments)*, despite the fact that it bore an *imprimatur* from the venerated Cardinal Elia Dalla

165

Costa. He censored a 'progressive' review, *Testimonianze*, and hounded its author, Don Ernesto Balducci, out of Florence. In July 1959 Pizzardo ordered the French bishops to put an end to the priest-workers once and for all (see Magister, p. 239 for these three examples).

Though the papacy is a monarchy and even, in some sense, an absolute monarchy, these powerful cardinals had great autonomy and behaved like English barons before the signing of Magna Carta. They did not feel beholden to the Pope. After all, they had elected him. Yet John annoyed them. On February 25, 1959, he gave an audience to Don Primo Mazzolari, a remarkably prophetic priest, who had had troubles first with the Fascists and then with the Holy Office. John imprudently called him 'the trumpet of the Holy Spirit in the plain of the River Po' (see Giudici, Marco, '*Il Coraggio della Speranza*', in *Vita e Pensiero*, February, 1980). Ottaviani was very displeased. He reminded everyone that the Holy Office, over which he presided, was 'the *supreme* Congregation'. The quip went the rounds: 'Tardini reigns, Ottaviani governs, John blesses'.

Of course John did have some supporters, but they tended to be younger and members of the papal household rather than the Curia. On February 18, 1959, Mgr Igino Cardinale, chief of protocol, had a long conversation with Sir John Lawrence, an Anglican and editor of *Frontier*. Cardinale was half-American, forty-three, promising, and the nephew of Don Giuseppe De Luca, who was now busily publishing everything by Roncalli that he could lay his hands on. Cardinale's comments reveal what was being discussed by Pope John's closest associates less than a month after the announcement of the Council.

Cardinale thought the Council might begin within two years. This was over-optimistic, but it expressed John's desire to hustle along. Press reactions to the announcement were being studied, and would help in planning the Council. An important decision of principle had already been taken: this would not be a 'doctrinal' council concerned with defining dogmas; instead, it would be a 'disciplinary' Council, by which Cardinale meant that it would deal with practical matters that were not immutable. But what reformable practical matters would figure on the agenda? At this early stage, it was difficult to say. But Cardinale boldly volunteered three examples of possible topics:

> 1. *Clerical celibacy.* The link between priesthood and celibacy might not be insisted upon in all situations. The example of the Uniate Churches in communion with Rome proved that celibacy was not absolutely essential to the priesthood. But it might be difficult to make this understood in 'Latin' countries.
>
> 2. *Liturgical reform.* Pius XII had already made changes in the Holy Week liturgy, had permitted 'evening' Masses and lightened the rigours of the eucharistic fast. There was much more to be done along these lines. The use of the vernacular and the place of the Bible in worship were bound to come up.
>
> 3. *Ecumenical concern.* 'The Holy Father has a great interest in reunion, and considers that some of the divisions of Christendom are based on trivial matters that became important only for historical reasons. In such cases, common sense could do much' (Lawrence, pp. 5–7).

This was the view from within the pontifical household in February 1959. As forecaster, Cardinale scored two out of three. Only clerical celibacy failed to get on the agenda of the Council for reasons we will discover in the next chapter.

Just how important the ecumenical dimension would be was a matter for debate. Fr Charles Boyer S.J., professor at the Gregorian University, might be expected to know. For over ten years he had been holding meetings with Anglicans, alternately in England and in Italy, always with permission and discretion. Boyer was rather perplexed. He stressed that the Council was an essentially Catholic event. The word 'ecumenical' used in its official title meant 'general' as contrasted with 'local'; of itself, it said nothing about inter-Church relations. Still, it might be possible, Boyer conceded, to invite 'schismatic' or even non-episcopal Churches to send 'observers'. Boyer thought that the doctrine of the Church would be high up on the agenda, but added: 'Until the Pope speaks, no one really knows what the Council will do' (Lawrence, p. 4). So the ball was thrown back into Pope John's court.

There was, however, another informal ecumenical group that felt its hour had come. Founded in Holland in 1952 by Fr (much later Cardinal) Jan Willebrands and Fr Frans Thyssen, the 'Catholic Conference on Ecumenical Questions', as it was vaguely called, sought to 'follow' the work of the World Council of Churches in Geneva. Willebrands met with many misunderstandings and obstacles. The conventional Catholic view was that the WCC was insufficiently 'theological' in its quest for unity. Willebrands was forbidden to attend the WCC meeting in Chicago in 1953 (Kaiser, p. 32) and rebuffed by Archbishop Cyril Cowderoy of Southwark, England. The participants in the Willebrands group fluctuated, but they included the Jesuit, Augustin Bea, rector of the Biblical Institute, the French Dominican Christophe Dumont and Pierre Dumont, monk of Chevetogne, Jean-François Arrighi, Cardinal Tisserant's secretary, and Mgr Josef Höfer of the diocese of Paderborn, theological adviser to the German ambassador to the Holy See. They were nearly all destined to play an important role later on.

Pope John had known Arrighi in Paris and thought highly of him. Legend has it that he gave Pope John lessons in Protestant theology. What is true is that they had many conversations on ecumenical matters in the run-up to the Council. Arrighi provided a link with French theologians such as Yves-Marie Congar who was still under a cloud. Congar thought the Catholic Church ought to have the decency to recognise that others had been ploughing the ecumenical field for some time. He wrote: 'At the moment when the Holy See emerged from semi-absenteeism, it found the ground tilled and sown and covered with thick-set and high-grown grain' (Congar, *Dialogue between Christians*, p. 41). Arrighi was already urging in February 1959 the setting up of 'a small, high-powered body to handle ecumenical matters' (Lawrence, p. 20). Until there was a body set up to deal specifically with inter-Church relations, the case would go by default.

If Arrighi, although a Corsican, provided the link with French theologians, Hofer knew the German ecumenical scene and had come to Rome at the request of his bishop, Lorenz Jaeger, with the intention of making it better known (Nash, p. 10). Jaeger, archbishop of Paderborn, was the founder and president of the Adam Möhler Institute whose purpose was 'to form specialists in Lutheran and ecumenical questions and to take part in inter-denominational conversations' (*ibid.*, p. 100). Höfer was familiar with the work of the thirty-year-old Swiss theologian, Hans Küng, who had written a thesis demonstrating that Luther's understanding of 'justification' was not incompatible with that of the Council of Trent (*Rechtfertigung*, 1957). Karl Barth wrote an admiring but somewhat baffled preface to Küng's book, admitting that if Küng were right, the Reformation reposed upon a mistake.

A key-word among all these Catholic ecumenists was 'collegiality'. It meant that the pope was not a solitary Atlas propping up the entire world — as some interpretations of Vatican I suggested. Rather, he was surrounded, sustained and assisted by the bishops of the whole world who shared with him in 'the solicitude of all the churches'. Pope John was known to be for collegiality. In Istanbul he had always tried to act collegially with the bishops of varied rites who shared his ministry.

The act of calling a Council was an extension of the same principle to the universal Church. On a humbler level, collegiality could be seen as an instance of what papal social teaching called 'subsidiarity': never put up to a higher level what can be dealt with on a lower level. John was already practising 'subsidiarity'. On February 23, 1959, Arrighi explained:

> John XXIII really applies the collegial system of government, and works with his fellow bishops. Unlike Pius XII, he trusts his subordinates. For example, I have to advise on matrimonial cases which involve the Uniate Churches. I make my recommendations to Cardinal Tisserant, who then puts them before the Pope. He says: 'Have you looked into this? Is it all right?' If the Cardinal says yes, the Pope signs (Lawrence, p. 19).

Arrighi also had some perceptive comments on Pope John's approach to ecumenical matters:

> He really cares about unity. His starting point is the Orthodox Church, but 'when you become ecumenical, you have to take in everybody'. . . . Recently he called the Congregation for the Oriental Churches together and said: 'I know that humanly speaking my plan is impossible, but God demands unity and we must do something about it' (Lawrence, p. 19).

It was a novel experience for the much-battered breed of Catholic ecumenists to have a pope on their side. So they made the most of it. However, nearly all Rome's ecumenists, and all those so far named, were non-Italian. This widened the gap with the watchdogs of orthodoxy in the Roman Curia, and introduced an ugly element of xenophobia into the clash of theological opinions.

Pope John made no immediate moves to reassure his supporters or clarify his intentions. Having announced his Council, he was surprisingly reticent about it. He seemed to lean back and watch things happen. He was discovering, the hard way, the limits of papal authority. 'I'm only the Pope around here' was partly a joke, partly a genuine lament at his impotence. The barons still ruled. The great event of the Council, now that it was decided upon and announced, did not monopolise his attention or his time. This was partly because he had to wait for the response from the local Churches — that was another aspect of collegiality. But it was also because he had to remain alert on so many other fronts.

In the first six months of 1959 he received in audience or state visits General Charles de Gaulle, Queen Elizabeth II, King Paul and Queen Frederika of the Hellenes, King Hussein I of Jordan and the presidents of Turkey, Indonesia and Tunisia, not to mention the Japanese prime minister and Prince Rainier of Monaco with his beautiful consort, Princess Grace (*Cronologia*, pp. 748–50). The whole world — with the exception of the Soviet bloc — appeared to be trooping to the Vatican. Cardinale kept the score. In seventeen years, Pius XII had ten visits from heads of state; John, who had the shortest pontificate of the century so far (apart from the 'flashing meteor' of John Paul I), had thirty-four (Cardinale, pp. 385–6). John was more inclined to talk with such personages about their children than about the Council. In any case, his more immediate concern on the Church front was with the Synod of the Rome diocese rather than the Council of the universal Church.

Pope John's first meeting with the Ante-preparatory Commission on June 30, 1959, gave him a chance to say what he hoped the Council would do. Its purpose was, he said, 'to demonstrate the striking diversity of rites together with the unshakeable unity of the Catholic Church'. This was the concept of the Council as 'spectacle' of which John was fond: it would speak to the world simply by meeting, and bring new energy and drive to the whole Church. But this was all rather vague – a bit like declaring that in future everything will be better. Equally vague was the pledge that the Council would both meet modern needs and be faithful to the past. There was, of course, no contradiction between fidelity and meeting the demands of the contemporary world. *Aggiornamento* and renewal would only be of value if they grew out of the authentic tradition. But the emphasis in his June 30, 1959, speech fell on consolidating and preserving the past rather than on responding to the present. What John said was perfectly compatible with the 'defensive' view of the Council represented by Tardini, Ottaviani and Pizzardo.

John's first encyclical, *Ad Petri Cathedram* (To the See of Peter) came out at the same time (June 29, 1959). It had been eagerly awaited: first encyclicals are usually programmatic, and it was expected to shed light on the Council. But this was a compromise, hybrid document whose final revision had been entrusted to Tardini. Pope John (or his script-writers) repeated Leo XIII's idea that class divisions are a law of nature. The encyclical was negative in tone, firmly anti-Communist, full of dire warnings about the mass-media, and it demanded obedience from all. It was difficult to square all this with the 'Good Pope John' so assiduously depicted by the very media he was berating. In an attempt to resolve this contradiction, commentators claimed that John had deliberately allowed himself to be influenced by Tardini as a way of soothing the Curia, still shell-shocked from the announcement of the Council. *Ad Petri Cathedram* proved that, despite his 'adventurism', he was a sound traditionalist at heart.

But that was a feeble explanation for *Ad Petri Cathedram*'s treatment of other Christians. Could this really be the voice of Pope John? He took his stand on Pius XI's 1928 encyclical *Mortalium Animos* which had ruled out Catholic participation in the international ecumenical movement and warned of the perils of indifferentism. He went on: 'Those who call themselves Christians, although separated from us, have held many congresses with the aim of establishing a closer relationship with each other, and to this end they have set up various bodies. These show that they are moved by the desire to reach some sort of unity' (No. 32). This was a rather lofty and apparently disdainful reference to the World Council of Churches. Its rather wishy-washy attempts to achieve unity were contrasted with the Roman Catholic Church which already has 'the unity willed by Christ' and so did not need to seek it (Nos. 33–8). *Ad Petri Cathedram* makes the point with elegant triplets: 'Unity, venerable brothers and beloved sons, should not be something evanescent, fleeting and hazardous, but rather something solid, stable and secure (No. 34). Solidity, stability and security could be found in the Roman Catholic Church, and only there. A conclusion followed, and John did not hesitate to draw it, even though it put in jeopardy the high

ecumenical hopes he entertained for his Council: if the papacy was the guardian of the
unity willed by Christ for his Church, then the solution to the scandal of Christian divisions was that all should 'return', repentant, to the sheepfold they had abandoned. After
reading *Ad Petri Cathedram*, it was reasonable to ask: would the real Pope John please stand
up? It seemed that with his first encyclical he had perpetrated an ecumenical *gaffe* of some
magnitude.

Or had he? The truth is that *Ad Petri Cathedram* was a duet for two voices. So far we have
heard from Tardini. Pope John certainly intended his encyclical to be an ecumenically
friendly document, and thought he had succeeded. This is clear even in the famous passage
that uses the obnoxious word 'return'. It is specifically directed to the separated brethren:
'Let me address you with ardent desire as brothers and sons. Let us nourish the hope of your
loving return with all the affection of a father . . . When we lovingly invite you to the unity
of the Church, we do not invite you to some strange house but to your own, shared paternal
home . . . "I am Joseph, your brother" '(Nos. 39–40). We have already seen the importance of
this text from Genesis 45.44. John uses it to express his readiness to step down from a superior position and place himself alongside and on the same level as his partners in dialogue.
The image of 'father', natural enough in a patriarchal figure of seventy-eight, is qualified by
that of 'brother'. And both images, father and brother, belong to John's *spiritual* vocabulary.

John and his team were now producing encyclicals at a great rate. There were three more
before the end of 1959: *Sacerdotii Nostri Primordia* (August 1, 1959, on the hundredth anniversary of the death of the Curé d'Ars, St Jean-Marie Vianney); *Grata Recordatio* (September 26,
1959, on the Rosary); and *Princeps Pastorum* (November 28, 1959, commemorating the six-
tieth anniversary of *Maximum Illud* in which Benedict XV reorganised missionary work).
They have been largely forgotten, and it cannot candidly be said that they created much of
a stir at the time. They confirmed the impression that John was a man of great piety, very
loyal to the enthusiasms and practices of his youth, and with half his mind in the past. This is
the sort of Pope he would have been had he not summoned a Council.

Tardini, meanwhile, was busily remedying the charismatic vagueness of his chief. He was
not over-keen on Pope John's notion of the Council as a 'new Pentecost' because it slotted
into no known juridical categories. Still brisk, brusque and apparently fit at seventy-one,
Tardini made most of the early running. On July 3, 1959, three days after *Ad Petri Cathedram*,
he addressed a meeting of rectors of Roman Universities and other theological institutes.
Tardini's telegraphic notes on the purpose of the Council have been preserved:

> It is more than likely from what can be seen as of now
> (a) that the Council will be more practical than dogmatic, more pastoral than
> ideological, and that it will provide norms for action rather than new definitions.
> However,
> (b) this does not take away the fact that
> > (i) we can (or should) recall and reaffirm those points of doctrine that are most
> > important and nowadays most threatened, or,
> > (ii) that we can (or must) move rapidly from a speedy and solid summary of doctrinal
> > principles to 'practical norms' (Nicolini, p. 193).

In Tardini's first point – he ticked them off on his fingers – one could just about discern the originality of this Council ('more pastoral than dogmatic') as John conceived it; but his second point seemed to transform it into an exercise for canon lawyers ('practical norms') that was hardly likely to interest still less inspire anyone.

Tardini's address, however, was the opening cannonade in the battle for the Council. He was addressing the rectors of Roman Universities because he expected them to provide the bulk of the 'experts' or *periti* who would be needed. The universities already provided most of the 'consultors' for the Roman Congregations. It would save time and money if they worked on the preparations for the Council. Thus − Tardini did not need to spell this out − there would be no need to invite experts from other Catholic universities whether they were in Washington DC, Louvain or Milan. Tardini was soon to appoint a 'Secretary' for the effective day-to-day control of the operation. Mgr Pericle Felici was forty-eight, professor of Canon Law at the Lateran University, and a member of the Roman Rota − the court that deals with disputed marriage cases. He was well-known, in a restricted milieu, for the elegance of his Latin verses. He later became secretary general of the Council itself. Tardini had carefully selected a man who shared his own juridical approach to the Council. His control, at this stage, was complete.

On October 30, 1959, Tardini summoned a press conference to tell the world what a Council was. This was unheard of: Roman Cardinals were not in the habit of meeting the press and exposing themselves to impertinent questions from the ignorant and the Anglo-Saxon. But Tardini blinded them with science. He held the press conference not in the Vatican but at his orphanage, Villa Nazareth, which ensured he got publicity for the place and showed what a pastorally-minded person he was. There are many accounts of what Tardini said on this occasion. His biographer reports that 'he gave an historico-doctrinal lecture on the nature of ecumenical councils with the dash and humour that are his wont, interspersing his remarks with witty asides' (Nicolini, p. 193). Bernard Wall, an English man of letters, described it rather more vividly:

> Cardinal Tardini came into the room with swift steps. He was a small man, with a thick brush of iron grey hair cut very short and businesslike. His spectacles were thick and gave him a peering look and these, with his mouth, which was not expressive of human sympathy, made him seem like a pedant or a schoolmaster, dried up, almost sour (Wall, p. 197).

Wall also gathered, accurately enough, that Tardini was not interested in ecumenism or Church reform, still less in 'learning from the world'. This raised a fundamental question: did Tardini really believe in the Council at all?

Pericle Felici tried to answer it some years later: 'Despite his gruff manner and his pungent Roman wit, Tardini was a man of great faith, and he lived by devotion to the Pope. Whatever exalted the Church and the Pope rejoiced his spirit. The positive response he gave Pope John when he announced the Council was dictated by such feelings' (Felici, p. 120). Though he wraps it up, Felici is here admitting that Tardini had little natural sympathy with the conciliar project as such, did not share Pope John's view of its aims, and obeyed only out of his elevated sense of the papal office. But his view of obedience did not exclude trying to hi-jack the Council preparations and divert them to his own ends. In a way, Tardini was probably the least suitable man to prepare Vatican II.

While Tardini was entertaining the press with his quips, Capovilla was giving lectures in Padua and Bergamo ostensibly to mark the first anniversary of Pope John's election. But what he was really doing was trying to put the record straight, in reply to the objection that Pope John was a dangerous innovator whose actions were an implicit criticism of his predecessors, particularly of the great and learned Pius XII to whom he could not hold a candle. It was also suggested – Tisserant used to go on about this at his exquisite dinner-table – that John was not very bright. So in his first lecture in Bergamo on October 20, 1959, Capovilla shows that, far from being an innovator, Pope John is still the good-hearted and traditionalist Catholic who had been so well-trained in the glorious Bergamo seminary. He was certainly reflecting Pope John's own feelings in this hymn of praise to Bergamo:

> His [Pope John's] Bergamo – as he sees and feels it – is a good, intelligent and hospitable city; solid in its faith, unshakeable in its traditions; jealous of its religious and civic heritage; sometimes seeming rather set apart in the austere beauty of its mountains and valleys, but proud of its natural beauties and its monuments. It is a blessed land. (*Letture*, p. 57).

Capovilla was really saying that a man who came from and remained loyal to such a background must be sound and trustworthy. As for Pope John's mind, he had received the grace of wisdom of the heart, which placed him in 'the order of charity' and so transcended the mere intellect (*Letture*, p. 62). That disposed of Tisserant's complaint that Pope John was none too clever.

In Padua on November 9, 1959, Capovilla presented John as the true heir of the popes of his lifetime, and indeed as the synthesis of their virtues. He had picked up traits from all of them: 'The enlightened Christian humanism of Leo XIII; the simple and attractive loveableness of Pius X; the general nobility of Benedict XV; Pius XI's longanimity; and from Pius XII the heart-beat of universal love' (*Letture*, p. 78). So John owed everything to the popes who had gone before. This was meant to be reassuring.

But at Padua in November 1959 Capovilla also dealt with a more precise and worrying question. The comparison with Pius XII was still being made, sometimes to John's credit, more often to his discomfiture. He had allegedly told the new bishop of Le Mans who was wondering how he could possibly succeed the remarkably wise, good and learned Cardinal Georges Grente: 'Don't worry. Just do what I do: the opposite of my predecessor'. It doesn't much matter whether John actually made this remark. It was *ben trovato* and it entered the oral tradition. It was also potentially highly damaging to him. So to scotch such stories Capovilla dug out a remark made by Patriarch Roncalli to Pius XII: 'Holy Father, you will leave a difficult heritage for any successor who tries to emulate you in your role as teacher and master of the word' (*Letture*, p. 37). Yet the more Capovilla stressed the similarities, the more one became aware of the differences.

John's journal confirms that after a year, he judged that he had not made a bad start: 'The experience of this first year gives me light and strength in my efforts to straighten out, to reform, and tactfully and patiently to make improvements in everything' (*Journal*, p. 321: dated November–December, 1959). But there was one particular reform he thought urgent. During meals on his retreat John had read to him St Bernard's *De Consideratione*, which was a diatribe against nepotism – showing favour to one relatives – and pluralism, the habit of holding several offices or benefices at once. John hated nepotism, as his nephew, Don Battista, had already discovered. Nepotism was not a problem in his pontificate.

Pluralism was. Roman cardinals often held several top posts at the same time. Pizzardo, for example, was both prefect of the Congregation for Universities and Seminaries and secretary of the Holy Office (*Lettere*, p. 173). Tisserant was Vatican librarian and had been prefect of the Congregation for Oriental Churches since he became a cardinal in 1936; he was sufficiently well dug in to believe himself immoveable. At first Pope John tried dropping gentle hints, such as that he was creating so many cardinals so that the burden of work might be shared out more equitably (*Lettere*, p. 173: Letter to Pizzardo, October 12, 1959). Pizzardo and Tisserant remained obstinately at all their posts and showed not the slightest inclination to move. Though it was against his temperament, John had to order them out. Accustomed to obeying all his life, John found disobedience hard to comprehend.

He wrote an official letter to each of them, published in *l'Osservatore Romano*, thanking them for spontaneously offering to resign. It was a white lie, but it was the usual form. But he was distressed at having to resort to such methods. 'They have refused the Pope', he said in sad disbelief, 'they have refused the Pope' (Trevor, p. 271). Cardinal Montini in Milan was also interested in the reform of the Curia. He was not even a member of the Antepreparatory Commission, but he wrote to Tardini to say that it would be a good thing 'if the Roman Curia were to abandon certain honorific or ritualistic or merely juridical ways of behaving, so as to set an example of Christian brotherhood and evangelical humility' (Monaco, p. 61). He was already set on curial reform.

Pope John wrote in his journal: 'I feel I am under obedience in all things and have noticed that this disposition, in things great and small, gives me, unworthy as I am, a strength of daring simplicity so wholly evangelical in its nature that it demands and obtains universal respect and edifies many' (*Journal*, p. 321). The 'strength of daring simplicity' so far from diminishing, grew as the pontificate went on. 'The whole world is my family', he noted in his journal (*ibid.*). Becoming pope had enabled John at last to become fully himself. It upset the usual law by which the old become ever more cautious and staid. In the New Year, 1960, there would be the Synod of the diocese of Rome. He was indeed starting at the beginning, at home and in Rome.

Chapter 16

At home and in Rome

Can Rome be true to itself if it remains merely a national capital? No, for
another Rome survives on another level, the Rome of the Catholic faith . . .
No one is a stranger in Rome.

(Cardinal Giovanni Battista Montini, speech in the Campidoglio, October 11, 1962,
opening day of the Council)

The official Vatican handbook describes the Pope's immediate entourage as belonging to a
home (*casa*) and a household or family (*famiglia*). These age-old terms can be contrasted with
curia which evokes royal courts and consequently courtiers and, indeed, flunkeys. The Pope
has both a *casa* and a *curia*.

Like his immediate predecessors, Pope John lived in the Apostolic Palace on the right of
St Peter's Square, on the same floor as the Secretariat of State (the so-called *terza loggia*). He
tried to create a family atmosphere in these lofty, marble-floored salons. Above the altar in
his private chapel was a Holy Family by a painter of the school of Paolo Veronese, a gift from
the Rome football team, Lazio (Capovilla: letter of January 31, 1984: the picture is repro-
duced in *Secolo*, facing p. 48). No doubt it reminded him of his own family and the Holy
House of Loreto. Pope John took it as a hint about how he should behave. He became the
father of the household rather than the monarch sitting on the throne. The three sisters from
Bergamo looked after the kitchen and the domestic arrangements but, warned by the fate of
Sister Pasqualina, they stayed in the background, discreet, almost invisible. Gianpaolo Gusso came down from Venice to join his brother Guido. They served at table and, after the
death of Angelino Stoppa, Pius XII's driver who had been tactfully kept on, took turns at
doing the driving (Capovilla, *ibid.*). They were both married men with children, but they
lived in the Vatican, not the Apostolic Palace. One or the other would always be present at
Pope John's Mass at 7 a.m.

A member of the papal household described its life:

> It is difficult for you Americans to comprehend how the Holy Father thinks of us and we
> of him. None of us have wives, children or social obligations. Nor do we lead a
> prescribed communal life like monks. Here in Rome we very often talk, read and listen
> to music together . . . The Holy Father is our real father; to him we are literally sons.
> Sometimes we tell him new things which interest him and he is proud of us. Sometimes
> he tells us to stop talking nonsense and to go away and learn wisdom (Spain, p. 5).

Unfortunately this idyllic picture is, according to Capovilla, not wholly true. John did
have the relationship described with a number of people on whom he liked to try out ideas.

But they did not form a community of work, and did not sit around of an evening listening to music. Sometimes John liked to listen to music during supper, but that was all. Otherwise his only relaxation was a walk in the Vatican gardens in the afternoon. This was also the time when, weather permitting, he read or browsed through books not strictly connected with his immediate work or, more usually, got Capovilla to read them out to him.

The same member of the papal household commented on the relationship between 'family' and Curia: 'Cardinal Ottaviani is not an enemy. To the Holy Father he is an uncle who is often difficult and must be circumvented, but who is still respected' (Spain, p. 6). That gets it about right. John once said of Ottaviani: 'Alfredo is a very dear friend: it's a pity he's half-blind and has jowls that wobble like a Venetian lagune in the sirocco' (Andreotti, p. 70). As for Tardini, John's household knew what to expect: everyone who had worked in the Secretariat of State for the last thirty years had passed through his hands. Nor was Tardini devoid of self-knowledge. He once described his original method of dealing with superiors in this way: 'I would suddenly blurt out a phrase, a question or a witticism that disconcerted, dismayed, embarrassed or sometimes demolished my interlocutor' (Nicolini, p. 229). Clearly Tardini was another difficult uncle who needed careful handling. Like Ottaviani, however, he was not a member of the papal family. He had to knock on the door.

But John still kept a line open to both men. Despite his general conservatism, Ottaviani was one of the first to declare nuclear weapons immoral. He applied the most traditional theory of 'the just war' and found it no longer fitted. Tardini's obstructionism was a nuisance and his explosions wearing, but at least he knew whole passages from Manzoni's *I Promessi Sposi* by heart (Nicolini, p. 221) which, in John's eyes, redeemed a lot of faults. The latest quips were reported to Pope John. We know that because he noted some of them down. Humour in the Vatican follows the Italian tradition and is not particularly funny: it makes a point economically. One day John noted the remark: *'Angelo regna, Carlo informa, Alfredo sorveglia, Domenico governa, Giovanni benedice' (Lettere*, p. 518). It was a more elaborate version of the 'joke' already reported. It means (full names and functions added):

> Angelo (Dell'Acqua, substitute) reigns, Carlo (Confalonieri, secretary of the
> Congregation for Seminaries and Universities) spies, Alfredo (Ottaviani, pro-prefect of
> the Holy Office) keeps watch, Domenico (Tardini, Secretary of State) governs, John
> merely blesses.

Though not exactly scintillating, the fact that it went into the Pope's private notebook suggests that he knew how the balance of forces in his Curia was perceived in Rome.

John tried to bring a personal touch to all his work. Much of it consisted in preparing documents or letters. As in all administrations, a draft was usually provided by someone else. John's commonest marginal comments were 'Redraft' or 'I can't possibly sign this as it stands' or 'I know this prelate personally and it matters a lot to me that you should let this come through' (*Lettere*, p. 23). Of course it was impossible for him to know personally every bishop in the world. But he prayed for them all.

Yet Pope John didn't just write to cardinals and bishops. He wrote to all his old friends, even if it was to say they must not expect to hear from him again. Among his strictly personal correspondence one letter, hitherto unpublished, stands out. It was to Adelaide Coari whom he had last met in Venice. There are not many letters from popes to non-royal women:

> Dear Miss Adelaide Coari,
> You won't think too badly of me if the state of life to which Providence has brought me does not permit me to say at any great length how fond are my memories of your activity half a century ago . . .
>
> There's a phrase of St Gregory Nazianzen that I love to repeat: God's will is our peace. This phrase follows me like the star of the Magi. Guided by its light we move towards Christ, with simplicity and courage, and reach out towards the certainty of eternal goodness. I'm writing this on St Catherine's eve, on the threshold of my 78th year. I'm in good health, and ready for anything, ready to serve the Church here below or to live on in the Church triumphant with our saints.
>
> I noticed with edification how faithful you were to the late Don Rebora of the Rosminians, and your fidelity to Mgr Radini. 'Your saints, Lord, bring us joy on all sides.' They stand by us, encourage and protect us, until the day of our final reunion.
>
> You will continue to pray for me, and I bless you from the heart. Ask Sts Peter and Paul never to draw me away from the two Johns who epitomise the light brought by the Old and the New Testament. (Bologna Archives: letter dated November 25, 1959).

Don Rebora was a poet whom Adelaide had helped to convert. The seventy-eight year old lady who received this unexpected and courtly letter in Milan outlived Pope John by three years. The day of the 'final reunion' came in 1966.

While trying to introduce a new family spirit into the papal apartments, the only physical change Pope John made was to have restored the Torre San Giovanni (St John's Tower), built in 848 to ward off the marauding Saracens. John turned it into a four-floor apartment with a lift. He wanted somewhere to withdraw to for prayer and reflection. It was his 'desert', though admittedly quite a comfortable one. The story of the tower in his own words is a good example of Pope John's table-talk:

> In the time of Pope Leo the tower that is now used by Vatican Radio was restored. That left the other tower in the southern corner of the gardens. Until 1926 it was used as an observatory. It was part of the fortifications that guarded the so-called Pertusa Gate. Pius XI thought of turning it into a place for retreat and recollection, and Pius XII had the same idea. But the work being done at Castelgandolfo and then the war meant that the project had to be laid aside. The abandoned tower spoiled that part of the gardens. So in 1960 the Commission for Vatican City examined a plan for the reordering of the whole area including the ponderous and rather tumble-down Lourdes grotto. The Commission had already set aside the money. I consulted a few people and was happy to give the go-ahead. But when the work began there were whisperings here and there, so I asked Cardinal Tardini what to do. He said: 'The restoration of the Nicholas V tower is a necessity, its conservation a duty, and its use a bonus for which your successors will be grateful'. It was given the name of St John in memory of Sotto il Monte, where I come from, which also has a Torre San Giovanni on the hill of the same name (*Letture*, pp. 470–1).

When future historians ask what difference Pope John's pontificate made to the Vatican and the Church, one can always reply: he turned a ruined, fortified tower into a place of prayer.

But John didn't have much time to linger in his tower. He was the bishop of Rome and took this, the foundation of his grander titles, seriously. But what, in practice, did it mean? The administration of the diocese was entrusted to a cardinal vicar. John inherited from Pius XII the eighty-year-old Clemente Micara, a crusty old gentleman whose age was beginning to show. He did not always see eye to eye with Pope John, perhaps believing that the Pope ought to get on with running the universal Church while leaving Rome to the man of experience, himself (see the hint in Caprile, '*Ancora su Giovanni XXIII*', p. 52). Micara, however, was flanked by a younger and more amenable pro-vicar, Luigi Traglia, who took over more and more of the work and was made a cardinal at the consistory of March 28, 1960.

There was much that needed attention in the diocese of Rome. When he announced the Synod for the diocese of Rome on January 25, 1959, he described in his own breezy way the changes that had come over the city since he ceased to live in it in 1925: 'In the suburbs especially houses, houses have been built, in which families, families are piled up on top of each other, families coming from all parts of the peninsula, from the islands and – we can say – from the whole world' (Alberigo, p. 274). The 'historic centre' of Rome was now surrounded on all sides by vast shoe-boxes of apartment blocks. Beyond them lay the shanty-towns, improvised huts for the poorest. In 1939 Rome had only 700,000 inhabitants served by sixty-two parishes. By the time John became Pope the population was over 2 million, the number of parishes had risen to 190, and the building boom showed no sign of slackening. Rome had never lacked priests. There were over 3000: but most of them worked in the Curia or were religious assigned to the Roman universities. Very few were engaged in pastoral work. At the Rome Synod John gave the statistics himself: there were 220 diocesan priests and 370 religious, making 590 priests in all (Alberigo, p. 310). Clearly Rome needed a bishop who would think seriously about its pastoral problems. Pope John joined in the hugger-mugger of the parishes of Rome, beginning in 1959 with the city centre and then gradually moving out towards the mushrooming suburbs. This was one of the causes of his popularity with the people of Rome: they did not have to go to St Peter's Square: the Pope had come to them.

However, his chosen instrument for the renewal of the diocese of Rome was not parish visits but the Synod. Throughout 1959 he devoted more time to the preparation of the Synod than to the preparation of the Council. He saw the Synod as a response to the changed situation in Rome, and a way of coping with the fact that these 'new Romans' were often uprooted peasants whose links and relatives were elsewhere. In a letter to Archbishop Traglia, president of the Synod Commission, he said: 'The new spiritual demands resulting from the present urban sprawl and development justify holding the Synod, and make something which in the past might have seemed superfluous now not only legitimate but necessary' (*Lettere*, p. 178: dated October 25, 1959). From which we may safely conclude that some in the Curia were arguing that there was no need for a Synod and – more boldly – that it was a waste of time and effort.

It has been suggested that the Synod was a 'sop' thrown by Pope John to keep the Curia happy while awaiting the Council, the real and decisive 'event of the Spirit'. Giuseppe

Alberigo has a more sophisticated version of this argument. He says that the Curia sought to delay the Council by concentrating on the Roman Synod and the revision of the Code of Canon Law. Given the great age of the Pope and the canonical fact that his successor would not be obliged to carry out any of his projects, this delaying tactic could perhaps lead to the scrapping of the whole idea (Alberigo, p. 74).

But Pope John wanted the Synod very much for the reasons already given. It is true that the Synod was not his original idea, but once put to him, he seized upon it eagerly. And the Synod also appealed to him because it was part of the post-Tridentine tradition. It was the constitutional way to reform a diocese according to Trent and St Charles Borromeo. Experience backed up history. Radini Tedeschi, his bishop, had held a Synod in Bergamo in 1910; he himself had organised a Synod in Venice in 1957. There had been Synods in many Italian dioceses and all over the world; yet Rome lagged behind. He liked the idea of this being the first Synod of the diocese of Rome. He was pleased to inaugurate it in the Lateran, as the cathedral of the diocese the proper place, exactly one year after announcing it.

And that was the link with the Council. The Synod was a practice run. It was designed to answer the question: can pastors and theologians work together harmoniously and at speed? The answer appeared to be 'yes'. The eight sub-commissions had worked well; religious and diocesan priests got on well. John was pleased. On June 18, 1959, he received all the Commission members and greeted them with the words of St Augustine: 'I've found you to be just the people I wanted' (*Lettere*, p. 182). On July 31, 1959, he wrote to Giuseppe Battaglia, bishop of Faenza: 'The sharing out of the work is proving highly effective, and the good will shown on all sides surpasses my expectations' (*ibid.*, p. 151). He had high hopes that the Synod would blaze a trail for the Council.

But nothing of the kind happened. There was a gap between Pope John's optimistic expectations and the actual event. His theology and theory of the Synod were fine, but its achievement was meagre. When the 755 pre-packaged articles that were the conclusions of the Synod were read out, without discussion or debate, the 'good will on all sides' he had detected the previous summer was dissipated. The only function of the Synod members was to applaud what had previously been decided upon. The Synod's detailed provisions, moreover, looked like an attempt to stem the tide of modernity; they did not suggest the rustle of a new Pentecostal springtime.

Roman priests were told to wear the cassock or black soutane at all times. The tonsure or shaven crown was insisted upon. Worldly events such as the opera and the race-meeting were placed out of bounds for clerics. Priests were not to use cars except in case of necessity, and never alone with a woman in any circumstances. They were warned off faith-healers and psychoanalysts. They were to show great prudence in their dealings with Communists, Freemasons and heretics (Prima *Romana Synodus*, Vatican Polyglot Press, 1960). Those who had hoped that the Council would be a great ecumenical event were mystified and appalled by the Roman Synod. It looked like the dashing of all their hopes. Conversely, those in the Roman Curia who did not like the idea of the Council – it meant foreigners in Rome - rubbed their hands with glee over the Synod. 'If the Council is going to be anything like the Synod', said one of them, 'it will be the most innocuous Council in the history of the Church' (see *L'uomo che non divenne papa*, p. 272).

Was Pope John disappointed by the world-wide hostile reaction to the Roman Synod?

He certainly felt it had been misunderstood. In an official letter to Cardinal Micara he thanked the old man for standing aside and allowing him to act as bishop of Rome, an elaborate and unnecessary courtesy. But then he goes on to explain that the Synodal Decrees, though they may seem a little arid or heavy, when read as a whole 'yield up their beauty and inner coherence, with occasional delicate touches that result in an unexpected psalmody, bringing clarity to the mind and savour to the heart' (*Lettere*, pp. 211–12: letter dated June 29, 1960). He also believed the decrees were written in excellent Latin. In an address to the Roman clergy, he rounded on his critics and dismissed them as so many 'doubting Thomases'. It was an anticipation of the way he would denounce the 'prophets of gloom' (see Abbott, p. 712) in his opening speech to the Council. It also showed his obstinacy or, less pejoratively, his resolution. In private he consoled himself with the thought that 'nothing is perfect in this world. If there are inadequacies or futilities my successor can always put that right by celebrating the *second* Roman Synod. It will always be the humble Pope John who celebrated the first' (*Lettere*, p. 182: to Capovilla).

But before the Synod is written off as a total failure, it should be noted that John's own personal contribution, discreet as it was, set it firmly on the path of pastoral charity. He felt very strongly about the way 'ex-priests' (the term is theologically improper, and he avoided it) were treated. The Church said that they should be avoided while the Concordat stipulated that they should not be employed in state posts. This excluded teaching, for which they were quite well prepared. Contemporaries of John at the Roman seminary had been caught in this trap. The problem was particularly acute in Rome where so many 'ex-priests' had been trained and whither they drifted in hope and anonymity. In this context, decree 35 of the Roman Synod, written personally by Pope John and undemocratically imposed on the Synod (like everything else), represented a dramatic new departure:

> Priests labouring under censure or other penalties, or who have perhaps unhappily left the Church, should never cease to trust in the mercy of the Lord or the humanity and decency of ecclesiastical superiors. Other priests, especially their friends, moved by heavenly charity, should strive to build up this trust. No one is to be denied the friendship of his fellow priests or consolation in his difficulties or even material help should it be needed (*Prima Romana Synodus*, Vatican Polyglot Press, 1960, p. 21).

That 'ex-priests' should be given money was a startling notion for its day.

John practised what he preached within the limits imposed by his office. His confessor, Mgr Alfredo Cavagna, and his secretary, Mgr Loris Capovilla, were bombarded with requests from priests who, impatient with the delaying tactics of the Curia, wanted the Pope to intercede on their behalf. John's instructions were clear: firmness on the principles, gentleness in their execution. His two aides were told that they must assure these men that their requests had reached the Pope, but that the 'proper channels' would have to be respected (*Lettere*, p. 532). Sometimes Pope John annotated these cries for help. Here is one case:

> X is an unhappy man who should not have been ordained. His psychological state justifies a release from priestly duties, and also financial support that will help him to resign without causing either scandal or shock. He deserves mercy before God and the people (*Lettere*, p. 531: May 1, 1962).

So X would have received an 'annulment' of his ordination. Y was less fortunate:

> I have read the memo of the unhappy Y. Evidently this is a pathological case, and I'm
> sorry that the act of mercy that would save him from despair is not being recommended
> to the Pope (*ibid.*, August 6, 1962).

He was 'only the Pope'. He could not bring himself to bend the rules or leap-frog over his subordinates – he was supposed to trust them.

For all his compassion, John had not the slightest intention of relaxing the rule of celibacy for the Western Church. We have already seen that in February 1959 Igino Cardinale thought that the abolition of mandatory celibacy might well be on the agenda of the Council. Aware of this opening to the future, an Italian Dominican, Fr Raimondo Spiazzi, published a 'sensational' article in the austere pages of the *Monitor Ecclesiasticus* (vol. no. 84, 1959). His argument was banal but astonishing to the media: the historical evidence for the present discipline of clerical celibacy was extremely shaky. This was a tabu topic. But Spiazzi made out a good case. Even the Fathers of the Council of Trent did not think that clerical celibacy was a matter of 'divine positive law', nor could they since there were validly ordained married priests in communion with Rome. Reporters, accustomed to reading the *Monitor Ecclesiasticus*, thrilled to this exciting topic, rushed to their telephones, and told their news editors that Pope John, the radical, was not averse to dropping the rule of celibacy.

They were hasty and wrong. He addressed the Roman Synod on the subject on January 27, 1960. The row over the Spiazzi articles was an invitation to show his hand. Some said that Pope John should not have pre-empted the judgement of the Council on so important an issue. But he may have felt that any hesitation on priestly celibacy would have given rise to dangerous expectations. Yet he was also a reformer. In the eleventh century, he claimed, the real reformers were those who *imposed* clerical celibacy after a period of scandalous corruption. So John's conclusion was: 'The law of ecclesiastical celibacy, and the concern to make it prevail, remain a permanent reminder of the heroic age when the Church of Christ had to do battle and succeeded to the extent that it earned the threefold title that is the emblem of its victory: "The Church of Christ, free, chaste, Catholic" ' (*Lettere*, p. 133).

In his Coronation homily Pope John had made it clear that he understood his office in pastoral and spiritual terms. The 'temporal' power of the papacy was gone for good, and he did not feel nostalgic for it. This allowed him to have a new relationship with the city of Rome and its civic authorities. They were no longer in competition. The Rome of Catholicism and the Rome, capital of Italy, could live together in peace, in what John always described by the almost untranslatable word *convivenza* (harmonious living together). John wrote in his *Journal*:

> What seems clear and providential is that all these crowds of Italians and still more of
> 'foreigners' who come to Rome know at once how to distinguish between the sacred and
> the profane; that is, Rome the capital of Catholicism and seat of the univeral Roman
> pontiff, and the Rome of ancient ruins and the whirlwind of secular and . . . worldly
> living which rages even on the banks of the Tiber. All this, however, with mutual respect
> among the various human elements, and no unfriendliness between Italians and non-
> Italians (*Journal*, p. 344: dated July–August, 1962).

This text indicates that the 'reconciliation' proclaimed in 1929 had by now become a reality. There was no longer, as in the 1930s, a grandiloquent dispute about which Rome was the true heir of ancient Rome. Nor did John emulate Pius XII in turning every election into a battle for the 'soul' of Rome. So, quite apart from anything else, John believed that the Council would be an opportunity to demonstrate to the world the *convivenza* that now prevailed: 'Government and municipal authorities are now busily co-operating so that the Council may be worthy of Rome as the spiritual centre of the world, and that Rome's arrangements for the accommodation, civic hospitality and the honourable treatment of guests from all over the world may excel all the finest achievements of her past' (*ibid.*, pp. 344–5).

The story of Pope John's relationship with Rome would be incomplete if a concern of the last year of his life were overlooked. He planned the transfer of the diocesan curia of Rome to its proper place in the Lateran Palace alongside his cathedral. The minutes of the Commission set up to consider the transfer have been published (*Lettere*, pp. 408–9). John said: 'The news has just reached my ears that it has been decided to transfer the diocesan curia to San Callisto and that furniture and equipment have already been moved in' (*ibid.*, p. 408). It was the familiar complaint: 'I'm only the Pope around here, nobody tells me anything'. The difference was that this time it was his position as bishop of Rome that had been usurped.

The minutes do not tell us why John opposed the move to the Palazzo San Callisto, but it is not difficult to guess. San Callisto is the monumentally huge 1930s neo-baroque barracks in the heart of Trastevere. It would no doubt have been convenient as a site for the diocesan offices. But it would have been symbolically all wrong, for it would have made the offices of the Roman diocese a mere appendage of the Roman Curia. John had his counter-proposal ready: move the diocesan offices to St John Lateran. He had been to St John Lateran on June 24, 1962, feast of St John the Baptist, and spoken at length about his desire, as Bishop of the Church of Rome, to make his cathedral the heart of diocesan life. 'From today onwards', he declared, 'the Lateran is no longer on the edge of the city, but at its effective centre' (*Lettere*, p. 408). Moving the diocesan curia there would revivify the place and make it what it ought to be, the true and living centre of the diocese of Rome.

So from Rome we move outwards to consider Pope John's Italian policies.

Chapter 17

The Italian connection

It came about that Italy took over the role once occupied by the Papal States.
But Italy still provided the providential earthly basis of the Holy See and its
point of insertion into the world. This is the link between 1848 and today.

(Arturo Carlo Jemolo, in *Chiesa e Stato in Italia negli ultimi cento anni*, Turin, 1963, p. 540)

No pope can fail to have an Italian policy. He has to make up his mind how much, or how little, he will involve himself in the affairs of the country he sees from his window. Pope John's originality was that he presented himself from the outset as a spiritual pope, a pastor, who made a clear distinction between the papacy and the republic of Italy. No longer in competition, they could live together in that spirit of harmonious collaboration he called *convivenza*. The result of making this distinction was that John's Italian policy was marked by 'disengagement' and 'reserve'. These are the terms he spontaneously uses whenever he thinks about the relationship between Church and state. He wanted the Church to withdraw from the immediate party-political battleground.

But this did not mean that he was washing his hands of Italian affairs or turning the Torre San Giovanni into an ivory tower. He thought that once the Church was detached from the hurly-burly of everyday politics, it would be better placed to speak about the rights and duties of Christians in the social and political sphere. Thus his 'disengagement' made *Mater et Magistra*, his first great social encyclical, possible. So although this chapter will be largely concerned with Italy, its significance is universal.

However, John's Italian policy soon ran into difficulties and had to be fought for. It was so utterly different from the policy of Pius XII who frankly exploited Catholic Action and the Christian Democrats to keep Italy safe from Communism (see pp. 242–3 above). Yet the 'men of Pius XII' were still at their posts. Ottaviani continued to threaten and bluster at the Holy Office. Ruffini reigned in Sicily. Cardinal Giuseppe Siri, archbishop of Genoa, was in complete control of the Italian bishops. He was president of the episcopal conference (CEI), president of its Catholic Action committee, president of the Italian social weeks, and much else besides. He preferred the precision of commitment to the vagueness of 'disengagement'. He held that through the Christian Democrats, the Vatican and the Church exercised a powerful influence for good on Italian society that it would be manifest folly to renounce. His friends in the Roman Curia were Tardini and Ottaviani.

So by the end of 1960 a strange situation was reached in which Italian churchmen, acting ostensibly in the name of the Pope, continued to propound a policy of which the Pope strongly disapproved. But since Pope John was for the most part silent on such issues, it was understandable that they should carry on as before out of habit, persuaded that nothing had changed. John's disapproval was patent, and precise and very painful events lay just beneath the surface. The whole story can now be told thanks to the hitherto unpublished material found in Giancarlo Zizola's two articles, *'Rapporti tra Moro e Giovanni XXIII'* (*Panorama*, May 10 and May 17, 1982).

On May 18, 1960, *l'Osservatore Romano* published an article under the heading *Punti Fermi* ('Here we stand'). It was unsigned, but Cardinals Tardini, Ottaviani and Siri had worked on it. The article reaffirmed the hierarchy's right and duty to issue commands in the political and social sphere. The bishops, it explained, were alone competent to judge the legitimacy of 'coalitions' or 'alliances'. This was a *moral* judgement that could not be left to the whim of the faithful. *Punti Fermi* recalled that there was 'an insurmountable opposition between Christian dogma and the Marxist system', and forbade Catholics to 'belong to, support or in any way collaborate with those who adopt and follow the Marxist ideology and its applications'. In the pontificate of Pius XII such an article would have been boring in its predictability; in the pontificate of Pope John it seemed disappointing and even faintly shocking. One could not both claim to be a 'spiritual pope' and interfere in politics in so blatant a fashion. It wasn't known who wrote the article. But it was assumed that the Pope approved of what appeared in his official newspaper.

Among those disappointed by *Punti Fermi* was Aldo Moro, leader of the Christian Democrats. For some time he had been trying to broaden the basis of his government by forming an alliance with the Socialists (PSI). This was the strategy known as 'the opening to the left'. Pope John was not unsympathetic towards Moro's case.

What was probably true in 1956 had become self-evident by 1960. Come what may, the Christian Democrats were going to remain in power. Foreigners might scoff at the annual musical chairs of ministers, but in reality Italian political life had great stability. But this stability was threatened. Moro's idea was that by the 'opening to the left' the Christian Democrats would cease to be merely the party of the Church and *Confindustria*, the employers' organisation, and their drift to the right where the neo-Fascists beckoned would be halted. The Christian Democratic Party would be revivified by being recalled to its origins when, far from being the Italian conservative party, it had been committed to social justice and reform. Italian democracy, still in 1960 a fragile growth, would be greatly strengthened if peaceful and democratic change were shown to be possible. Then the siren voices of totalitarianisms to left and right would lose their alluring charm. The 'opening to the left', finally, offered a more palpable advantage: it was hoped that in alliance with the Socialists the Christian Democrats might reverse the appalling losses they had suffered in the November 6, 1959, municipal elections when they lost over a million votes.

But such was the power of the Church in Italy that Moro's whole scheme would fail if it were opposed by the bishops. *Punti Fermi* made it clear that they would oppose it, vehemently. It talked about Marxists rather than Communists: this was to make the point that the Socialists were considered to be Marxist fellow-travellers. Also at issue – and indeed the heart of the matter – was the autonomy of the laity in politics. If the Christian Democrats were not to be allowed to make up their own minds about alliances and coalitions, then they would remain tied to the episcopal apron-strings and never attain the kind of political maturity that French or American Catholics considered normal. Where did Pope John stand?

It was quite evident where the official spokesmen of the Italian bishops stood. The local Catholic papers, almost invariably edited from the diocesan curia, attacked Aldo Moro as both heretic and traitor. *Verona Fedele* assured its readers that the Lord had already condemned Moro to hell-fire (an ironical judgement in view of his eventual death, tortured and murdered by the Red Brigades in 1978). Cardinal Siri inspired an article in his own paper, *Il Nuovo Cittadino*, called 'An Open Letter to Moro' that was a litany of insults and abuse. He followed this up with a personal letter, soon published, informing Moro in case he did not know that the Church's attitude to Communism had not changed. It ended: 'What has happened makes one deeply fearful for the future. In the name of God I beg of you to reflect on your responsibility and the consequences of your actions' (*Panorama*, May 10, 1982, p. 251).

But no matter how hard he reflected in his office in the Piazza del Gesù, Moro could be forgiven for feeling that these attacks were directed to the wrong address. He was not, in 1961, proposing an alliance with the Communists. His Christian conscience was clear. As he understood Catholic social doctrine from his old mentor Cardinal Montini, its guiding principle was the common good rather than the defence of sectional interests.

Moreover, the 'alliances' and 'coalitions' denounced by *Punti Fermi* were no longer just a theoretical possibility: they were actually being set up in Milan, Florence, Genoa (Siri's own fief) and forty other large Italian towns. But this merely increased the venom of the attacks on Moro. He desperately needed some ecclesiastical support. In Milan, the curially influenced newspaper, *Italia*, had joined the pack in condemning him. But Cardinal Montini promptly sacked its clerical editor and replaced him with a distinguished lay historian, Giuseppe Lazzati, whose democratic credentials were unimpeachable. That was encouraging. Even more encouraging was the total silence of *l'Osservatore Romano* which feigned not to know that anything at all was happening. It was assumed, correctly, that Pope John was responsible for this diplomatic silence.

But Moro needed more than silent acquiescence. He needed Pope John on his side. On January 27, 1961, Moro met Mgr Andrea Spada, since 1938 the editor of *l'Eco di Bergamo*, the only paper Roncalli read every day of his adult life, and a friend of the Pope. Spada suggested that he should state his case in a personal memorandum for the Pope. Moro wrote his report, Spada delivered it to Pope John and told him that in his judgement the Christian Democratic leadership should be trusted and that the unjust attacks on them should cease.

However, Moro's memo and Spada's audience had no immediate or perceptible effects. The project for a coalition in Sicily brought a thunderous condemnation from Cardinal Ruffini. Siri sent him a telegram of 'heartiest congratulations'. It seemed that an impasse had been reached which Pope John was unable to breach.

But although John did not intervene directly on the 'opening to the left' issue, he was not inactive. He tried to raise the level of debate above sterile polemics. On April 11, 1961, he received the Prime Minister, Amintore Fanfani, and made his clearest statement to date on the relationship between the Church and Italy. The *Risorgimento* which had unified Italy at the expense of abolishing the Papal States, was a providential event. No Pope had dared to say that before:

The celebration this year of the hundredth anniversary of Italian unification is a cause of great joy for Italy, and both of us, on the two banks of the Tiber, share the same feeling of gratitude towards Providence who, despite vicissitudes and conflicts which enflamed passions, as happens in every age, had guided this most favoured part of Europe towards a position of respect and honour in the concert of nations . . . If we look serenely at the events of a more or less distant past, the truth of the maxim comes home: history conceals and reveals all (DMC, III, p.205).

John recalled Pius XI's achievement in signing the Lateran Treaties and said that they had paved the way for 'the true and perfect unity of race, language and religion that had been the hope of the best Italians'. However, this did not mean, he hastened to add, that there was any confusion between the roles of Church and state:

The special situation of the Catholic Church and the Italian State – two organisms which differ in structure, character, level and aims – presupposes a certain reserve in the relationship which, based on courtesy and respect, makes the occasions on which their representatives do meet from time to time all the more agreeable (*ibid.*).

This speech was a landmark. It became known as 'The Wider Tiber' speech.

Since Fanfani the prime minister had fully endorsed the line of Moro on the need for an 'opening to the left', Pope John's 'reserve' meant in effect that he did not propose to interfere in political choices which properly belonged to the electors and their chosen representatives. He was abstaining. He would not seek to exercise jurisdiction in political matters. He was repudiating *Punti Fermi*. It followed that Siri and his supporters in the Roman Curia were being dropped, however gently, by the Pope.

This context helps to explain the significance *of Mater et Magistra*. Intended for May 15, 1961, to mark the seventieth anniversary of Leo XIII's *Rerum Novarum*, it did not in fact appear until July 15. Though delay usually meant fierce off-stage arguments, in this case it was due to translation difficulties. *Mater et Magistra* was eagerly scrutinised by Italian bishops and politicians to see on whose side Pope John had come down. On the whole Moro and his friends felt encouraged while the Siri camp was discomfited.

Mater et Magistra calmly accepts 'the welfare state' as an expression of the common good'. That may sound unremarkable, but Pius XII had recoiled from the prospect of 'communal kitchens, free health services and free education' (see Hales, p. 45). John, on the other hand, welcomed the fact that there had been 'an increase in social relationships' and 'a development in social life'. He called this process 'socialisation', a term borrowed from Pierre Teilhard de Chardin. Commentators who wished to stress 'the continuity of Catholic social doctrine' tied themselves into intricate semantic knots as they tried to explain that 'socialisation' did not and could not possibly mean 'socialism', since 'socialism' had been condemned by previous popes. The word 'socialisation' did not even appear in the Latin text which used expressions like *socialium rationum incrementa* or *socialium rerum progressus* (see Campbell-Johnston, p. 382). But it *was* found in the translations.

Whether 'socialisation' implied 'socialism' was largely a matter of definition. But if 'socialism' meant the welfare state, then it was plain that Pope John approved of it: 'It (socialisation) is an effect and a cause of the growing intervention of the state even in matters of such intimate concern to the individual as health and education, the choice of a career, and the care and rehabilitation of the physically and mentally handicapped' (*Mater et Magistra*, No. 48). But doesn't this, Cardinal Siri was soon to ask, subordinate the individual to the amorphous mass, the monstrous Leviathan evoked by Pius XII in his broadcast to Austrian Catholics on September 14, 1952? Had not this great pontiff precisely warned them not to submit to 'an all-embracing socialisation'? He had (see AAS 44, 1952, p. 792).

Pope John anticipated this objection, and put it in his encyclical: 'Must we then conclude that increased social action necessarily reduces people to the condition of being merely automatons? By no means' (No. 48). The safeguard against the potential evils of state control and excessive bureaucracy were twofold. First, 'a healthy view of the public good must be present and operative in those invested with public authority' (No. 51). Second, 'the numerous intermediate bodies and corporate enterprises' should enjoy real autonomy (No. 52). It was the classic 'liberal' defence against the totalitarian state. The 'numerous intermediate bodies' – political parties, trades unions, the judiciary, the broadcasting services, the press – should be genuinely independent, and through their stimulating inter-play the common good would be served.

But the acceptance of the welfare state was not the only originality of *Mater et Magistra*. Though it is disingenuously presented as merely 'confirming and making more specific the teaching of our predecessors', its whole approach was novel. It is clearly referring to the real world of 1961. Gone is the semi-feudal world evoked by Leo XIII in which 'the simple workman, surrounded by his family, settles down to his frugal but sufficient meal, the just reward of his labour' (Hales, p. 45). John's world is that of colleges of further education, the European Economic Community (which Italy joined from the outset) and the United Nations. He was optimistic about them all.

This marked a new tone in 'Catholic social teaching'. John does not scold. He welcomes the good wherever he finds it. In Pius XI and Pius XII one sometimes got the impression that the world was being lectured at and castigated from the outside by an irate headmaster who knew better. 'Catholic social doctrine' in the 1930s and 1940s brought comfort to Latin dictators like Franco in Spain and Salazar in Portugal, both of whom claimed to be implementing its principal of *interclassismo*, the harmonious collaboration of all that was the Catholic response to the Marxist class-war. John did not speak from the outside or adopt a superior tone. The Church was *Mater* (Mother) as well as *Magistra* (Teacher). John eventually revealed that he had got the phrase *Mater et Magistra* from Pope Innocent III's address to the Fourth Lateran Council (Alberigo, p. 348). He consulted widely, seeking the views of Cardinals Paul Richard of Bordeaux, Franz König of Vienna, Canon Joseph Cardijn, founder of the YCW, and Mgr Pietro Pavan, professor of sociology at the Lateran University (John had raised his old college to this dignity on May 17, 1959).

It was in Italy that *Mater et Magistra*, though addressed to the whole Catholic world, had its most immediate application. Not that it settled all the controversies. The human mind is endlessly resourceful in rejecting what it finds uncongenial. Cardinal Siri continued his anti-Moro campaign, but he seemed more and more to be beating the air.

Pope John's journal for August 13, 1961, reflects the strength of his disapproval:

> It is very important to insist that all bishops should act in the same way: may the Pope's example be a lesson and encouragement to them all. The bishops are more exposed to the

temptation of meddling immoderately in matters that are not their business, and this is why the Pope must admonish them not to take part in any political or controversial arguments, and not to declare for one faction or section rather than another. They are to preach to all alike, and in general terms, justice, charity, meekness, gentleness and the other evangelical virtues, courteously defending the rights of the Church when these are offended or compromised (*Journal*, p. 331).

From this we may infer that John had 'admonished' the Italian bishops, and no doubt their president, Cardinal Siri, but to little avail. The theocratic habits instilled by Pius XII could not be eradicated so easily. What Pope John described as 'immoderate meddling', Siri considered to be his ordinary, everyday and – he would have added – *sacred* duty. Not much room for compromise there.

'Disengagement' meant not only steering clear of interference in political matters but also giving up the intrigues to which prelates in the land of Niccolò Machiavelli were particularly prone. It would be wrong to suggest that the whole Italian Church was sunk in corruption; but it would be equally wrong to imagine that such temptations had not invaded the Vatican itself. John knew what was going on about him as the following story, from an impeccable source, illustrates. Any vagueness in the narrative is deliberate.

At about this time, summer 1961, a certain cardinal of aristocratic origins was on his death-bed. He had been engaged in the financial operations of the Vatican for many years. Pope John suddenly became worried that the aged cardinal might die unshriven, his soul in agony as much as his body. So he sent along a friar (usually described in hagiography as ' a humble friar') to hear the cardinal's last confession. The friar returned, rather crest-fallen, and reported that the relatives were blocking the ante-chambers, and refused to let him through. 'Just as I thought' said Pope John, by now angry, 'find an archbishop, they surely will not refuse an archbishop'. But they did. This was work for a cardinal. A cardinal was found who was able to pull rank, make his way through the relatives and hear the dying man's confession. The point of this puzzling story is that the nephews and nieces of the cardinal feared that if he made a final confession, he might feel obliged in conscience to change his will.

John's own will was already carefully drawn up. No relatives would crowd around his death-bed. 'Born poor', he wrote, 'I am particularly happy to die poor' (*Journal*, p. 367). 'Disengagement' had moral as well as political implications.

But it did not mean that he was uninterested in the details of practical politics. On the contrary. In February 1962 he called for and studied with great care Aldo Moro's prolix report to the eighth Christian Democratic Congress that had just met in Naples. It put the case for the 'opening to the left'. Pope John found that Moro's report made sense. But just to make sure, he submitted it to the judgement of experts who concluded that it was 'not only in harmony with revelation but with the social doctrine of the Church' (*Panorama*, May 17, 1982, p. 246). That was an accolade. Moro was informed of this *nihil obstat*. He wrote to Pope John, thanking him for his 'paternal interest and understanding'. Moro pledged his loyalty to the Pope, the hierarchy and the social doctrine of the Church, declared that under his leadership the Christian Democrats would always strive to work for the real good of Italy, and asked for a blessing on himself, his family and his party (*ibid.*, p. 257). But he did not at this stage crave an audience. That would have been immediately seized upon by his critics. For the time being 'reserve' continued to be the best papal policy. And Moro understood perfectly well why.

Moro wrote his letter to Pope John on February 3, 1962. The same day John published the *motu proprio* fixing the start of the Ecumenical Council for October 11 of that year. This ought to have concentrated the mind of Cardinal Siri on the impending 'event'. Far from it. He soon hurled himself into a fresh political battle. On March 2, 1962, Amintore Fanfani presented his reformist programme to the Italian parliament. This time round he was Prime Minister in a 'centre-left' administration which meant that he was in power thanks to the abstention of the Socialists; they would not vote with him, but neither would they bring him down. Fanfani's main proposal was for the nationalisation of the electricity industry. Siri sniffed the most sinister implications in this measure. He set down his worries in a memorandum which landed on Pope John's desk in June, 1962.

It was a passionate document. Siri denounced nationalisation in general as immoral be- cause it set limits on freedom and opened the door to tyranny and dictatorship. These evils would inevitably follow if political and economic power were concentrated in the same hands. The Leviathan loomed once more. It was not altogether clear why nationalising electricity should be deemed to have such devastating effects, but it was now too late to halt Siri in his tracks. Insofar as the Christian Democratic Party had abandoned Catholic social doctrine, it had forfeited the right to the title 'Christian'.

But Siri was not yet finished. Chagrined at not being able to convince the Pope himself, he tried an indirect approach. On July 7, 1962, Capovilla received a letter from the President of *Confindustria*, Furio Cicogna, requesting an audience for himself and his deputy, Angelo Costa. They did not need to say why they wanted an audience: it was too obvious that they were going to protest about the electricity nationalisation bill. Pope John refused them an audience. On July 9, 1962, he typed out a note which Capovilla was to commmunicate to Cicogna. It is a classic – and hitherto unpublished – statement of Pope John's political 're- serve':

> The Holy Father wishes to remain outside conflicts of a politico-social nature between sons whom he respects and loves with an equal measure of comprehension. It is the Lord who searches out all our hearts. So you will understand the Pope's silence in the discussions that have been going on in the last few months, discussions between brothers whom the father holds equally dear . . .
>
> In the four years that Pope John has exercised his ministry he has never once had, sought or exploited any meeting with government ministers, trades unionists or any other concerned party to emerge from his reserve. In this he follows the example of the patriarch Jacob who, in the midst of his quarrelling sons, confined himself to watching, suffering and keeping silent.
>
> These explanations are also a request that the president and vice-president of *Confindustria* may dispense the Pope from an audience that could not remain confidential and could not fail to give rise to various speculations (*Panorama*, May 17, 1982, pp. 256–7).

John remained unfailingly courteous, even when he had to say no.

Yet the patriarchal pope was not quite so neutral as he appeared. On August 3, 1962, he gave to Aldo Moro the audience that he had refused to the chiefs of industry only a month before. It was a meeting that both men had long desired. It took place at Castelgandolfo, which was more discreet and less supervised by the media, and lasted about an hour. There were no speeches and protocol was at a minimum. In a note written later the same day Pope John described Moro as 'an excellent Catholic, a statesman, a man of great social concern' (Capovilla, letter to the author, May 13, 1983). This meeting on the eve of the Council with someone who was still being publicly attacked by Siri spoke for itself. It did not need elaborate commentary. 'It was', remarked Giancarlo Zizola, 'a metaphor for the Pope's recognition of the political liberty of Italian Catholics' (*Panorama*, May 17, 1982, p. 259).

Meantime, Siri's monopoly of power was broken. Little wonder that he was heard to complain that Pope John's pontificate was 'the greatest disaster in recent ecclesiastical history', explaining that by 'recent' he meant in the last five hundred years. (In his evidence to the beatification process of Pope John, Siri withdrew this judgement and said that he had been wrong.)

John's reform of the Italian episcopacy through new statutes of 1959 brought the Italian bishops into line with other episcopal conferences who did not enjoy a 'special relationship' with the Vatican. Naturally, since the Holy See was in Italy, the relationship would still be unique; but the umbilical cord had been cut, and the Italian bishops could thrive and grow up. E. E. Y. Hales' conclusion about Pope John's approach to Italian politics is entirely justified: 'He was largely free from the Renaissance habit of using politics to strengthen the papal position in Italy, and from the mediaeval habit of using politics to build a papal ascendency over Europe' (Hales, p. 63).

What the Council's document *Gaudium et Spes* would soon have to say about politics reflects Pope John's practice as much as his theory. Clerics are not omnicompetent (No. 43), lay persons have 'freedom of enquiry and thought' (No. 62), the Church is prepared to renounce 'privileges' once sanctioned by concordats (No. 76), and it is in the profoundest sense 'the Church of the poor' (No. 1). The Council could have arrived at these conclusions unaided; but it was helpful to have the example of Pope John.

But it is time to pick up the threads of the Council. It was being assiduously prepared. Many of the same actors who have already been met in this chapter were involved, but others were new.

Chapter 18

Enter Augustin Bea

The first opinion of a ruler's intelligence is formed on the quality of the men
he has around him.

(Niccolò Machiavelli, *The Prince*, Penguin Classics, 1961, p. 124)

Getting the Council under way was like cranking up some enormous machine. The Ante-
preparatory Commission had been set up at Pentecost 1959. Out of 2812 prelates or institutions (like Catholic universities) consulted, 2150 replied. This was 76.4 per cent – a good
'market response'. Their replies will be invaluable to future historians who want a graph of
Catholic leadership mentalities in 1960. A sampling suggests that they had not yet grasped
the possibilities put within their reach by the Council. They confined themselves to minor
reforms: the Holy See should concede more 'faculties' to the local bishops (Rouquette, I, p.
88). One English bishop shared his ambitions for the Council with his people. He assured
them that 'there were great hopes of new definitions' such as that of Our Lady as 'Mediatrix
of All Graces' (Pawley, p. 430). It was difficult to be more wrong than that. All these suggestions and requests, known as *voti*, were confidential at the time, but were later published by
the Vatican Press in fifteen massive volumes (*Acta et Documenta Concilia Oecumenico Vaticano
Secundo apparando*). Subsequent studies, such as *A la Veille de Vatican II, Vota et Réactions en Europe
et dans le Catholicisme Oriental* (eds. M. Lamberigts and Claude Sotens, Leuven, Theology
Faculty, 1992), reveal occasional flashes of John's 'new Pentecost'.

Although John chose the eve of Whitsunday, June 5, 1960, to announce the setting up of
the Preparatory Commissions proper, they did not set to work until November 13, 1960.
There was a suspicion that Cardinal Domenico Tardini was deliberately spinning out the
preparations for whatever reasons; if he thought that John might not last much longer, he
fell victim to a divine irony, dying himself on July 30, 1961, almost two years before the
Pope. Even for an institution which 'thinks in centuries', the delay was disquieting with so
many old men around. Still more disquieting was that the Central Theological Commission and its ten sub-commissions were largely under curial control.

This was the result of a decision taken by Pope John himself. He decided that the president of each sub-commission would be the prefect of the corresponding Roman Congregation (or dicastery). So Cardinal Gaetano Cicognani, of the Congregation of Rites, was
responsible for liturgy while Cardinal Marcello Mimmi from the Consistorial Congregation dealt with episcopal matters. Cardinal Alfredo Ottaviani presided over the Theological
Commission, and held that it had a right of veto over everyone else because the Congregation to which it corresponded, the Holy Office, was traditionally known as 'the *supreme*
Congregation'. (Ottaviani was strictly its 'pro-prefect' because the Pope himself was its 'pre-

fect': but this was a distinction without a difference.) The effect of these arrangements was that the control of the preparations for the Council was firmly vested in the hands of the Roman Curia.

This became perfectly clear when the names of the members of the preparatory commissions were unveiled. There were over 800 of them. Generalisations about so vast a group are not easy, but critics were soon claiming that in the main they represented the 'Roman school' for which theology was the exposition and defence of known truth rather than an exploration on the frontiers of knowledge. However, there were plenty of individual exceptions. Cardinal Giovanni Battista Montini managed to smuggle his mentor, Oratorian Fr Giulio Bevilacqua, onto the Liturgy Commission (Bugnini, p. 27). But Montini himself was still excluded at this stage. But the names of those not summoned to serve formed a roll-call of 'the great and the good' of the period: uninvited were the Jesuits John Courtney Murray and John L. McKenzie from the United States, the brothers Karl and Hugo Rahner from Bavaria, and Frenchmen Henri de Lubac and Jean Daniélou; also absent were the French Dominicans Yves-Marie Congar and Marie-Dominique Chenu. In short anyone touched even lightly by the fall-out from *Humani Generis* or who had otherwise had problems with the Holy Office was rigorously excluded.

Moreover, John's instructions provided only a mild incentive to seek outside help. The fact that the Curia is responsible for the organisation of the Council, he explained on June 5, 1960, 'does not exclude from time to time the co-operation of enlightened wisdom from ecclesiastics invited in view of their acknowledged personal competence'. Note the absence of lay men and women. It is assumed that male ecclesiastics hold a monopoly of 'enlightened wisdom'. It would be easy but unjust to make Tardini alone the scapegoat for these arrangements. Pope John bore his share of responsibility. The upshot was that many feared the Council would be a packed assembly, lacking the best available scholarship and the essential attribute of freedom.

Had John made a bad mistake? Should he have foreseen what would happen? It seems that he half-foresaw it, tried to forestall its worst effects, but persisted because he thought if the curialists were involved in the work of the Council they would be committed to it. It would not suddenly burst upon them as a threat to be resisted or a foreign invasion to be repulsed. This part of John's plan did not altogether miscarry. Mgr Dell'Acqua claimed that there was a new spirit in the Curia:

> In the Secretariat of State no one any longer feels they have to go out and do pastoral work to keep themselves sane. They realise that their work in the Secretariat of State is itself pastoral. Pope John had changed the outlook of the Church's central administration, while its juridical position remained unchanged (*L'Uomo che non divenne Papa*, p. 265).

Well and good. But it seems rather odd that working on the preparations for a would-be 'pastoral' Council should lead one to abandon pastoral work outside; and what Dell'Acqua said was only patchily true. Bureaucracies have their own in-built inertia and resistance to change.

Yet one reason why Pope John was not particularly worried at this stage was that alongside the laborious official preparation for the Council, so tightly controlled by the Curia, there was another form of preparation that was free, unofficial, independent, and above all public. Unlike the official preparations that were secret and therefore invisible, the books, articles and television interviews about the Council carried the discussion to everyone in the Church and beyond. This media activity created expectations, gave rise to arguments about the purpose of the Council, and reflected in however crude a manner the *sensus fidelium*, that instinctive sense of what is right doctrine lodged in the hearts of all the faithful. From this vast output, two contrasting works may be selected because in different ways they directly influenced the Council.

Lorenz Jaeger, archbishop of Paderborn, has already been mentioned as the founder of the Adam Möhler Institute. As soon as the Council was announced on January 25, 1959, he embarked on an historical study of the Council, called in English translation *The Ecumenical Council, The Church and Christendom*. Jaeger's solid and dependable book had a considerable influence. It clarified the questions and changed some perceptions. He pointed out that there was no fixed or prescribed historical 'model' for a Council. They had all been time-conditioned events dependent on all manner of external factors such as, for example, the role of the emperor. Another variable in a Council was the Church's own self-understanding at the time; for there could not be a council at all without some implicit ecclesiology or doctrine of the Church.

This was dynamite. For the way the Council was actually being organised, apparently at the behest of Pope John, reflected a centralising, authoritarian, clerical, juridical, un- or anti-ecumenical and world-defying understanding of the Church that could have the most appalling consequences. There would be no point at all in meeting merely to repeat the Syllabus of Errors. Vatican I, Jaeger went on, had been a monarchically run Council reflecting the autocratic spirit of the age, and it reacted against all contemporary movements. Vatican II would have to reflect the more 'democratic' or – if that word were alarming and improper – 'collegial' temper of the mid-twentieth century. It followed that there would have to be 'free and close discussion of all objections and difficulties' (Jaeger, p. 86) This was aimed at Cardinal Ottaviani who held that controversial matters should not be discussed at the Council lest the faithful be disedified. Jaeger also argued that there should be some kind of 'lay participation' in the Council as a reminder that, in the last analysis, the teaching of the Church reposed upon the *sensus fidelium*. Jaeger, in short, invited Pope John to supply the vision and organisational savvy to see that the Council got under way in the right spirit. John might ruefully complain, 'I'm only the Pope around here'. But there were some things that only the Pope could do.

Another German-speaking theologian, Swiss-born Hans Küng, responded with equal alacrity to the announcement of the Council. The German edition of *Konzil und Wiedervereinigung. Erneuerung als Ruf in die Einheit* appeared in 1960 (translated in England as *The Council and Reunion* and in the United States as *The Council, Reform and Reunion*). That same year Küng was appointed professor of Theology at Tübingen at the remarkably early age of thirty-two. Unlike Jaeger's rather heavy tome, Küng's book was lively and readable. Moreover, he ventured to set out an agenda for the Council. Needless to say, it was not quite the programme the Roman Curia had in mind – and his book had to wait until 1965 for an Italian translation. For Küng the plain purpose of the Council was the reform of the Church. If this reform were properly done, it would lead to reunion on equal terms with the 'separated brethren'. Küng catalogued the steps that would have to be taken to meet the *valid* demands of the Protestant Reformation: some appreciation of the Reformation as a *religious* event (not reducible to political or psychological factors like Luther's libido); growing esteem for and use of the Bible in theology and worship; the development of a 'people's liturgy', naturally in the vernacular; an understanding of the 'universal priesthood' of all the faithful; dialogue between the Church and other cultures; the liberation of the papacy from political entanglements; the reform of the Roman Curia and the abolition of the Index of Forbidden Books. Küng proved an accurate and far-sighted prophet: all of his seven demands were embodied, even if in modified form, in the final documents of the Council.

Moreover, Küng skilfully appealed to Pope John who, he assumed somewhat gratuitously, would share his enthusiasm for all these causes. Küng contrasted the wide-awake Pope with slumbering Christendom:

> Schism is a scandal. But it is perhaps an even greater scandal that the majority of Christians, in all communities, even today, and including theologians and pastors, are profoundly indifferent to this scandal; that they feel the division of Christendom at most as a deplorable imperfection, not as an immeasurably crippling wound which absolutely must be healed; that they are deeply concerned over a thousand religious trivialities, but not over Our Lord's desire that 'all may be one'. Will the words and actions of the Pope be enough to waken these sleepers? (*Council and Reunion*, p. 57).

It was, in every sense of the term, rousing stuff. Especially when repeated to crowded audiences across Europe and the United States.

Shrewd, too, and well calculated to appeal to Pope John, was Küng's presentation of the sixteenth century Council of Trent as essentially a *reforming* Council He did not make the mistake of those who used Trent as a bogey and blamed everything corrupt on its bigoted narrowness. Kong explained that it had some good effects: 'It hardly needs stressing that for all their limitations, these acts of restoration were productive of immeasurable good. It is thanks to them that the Church of the Baroque period displays a purity and a strength that are very different from the Church of the Renaissance' (*Council and Reunion*, p. 120). This was exactly the thesis of Roncalli in his edition of the *Acta* of St Charles Borromeo. True, Küng went on to say that after Paul IV, the polemical atmosphere and political manoeuvrings led to an inquisitorial repression of error that was less admirable. But John as historian could not quarrel with that either.

He never made any public comment on Küng. There was no reason why he should. But already what may be termed the 'first battle of Küng' was being waged. The Curia was furious at the way this jumped-up young man was denouncing the Holy Office and waving his personal programme for the forthcoming Council in the press and on television while sound theologians and serious-minded persons like themselves were exchanging decent Latin memos on the limits of religious 'exemption'. It was intolerable. (To tell the truth, there were some in the Curia who were delighted at the thought that Ottaviani had at last met his match.) But Küng had a lot of support. Cardinal Franz König, archbishop of Vienna, a scholar with whom few in the college of cardinals could compete, introduced the German edition and called the book a 'happy omen'. In his introduction, Cardinal Achille Liénart of Lille stressed its ecumenical importance (see Nowell, p. 82). It was reasonable to conclude that whatever the Preparatory Commission might be doing, Küng had provided the real agenda for the Council, and drawn up the battle lines for its first session. Never again would an individual theologian have such influence.

There did not seem to be any easy way in which the various streams of preparation could merge. Yet if they did not, the Council would fail to live up to the expectations aroused by theologians like Jaeger and Küng. Was there anyone in Rome who knew German theology and knew his way about the Vatican? There was Fr Augustin Bea S.J., rector of the Biblicum. But he was six months older than Pope John, and already looked so frail that it seemed a puff of wind would blow him over. He was stooped and his tortoise-like face was deeply lined. As a Jesuit he would have to refuse a cardinal's hat at first, but if Pope John insisted under obedience, then he would accept without enthusiasm or demur. Bea was created cardinal on January 28, 1960, though his precise role was not yet clear. He did not look like a man who would launch the Church on a radically new course. Yet without Bea, it is unlikely that Pope John would have got the Council he wanted.

The idea of a small, high-powered body dealing exclusively with ecumenical questions had been canvassed early on. But it was Jaeger who drew up the detailed plan which Cardinal Bea presented to the Pope in a letter dated March 11, 1960. John annotated the letter:

> Heard the views of the cardinal secretary of state [Tardini] and of cardinal Bea (12 and 13 March). The project is approved. Cardinal Bea will be president of the proposed Pont. Comm. Answer and reach an agreement with the Bishop of Paderborn [Jaeger].
>
> Prepare everything but wait till after Easter for the official publication: this will bring it into line with the other commissions which will be named on various other matters.
> *Ita. Die XIV Martii*, 1960 (*Lettere*, pp. 495–6).

Ita, wrote John, yes, so be it. Did he realise that he had just made the most important appointment of his pontificate? He seems to have taken it in his stride as one of his 'silent inspirations from the Lord'. Though he entrusted the future to the Lord and refused to be 'curious and anxious about the shape of things to come' (*Journal*, p. 336), he was perfectly capable of thinking and planning ahead.

His *motu proprio, Superno Dei Nutu*, which set up the Secretariat for Christian Unity, defined its purpose in clear and ungrudging tones:

> In order to show in a special manner our love and good will towards those who bear the name of Christ, but are separated from this Apostolic See, and in order that they may be able to follow the work of the Council and find more readily the way to attain that unity for which Jesus besought his heavenly Father, we have established this special Office or Secretariat (*Unity of Christians*, p. 166).

It was the hoisting of a signal. It let the separated brethren know that they too were officially invited to take part in what Karl Barth was soon to call 'the event' (of the Spirit). The Secretariat for Christian Unity was something totally new from the start, and it needed new men. Bea scoured the Catholic universities and seminaries for members and consultants chosen for their biblical, ecumenical or patristic competence. Some, like Fr Maurice Bévenot SJ, of Heythrop College, England, had led a blameless life entirely dedicated to the study of the transmission of the St Cyprian manuscripts. Others were too young to have incurred Holy Office displeasure. Bea spotted for example the thirty-seven year old Canadian Augustinian, Gregory Baum, whose Fribourg, Switzerland 1956 thesis, *That all may be One*, had been followed by work on the anti-semitism of the Gospels. Thus the organisation, method of work, personnel and spirit of the Secretariat for Christian Unity were something utterly foreign to the Roman Curia. They even talked different languages, preferring German, English and French to Italian. This was not out of anti-Italian prejudice but simply because few native Italian-speakers had much experience of ecumenism.

So this ecumenical 'cuckoo in the nest' was unwelcome to the Roman Curia. With it Pope John had out-flanked and by-passed the Curia that was supposed to be preparing the Council. He had introduced a wholly new criterion into the preconciliar discussions: what will other Christians think? For the first time the Council preparations were on course and heading in the direction Pope John had hoped for from the start.

The purpose of the Council came into clearer focus. John had always known that Vatican II would not be a 'council of reunion' in the sense that Lyons in the thirteenth and Florence in the fifteenth century had attempted to be. The time was not yet ripe. Cardinal Bea stated very clearly what Pope John had in mind:

> The Holy Father hopes that the forthcoming Council may be a kind of invitation to our separated brethren, by letting them see, in its day-to-day proceedings, the sincerity, love and concord which prevail in the Catholic Church. So we may say, rather, that the Council should make an indirect contribution to union, breaking the ground in a long-term policy of preparation for unity (*Unity of Christians*, p. 158: originally *Katholische Nachrichten Agentur*, January 22, 1961).

Those whom Tardini only nine months earlier had described as 'dissidents' were transmuted into 'separated brothers'. Instead of being kept at barge-pole length with condemnations, they were invited to 'Come and see' (John 1.39). And their responses and expectations would help to shape not only the nature and extent of their own participation but the agenda itself. Bea and his secretary, Mgr Jan Willebrands, embarked on a vast programme of correspondence and travel to discover the answers to these questions and build up their team. Bea was rejuvenated. There were many stories of old men being transformed and throwing away their sticks on becoming cardinals. 'SEE THE WORLD WITH BEA' was a Roman joke of the time (BEA being the current acronym for British European Airways).

In the midst of the consultations that led to the setting up of the Secretariat for Christian Unity, Cardinal Francis J. Spellman, archbishop of New York, military vicar, showed that his sense of timing had gone awry. He petitioned Pope John to start the historical investigation that might eventually lead to the beatification and canonisation of Pope Pius XII (*Lettere*, p. 499). John tried to reply, but found it difficult. 'The feelings of devoted esteem and admiration', he bravely began, 'that so many in the Church have for Pius XII, are well-known'. But there he laid down his pen. He left the matter to his successor. He did not think that canonising popes was of much help to the mass of Christians. On this occasion he could not find a formula to say 'no' to Spellman without letting him down badly.

But the petition had a pharisaic aspect. The comparison between John and his predecessor continued to be made. It was made even more sharply after the creation of the Secretariat for Christian Unity and Bea's appointment as its first President. For by this act – it was whispered – the ecumenical rules laid down in his instruction *Ecclesia Catholica* (December 20, 1949), were being manifestly flouted. And this was Pope John's doing. However, since it was not good form to attack the Pope directly, Bea became the target. But Bea, despite his frail shoulders, was a tough man to bring down. He had lived in Rome since 1924 and knew the ropes. It was particularly difficult to drive a wedge between him and Pius XII since he had been the Pope's confessor. Indeed, this is what alarmed some ecumenists when they heard of his appointment as president of the Secretariat for Christian Unity: he seemed to be too much a 'man of Pius XII', another venerable survivor from the *ancien régime*. This was one reason why he could be useful to Pope John. Bea formed a bridge between the two pontificates. No one could fault Bea on loyalty to Pius XII. He would therefore have to be attacked on other grounds.

Ottaviani emerged as his principal opponent. Not very scrupulous when it came to in-fighting, Ottaviani probed for weaknesses and throughout the next three years varied the point of attack as occasions arose. Bea was deemed unsound because he had contributed to if not drafted the Pius XII encyclical, *Divino Afflante Spiritu* (1943) which conceded that the study of ancient literary *genres* could help in the understanding of the Bible: this innocuous proposition was believed to 'give in to form-criticism' as practised by Rudolf Bultmann. Bea's second weakness was that he was supposed to be unfaithful to the *Ecclesia Catholica*, which stressed the need for great caution in ecumenical contexts (known humorously at the time as 'mixed bathing'), and the peril of taking actions which might 'compromise the revealed doctrine of the Church'. Since *Ecclesia Catholica* had not been rescinded, it was as-sumed with impeccable logic that it was still in force. Nuncios and Apostolic Delegates were on the look-out for rash or indiscriminate bathers in ecumenical waters. These two charges against Bea will recur with tedious repetitiveness. John made no attempt to curb Ottaviani. But he encouraged Bea to reply in a reasoned manner to criticisms. So Bea gave endless interviews and wrote articles, notably in *Civiltà Cattolica*.

This estimable Jesuit fortnightly had been founded to defend the Ultramontane case and the Syllabus of Errors. In the twentieth century it had become, as it were, the adult version of *l'Osservatore Romano*. It had the rule that no non-Jesuit could write in it, and it was cen-sored by the Secretariat of State. At the start of 1961 Bea published an article called 'The Catholic Attitude to the Problem of Christian Unity' (*Civiltà Cattolica*, I, 1961, pp. 113–29: *Unity of Christians*, pp. 19–46). It was a boring and rather conventional article that did not yield up its meaning straight away. The New Testament, he pointed out, shows great 'sever-ity' towards heresy and schism. He quotes a cluster of fierce Pauline texts to illustrate what happened to the incestuous Corinthian (he was 'handed over to Satan': I Corinthians 5.4–5) and those who have 'made shipwreck of their faith' (I Timothy 1.19-20). St Matthew's Gos-pel says of the recalcitrant: 'If he will not listen to the Church, then count him all one with the heathen and the publican' (Matthew 18.17).

It is easy to imagine Ottaviani reading this passage and suspecting a catch somewhere. This was only the first part of the dialectic, the thesis to be followed by the antithesis. Bea went on to say that the New Testament severity that he had so vividly illustrated applies *only* to those who have individually and deliberately withdrawn from the true faith. 'As it is no merit of ours to have been born and brought up in a family belonging to the Catholic Church, so it is no fault of theirs that they are children of parents separated from our

Church. Accepting in good faith the inheritance handed on by their parents, these non-Catholics can sincerely believe that they are on the right path' (*Unity of Christians*, p. 27). The remainder of Bea's article was concerned with the common faith in which all Christians shared. 'Non-Catholic Christians must not, therefore, be put on the same plane as the non-baptised; for they always bear, not only the name of Christ on their foreheads, but his actual image in their souls, deeply and indelibly imprinted there by baptism' (*ibid.*, p. 32). More than twenty years later, these are banalities, blunted by endless repetition. In the early 1960s they were liberating discoveries, enlightening truths. Then Bea quoted Pope John's address to the preparatory Commission on November 13, 1960: 'One great point to be held by every baptised person is that the Church remains for ever his Mystical Body. He is the Head, to it each of us believers is related, to it we belong' (*Unity of Christians*, pp. 32–3). The syntax was tortured but the meaning clear: this was a decisive move from an ecclesiology that excluded other Christians to one that embraced them.

Within two weeks of making this liberating statement, Pope John received Dr Geoffrey Fisher at the Vatican. It was on December 2, 1960, that a pope and an archbishop of Canterbury met for the first time since the Reformation. It was also the first-fruits of Bea's indefatigable letter-writing and the first response to Pope John's invitation to 'Come and see'. The Curia was hostile to this hob-nobbing with 'dissidents'. Tardini scarcely bothered to conceal his hostility and did everything he could to cut the visit down to size. Bea was not even allowed to see the archbishop, still less to be present at the audience. Tardini sent along a relatively junior member of his staff, Mgr Antonio Samorè, to keep an eye on Pope John and report back. No ecclesiastical title was accorded to Fisher who was addressed throughout as *Dottore*, as though he were some kind of university professor (all these details from Col. Robert Hornby, in a letter to the author, February 23, 1982: he was Dr Fisher's press officer). As Peter Nichols put it: 'The visit was treated like a guilty secret. No photograph was permitted, and every effort made for the event to pass off as unobtrusively as possible' (*Politics*, p. 314). 'Behind those walls', a frustrated television commentator was reduced to saying, 'history is being made'.

If there was official coolness on the Roman side – Pope John excepted – Archbishop Fisher displayed a certain amount of Anglican truculence. He pointedly included the visit to Rome in a journey that led him to Istanbul to see the ecumenical patriarch. Having arrived in Rome, he then preached a sermon in the Anglican Church in which he contrasted the 'Anglican' concept of 'collegiality' with the 'Roman' idea of papal monarchy. Collegiality, he declared, was admirably reflected in the unity and diversity found in the British Commonwealth, while the papal monarchy, if unchecked, could lead straight to dictatorship. Moreover, Fisher fully intended to lecture Pope John on the ineptitude of the 'Return-to-Rome' theory enshrined in *Ad Petri Cathedram* of the previous summer. He told Pope John that 'the two Churches are running in parallel – maybe they are two straight lines that will merge in eternity' (Hornby, as above). Pope John told Giuseppe De Luca that they talked of St Gregory the Great and of St Augustine's mission to Canterbury (*Lettere*, p. 165). That was predictable enough.

Cardinal Bea shrugged off his humiliations as all part of the ecumenical cross, and rejoiced that the visit had taken place at all. It was officially described as a 'courtesy visit' and no 'negotiations' had taken place. After four centuries, the ice was broken and contact was re-established. For Dr Fisher the visit was an undoubted success. He was charmed by Pope John's evident goodness, but he had stuck to his Anglican principles and protected his flanks. He was able to return home and resign, as he had already decided to, on a high note. A six-hour debate in the House of Lords showed that the majority of Anglican peers were strongly in favour of the ecumenical cause as they perceived it, and wished to banish bigotry. The visit did a great deal to establish the Anglican Communion as an original body, distinct both from the Orthodox and the Protestants. To drive home this point, the archbishops of Canterbury and York appointed Canon Bernard Pawley to be their 'personal representative' to the Vatican. He was received by Pope John on July 12, 1961. No other Church or Communion had the wit to have its own ambassador in Rome.

The Fisher–Roncalli meeting had another sequel: an anecdote. On January 4, 1961, Evelyn Waugh, the master novelist, wrote to Elizabeth Pakenham (now Lady Longford): 'Did you know that Archbishop Roberts had an audience with the Pope a week after Dr Fisher had gone charging in crying: "Your Holiness, we are making history"? The Pope said to Roberts: "There was another Archbishop from your country here the other day. Now who was he?"' (*Letteres*, p. 558; also, less elaborated, *Diaries*, p. 777). Anyone who knew Thomas d'Esterre Roberts, the sometime archbishop of Bombay, would realise that inventing such a story would have given him as much puckish pleasure as Waugh derived from repeating it.

In the Evelyn Waugh fiction, however, can be seen the beginnings of the conservative myth that presents Pope John as an amiable but bumbling old boy who could not remember from one day to the next who he had been talking to. From that it is only a step to saying that he was being manipulated by Capovilla or Bea for their nefarious schemes. All the evidence is to the contrary. John was perfectly lucid and alert. But John was approaching eighty, four score, and that makes anyone pensive.

Chapter 19

Getting on for eighty

A conservative in all but essentials.

(A.J. Balfour on Mr William E. Gladstone, quoted by Paul Johnson in *Pope John XXIII*, p. 53)

The summer of 1961 marked the turning-point in Pope John's pontificate. He had grown in confidence and sureness of touch, and he had a fresh Secretary of State in Amleto Cicognani. The 'new tone' struck in *Mater et Magistra* had been a success. He had found his own voice. In June 1961 he addressed the first session of the Central Commission, and so launched the immediate preparations for the Council. In July he sent a message to Pax Christi that was a first signal to the Soviet Union, made all the more necessary in that relations between Nikita Khrushchev and the new American president, John F. Kennedy, were increasingly fraught. The rhetoric of Kennedy's inauguration had been followed by the Bay of Pigs disaster. While John spent his summer at Castelgandolfo reflecting on his pontificate, Berlin was in turmoil, thousands were crossing daily to the West, and on August 13 rubble and barbed wire were unloaded in the deserted streets of East Berlin. Four days later the 'Berlin Wall' was complete. From now on international events counter-pointed the pontificate.

The meeting of the Central Commission in June 1961 marked the beginning of the final stage in the preparation of the Council. In his address on June 20, John listed the practical matters that would have to be solved before it could start: the choice of theologians and canonists to serve as experts; the rules of debate; the voting procedures. One question was already settled: 'It is obvious that Latin should be the official language of the Council; but on occasions, and where necessary, the use of modern languages will be permissible in speech' (DMC, 3, pp. 574–5). He meant that *documents* would have to be in Latin. The idea that Latin was 'the official and ordinary language of the Church' had been put forward in *l'Osservatore Romano* almost as soon as the Council was announced. Cardinal Antonio Bacci, the Latinist, was making a pre-emptive strike against those monoglot Anglo-Saxons who would undoubtedly demand simultaneous translation facilities. Later, Cardinal Richard J. Cushing, Archbishop of Boston, offered to pay for them. 'In Latin', he is supposed to have said, 'I represent the Church of silence'. Mgr Alfredo Cavagna, Pope John's confessor, argued for the use of modern languages, but he was outvoted in the Central Commission (Alberigo, p. 85; also Rynne, p. 101).

The great interest that the world was taking in the Council, John went on, meant that the media would come to Rome in force to report it. What was to be done about the press and the electronic media? Vatican I offered no helpful precedents: in 1870 the best that happened was that a well-connected reporter might dine with a bishop or corner a *monsignore* in the fire-engine room of the Apostolic Palace. John stated a simple principle that, had it been generously interpreted, would have averted much frustration: 'Nothing which helps souls should be hidden. But in dealing with grave and serious matters, we have the duty to present them with prudence and simplicity, neither flattering vague curiosity nor indulging in the temptation of polemics' (*ibid*.). The trouble was that the maxim 'Nothing which helps souls should be hidden' was ambivalent: who was to decide what was edifying and what not? How did one know one was dealing with vague curiosity'? There were already those who thought that the best way the press could help souls was by shutting up.

More important than these practical questions was John's clear statement that the purpose of the Council was the *aggiornamento* or bringing up to date of the Roman Catholic Church. This of itself would set up ecumenical vibrations. He reminded the Central Commission that 'the Council is not a speculative assembly, but a living and vibrant organism which embraces everyone in the light and love of Christ' (DMC, 3, p. 575). It was not a Council of reunion, but it could be called a Council for reunion leading to 'the recomposition of the whole mystical flock of Christ'. He freely admitted that to achieve this great goal would involve 'a change in mentalities, ways of thinking and prejudices, all of which have a long history'. So he anticipated that some would feel threatened and disturbed.

At this point Cardinal Domenico Tardini, Secretary of State and the principal link with the previous pontificate, was struck down by a massive heart attack. He died on July 30, 1961, and was buried in the Carmel at Vetralla. The death of Cardinal Nicola Canali, for so long the financial wizard of the Vatican, on August 3, 1961, heightened the feeling that an era had come to an end. Nor was it entirely a matter for regret. John remembered the time early in 1960 when Tardini had tried to get rid of Mgr Angelo Dell'Acqua by 'promoting' him to the Paris nunciature. Having failed, Tardini called a press conference in his flat to announce that either Dell'Acqua went or he would. 'When one understands that one is no longer useful', said Tardini in his usual blunt fashion, 'one goes away' (Magister, p. 254: the date was March 16, 1960). Well, now Tardini had finally 'gone away'. John went to both funerals, but they did not fill him with thoughts of mortality. He wrote: 'The departure to the highest sphere of two cardinals, both most distinguished servants of the Holy See, has caused me many grave preoccupations' (*Journal*, p. 341). He makes it sound as though the two cardinals had gone up to some celestial House of Lords.

It would be going too far to say that Cicognani's appointment as the new Secretary of State was, in any sense of the word, 'inspired'. John chose him because he wanted someone whose hands were clean of the clinging mud of Italian politics. Like Pope John a country boy from a north Italian village, Amleto Cicognani was two years younger. Their paths crossed in 1928–33 when Cicognani worked in the Congregation for the Oriental Churches and sometimes dealt with tangled Bulgarian and Uniate affairs. In 1933 Cicognani became apostolic delegate in Washington where he remained for a wholly unprecedented twenty-five years. When his brother Gaetano was made a cardinal, according to canon law that ruled out a red hat for Amleto. In 1958 Pope John cheerfully disregarded this anti-nepotism rule and made Amleto a cardinal in his first consistory. As soon as the formidable Tisserant could be dislodged, Amleto Cicognani was put in charge of the Congregation for the Oriental Churches. Though not a brilliant man, and by now past his best, Cicognani was loyal, was believed to know English, the United States and even the Kennedy family and, having fewer ideas of his own, was much more comfortable to work with than Tardini. The CIA report says he was regarded as 'an old friend of great experience who has become one of the family, like a trusted doctor' (Spain, p. 6).

August 1961 was also the opportunity for John to do some spiritual stock-taking, in his Castelgandolfo retreat. He is still turning to the future, and can now comment ruefully on the theory that he would be a 'stop-gap' Pope:

> When on October 28, 1958, the cardinals of the Holy Roman Church chose me to
> assume the supreme responsibility of ruling the universal flock of Jesus Christ, at
> seventy-seven years of age, the idea was abroad that I would be a provisional and
> transitional pope. Yet here I am, already on the eve of the fourth year of my pontificate,
> with an immense programme of work ahead of me to be carried out before the eyes of
> the whole world, which is watching and waiting (*Journal*, p. 325).

He sketched out an understanding of the Petrine ministry that would prove to have great ecumenical importance. He probably did not intend this consciously: as far as he was concerned, he was merely reflecting on his own experience:

> What is important is to co-operate with God for the salvation of souls and of the whole
> world. This is our true mission, which reaches its highest expression in the pope.
>   'In all things look to the end.' I am not here thinking of death, but of the purpose and
> divine vocation to which the pope has been summoned by a mysterious decree of divine
> Providence. This vocation is shown in a threefold splendour: the personal holiness of the
> pope, which gives its own glory to his life; the love which the universal Church bears
> him, in the measure of that heavenly grace which alone can inspire him and assure his
> glory; finally, his obedience to the will of Jesus Christ, who alone rules, through the
> pope, and governs according to his own pleasure, for the sake of that glory which is
> supreme on earth as it is in heaven. The humble pope's most sacred duty is to purify all
> his own intentions in the light of this glory, and to live according to the teaching and the
> grace of Christ (*Journal*, p. 333).

Glory: the word occurs four times in this passage. It refers not to the sound of heavenly trumpets or hosannas, but to God himself in the splendour of his presence and the energy of his light. How to live *Ad majorem Dei gloriam*, to the greater glory of God, was the first lesson of his seminary; it was the final key to his life. In being brought closer to death, he was brought closer to glory.

As Pope John sat in the shade of the Castelgandolfo cedars, he had never written such extensive retreat reflections, occupying eighteen pages in the English translation. (Manuscript comparison does not help, since the pages are of irregular sizes.) Before then his longest retreat notes had been: Roman seminary, 1902, fourteen; Istanbul, 1942, five; Algiers, 1950, five. His prolixity, better, his expansiveness, is part of his attempt, as he moves towards his eightieth birthday, to see his past life and his present ministry in the light of the divine vocation by which he is absorbed. His stock-taking had an aspect of leave-taking.

He interrupted his retreat on August 15 because of 'some anxieties about the problem of preserving world peace'. He said Mass in the parish church of Castelgandolfo and urged everyone to join him in prayer to Mary, 'the Queen of peace and peacemaker of the whole world' (*Journal*, p. 337). Then he stayed on at Castelgandolfo until the end of September 1961. From there on September 10 he despatched a message of peace and good will to all while the Conference of Non-aligned Nations was meeting in Belgrade. He reminded the world leaders of their 'dreadful responsibility before history, and, more importantly, before God's judgement' (Stehle, p. 302). This message evoked interest in Moscow, so much so that on September 21, 1961, *Pravda* published an interview with Khrushchev who said:

> John XXIII pays tribute to reason. From all parts of the world there rises up a desire for peace that we can only approve of ... It is not that we fear God's judgement, in which as an atheist I do not believe, but we welcome the appeal to negotiate no matter where it comes from. Will ardent Catholics like John F. Kennedy, Konrad Adenauer and others heed the Pope's warning? (*ibid.*).

There was a blatant element of propaganda in the contrast between the 'peace-loving' Pope and the 'war-mongering' lay Catholics (who were a little less 'ardent' than Khrushchev imagined). But it was an historic statement: for the first time since the Revolution a Russian leader had brought himself to say something good about the Pope. *Pravda* had dismissed Pius XII as 'the Pope of the Atlantic Alliance' and Stalin scornfully enquired how many divisions he could deploy. Khrushchev's interview had a more general international importance: it was a sign that for all his bluster, he was not prepared to push the world to the brink of nuclear war for the sake of getting the Allies out of Berlin. On October 17, 1961, he told the Communist Party Congress that 'the Western powers are showing some understanding of the situation' and so he would not insist on December 31 as the deadline for their departure from Berlin. That was a major concession.

The art of diplomacy consists in profiting from the slightest change in the wind. John took a discreet initiative. He knew that Palmiro Togliatti, secretary of the Italian Communist Party, was due to go to Moscow. He authorised Don Giuseppe De Luca to meet Togliatti in secret to discuss how Moscow–Vatican relations could be improved. He suggested, and Togliatti agreed, that a telegram of congratulations on John's eightieth birthday would be an effective and non-committal sign. It would be well received in the Vatican, and need not be compromising for Khrushchev: to reach eighty and still be active was a remarkable human and non-ideological achievement (Magister, p. 272).

Khrushchev's telegram, therefore, was not a bolt from the blue – though that is what the world was allowed to think. It duly arrived, in Russian with an unofficial Italian translation, at 1.30 p.m. on Pope John's eightieth birthday, November 25, 1961. The Soviet Ambassador to the Republic delivered it to the papal nuncio to Italy who brought it along to the Secretariat of State. Pope John's telegrammed reply to Khrushchev read: 'His Holiness Pope John XXIII thanks you for your good wishes, and for his part sends to the whole Russian people cordial wishes for the increase and strengthening of universal peace by means of understanding based on human brotherhood: to this end he prays fervently' (*Lettere*, p. 336). It went by the reverse route to Khrushchev's telegram, and was in Italian, with a Russian translation. *L'Osservatore Romano* feigned to ignore the exchange of telegrams until December 17 – three weeks late.

In his short notes during a brief Advent retreat he does not reflect any excitement about what had just been happening. For the first time he confesses that he is beginning to feel his age: 'I notice in my body the beginning of some trouble that must be natural for an old man. I bear it with resignation, even if it is sometimes rather tiresome and also makes me afraid it will get worse. It is not pleasant to think about this; but once again, I feel ready for anything' (*Journal*, p. 342). Was he already being affected by stomach cancer?

Despite these worries about his health, he resolved to do some reading: 'In recent months I have felt very much at home with St Leo the Great and with Innocent III. It is a pity so few ecclesiastics study these writers, who abound in theological and pastoral doctrine. I shall never tire of drawing from these sources, so rich in sacred learning and sublime and delightful poetry' (*ibid.*, pp. 342–3). John treated the popes of the past not as dead butterflies trapped in the pages of a book but as living voices that sprang up from the page and witnessed to the continuity of the Petrine office. John wrote one of his minor encyclicals, *Aeterna Dei*, for the fifteenth hundred anniversary, to the day, of Leo's death, November 11, 1961.

But it was the Council that now took up most of his time. On December 2, 1961, he notes laconically:

> A great deal of my work is in preparation for the Second Vatican Council. There begins to take shape in my mind the desire of gathering around me in my daily prayer the prayers of all the clergy, secular and religious, and of all the women's religious congregations, in some official and world-wide form (*Journal*, p. 343).

His request for prayers was extended to the whole Catholic and indeed Christian world in *Humanae Salutis*, the solemn apostolic constitution which convoked Vatican II. It appeared on Christmas Day 1961. The most important feature *of Humanae Salutis* is the way it emphasises, more clearly than ever before, the idea that the Council will be *at the service of the world*. Pope John, in a single sentence, provided his Council with a method and commentators with material for a lifetime. He spoke of the need to 'discern the signs of the times': 'We should make our own Jesus' advice that we should know how to discern "the signs of the times" (Matthew 16.4), and we seem to see now, in the midst of so much darkness, a few hints which augur well for the fate of the Church and humanity' (Abbott, p. 704). Most exegetes think that 'the times' in Matthew's text means the new Messianic age inaugurated by Jesus, and that the 'signs' are his miracles. Pope John gave this an accommodated meaning to express his confidence that the Spirit was still at work in the world. He acts through the men and women, the trends and the movements of the present age.

Pope John did not deny the negative factors. There was enough gloom and darkness in the world of late 1961 to make anyone pessimistic: the Berlin crisis was not resolved, nuclear weapons were being tested, and sites for them were already being prepared in Cuba. Jürgen Moltmann accused Pope John and Marie-Dominique Chenu OP, who influenced him, of ignoring the apocalyptic signs of disaster and concentrating on those that could be given a more optimistic reading (*Church in the Power of the Spirit*, p. 368, fn. 64.) It is true that John was not very interested in the signs that the end was nigh: there wasn't much he or anyone else could do in the face of the world's end. In the meantime, he was concerned with what the Holy Spirit was saying to the Churches.

Humanae Salutis marked a victory for Cardinal Bea. Pope John no longer prayed for the return of the separated brethren to Roman obedience, but for 'the return of unity and peace, according to the prayer of Christ to the Father'. Again, John noted that other Christian

Churches had welcomed the Council 'and hope to send representatives of their communities to follow its work at close quarters' (Abbott, p. 709). This was the first discreet yet official recognition of the fact that there would be non-Catholic 'observers' at the Council.

Bea had come a long way in a short time. Only a year earlier his first meeting with Willem Visser't Hooft, secretary general of the World Council of Churches, took place in secret and in a cloak-and-dagger atmosphere (Nash, p. 108). With Tardini gone, the need for such precautions was removed, and five Roman Catholic 'observers' were able to attend the Third General Assembly of the WCC in New Delhi. The welcome they received and the access they were given to documents and debates, encouraged Bea to make comparable arrangements for the Council.

The only matter *Humanae Salutis* failed to clear up was the date of the Council. It was going to be vaguely 'some time in 1962'. But John, now past eighty, was nearly there. 'Three years have passed', he wrote, 'during which we have seen, day by day, the little seed develop and become, with the blessing of God, a mighty tree' (Abbott, p. 707). It was a mighty tree, and it had some pretty tangled branches.

Chapter 20

The dress rehearsal

*The meetings of the Central Preparatory Commission of the Council will
be more important than the sessions of the Council itself, since greater
frankness and sincerity may be expected in them.*

(Cardinal Bernard Alfrink, Archbishop of Utrecht, in *Herder-Korrespondenz*,
XVI, 2, 1962)

Few could have known at the time how heart-felt were Cardinal Alfrink's words early in
1962. For the meetings of the Central Commission were held behind well-locked doors.
They were so impenetrably secret that the reports on them in *l'Osservatore Romano* were written in advance so that nothing untoward might leak out. They had a feature shared by many
Vatican press office hand-outs then and later: they were strong on insignificant detail. The
Central Commission, the world learned, was made up of 102 members and 29 consultors;
among them were 60 cardinals, 5 patriarchs, 27 archbishops, 6 bishops and 4 general super-
iors of religious orders. They came from 59 countries (the complete list followed). The Hall
of Congregations in which the Central Commission gathered had been redecorated. It was
described in detail from the chandelier, a gift of the Murano glass-blowers of Venice to Pius
IX in 1877, to the central tapestry which, measuring 9 by 5.30 metres, depicted the Last
Supper: it was here because Pius VI had washed the feet of the poor in this hall on Maundy
Thursday (Caprile, I, 2, p. 225).

But that was in 1780. *L'Osservatore Romano*'s reports in 1961 and 1962 were less exhaustive.
They presented a picture of the meetings of the Central Commission in which all was sleep-
inducing sweetness and light. Needless to say, this was nonsense. To those who took part in
them, the meetings of the Central Commission acted as a kind of 'little Council' and were a
dress rehearsal for the real thing.

That the Central Commission would have such an important role had not been anticipated.
Busy cardinals with full diaries thought they could dispense themselves from attending. But
they were 'chased up' (as one of them said) by Pericle Felici, secretary general of the council,
who revealed himself as a highly efficient man who kept the paper moving – or rather the
thick, red-bound volumes. Its members were soon disabused of the notion that the Central
Commission was a kind of Honorary Committee of notables which left all the hard work of
drafting to the sub-commissions. This complacent theory was wrecked first because Cardinal
Alfredo Ottaviani, who since the death of Cardinal Domenico Tardini had assumed the mantle of leader of the conservatives, claimed for the Central Commission the right of veto over
the work of all the other commissions. It had the same function in the Council preparations as
the Supreme Congregation of the Holy Office had in the Curia generally.

Moreover, the main immediate task of the Central Commission was to judge whether the input from the other commissions was 'worthy of a Council'. It was not an easy criterion to apply. The meetings got longer and longer. They began at 9.30 a.m., and often lasted well beyond one o'clock. At the May session, Cardinal Pietro Ciriaci broke up the meeting at 1.50 by noisily gathering up his papers and saying to the acting chairman, Pizzardo: 'It is time. Lunch. No more today'. If Roman cardinals found the pace hard to bear, those who were jetting back and forth across the Atlantic or the Pacific almost once a month found it even more taxing.

The 'foreigners' grumbled when they noticed that Curial cardinals only came to meetings when the matter in hand concerned them. This prepared the ground for the dramatic clash in November, 1961. The question, what is the Council for? had still not been given a full answer. Ottaviani laid a proposal before the November, 1961 meeting of the Central Commission. With a naïveté far out-stripping that alleged to have been displayed by Pope John, he proposed a new 'Profession of Faith' for the forthcoming Council that would repeat the anti-Modernist oath, repudiate the errors condemned by *Humani Generis* as well as those subsequently circulating about Mary's virginity, solemnly affirm that there was an essential difference (and not merely a difference of degree) between the hierarchical priesthood and the general priesthood of all the faithful and, finally, denounce those who spoke 'with ex-aggerated emphasis about the Church's guilt and sinfulness *etc*' (Caprile, I, 2, p. 229).

Ottaviani succeeded in uniting against him a majority of the diocesan cardinals and bishops. It was not so much that anyone disagreed with what he was saying; they just could not see the point of saying it all over again in a Council that was supposed to be dedicated to 'renewal' and *aggiornamento*. Ottaviani, accustomed to speak in the name of the Holy Father for over fifteen years, had the disagreeable experience of being attacked. Moreover, whereas he habitually spoke as one who had authority, he was now treated as an equal, one member of the college. Cardinal Bernard Alfrink of Utrecht, the Netherlands, led the attack. He was quickly backed up by the Germans and Cardinal Franz König of Vienna; the French bided their time; the Americans who took it in turns to come, found it hard to follow the Latin debates and tended to trust Cardinal William Godfrey, of Westminster, by now a very sick man, who was an excellent Latinist. Suspicious of all things new or strange, he tended to take Ottaviani's side on disputed questions.

There were so many disputed questions at this November, 1961 meeting. Cardinal Augustin Bea presented his scheme for having non-Catholic observers at the Council (Caprile, I, 2. p. 229). Ottaviani tried to ensure that these 'observers', supposing they came, should know as little as possible about what was going on. The Council was an essentially *Catholic* event. *Per se* it did not concern anyone else. It was at this November, 1961 session that Ottaviani also launched the first version of his ill-fated *schema* (or draft text) on 'The Two Sources of Revelation'. A year later it would suffer a terrible battering at the Council and be withdrawn, along with most of the other prepared texts. The Council was to confirm what the meetings of the Central Commission had already suggested: the Roman Curia could no longer impose its will on the Church as a whole. The dress rehearsal took place in private, but the characters already had their allotted roles; a year later they played them out before the eyes of the world.

Had Pope John already guessed what would happen at the Council? There is no evidence that he expected, still less hoped, that the Curia's draft texts would be rejected when the Council met. Yet this is what the liberal or 'progressive' myth presupposes. It assumes that Pope John, with his peasant shrewdness, out-manoeuvred the Curia, artfully leaving it the illusion of control while knowing full well that it would shortly be routed. All the evidence goes the other way. No wedge can be driven between Pope John's preparations for the Council and the Curial preparations. They went hand in hand at every stage. He read all the draft texts personally, and annotated them. His notes are usually on minor points or else record simply that he had read them attentively and, sometimes, with joy. Moreover, on January 23, 1962, he praised the draft texts rather lavishly. At their last meeting on June 20, 1962, he was even more fulsome: 'Three years of magnificent, edifying and most devoted hard work'. If the progressive myth were true, all this was a Machiavellian feint.

The problem is deepened if we consider the unexpected bombshell of *Veterum Sapientia* (The Wisdom of the Ancients) which burst upon an astonished world on February 22, 1962. It was a eulogy of the Latin language which was said to be *the* language of the Church. It was therefore imposed or re-imposed as the teaching medium of philosophy and theology in seminaries. It was surely the most ineffectual document ever published by Pope John. For the rest of that academic year – rarely longer – tongue-tied Anglo-Saxon professors exercised their rusty Latin on bewildered and sometimes uncomprehending students. This was all in the name of 'good Pope John' who despite his liberal image was now engaged in 'putting the clock back'. His admirers had a hard time making sense of it. Some claimed it had been imposed on him by the Roman Curia – a fact Pope John vigorously denied whenever he got the chance; others used it to illustrate the difference between 'Roman' and 'Anglo-Saxon' attitudes to law – the authors of the document did not expect it to be taken literally, while those who received it did (Trevor, p. 295).

Pope John's interest in Latin was because it was the language of the 'old fathers' among whom he loved to browse to avoid 'superficiality' (*Journal*, p. 342). Moreover, since it had been decided that Latin would be the language of the Council, he thought it not unreasonable that priests and bishops of the future ought at least to be able to read it fluently. He himself did not find conversing in Latin at all easy or natural, and as the Council approached practised twice a day with Fr Luigi Ciappi OP, the gaunt Master of the Sacred Palace, and Mgr Alfredo Cavagna, his confessor (*Journal*, p. 345 and p. 348).

The timing of *Veterum Sapientia* makes more sense if we relate it to an inner curial battle over liturgy. The Liturgy Commission was much better organised and broadly-based than any of the other commissions. It escaped from curial control and generated a measure of reforming enthusiasm in its members. As Mgr Annibale Bugnini remarked after their spring, 1961, meeting: 'One felt the contribution of different cultures and experiences; local situations coloured and refined our thinking and our way of expressing ourselves. We formed a true family in which the "sense of the Church" was vividly alive' (Bugnini, p. 29). Bugnini was not making this up: in the Liturgy Commission they had the true experience of 'the Council before the Council' and their draft text was the only one – of seventy – to survive. But their proposals for a modest use of the vernacular were already causing alarm in the Curia.

The real drama came on January 22, 1962, when the aged Cardinal Gaetano Cicognani, who was president of the Liturgy Commission because he was Prefect of the Congregation of Rites, was presented with the text that would be laid before the Council. 'He welcomed it', said Bugnini, who was Secretary of the Commission, 'with joy and apprehension' – joy because the work was complete, apprehension because whenever he had to commit himself, he became nervous, and wanted more time to re-read and consult. But he took the plunge, signed on February 1, 1962, and died four days later on February 5. Bugnini concludes his account: 'If Cardinal Cicognani had not signed this document, humanly speaking it would have been a disaster, for everything would have been thrown into the melting pot yet again. But who knows the ways of the Lord?' (Bugnini p. 37). Bugnini's question has a note of personal pathos. Regarded by the Curia as a dangerous iconoclast, within the year he was disgraced and forbidden to teach (Rouquette, I, p. 234). Paul VI rehabilitated him in 1967 by making him Secretary of the Council for the implementation of the liturgical reforms.

As soon as Gaetano Cicognani had appended his last and most fateful signature on February 1, the way was open for the release of the *motu proprio, Consilium Dei Nostri*, which fixed the start of the Council for next October 11. Twenty days later, *Veterum Sapientia* appeared. It was therefore a concession made to those powerful curial forces who regarded the work of the Liturgy Commission as highly dangerous. On another level, however, the argument over *Veterum Sapientia* was not about Latin at all: it was about who would control the Council. The use of Latin gave the Curia a built-in advantage that it did not propose to throw away. Felici, the secretary general, was perfectly at ease in Latin, could dazzle and make jokes that at least his cronies appreciated. The journalists' Latin proved non-existent or rusty. Cardinal William Godfrey of Westminster, having struggled to get out the phrase '*Debemus levare Latinam*' (by which he meant raise its status) was astonished to read in *Il Tempo* the next day that he had called for Latin to be abolished (*levare* in Italian means to take away: Archbishop Derek Worlock, letter of December 28, 1993).

On a still deeper level, *Veterum Sapientia* was about the relationship of language to faith. Precisely because Latin is a dead language, *Veterum Sapientia* claims, it is 'fixed and invariable' (No. 8). In short it is the perfect language for a scholastic theology preserved – so it believes –from the ravages of time and history. But this was not Pope John's last word on the subject. In his opening address to the Council he said that 'the substance of the ancient deposit of faith is one thing and the way it is presented is another'. Without actually contradicting *Veterum Sapientia*, this statement is hard to reconcile with it. John's mind could accommodate puzzling incompatibilities. His thinking about the Council moved on many levels, and was never the realisation of a clear-cut and well-formulated blue-print. His essential role was to be an enabler and an improviser. He was happy to accept the curial plans – until something better came along. When something better came along, he pounced upon it and made it his own. He seized eagerly upon ideas put forward by Cardinals Wyszyński of Warsaw, Suenens of Malines-Brussels, Bengsch of Berlin and – last, not least – Montini of Milan. What they brought to him will be the subject of the rest of this chapter.

On February 17, 1962, John gave an audience to Cardinal Wyszyński and discussed with him what could be done about Mgr Josef Slipyi, major archbishop of the Ukrainians, who had vanished into a Soviet labour camp after the enforced destruction of his Church in 1948. John had noticed that it was Slipyi's seventieth birthday. He said to his secretary, Mgr Loris Capovilla:

The Council is approaching. I've been thinking of the bishops who are in prison or in exile and who can't come. We have to try to do something for them . . . The exchange of greetings on November 25, 1961, my eightieth birthday, should not lead sensible people to fantastic conclusions; but it was a step towards prudent contact. We should let the East Europeans know this: they have shown respect for the pope as the head of the Catholic family, and for the first time they have paid tribute to his work for peace. . . . So without using protocol and strict diplomatic forms, it would be good to let them know the pope's sorrow at being unable to welcome the bishops from certain countries (IME, p. 170).

But who should be approached informally? And through whom? There were no ordinary diplomatic relations between the Vatican and any communist country. Pope John's Secretary of State, Amleto Cicognani, reminded him of Mgr Francesco Lardone, who was now in Pope John's old post in Istanbul. It had been raised to the status of a pro-nunciature and was still a good window on the East. A straightforward man, now aged seventy-six, Lardone had an unusual background for a diplomat. When invited to take a holiday in Rome in February, 1962 he replied that he had work to do in Ankara and didn't need a holiday. A phone call told him that he was needed urgently. He arrived lackadaisically in mid-March. A few precious weeks had been lost.

Pope John surprised Lardone by receiving him not in his library but in the Vatican gardens. It was easier to talk there. As they strolled, Pope John said, 'For me you are the top diplomat of the Holy See' (*Utopia*, Italian p. 249). Then Lardone discovered his mission: working through the Soviet ambassador to Turkey, he was to try and find out whether there was any hope that bishops from Eastern Europe would be allowed to come to the Council. Back home in Turkey, Lardone got in touch with the Soviet ambassador Nikita Ryjov who was affable and within a week reported that he had an answer from Moscow: agreed. Lardone then handed over the official invitations to the Catholic bishops of the Soviet Union who were mostly in the Baltic republics. The ambassador took them personally to Moscow – to avoid losing them in the post, he explained, possibly humorously. Emboldened by this success, Lardone presented his respects to the other ambassadors of the Soviet bloc and invited their bishops to come to the Council. They all agreed to pass on the Pope's request. Khrushchev's example was the determining factor.

On June 2, 1962, Lardone was back in Rome to report on the apparent success of his mission. Although the audience had been fixed for the next day, John received his 'top diplomat' immediately and explained: 'This time you've taken the place of the Princess Maria Gabriella. This is how it came about. While I was shaving I heard on the news this morning that today is Italy's national feast, and I thought it wouldn't be proper to receive a princess of the house of Savoy on the feast of the Republic' (*Utopia*, Italian, p. 248). This is an example of Bergamesque humour: dry, but with a twinkle in the eye. But the main point of the whole Lardone episode is that Pope John was not only prepared but was delighted to depart from official channels – in this case the Secretariat of State – when it suited him. He had a certain conspiratorial pleasure in outwitting his officials.

He was equally open to the unofficial when it came to preparing the Council. If a bishop's pastoral letter seemed to him to sum up the spirit of the Council, he wrote to him immediately to ask for advice. This happened twice. The first pastoral letter to catch his eye was written by Cardinal Léon-Joseph Suenens of Malines, Belgium. He liked it so much that he asked Suenens to pen a memo on how the work of the Council should be organised (De Riedmatten, p. 53). Suenens promptly obliged with a lucid document in two parts: (i) what the Council should not attempt to do; (ii) what the Council should do. Suenens argued that a Council that appeared obsessed with inner-Church matters would disappoint the expectations of the world. It would have to face up honestly to questions of war and peace, the morality of nuclear war, birth-control and 'the population explosion'. Suenens did not mean that questions like collegiality and ecumenism were not important. But he wanted to distinguish and keep in balance the inner life of the Church (*ad intra*) and the Church seen in relation to the world and its problems (*ad extra*). This put neatly what Pope John had tried to say in *Humanae Salutis*, and it affected all later statements. From now on Suenens became one of Pope John's confidants.

Cardinal Montini's Lenten pastoral, written from Rome, was an epistle to the Milanese. It was called *Pensiamo al Concilio*, Let us think about the Council. He had evidently read and assimilated all the literature and, like Suenens, was backed up by a Catholic university, the Sacred Heart university of Milan. He set himself the task of answering a simple question: 'What are the Pope's intentions concerning the forthcoming Council?' Though he did not claim any inside knowledge, it was obvious to all that he knew Pope John's mind and emphasised what he wanted emphasising. He said that the central theme of the Council would be the mystery of the Church. 'It is the whole Church that expresses itself in the Council', said Montini, explaining why the Milanese were involved in it, 'and we are the Church'.

Montini says bluntly that 'the Council is not likely to define any new dogma as part of revelation' (*Pensiamo al Concilio*, No. 46). The Council should 'enter into a dialogue with history' (*ibid.*, No. 54) and its main business would be renewal and *aggiornamento*. He found a metaphor for *aggiornamento* which in a way summed up what Pope John's pontificate had already achieved: 'The Church will divest itself, if need be, of whatever royal cloak still remains upon its sovereign shoulders, so that it may put on the simpler forms modern taste demands' (*ibid.*, No. 55). Montini was clear, finally, on the vexed question of how to deal with errors. He wrote: 'We shall have a Council of positive rather than punitive reforms, and of exhortation rather than anathemas' (*Pensiamo al Concilio*, No. 37). Moreover, he linked this positive attitude to Pope John's 'optimism' which, he claimed, 'has spread throughout the whole Church, deepening our sensibility' (*ibid.*, No. 39). Both Montini and Suenens would play a discreet yet decisive role when the Council met in six months' time.

Optimism in the sense of a heightened sensitivity to the action of the Spirit, was gaining ground in the ecumenical sphere. With Tardini out of the way, Bea could arrange audiences for any Church leader who cared to come. The complete list of ecumenical meetings before the Council is as follows: Dr Arthur Lichtenberger, president of the American Episcopalian Church (November 15, 1961); Dr Joseph Jackson, president of the National Baptist Convention of the United States (December 20, 1961); Dr Archibald C. Craig, moderator of the General Assembly of the Church of Scotland (March 28, 1962); Dr Mervyn Stockwood, Anglican bishop of Southwark, London (April 7, 1962); Professor Edmund Schlink, of Heidelberg University, representing the Council of the German Evangelical Church (April

27, 1962); Dr Arthur Morris, Anglican bishop of St Edmundsbury and Ipswich (May 10, 1962); Metropolitan Damaskinos, of Volos, Greece (May 17, 1962); and Dr Joost de Blank, Anglican archbishop of Cape Town, South Africa (June 20, 1962) (listed in *Natale 1975*, pp. 51–3).

Bea's secretary at the time, Jan Willebrands, explained why these meetings were important. They suited John's style. He preferred people to books, and radiated goodness and friendliness. He has sometimes been presented as anti-intellectual and mistrustful of the subtleties of theologians. But that judgement was based on the false premise that he was a shrewd but ignorant old peasant. What is true is that he thought theological dialogue alone was insufficient. He needed this personal contact with Church leaders to begin to understand the historical context in which they had emerged and their present positions. History held the key to understanding. From his previous experience, Pope John knew a great deal about the Orthodox Churches; but now he was learning fast about Canterbury, Geneva, Moscow, Cairo and so many other places.

One might conclude from all this that Bea was riding high. He was educating the Pope and shaping the course of the Council. Precisely for that reason, the curial attacks on Bea redoubled. One episode, tedious enough in itself, is worth recalling to show how the battle-lines were drawn up. In December, 1960 *Divinitas*, the learned journal produced by the staff of the Lateran university, launched an intemperate attack on the Biblical Institute (the 'Biblicum'), of which Bea had for so long been the Rector. Two of its professors, Frs Stanislaus Lyonnet and Maximilian Zerwick, were reproached for holding that 'the study of the literary forms of ancient Oriental literature' was essential to understanding both the Old and the New Testaments. In this way they challenged those 'dogmatic theologians' who for centuries had expounded the meaning of scripture without having the slightest knowledge of ancient literary forms. The author of the article, Mgr Antonio Romeo, was working in the Congregation for Seminaries and Catholic Universities, and would not have written such an attack without the approval of his chief, Cardinal Giuseppe Pizzardo.

Pope John only found out about the anti-Bea, anti-Biblicum campaign by accident, and he was very angry. He told Capovilla to phone the Rector of the Biblicum at once and assure him that 'the Pope has complete confidence in the orthodoxy of the Biblicum'. Then John ordered Pizzardo to write a letter of apology to Bea, disclaiming any fore-knowledge of Romeo's article. Pizzardo complied, but it made no difference to his behaviour. The principal instrument of the 'fundamentalists' was the Biblical Commission presided over by Cardinal Eugene Tisserant. Although Bea was one of the twelve cardinal members, the dominant tone was set by the trio of Pizzardo, Ruffini and Ottaviani.

On May 21, 1962, Pope John decided that enough was enough. He would have a showdown with the Biblical Commission. He wrote a memo to Cicognani, Secretary of State, that bristles with impatience: 'The time has come to put a stop to this nonsense. Either the Biblical Commission will bestir itself, do some proper work and by its suggestions to the Holy Father make a useful contribution to the needs of the present time, or it would be better to abolish it and let the Supreme Authority replace it in the Lord by something else' (*Lettere*, p. 536). This was the toughest language ever used by Pope John, and the only time he uttered a threat. An unreformed Biblical Commission was worse than useless. Its intolerance was creating needless anxieties, uncertainties and absurdities. Though he preferred to be an enabler, he would have to intervene. 'Reforms have to begin from above', he noted on Maundy Thursday 1962 (Alberigo, p. 87). Moreover, the ecumenical dimension of the Council, which was becoming more and more apparent, required that the best Catholic biblical scholarship should be available. Otherwise, the Protestants would not be able to take the Council seriously. The fierce memo went on:

> Those who have the charge – better, the honour – of promoting the Bible as the most sacred treasure of the Church, alongside and after the apostolic Tradition, should take care not to fail in their vocation.
>
> It would be very consoling for the humble servant of the servants of God if in preparation for the Council there was a Biblical Commission of such reputation and integrity that it would be a resource which our separated brethren could rely on and respect (*Lettere*, p. 537).

Pope John's own use of scripture was devotional rather than critical. He never posed as a scripture scholar. But he could see how harmful these polemics were both to individuals and to the prospects for the Council.

Pope John carried out his threat. The Biblical Commission was provided in July, 1962 with a new secretary and 'consultors' as eminent as Rudolf Schnackenburg, Bernard Rigaux and Xavier Léon-Dufour. But the 'battle of the Biblicum' was still not finally won. Its climax would come during the first session of the Council.

Getting the Council on the road was hard work. Pope John ordered that the *schemata* (drafts) should be circulated to all the members of the Council not in September, as had been originally foreseen, but in July and August. Some bishops had complained that they were being kept in the dark and would arrive at the Council in ignorance. Others had the impression that the Central Commission – made up when all were present of 102 members and 29 consultors – had decided everything in advance, and that the Council would have nothing to do except rubber-stamp what was laid before it. Pope John wrote: 'It would be good to let them know as soon as possible that they will be receiving this material earlier. This will put a stop to certain reactions that have been noticed here and there. It will prevent unprofitable, wearisome and harmful chatter that merely results in wasted time and wasted energies' (*Lettere*, p. 536: May 20, 1962). Those were not the words of a man who expected still less hoped that the bishops would turn down the draft texts when they saw them. On the contrary, at the end of the fifth session of the Central Commission in April, 1962 Pope John remarked that 'the consent of the Bishops will not be difficult to obtain and their approval will be unanimous' (Rouquette, I, p. 114).

This confidence raised another problem. It had all along been assumed that the Council would complete its work in a single session from October 11, feast of the Maternity of Our Lady, to December 8, feast of her Immaculate Conception. Yet the *schemata* were piling up: the feat of discussing, amending and re-writing seventy of them in two months made pouring a quart into a pint pot look easy by comparison. There were hints that a further session might be needed. The Curia wanted a short, sharp Council, after which the foreigners would depart and normality would return. Pope John, however, always encouraged those from outside Rome to 'hang on' and not let the Curia run everything. Cardinal Franz König, of Vienna, thought that 'several sessions' would be needed. He was proved right. But for

Pope John personally, there was a dilemma: however much he wanted to see the Council through, the Council was sovereign and had to be free to take its time, even if that meant he might not see its end.

But general satisfaction with the preparatory work certainly did not exclude the desire to improve the drafts. Pope John was particularly impressed by a confidential document, dated May 4, 1962, drawn up by Cardinal Alfred Bengsch who lived in East Berlin. It was a devastating critique of *De Animarum Cura in Particulari* (On the Pastoral Care of Special Groups). Bengsch addressed himself to the section on 'the pastoral care of those afflicted by communism' (*de cura pro Christianis communismo infectis*). He thought its tone and approach were disastrous. He offered a lexicon of terms to be avoided in conciliar documents. They should not speak of 'fear of Soviet power', 'the free world', 'hatred of communism' or the 'iron curtain' (Stehle, p. 444, where Bengsch's full text was published for the first time). Bengsch's remarks were based on the common sense view that if the decisions of the Council were to be applied in Eastern Europe, it would be better not to begin by alienating and insulting its rulers. But that was what one did every time one spoke of 'the free world' for example.

Moreover, a more general principle was involved of the utmost importance for the Council: it would be impossible to 'enter into a dialogue with history' if one began with condemnations. This was where Pope John really did begin to diverge from some of the preliminary drafts. One day, he measured a page with his ruler and said: 'Seven inches of condemnations and one of praise: is that the way to talk to the modern world?' It was Cardinal Montini who was given the task of making this point at the decisive final meeting of the Central Commission in June, 1962. Anathemas and condemnations, said Montini, were not the answer to contemporary errors. It was after this speech that Cardinal Ottaviani was heard to murmur: 'I pray to God that I may die before the end of the Council – in that way I can die a Catholic' (*Panorama*, p. 257).

Cardinal Suenens is the source for the following story. Pope John had spent the day in the garden at Castelgandolfo, pen in hand, studying the draft texts for the Council. It was the task he had imposed on the bishops; he had to give them a lead. Suenens met him, and Pope John tried out some of his marginal comments on him. But then John suddenly stopped and said: 'Oh, I know what my personal part in the preparation of the Council will be . . .'. After a pause, he added: 'It will be suffering' (Novak, p. 19: from Suenens' tribute to Pope John in St Peter's, October 28, 1963).

As usual, Pope John under-rated himself.

Chapter 21

On the slopes of the sacred mountain

After three years of preparation, certainly laborious but also joyful and
serene, we are now on the slopes of the sacred mountain.

(Pope John, *Journal of a Soul*, p.349, September, 1962)

Despite all Pope John's urgings, only seven draft texts were ready to be sent to the bishops in
August 1962. Four came from Cardinal Alfredo Ottaviani's Theological Commission: The
Sources of Revelation, The Moral Order, The Deposit of Faith and The Family: all would be
rejected by the Council. The Liturgy Commission had worked well, and though its draft
annoyed the devotees of Latin, it cunningly presented its proposals as in continuity with the
liturgical reforms begun by St Pius X and Pius XII. There remained a derisory draft on 'the
means of social communication' presented by the Secretariat of that name, and a draft on
The Unity of the Church prepared, some thought eccentrically, by the Oriental Churches
Commission.

Pope John spent his summer at Castelgandolfo. But it was not much of a holiday. He was
still working through the prepared texts; and even at this eleventh hour, he had to defend
the Council against Cardinal Joseph Frings of Cologne and Cardinal Julius Döpfner of Munich who begged him to postpone it. But John was not going to be deprived of his Council
at this late stage. The 'suffering' that he had talked about to Cardinal Suenens was a premo-
nition of the illness that would kill him. He had already revised his last will and testament
the previous summer. 'I await the arrival of Sister Death', he had written, 'and will welcome
her simply and joyfully in whatever circumstances it will please the Lord to send her' (*Journal*, p. 369: September 12, 1961).

On August 2, 1962, he completed the preparations for his death by drafting a *motu proprio*
to deal with the *sede vacante* period, when the chair of Peter would be empty. Its chief concern was to avoid any repetition of the grisly scenes that followed upon the death of Pius
XII. Its main provisions were that no photographs should be taken of the Pope on his
deathbed, that only those strictly needed should be allowed into the crypt for the burial,
and that no one at all should live in the papal apartments at this time (*Lettere*, pp. 549–50).
All three points were embodied in the *motu proprio, Summi Pontificis Electio* (The Election of a
Supreme Pontiff) of September 5, 1962 (AAS, 56, n. 11, pp. 632–40) and were retained in
Paul VI's *motu proprio* of October 1, 1975, *Romani Pontificis Eligendo* (On Electing the Roman
Pontiff).

But although Pope John accepted the prospect of suffering and death, this did not mean that he was inactive. On the contrary, he 'took charge' of the final preparations for the Council in the most effective way open to him: he worked hard on the two speeches that would give it impetus and direction. He knew that his address on October 11 would be the most important of his life. As he went into retreat in his beloved Torre San Giovanni, he explained why this would be no ordinary retreat: 'This time, everything is with the intention of preparing the Pope's soul for the Council; everything, including the preparation of the opening speech which the whole world gathered in Rome awaits' (*Journal*, p. 346). But with the international situation so menacing, it was difficult to concentrate. Attention had moved from Berlin to Cuba where, according to refugees, Soviet offensive missiles were already in position or would shortly be. Pope John had a first-hand report from Vice-president Lyndon B. Johnson who had an audience on September 7, 1962.

Cardinal Gustavo Testa, now prefect of the Congregation for the Oriental Churches, and his predecessor, Cardinal Eugène Tisserant, were engaged in secret negotiations designed to permit 'observers' from the Russian Orthodox Church to attend the Council. This was what Pope John wanted more than anything else. Since the Russian Orthodox Church was subservient to the Soviet state, the presence of Russian Orthodox observers would be a sign not only of the improved ecumenical climate but of East-West *détente* – and it might get Slipyi out of his labour camp in Siberia. The United States and the USSR were already scowling at each other over Cuba. If there were observers present, the Council would at least be one forum in which East and West were still conversing. Provided he had a long enough spoon, Pope John was prepared to meet Khrushchev: 'If this good fellow came to Rome and asked to see me, why should I refuse? I would listen to him and then, calmly and politely, give him my thoughts on the Church's claims at the present time: we don't want protection or privileges, but we simply want freedom to preach the Gospel' (IME, p. 68).

Still, if he couldn't meet Khrushchev, he could at least try to entice some Russian Orthodox observers to Rome. *The Journal of the Moscow Patriarchate* had already rejected the idea on the grounds that the Council was merely another instance of Roman Catholic imperialism. John, the old diplomat, regarded this as a predictable opening gambit. Cardinal Gustavo Testa and Bea's number two, Mgr Jan Willebrands, were instructed to try anything they could think of to reopen the question. Cardinal Eugène Tisserant, his earlier clinging to power now forgiven, was brought in to help because of his immense experience of the East. He began to enter into the spirit of the pontificate with some zest. The Secretariat of State was by-passed.

Nothing happened for many weeks. Then in August Metropolitan Nikodim of Leningrad, who was officially responsible for the 'foreign relations' of the Russian Orthodox Church, let it be known that he would like a confidential meeting with top Vatican officials. Willebrands met him in Paris, and Tisserant in Metz: meetings in France escaped the prying eyes of the Roman press. The gist of Nikodim's message was that the Russian Orthodox Church would consider sending observers to the Council provided an assurance was given in advance that it would be a strictly apolitical event (that is, that it would not condemn atheistic Communism). Since the principle of 'no condemnations' had already been established as one of the ground-rules of the Council, this assurance could be given. Nikodim would deliver the invitations himself.

But Pope John had a scruple about this. He did not need the wily Tisserant to point out that invitations to *all* Orthodox Churches ought to be sent through the Ecumenical patriarch in Constantinople, Athenagoras. There was a grave danger of getting embroiled in an inner-Orthodox dispute. Late in September he sent Willebrands to Moscow. His mission was to inform Patriarch Alexis and the Holy Synod that the Council had no political objectives and would issue no anathemas (*Utopia*, Italian, p. 184). Willebrands set off on September 28, but his journey was kept secret. So it was that on October 8, just three days before the start of the Council, having received no word from Moscow, Athenagoras announced that the Orthodox Church would not be sending observers to the Vatican Council. Athenagoras was very sad about this. He was the man who had greeted Mgr Giacomo Testa with the words: 'There is a man, sent from God, whose name is John'. But although he had the primacy of honour over the Orthodox Churches, he also had to defer to the Russian Orthodox Church as 'the largest and the least free' (to borrow Stehle's excellent phrase: p. 303). So on the eve of the Council, it looked as though all these strenuous efforts had come to nothing.

Still, there was some sort of communication with the Russians. To Pope John's intense disappointment China, the other great Communist power, proved totally impenetrable. There had been two million Chinese Catholics in 1949; their friends in Hong Kong gave him the gift of an altar for the first anniversary of his election. He had it set up in the new chapel in the Torre San Giovanni. He called it 'my Chinese altar' and said 'it will always remind me of the missionary activity to which the Pope is called' (*Journal*, p. 347: September 10, 1962). The altar was also a reminder of how little he could do for the Catholics of China. In 1962 little was known about them.

Most of the twenty or so Bishops who were alive when Mao took over in 1949 had vanished. In 1956–7, at the time of the 'hundred flowers' campaign ('Let a hundred flowers blossom', declared Mao, 'and let a hundred schools of thought contend'), forty-two 'patriotic' bishops were appointed with government approval. Pius XII promptly pronounced them to be in schism. At first Pope John echoed this usage, causing distress in China and delight in Taiwan. Then he had a meeting on February 26, 1960, with Charles Joseph van Melckebeke, who had been bishop of Ning-sia in Outer Mongolia. After the revolution he had distributed church property and gone to work on a farm. He told Pope John that the term 'schism' was not strictly applicable to the Chinese bishops, since they had not deliberately and obstinately broken with the Church of Rome. They had never had a chance to explain their position and the pressures they were under (*Utopia*, English, p. 191). After this conversation, Pope John never again used the term 'schism' in speaking of China. But this was not enough to allow Mao's government to let Chinese bishops go to the Council. Instead, ten bishops from Taiwan and the *diaspora* arrived at the last minute on October 11. Pope John did not solve the 'two Chinas' problem.

Pope John's thinking and prayer extended to embrace the whole world. From time to time he was made aware of some squalid manoeuvre happening beneath his very eyes. He followed St Bernard's principle: 'To notice everything, to turn a blind eye to much and to correct a few things'. In June 1962 Cardinal Giuseppe Pizzardo finally secured the suspension from teaching of the two Biblicum Jesuits attacked in the article in *Divinitas* (see last chapter), Stanislaus Lyonnet and Maximilian Zerwick. Pope John's trust in subordinates meant that he would not undo the suspension. But he found a diplomatic solution by allowing Lyonnet to continue acting as vice-dean of the Biblicum and encouraging Zerwick to carry on teaching biblical Greek (which was his speciality).

In August Cardinal Alfredo Ottaviani bagged an even bigger prize for the Holy Office: he published a *monitum* or warning that reading the works of the late Pierre Teilhard de Chardin SJ could prove damaging to Catholic minds (AAS, 54, 1962, p. 526). Pope John had never read Teilhard de Chardin but Léopold Sédar Senghor, the poet-president of Senegal, had enthused about the inspiration the French Jesuit brought him. John pointed out that a *monitum* was more an alarm-signal than a condemnation. But strangely enough 'Teilhardian' phrases began to enter the speeches he was working on at the time. The optimism of his inaugural address to the Council, his fascination with space travel which allowed the world to be seen as 'one planet', and his reference to 'a new order of human relationships' (Abbott, p. 712) all echoed Teilhardian themes.

On September 11, 1962, exactly a month before the Council was due to start, he broadcast a speech on Vatican Radio in which he at last indicated the direction he wanted the Council to take. According to the progressive myth, this was the moment when he cast aside the mask and rejected all the preparatory work. This judgement is surprising in view of Pope John's opening remark:

> In the course of three years of preparatory work, a host of distinguished minds chosen from every nation and language, united in affection and determination, has brought together a superabundant wealth of doctrinal and pastoral material worthy to be offered to the Bishops of the whole world who, gathered beneath the vault of St Peter's, will find grounds for the wisest applications of Christ's evangelical *magisterium* which for twenty centuries has enlightened the humanity redeemed by his blood (Alberigo, p. 354).

It is true that this encomium on the preparatory work is studiously vague. No examples of this 'wealth of doctrinal and pastoral material' are given. He damns with faint praise. But it would not have been proper to anticipate the Council on particular controversial points, and Pope John had a keen sense of what was proper.

'From every people', said Pope John, 'we expect a contribution based on intelligence and experience that will help to heal the *scars* of the two World Wars that have so profoundly changed the face of all our countries' (Alberigo, p. 357: italics in the original). Just as mothers and fathers detest war, he went on, so 'the Church, the Mother of all without exception, will once more repeat the proclamation that echoes down the centuries from Bethlehem, *pacem in terris*, peace on earth' (*ibid.*, p. 358). And peace was inseparable from justice. It will be illuminating, he says, to present the Church 'in the under-developed countries as the Church of all, and especially of the poor' (*ibid.*, p. 357). The 'Church of the poor' was not a theme that any of the draft texts, composed almost entirely by 'first world' theologians, had even alluded to.

Finally Pope John reflected on the experience of preparing the Council. He did not see it as negative at all. In fact he was starry-eyed about it. The bonds of love which had held the Church together in Europe and the known world in the first centuries had been subsequently weakened or even broken. But the project of the Council had brought almost everyone together in fraternal recognition in the arms of their common mother, the holy and universal Mother Church (Alberigo, p. 359). The theme of the Church *ad intra* and *ad extra* was vividly summed up in the contrast between St Peter, concerned with order and stability, and St Paul, concerned with missionary endeavour and reaching out towards 'those who had not yet received the Gospel' (*ibid.*). The Council would have to be both Petrine and Pauline.

But did Pope John write this speech himself? This question was sometimes asked by his curial 'opponents' who wanted to hint that he was incapable of having such ideas unaided and must therefore have delivered himself uncritically into the unsafe hands of 'outsiders' like Cardinal Suenens. Henri de Riedmatten OP, known to his brethren as 'Henry the Navigator' for his skill in negotiating choppy Vatican waters, said bluntly in 1967: 'It is no longer indiscreet to say that the September 11, 1962, speech was very largely inspired by the second of Cardinal Suenens' memoranda, so much so that the very next day Pope John gave Cardinal Suenens a gift of his works as a pledge of his agreement and gratitude' (De Riedmatten, p. 53). But 'very largely inspired by' does not mean that Pope John simply copied down a Suenens text: as was his practice with a draft that he liked, he thought it through, made it his own, and added personal touches. One effect of this collaboration was that from now on Cardinal Suenens became still closer to Pope John.

He needed all the calm he could muster. On Sunday, September 23, 1962, he submitted to an x-ray and other tests at the hands of specialists and his doctors. Available already that same evening, the gloomy verdict was given to Capovilla who immediately informed Cicognani, secretary of state, and Dell'Acqua, his *sostituto* (Letter, January 30, 1989). That afternoon, and without knowing his fate, John went down to the crypt of St Peter's to pray at the tombs of his predecessors. Then Capovilla explained that the threat was not so much to his health as to his life. 'The Pope appeared calm', Capovilla went on, 'when he asked for explanations about the x-rays and the gastric pains that troubled him'. He knew what it all meant. However, it was decided to say nothing publicly about his state of health, since that would trigger off pre-conclave speculations and be a distraction from the Council. Pope John would behave 'as if' nothing were wrong.

Pope John's remark that his contribution to the Council would be suffering took on a deeper and more poignant meaning. From now on he would be living on borrowed time. He had said of Pius XII that 'Sister Death came to him swiftly'. That would not be his experience. Cancer was the Roncalli family disease. Not only his sisters Ancilla and Maria had died of it, but also Teresa (in 1954), and his brothers Giovanni (in 1956) and Giuseppe would (in 1981). He was approaching eighty-one, and in old age stomach cancer is slow to develop, painful and ineluctable. From now on every day he lived was a bonus, a gift from the Lord, a grace that was granted for a purpose. This brought an added edge of urgency to all his projects. It also gave him the freedom that came from knowing that, humanly speaking, he had nothing more to lose. Pride, self-will, even vanity no longer meant much.

Fortified by his new knowledge, he decided to go on pilgrimage to Loreto and Assisi on October 4, 1962. Apart from visits to his own property at Castelgandolfo, it was the first time a pope had left Rome officially since 1870. He boarded the presidential train at 6.30 a.m. at the Vatican's neo-classical station. Normally it has no passengers. He was joined at the Trastevere Station by Amintore Fanfani, the prime minister. President Antonio Segni took a plane and was waiting to greet him in Loreto. So the event had a political significance within Italy: it was the final seal set on the reconciliation of 1929. At every halt along the route – at Orte, Narni, Terni, Spoleto, Foligno, Fabriano, Iesi, Falconara and Ancona – enthusiastic crowds greeted Pope John with vivas. There were tears in his eyes. 'This conversation without intermediaries between a father and his children revealed that Italian attitudes had indeed changed for the better' (Capovilla: letter to author, February 2, 1983).

But that was not what Pope John's pilgrimage meant to non-Italians. That he should go to Assisi to pray for the coming Council was understandable. If the Council was going to stress the 'Church of the poor', as he had suggested in his September 11 broadcast, then St Francis, the poor man of Assisi, was a fitting patron. Moreover, in his Assisi sermon John linked poverty and peace: only when 'the good and beautiful things that Providence has placed in this world' were equitably shared out could there be true peace. Few could quarrel with that. And everyone loved St Francis.

But Loreto was a different matter, with its dubious story of the holy house of Nazareth being transported by angelic removal men to a rocky eminence overlooking the Adriatic. It would, however, have been insensitive to deny to an old man – no one knew he was dying – the right to return to a place he had first visited sixty years before on September 22, 1900. Far from encouraging mariological excesses, he talked very simply and directly on three points: the Incarnation, the family and work. Everything he said was directed towards the Council. His prayer for the Council was that it would be 'a joyful proclamation of the Gospel, leading to brotherly harmony between all peoples and ever more generous justice, so that the light of God's mercy may shine on everyone' (*Rosario*, p. 141). Even the most rigid Protestant could not object to that.

Bishops were by now pouring into Rome. There were about 217 from the United States who mostly installed themselves in grand hotels on the Via Veneto. The Rome Hilton was not yet built. According to Robert Kaiser, of *Time* magazine, they were accompanied by 'two or three clerical buddies, whom they called "theologians" ' (Kaiser, p. 76). The 531 Latin Americans economised by staying at their own colleges. The Europeans were still the largest group: over 400 Italians who scarcely knew each other scattered round the city, except for Cardinal Montini who, it was noticed, was given a room in the Vatican; 159 French who claimed to know Pope John at first-hand; 95 from Spain, still wondering what *Mater et Magistra* meant for the Franco dictatorship; 68 Germans aware of their responsibility to theology and learning; 33 from Catholic Ireland; 27 from Portugal living with apparent contentment under Salazar and Our Lady of Fatima (the single dissident bishop was exiled to the Azores); 24 from England and Wales (including the Ukrainian Exarch) many of whom were staying at the Venerable English College where they had been students.

There were many surprises. Although the Netherlands had only 9 bishops, the total list of Dutch bishops, once the missionaries were counted in, came to 76. They had worked hard on the preparatory documents, and had commissioned Edward Schillebeeckx OP to write a theological commentary on them. His *Animadversiones*, a manuscript of 47 pages, were devastating; the only draft for which he had a good word was that on liturgy. Again, though Belgium itself had only 15 bishops, the full list of Belgians had 59 names. All in all the number of missionary bishops came to over 800 out of an official total of 2449. If the North European bishops supplied the intellectual input to the Council, the missionaries were to act as its conscience.

There were 296 bishops from Africa, 93 from the Philippines, Japan and Indonesia, and 84 from India who left a country at peace and returned to find it at war with China. Additional colour was provided by the Uniates: Maronites from the Lebanon led by their Patriarch Meouchi of Antioch, proud of their 700-year-long resistance to Turks and Arabs; their neighbours the Melkites headed by 84-year-old Patriarch Maximos IV Saigh who refused to speak Latin on the grounds that Arabic was the language of his Church – he spoke French instead; and the bearded representatives of the Malankars, the Copts, the Chaldeans and Armenians – all seeming exotic to the Latins and yet familiar to Pope John from his time in the East. Before a single word had been spoken, the gathering said something about the true nature of Catholicity: it could not be reduced to the monochrome uniformity demanded by the Curia.

But one element in the spectrum of Catholicism was still missing. Where were the East Europeans? On Sunday October 7 Pope John regretted the absence of Stefan Cyril Kurtev, whom he had appointed forty years before and who was still exarch of the Bulgarians, and of another Bulgarian bishop whom he mis-remembered as Popov (in fact Simeon Kokov) (*Lettere*, p. 552). John was reminded of these old friends by ex-King Simeon of Bulgaria, whom we last met at the age of six in 1944, who now wanted a ticket for the inaugural Mass. Of course he should be admitted, John noted, provided he does not remind everyone of his former title.

The next day, October 8, Cardinal Wyszyński arrived with thirteen Polish bishops, among them Karol Wojtyla from Kraków. Nine more were to arrive later. Pope John was delighted to see them. In a speech that was not made public at the time, but which was relayed to Moscow, Pope John mentioned almost casually 'the Polish Western territories recovered after centuries', which was code-language for recognising the post-war frontiers of Poland and Germany (Stehle, p. 304). The next day three Hungarians and two Yugoslavs arrived and, even more remarkably, on Wednesday, October 10, Pope John was able to embrace three Czech bishops and Petras Mazelis, Apostolic Administrator of Telsiai, Lithuania, now a republic of the Soviet Union. These were all signs of the improving relations with the Communist bloc. On the other hand, Willebrands had returned from Moscow, apparently empty-handed, on October 4.

So now by October 10, 1962, the eve of the Council, most of the cast had been assembled. Not all of them were sure what for. Archbishop Aston Chichester SJ, always known as 'Chick', an Englishman who had spent most of his life in what was then Southern Rhodesia (now Zimbabwe) and who at eighty-three was not only older than Pope John but fatter, was seen wandering round the Jesuit Curia enquiring: 'Just who is this bloke Otto ... Ottoviani?' (Kaiser, p. 76: amended by oral tradition). He didn't have much time to find out, for he died as he entered St Peter's on October 24, and was thus spared a Council he might have found hard to comprehend.

It was drizzling on the morning of October 11, 1962, the first day of the Council. Someone recalled the violent thunderstorm that had marked the end of Vatican I. Pope John's opening address to the Council made October 11 the date to remember it by. It acted as a criterion or yard-stick: this or that is to be rejected because it is not in accord with the spirit of October 11. Archbishop Thomas Roberts once said: 'Whenever I get depressed during the Council, I reread Pope John's opening address, and have my spirits lifted'. In this speech

Pope John, having toiled to the upper slopes of the sacred mountain, pointed to the promised land beyond.

But Pope John's speech came only at the end of a long ceremony that began at 8 a.m. Until he began to speak, October 11 meant simply a baroque endurance test. Cardinal William Godfrey's train-bearer sets the scene:

> The contrast between the grand ceremonial of the past and new demands of the Council was evident as the procession of Bishops entered St Peter's. The entire length of the basilica up to the papal altar under the cupola had been transformed into a mighty council chamber with tiers of seating raised high on either side, and with tribunes aloft for religious superiors and *periti* [experts]. This constituted an unforeseen practical difficulty: where to put the cardinals' secretaries and train-bearers who could no longer occupy their privileged position sitting on the floor at the feet of their masters. For there was no more floor.
>
> As we arrived at the doors of the basilica, papal masters of ceremonies tucked scarlet silk trains over cardinalatial arms, and then clapped their hands at us in the vain hope that we might vanish. We were driven hastily round the back of the tiered seating and up into the tribunes from which we were swiftly evicted by the self-righteous *periti*. Next we were tucked into a corner near the diplomatic corps and ecumenical observers, who were having a splendid time with their cameras . . . Then Mgr Willebrands came along, shook my hand, and called out to the Swiss Guard: 'They cannot remain here'. Thus cardinals' train-bearers were significantly the first victims of renewal and ecumenism . . . We joined the attendant members of the papal household, and for the next few hours stood unseeing, close at hand
>
> (Worlock, Archbishop Derek, 'The Sharing Church', in *The Tablet*, October 9, 1982, pp. 1005–6).

History in the making always tends to be uncomfortable. The less stout-hearted could always watch on television as Pope John, having arrived at the door of the Basilica, descended from his undulating *sedia gestatoria*, and *walked* up the main aisle, casting a glance towards the statue of St Peter on the right.

After the *Veni Creator*, Cardinal Eugène Tisserant said the Mass. The Sistine Choir sang Palestrina's *Missa Papae Marcelli* with its customary *vibrato:* the Counter-Reformation at its best. The bishops neither participated nor communicated at the Mass: liturgy as spectacle. Mass over, the cardinals made their obeisance to the Pope. Then Pope John read out, as canon law demanded, the fierce and formidable profession of faith of Pius IV, dating from 1564. 'I confess and hold the Catholic faith', Pope John solemnly swore, 'outside of which no one can be saved'. Mgr Pericle Felici then recited the oath in the name of all the Council Fathers. It was said that the 'observers' were profoundly shocked by this oath; but more often than not, it was Catholic theologians and reporters who were shocked on their behalf. Anyway, it didn't matter, for Pope John's speech dissipated whatever bad impression had been made.

Or did it? Here again, hindsight plays tricks with memory. The speech came at the end of a very long morning. It lasted thirty-seven minutes. It was in Latin. Not everyone grasped its meaning straightaway. It made its real impact only when it was translated and published in the press. But for those who could understand, it was a *tour de force*. With his 'robust and harmonious voice' (Falconi), Pope John seemed to shed his years and obesity and become a youthful prophet launching the Church on a great adventure of the Spirit.

But – the question recurs – was it all his own work? Capovilla assures us that it was. He quotes Pope John saying: 'I would like the first Italian draft of this speech to be published, not because I want to be praised for it but because I want to take responsibility for it; it should be known that it belongs to me from the first to the last word' (*Letture*, p. 197). One could hardly be more emphatic than that. The ideas it contains had long been familiar to him. This speech summed up his entire life (see Alberigo, Giuseppe, *'Dal bastone alla miseri- cordia'*, in *Cristianesimo nella storia*, October 1981, pp. 487–521, for the best study of its impor- tance and originality).

The October 11 speech contained four main themes which lifted it above banality and shaped the future course of the Council: the idea of a council as the celebration of faith ever-old, ever-new; an optimism in the Spirit which involved a denunciation of the 'pro- phets of misfortune' (usually translated indiscriminately as 'prophets of gloom' or 'of doom'); a clear statement on what the Council was for and what not; and a novel approach to errors.

The Council was to be a celebration of Catholic faith. The Council celebrated Catholic faith simply by assembling; and it renewed this celebration of faith in its daily liturgies which reflected the fact that Catholicism was 'reconciled diversity' rather than bland unifor- mity. Catholic faith and Christian faith were not distinct in their object: but Christian faith expressed a fidelity to the Gospel, while Catholic faith drew attention to continuity with the past ('tradition'). So they were not in contrast still less in contradiction with each other. This made possible both the renewal of the Catholic Church and a spirit of ecumenical openness.

Pope John's hearers, however, only began to wake up when he spoke directly of the Ro- man Curia. This retranslation of his Italian text is designed to bring out its vigour and fresh- ness:

> In the everyday exercise of our pastoral ministry, greatly to our sorrow, we sometimes
> have to listen to those who although consumed with zeal do not have very much
> judgement or balance. To them the modern world is nothing but betrayal and ruination.
> They claim that this age is far worse than previous ages, and they go on as though they
> had learned nothing at all from history – and yet history is the great teacher of life . . .
> We feel bound to disagree with these prophets of misfortune who are for ever
> forecasting calamity – as though the end of the world were imminent (*Lettere*, p. 426: see
> Abbott, p. 712 for the familiar translation).

Pope John's 'sense of history', however, was not merely a strategy for dealing with em- battled misanthropes who sought security by returning to the past and denigrating the pre- sent. It also made him see the importance of responding to the Spirit *now*. This defined the purpose of the Council, negatively and positively:

> Our task is not merely to hoard this precious treasure, as though obsessed with the past,
> but to give ourselves eagerly and without fear to the task that the present age demands of

us – and in so doing we will be faithful to what the Church has done in the last twenty centuries. So the main point of this Council will not be to debate this or that article of basic Church doctrine that has been repeatedly taught by the Fathers and theologians old and new and which we can take as read. You do not need a Council to do that. But starting from a renewed, serene and calm acceptance of the whole teaching of the Church in all its scope and detail as it is found in Trent and Vatican I, Christians and Catholics of apostolic spirit all the world over expect a leap forwards in doctrinal insight and the education of consciences in ever greater fidelity to authentic teaching. But this authentic doctrine has to be studied and expounded in the light of the research methods and the language of modern thought. For the substance of the ancient deposit of faith is one thing, and the way in which it is presented is another *(Altra è la sostanza dell'antica dottrina del* depositum fidei, *ed altra è la formulazione del suo rivestimento) (Lettere*, p. 427: see Abbott, p. 715 for comparison).

The last sentence became, understandably, an object of controversy. Those who held an 'immobilist' view of language regarded it as pernicious neo-modernism; those on the other hand who thought that history was a necessary dimension of all theology found it liberating.

There can be no doubt about what Pope John said and meant. The above translation is based on the Latin transcript provided by Vatican Radio, and can be checked in its archives. Yet when the Latin version of the inaugural speech appeared in *Acta Apostolicae Sedis*, the official collection of papal documents, the text had been tampered with and censored. The idea of the 'substance' of faith vanished, and cautious qualifications were introduced. They are italicized in the following text and in the translation which immediately follows:

> For the . . . deposit of faith itself, *or the truths which are contained in our venerable doctrine*, is one thing, and the way in which they are expressed is another, *retaining however the same sense and meaning.*

The last clause, not by chance, comes from the anti-Modernist oath of 1910 which also speaks of holding fast to 'the absolute and immutable truth' (Daly, pp. 235–6). So the censoring of Pope John can be safely attributed to those who were still trying to preserve language in aspic and deny history.

This was not the only sentence on which the translators acting as censors distorted John's thought. When he discovered these outrageous changes in late November 1962, he was too canny to sack the editor of *Acta Apostolicae Sedis*. He simply quoted himself, in the original non-edited version, in important speeches. (*Time* magazine for October 5, 1962, quoted an anonymous editor on *l'Osservatore Romano* who frankly admitted that he 'changed the Pope's words, whenever he said something which caused raised eyebrows'.)

If curial theologians were alarmed by the apparent 'relativism' of Pope John's remarks on language and faith, his comments on how to deal with errors sent shivers down the spine of the more politically inclined. No resourceful editing could alter the fact that in refraining from condemnations he had broken with a tradition at least four centuries old. Yet Pope John did it with great tact and skill. He did not deny that errors existed in the contemporary world; indeed, they positively abounded. In a characteristic image he said that 'errors often vanish as swiftly as they arise, like mist before the sun'. It was an experience he had often had as he sat on his balcony at Sotto il Monte. So the Council was not being summoned to condemn errors: 'Today the Spouse of Christ prefers to use the medicine of mercy rather than severity. She considers that she meets the needs of the present age by showing the validity of her teaching rather than by condemnations' (Abbott, p. 716: retranslated). Pope John modestly described this new attitude as a 'preference'. But he knew perfectly well that if one looked at the history of the papal *magisterium* in the last 150 years, it was little short of 'revolutionary'. The results would be seen very shortly. The new approach meant that the nineteenth-century thesis, still defended by Cardinal Alfredo Ottaviani, that error has no rights, would have to be revised.

Two events, very disparate in nature, sum up the 'spirit of October 11'. Train-bearer Derek Worlock went in search of his cardinal and found him standing beneath the statue of St Peter with its toe well-worn by the devoted touch of the faithful. Also present was Cardinal Pietro Ciriaci. 'When this Council is over', announced Cardinal Godfrey, who like Pope John was dying of cancer, 'Peter will still be there, serene and true'. 'Yes' replied Ciriaci, prefect of the ominously named Congregation for the Discipline of the Clergy and the Faithful, 'but we are not all made of bronze'.

The next day two observers from the Russian Orthodox Church, Archimandrite Vladimir Kotliarov and Vitalij Borovoi of Leningrad, arrived in Rome. This time the overworked word was justified: it was 'sensational' news. It meant that Pope John's olive branch had been picked up. The Council was now ready to begin.

Chapter 22

Sixty days to change the Church

When the Fathers of Trent met in Council, under the guidance of the Holy
Ghost, they did not quash their differences or silence objections, but let each
opinion assert itself manfully, and even rudely, in what may be justly called a
trial of strength.

(Lord Acton, *Essays on Church and State*, p. 170, written in 1863)

Everything – nearly everything – that was publicly said and done at what came to be
known as the 'first session' of Vatican II can be found in the four massive volumes of the *Acta
Synodalia Concilii Vaticani II* (ASCV from now on) or in Giovanni Caprile's *Il Concilio Vaticano
II, Primo Periodo* (Caprile II).

The most delightful item is the conversation – to call it a speech would be pompously
misleading – Pope John had with the crowd gathered in St Peter's Square on the night of
October 11, 1962, the date the Council began. The police estimated that two hundred thousand people were present. The youths of Catholic Action, bearing torches, formed a huge
cross around the central obelisk. There was much chanting and singing. The object of the
exercise was to get Pope John to appear at his window on this the greatest day of his life. It
worked. John appeared at his window and cried: 'Dear children, dear children, I hear your
voices'. In the simplest language, he told them about his hopes for the Council. He pointed
out that the moon, up there, was observing the spectacle. 'My voice is an isolated one', he
said, 'but it echoes the voice of the whole world. Here, in effect, the whole world is represented'. He concluded: 'Now go back home and give your little children a kiss – tell them it
is from Pope John' (ASCV, I, 1, p. 202). One could almost touch the emotion. The 'patriarch'
gave and generated love with all his being.

With the Romans on his side, Pope John turned his attention next day to the diplomats
who had come to Rome for the opening of the Council. Seventy-nine nations were represented in one form or another. He told them that although the Council was a religious
event, he hoped that it would contribute towards world peace, 'peace based on growing
respect for the human person and so leading to freedom of religion and worship'.

The speech was a sketch for *Pacem in Terris*. Perhaps only the US Ambassador, G. Frederick
Reinhardt, knew or suspected that within a week the Cuban missile crisis would bring the
world to the edge of doom.

Next day, October 13, Pope John met the 'observers' in the Consistorial Hall and the journalists in the Sistine Chapel – so that the awesome responsibility might strike home. Between them, observers and journalists were to ensure that this Council would be different
and known about. All these speeches were in French, the language John invariably used on

'international' occasions. *Chers messieurs* (dear sirs), he began his address to the observers, continuing: 'I don't like to claim any special inspiration. I hold to the sound doctrine: everything comes from God' (ASCV I, 1, p. 197). Then John talked about his feelings on the morning of October 11: 'I couldn't help looking round at so many sons and brothers. And when my eyes fell on your group, and on each of you, I felt comforted by your presence' (*ibid.*). The observers were captivated.

Marshalled and chaperoned by Cardinal Bea's men, the observers soon got the hang of things and picked up the jargon about the *aula* (the Council chamber) and the *schemata* (the draft texts). They sometimes had the painful experience of being misrepresented in the *schemata* and abused in the *aula*. Cardinal William Godfrey, for example, argued against the use of the vernacular on the grounds that the Anglicans had tried it and, despite the beauty of their worship, 'their churches are empty while ours are full' (ASCV, 1, 1, p. 374: October 23, 1962). Bea's men consoled the observers with the thought that things had been much worse at Vatican I: when Bishop Joseph Strossmayer of Bosnia said that there were many Protestants who 'erred in good faith', he was shouted down with cries of 'Shame: heretic: get down from the pulpit! *Anathema sit!*' (McGregor, p. 36). The observers believed that they had Pope John on their side and knew that through Bea and Bishop Emile Josef de Smedt of Bruges they could make their views known in the *aula* itself. Their title, observers, suggested a passivity that did not accurately describe their real role. It developed enormously in subsequent sessions.

Then came the journalists. Over 1200 were accredited for the opening session, but only about 200 stuck it out for the whole period. For the theologically untrained, it was utterly bewildering. Pope John addressed this motley and restless crew on October 13. 'You can bear witness', he said with a smile, 'that the Church has nothing to hide'. That remark, remembered later, caused raised eyebrows. If there was nothing to hide, why was it that speeches at the Council were baldly summarised and never attributed? 'The following opinions were expressed' was the discouraging formula adopted in the official hand-outs. And why was it that everything remotely interesting was covered by something called 'the pontifical secret', which was a super-secret secret. Thus Fr Sebastian Tromp SJ, a Dutchman and Cardinal Ottaviani's favourite theologian, when asked about the relationship between the Holy Office and the Secretariat for Christian Unity, replied with horror: 'This is a very delicate matter; I thought it was supposed to be secret' (*De Gelderlander Pers*, December 18, 1962).

Some reporters took a high and mighty tone about the obstacles placed in their path. Here, for example, is the witness of the eminently respectable Christopher Hollis, former member of parliament, man of letters, son of an Anglican bishop, brother of a chief of the British secret service:

> The press relations of the Council were in the hands of Curial officials. It would perhaps be a discourteous exaggeration to say that this is as if one were to ask the prisoner in the dock to report on his own trial . . . They cannot understand it, and are not the best people to interpret what they cannot understand (*The Critic*, Chicago. February–March 1963).

Resourceful reporters solved their problems in characteristic ways. Patrick O'Donovan, of *The Observer*, London, eschewed theology and wrote divinely. He surveyed the bishops as they went into St Peter's and saw 'executive faces and kindly faces and imperious faces and ascetic faces, and faces that have known good tables' – including his own, no doubt.

Others knew they had a book in the making. Bob Kaiser, from *Time*, made friends with Archbishop 'Tommy' Roberts who left confidential documents strewn about his flat. Antoine Wenger, a French Assumptionist priest and editor of *La Croix* was actually inside the Council as an expert on communications. This led him into agonised hairsplitting about what he could and could not say. There was a joke circulating: 'Why conciliar secrecy?' Answer: 'Because secrets travel faster.'

The odd thing was that the rule of secrecy did not seem to apply, or at any rate was not respected, in the case of the Italian press. The professional *Vaticanisti* or Vaticanologists had sources not available to anyone else. At the same time most of them were ideologically committed to an alarming degree. The only reliable Italian source was *Civiltà Cattolica*, the Jesuit fortnightly. The Jesuits knew everything, and sometimes shared their knowledge. They were firmly on the side of Bea and Pope John.

Among those who made light of the journalistic problems was the mysterious 'Xavier Rynne' who wrote copiously in *The New Yorker*. With admirable candour, 'Rynne' claimed no inside knowledge and confessed that his eventual book was based 'on sources available to the general public' (Rynne, p. xi). Fr Francis Xavier Murphy CSSR, who with a twinkle in his eye denies that he was 'Xavier Rynne', wrote in 1984: 'Any journalist incapable of cracking a Vatican secret after diligently reading the Italian press, scrutinising *l'Osservatore Romano*, and attending an embassy reception or two, should change his profession' (Murphy, FX, 'Vaticanology: separating fact and fiction', in *National Catholic Reporter*, February 24, 1984, p. 7).

All these writers recounted the dramatic events of October 14, the first working day of the Council. The Council asserted itself by deciding to elect its own Commission members rather than meekly accepting the 180 names provided by the Curia. Cardinals Achille Liénart of Lille and Joseph Frings of Cologne delivered this blow to Cardinal Alfredo Ottaviani. He was visibly shaken, as could be seen on television news, which had pictures without sound (Wenger, p. 59). The politically-minded said the Council had made a bid for independence; theologians preferred to say that it illustrated the meaning of 'collegiality'. This was certainly fun, and there was a mood of almost schoolboy exhilaration. During the summer holiday, the archbishop of Toulouse, Gabriel-Marie Garrone, had carefully studied the *regolamento* or rules of procedure for the Council. He quickly realised that the make-up of conciliar commissions was a matter of the utmost importance. For if the draft texts were to be referred back − and there was every likelihood of that happening − there was not much point in sending them back to the same people. As Yves-Marie Congar duly remarked: 'An apple tree produces apples, a cherry tree cherries'.

Who was really organising the Council? In theory, its day-to-day management was in the hands of the 'Council of Presidents.' But this was a largely notional body. It held no regular meetings. As far as can be discovered, the only decision of any importance taken by the Council of Presidents was that the first *schema* to be examined was that on liturgy. As Liénart explained: 'We ought really to have started with a doctrinal *schema*, but we thought that an easier *schema* would allow us to play ourselves in' (Grootaers, Jan, 'L'attitude de l'Archevêque Montini au cours de la première période du concile', a paper given at the Paul VI colloquy in Milan, September 23–5, 1983). The idea was that everyone, however obtuse, would have something to say about worship.

Although very few were aware even of its existence, authority at the Council was vested in the seven cardinals who sat on the Secretariat for Extraordinary Affairs. In theory the Secretariat was the hourglass connecting Pope and Council. We already know three of its seven members: Montini, Suenens and Wyszyński. The others were Carlo Confalonieri, a curialist who prided himself on his independence of mind, Albert Meyer of Chicago, a scripture scholar who won the esteem of Fr Andrew Greeley, Julius Döpfner of Munich who balanced Giuseppe Siri of Genoa, later described as 'the arch-conservatives' conservative'. But there is not much evidence that this body met very often or decided anything of consequence. Much more influential was an unofficial group headed by Montini and Suenens that had no name. If it has to be labelled, it could be called the 'friends of Pope John'.

They were worried right from the start of the Council because it seemed aimless and without a plan. On October 18, 1962, Montini put his worries in writing in the form of a letter addressed to Cicognani. That was what protocol demanded, but it was meant for Pope John's eyes. He appended Suenens' attempt, based on the distinction between the Church in itself and in its mission, to synthesise the draft texts. He was critical of the Council of Presidents. 'The choice of the liturgy as the first topic for discussion', Montini wrote, 'although it was not placed first in the volumes distributed to us and although there was no need for it to come first, confirms the fear that there is no pre-established plan' (*l'Osservatore Romano*, January 26, 1984). One could not discuss the prayer of the Church without knowing what the Church was. So the Church was the only logical starting-point. He had made this point with some heat to Felici after a meeting of the preparatory commission (Caprile, II, p. 251).

Montini thought the hope of completing the Council in a single session was illusory and would have to be abandoned. At least three sessions would be needed to bring order into chaos. This was bad news for Pope John. He already knew that he was dying. But he had to admit that Montini's plan, which was backed by Suenens, made sense. And there was no other.

Montini's programme for the Council as outlined in his October 18, 1962 letter may be summarised as follows:

> 1. The Council should focus on one theme: the nature of the Church. Why? Because it was the completion of Vatican I which had half-dealt with ecclesiological questions, and because in the twentieth century there had been a renewal in the Church's self-understanding, illustrated by the encyclical *Mystici Corporis*.
>
> 2. But while dealing with the Church, the Council should not be introspective. 'The image of Christ, like the Pantocrator in the ancient basilicas, should rule over the Church which gathers around him and in his name'.
>
> 3. The Council should recognise the 'acquired certainty' about the primacy of Peter and his successors. 'After the definition of papal primacy and infallibility, there were some departures' [he means the Old Catholics under Johann Döllinger] 'and some hesitations, but now there is docile acquiescence'. Since in order to 'complete' Vatican I they had to discuss collegiality and the role of bishops, why not say 'briefly, clearly, solemnly and in heartfelt fashion' that the papal office was not being called into question?
>
> 4. Then the Council should concentrate on the 'mystery of the Church'. It would have

to deal with different tasks or roles in the light of the renewed self-understanding of the Church: bishops, priests, religious, lay people. The point was to arrive at a vision of the Church that was not merely juridical but to see it rather as 'humanity living in faith and love, animated by the Holy Spirit . . . It seems to me that this was the original intention of the Pope when he called the Council'.

5. The *second session* should consider the mission of the Church, or what the Church does. Montini suggests that this would be the right place to deal with liturgy (the Church at prayer) or the 'young Churches' (the Church as mission).

6. Finally a *third session* would be needed to deal with the Church's relationships with other human groups. This would include:

    (i) 'relationships with the separated brethren – to try to deal with this at the start of the Council seems to me to make any solution impossible'.

    (ii) relations with civil society (peace and war, relations with states etc).

    (iii) relations with the world of culture, the arts and sciences.

    (iv) relations with the world of work, economics etc.

    (v) relations with the Church's enemies etc.

At this point Montini added that the texts for the 'third session' he envisaged would have to be written in a different style. They would have to be more like prophetic messages addressed to our contemporaries, whether they were believers or not' (*l'Osservatore Romano*, January 26, 1984: letter dated October 18, 1962).

Montini's letter is the single most important document for understanding not only the first session but the whole Vatican Council. The fact that it was virtually unknown until September 1983 – when Suenens gave his copy to the Paul VI archives in Brescia - means that hitherto historians have lacked the key that would have unlocked the Council. It was to go more or less the way Montini proposed only a week after it started. True, it needed four sessions rather than the three he thought needed – but that was a trifling error since Pope John and the majority of Council Fathers optimistically believed that the Council would be over by the following Christmas. The letter was designed to fill the 'leadership vacuum'. Suenens recalled a conversation with Pope John the previous March. 'Who is organising the Council?' Suenens asked. 'Nobody', replied John, meaning (says Capovilla) that nobody was dominating it. Freedom was no doubt a good thing, but unrestrained freedom led to confusion. Pope John grasped this in late November when he asked Montini and Suenens to say in the *aula* what they had said privately in October. They duly obliged. Pope John could not have drawn up such a plan himself. He had not the scholarship. But he could recognise and appreciate lucidity in others. His own, more modest role, was not in doubt. He told Cardinal Gabriel-Marie Garrone, in a metaphor that would have delighted Archbishop Roberts, that his task was that of launching this big and heavy ship. 'Another', he said sadly and prophetically, 'will have the task of taking it out to sea' (*l'Osservatore Romano*, English edition, February 1, 1982).

Barely more than a week after Pope John's opening address, there was further evidence of inept planning when the Council of Presidents acting 'in the name of the Holy Father' invited the Council to endorse a 'Message to the World'. It seemed rather presumptuous to be addressing the whole world before they had actually done any work. Archbishop John

Carmel Heenan was briskly dismissive: 'I believe it is not yet time to be sending a message to all men, and it makes me sad to see a first message that is so vapid and long-winded. I am quite sure the press will pay very little attention to it' (ASCV, I, 1, p. 237). Heenan was right. The message quickly passed into oblivion.

But lodged in Pope John was the dream of a text that would be addressed not just to Catholics but to all humanity. Such a text was urgently needed, for the world had suddenly become notably unsafe. On October 15 reconnaissance photographs proved beyond doubt that Soviet missiles were in Cuba, within easy reach of the United States (Schlesinger, p. 506). On October 20, the day the Council debated its ineffectual 'message', President John F. Kennedy announced a quarantine or blockade on the Soviet ships that were known to be heading for Cuba. There followed a hectic week in which it seemed quite likely that a nuclear war might engulf the world. Families of politicians were evacuated from Washington. In Rio de Janeiro, Dr Billy Graham announced the end of the world, prematurely as it turned out, but not unreasonably.

Pope John played an important pacifying and reconciling role in this fateful week. Khrushchev acknowledged this later. 'What the Pope has done for peace', he told Norman Cousins, editor of the *Saturday Review*, on December 13, 1962, 'will go down in history' (Stehle, p. 306). But what Pope John did has not gone down in the history of the Kennedy era. One searches in vain for any mention of Pope John in the biographies of John F. Kennedy or the accounts of the Cuban missile crisis. One can only speculate that having their first ever Catholic president made American historians reluctant to admit that the Pope might have had some influence on him. At the other end of the spectrum, *Vaticanisti* exaggerate Pope John's role. They present him as a last-resort mediator when all other diplomatic channels had broken down. But to inflate his role is just as bad as to underestimate it.

The key day in the story was October 23, 1962. Having made his strong stand and imposed the blockade, John F. Kennedy tried gentleness. His brother Robert had built up a friendly relationship with the Russian ambassador in Washington, Anatoly Dobrynin. The president sent his brother along to explain how he read Khrushchev's intentions. No threats were uttered. Robert pointed out that John F. was far less hawkish than others in the administration, and that although he and Khrushchev did not agree on many issues, 'there was now a measure of mutual trust and confidence between them on which he could rely' (Schlesinger, p. 514). That same day the president, pulling out all the stops for peace, called Norman Cousins, author of a book which argued that the only 'third force' in bi-polar world was the papacy. President Kennedy said he wanted to make contact with the Vatican. Cousins consulted the enigmatic Belgian Dominican, Fr Félix Morlion, then engaged in dialogue with Soviet scientists in Andover Massachusetts, who had contacts in the Vatican. He eventually got through on the evening (Rome time) of October 23 and talked to Mgr Igino Cardinale, chief of protocol, who assured him that Pope John would be willing and anxious to help in any way he could.

The Russians at Andover were apprehensive and wanted to go home. Cousins persuaded them to talk to Morlion. Talking to a priest was a new experience for them. They knew Khrushchev personally and transmitted portions of a coded telegram: 'We really believe that you are a friend of peace and do not want the death of millions'. In the Vatican, meanwhile, Pope John had received Morlion's request for intervention. With Dell'Acqua he worked throughout the night on a message to be broadcast the following day. From time to time he went off to his private chapel to pray. He knew exactly what was expected of him. What was it he had said on the night of October 11? 'The Church's voice is an isolated one, but it echoes the voice of the whole world'. Some public sign of papal esteem would help Khrushchev persuade the Kremlin hawks that peace was the wiser course. John's previous discretion now stood him in good stead. He had stopped talking about 'the Church of silence'; he had welcomed the Cuban ambassador to the Holy See, Amado Blanco; he had made it clear that the Council would not issue condemnations. In other words, he had earned the right to be listened to.

The following day, Wednesday October 24, there was the usual weekly audience. At the end of his address, Pope John added a loosely linked sentence on the good will of statesmen: 'The Pope always speaks well of those statesmen, on whatever side, who strive to come together to avoid war and bring peace to humanity'. Banal enough, but it was a first signal to Khrushchev. The second signal was Pope John's message which was delivered to the Soviet Embassy in Rome for transmission to Moscow. It read:

> I beg heads of state not to remain insensitive to the cry of humanity, peace, peace. Let them do all that is in their power to save peace; in this way they will avoid the horrors of a war, the appalling consequences of which no one could predict. Let them continue to negotiate. History will see this loyal and open attitude as a witness to conscience. To promote, encourage, and accept negotiations, always and on every level, is a rule of wisdom that draws down both heavenly and earthly blessings (DMC, pp. 614–15).

John broadcast his message on Vatican Radio that afternoon. By Friday October 26, it made page one of *Pravda* under the banner headline: 'We beg all rulers not to be deaf to the cry of humanity'. This was unheard of. It meant that Khrushchev was preparing his retreat. Pope John's intervention helped to let him off the hook. He could appear as a lover of peace.

On Sunday October28 Khrushchev replied to Kennedy. He declared that work on the missile bases would be suspended, that the weapons would be sent back to the Soviet Union, and that he would begin negotiations within the framework of the United Nations. The Soviet ships had already turned back. In his private chapel, Pope John celebrated a Mass for peace. Soon after, Dell'Acqua, substitute at the Secretariat of State, brought him a message that had just arrived from President Kennedy. He thanked Pope John for his help. Not only was the immediate crisis resolved, but Khrushchev wanted further contacts to discuss disarmament and *détente* (*Utopia*, English, p. 9). It was the fourth anniversary of John's election and the feast of Christ the King.

The Rome newspapers that Sunday morning had not got the latest news and were still alarmist. So Pope John's words to an anxious crowd at the Angelus brought news as well as hope:

> There have been four years of prayer and service, of meetings and conversations, of joy but also some suffering; but every day has been lived with a readiness to do the divine will, and in the confidence that all things work together for the edification of all.
>
> On today's feast of Christ the King, I feel deeply moved and my spirit is led to serenity and calm. The word of the Gospel has not changed; but it rings out to the ends of the

earth and finds its way into human hearts. Dangers and sufferings, human prudence and wisdom – all these should issue into a canticle of love, and a renewed plea, addressed to all men, to seek and restore the Kingdom of Christ . . . A new spirit is beginning to enter the minds of politicians and economists, scientists and men of letters (AAS, 54, 1962, p. 860).

Capovilla dates the origin of *Pacem in Terris* to October 25, 1962, when Pope John was working on his message (IME, p. 180). The Council was wondering how to address the people of the modern age. John would talk about what most concerned people– war and peace. So the encyclical was conceived at the height of the Cuban missile crisis. His 'readiness to do the divine will' led him to this at a time when illness and preoccupation with the Council ought to have dispensed him from extra effort.

No one would have blamed him if he had not written *Pacem in Terris*. He had quite enough to do as it was. But he wanted, before it was too late, to deliver his last will and testament. His old diplomatic habits began to operate once more: when you sense an opening, hasten to exploit it. Khrushchev and Kennedy, the two most powerful men in the world, were well-disposed towards him and even, relatively, towards each other. So keep up the pressure for peace. There was a sense in which this work was more important than the Council. Its debates on the liturgy were dragging on repetitively and interminably. Cardinal William Godfrey produced the 'argument from lipstick' *(labia tincta rubri coloris)* against conceding the chalice to the laity. The 'argument from tourism' against the use of the vernacular plodded its weary way. There had already been some furious clashes in the *aula*. This was an additional reason for working on *Pacem in Terris:* it would be a hint to the Council that the Church existed not to contemplate its navel, but to serve the world. So Pope John did not find it necessary to follow everything that was being said in St Peter's. He kept his closed-circuit television on all the time, of course, but he only switched up the sound when someone who interested him appeared.

But Pope John's physical absence from the *aula* did not mean that he was uninfluential in it. During the debate on the liturgy, his October 11 speech was quoted time and time again by those who wanted freedom, adaptation and changes. His key-terms and attitudes were echoed repeatedly: renewal and optimism, pastoral and ecumenical. This was what Pope John had taught the bishops. Those opposed to change, on the other hand, were unable to quote the October 11 speech. Cardinal James F. McIntyre, of Los Angeles, went directly against it when he claimed that 'the attack on the Latin language in the liturgy is indirectly, but no less truly, an attack on the fixity of sacred dogmas' (ASCV, I, 1, p. 370).

The reformers were neither crude nor foolish. Their strategy was to claim that they were merely continuing the liturgical reforms that had started with St Pius X and been further extended under Pius XII. Ottaviani, who saw himself as the faithful guardian of Pius XII's memory, opposed them. But he made a tactical blunder, however, when he said that priests would soon lose their enthusiasm for this 'new-fangled concelebration', when they learned it would mean forfeiting their Mass stipends. At this point he was stopped by Cardinal Bernard Alfrink not because he had made a petty and stupid remark but because he had run over the allotted fifteen minutes. 'I've finished now,' he cried as he departed, jowls quaking and leaving his hearers uncertain whether he meant he had had his say or had enough. He was not seen in the *aula* for another two weeks. Though Alfrink was merely doing his duty, the fact that a Dutch cardinal should have halted Ottaviani in his tracks provided a symbolic vignette of how much the Church was changing. This happened on October 30, 1962.

Deprived of the presumed approval of the *reigning* Pope, the conservatives were at a loss what to do next. They clumsily put the ball in their own net. Cardinal Antonio Bacci alleged that some passages in scripture, such as the story of the chaste Susannah and the libidinous old men, not to mention the Canticle of Canticles, were best left in the decent obscurity of the Latin (ASCV, I, 1, p. 408).

Bacci was closely followed by Archbishop Pietro Parente, secretary of the Holy Office:

> We are true martyrs at the Holy Office. We know how much patience, how much work, how much prudence is needed to prepare *monita* (warnings), decrees etc. It's very hard work. You've no idea. And all this work is done in Latin, and a good thing too. All you innovators should learn from the Holy Office, which rightly holds fast to tradition and embarks on new ways only with the greatest prudence, a serene heart and calm nerves. So to attack the Latin language would be a very serious matter. (ASCV, I, 1, p. 425).

Like his master Ottaviani, he accepted the diagnosis which said that the trouble with the Church was 'the itch for novelties', known in Latin as the *pruritus innovationum*, which made it sound like a particularly repugnant disease, highly contagious, found most commonly in the Netherlands, and spread by contact with the works of Edward Schillebeeckx OP, whose critique of the draft texts had been devastating and was resented.

So everyone inside the Council had to react, positively or negatively, to the aims which Pope John had fixed for his Council. However, on the details of the debates that were engaging the Fathers in the *aula*, Pope John made no comment. Meeting the French bishops on November 19, the most critical and controversial moment of the session, he described himself once more as the Patriarch Jacob who refused to be drawn into taking sides between his quarrelling sons. But he acknowledged: 'Yes, there's an argument going on. That's all right. It must happen. But it should be done in a brotherly spirit. It will all work out. I am an optimist' (Wenger, p. 114). These almost daily meetings with groups of bishops were his means of sharing in the work of the Council. John had just completed the first round of audiences, and was about to begin the second – starting with the East Europeans – when illness forced him to stop.

So Pope John was 'present' to the Council even though he was not in St Peter's. And although his views on liturgy in the vernacular or communion under both kinds were officially 'unknown', everyone knew that the Patriarch Jacob had some favourite sons. Montini or Joseph reminded the Council on October 22 why liturgical changes were being proposed: it was so that the prayer of the Church might be more pastorally effective. This was the golden rule. He quoted St Augustine: 'It is better that we should be blamed by literary critics than that we should not be understood by the people' (ASCV, I, 1, pp. 314–15). Having said this on October 22, Montini who – it must not be forgotten, thought liturgy the wrong starting point – fell silent in the *aula* until December 5.

There was another way in which Pope John could influence the Council: by dropping hints. The broadest hint was dropped on November 4, 1962, feast of St Charles Borromeo and fourth anniversary of his coronation. It conveniently fell on a Sunday. Mass was celebrated in the ancient Ambrosian rite of Milan by Cardinal Giovanni Battista Montini. But Pope John himself preached the homily. He lavished praise on the Ambrosian rite as an instance of that liturgical diversity which greatly enriched the Church. He quoted the Latin tag *ars una, species mille* —which means that though the creative impulse is one, it produces manifold forms. It must have been evident to all but the most dull-witted Council father that Pope John was saying he was in favour of moderate liturgical change. Moreover, Pope John explained that Rome had learned from Milan: the washing of the feet on Maundy Thursday was not originally a Roman custom; it came from Milan, as St Ambrose testifies in his *De Sacramentis (On the Sacraments*, 3,1,5: DMC, V, p. 10). Finally, by his presence and warm words about 'the first cardinal whom we created', Pope John seemed almost to be designating Montini as his successor.

Montini had a plan. Yet he was silent in the *aula*. He was waiting for the crisis to mature. The debate on the liturgy had exposed contrasting positions. A clear majority was emerging in favour of change. The debate on the two sources of revelation was likely to be even more acrimonious. Montini kept his diocese informed by articles in the Milan newspaper, *l'Italia*. On the eve of the debate, he made it clear that the crunch had been arrived at: 'Only those who are familiar with the development of theology, the progress that has been made in biblical studies, and the controversial heat generated by these questions, both within and without the Church, can appreciate the apprehensions, hopes and fears which this new topic brings to the Council' (Montini, GB, *Discorsi e scritti sul Concilio*, p. 194).

The debate on the 'two sources' began on November 14 and lasted a week. At its centre was the question: is the revelation made in Christ contained in Scripture or Tradition or partly in both? Ottaviani's draft text subordinated both Scripture and Tradition to the *magisterium*. Most theologians thought this was a mistaken approach and ecumenically disastrous. The 'progressives' attacked the view that revelation was embodied in propositions rather than in the person of Jesus. The 'conservatives' launched a vicious attack on scripture scholars who were thought to be tearing the heart out of the Gospel.

The loquacious Ruffini – he spoke twice as often as anyone else in this first session – said the draft text could not be rejected because there was nothing to put in its place. 'It would be', he declared in a revealing metaphor, 'as though a calamitous storm suddenly swept away the foundations of a great building' (ASCV, I, 3, p. 37). A few days later Cardinal Valerian Gracias of Bombay, just back from India and war, replied that it was often more economical to demolish an old house and build a completely new one than to patch up the old. There were dozens of theologians in Rome at that time who could produce an alternative text at the drop of a biretta. Without waiting for an invitation Karl Rahner had already done so. Before coming on to 'the presence of God revealed in the Church's preaching', he had a characteristic section on 'the hidden presence of God in the history of mankind', which anticipated his theory of 'anonymous Christians'. A furious Ottaviani harangued the Theological Commission about 'unauthorised documents that were against the rules and only caused trouble' (Wenger, p. 106). It was just as well that burning dissidents had gone out of fashion.

When Ruffini, Ottaviani and Bacci went to Pope John with their grumbles about the allegedly monstrous behaviour of the 'progressives', he consoled them with history. Things had been far worse at Trent, where an irate Latin bishop tore the beard off a Greek. So there was no need to get upset. Pope John would not use his authority to save the *schema* from defeat; but he would use it to spare its authors from humiliation.

Yet there was still a lot of gloom in the Council. On November 12 it was announced that there would be a second session in 1963 from May 12 to June 29. It seemed likely that the first session would end in chaos, with nothing to show. Bishop James H. Griffiths, an auxiliary of New York, quoted scripture on November 19: 'Lord we have laboured all night and caught nothing, but in your name we will let down our nets' (ASCV, I, 3, p. 203). He evidently didn't expect to find anything in the nets. Yet this was the day on which Pope John was saying to the French bishops, 'I am an optimist'.

On November 21, the forty-two-year-old Bishop of Kraków, Karol Wojtyla, made his maiden speech on the much criticised draft, *De Fontibus Revelationis* (On the Sources of Revelation). He pointed out that a freshwater spring was a 'source' in the strict sense, and that wells and cisterns were only improperly and analogously called 'sources'. In this way he sought to abolish the problem the Council had been debating. The only true and proper 'source' was God speaking. Tradition and Scripture were not 'sources' in the strict sense. Therefore if the document were to be retained, its title would have to be changed (ASCV I, 3, p. 294). It cannot truly be said that on hearing this Barthian mini-lecture, the Fathers of the Council nudged one another and said: 'One day Kraków will be Pope'. But at least they were able to distinguish him from his Polish colleague, the auxiliary of Gniezno, who wanted to change the creed to 'I believe in the Holy, Catholic and *Petrine* Church' (Caprile II, p. 240).

Pope John now took some decisions of crucial importance for the future. First, the *schema* was clearly not a text that could win unanimous assent. Second, the topic of revelation would be entrusted to a 'mixed commission'. This was announced in *l'Osservatore Romano* on November 24. Its co-presidents were Bea and Ottaviani, its co-vice-presidents were Liénart and Cardinal Michael Browne, and its co-secretaries were Fr Sebastian Tromp SJ and Mgr Jan Willebrands. This symmetry was maintained all down the list. This, says Heenan in his free-booting style, 'was Pope John's way of banging our heads together: he shrewdly judged that men who made flaming and intransigent speeches in the *aula* might behave more reasonably in private' (*Crown of Thorns*, p. 356). The real point of Pope John's decision was that the monopoly of the Holy Office was broken.

The final two weeks of the session confirmed the need and the wisdom of enhancing the role of the Secretariat for Christian Unity. First the *schema* produced by the Oriental Churches Commission, *Ut Omnes Unum Sint* (That all may be one), was referred back. Then Ottaviani's *De Ecclesia* was rejected. From Pope John's point of view, the snag was that all this reworking would take time; and yet there was not much time between December 8 and May 12 when the second session was due to begin. Moreover, bishops would hardly have resumed their pastoral programme before it was time to return. So on November 27 Felici announced that 'many Bishops have asked, on pastoral grounds, that the second session should not begin in May but in September. The Holy Father in an audience with the Secretary of State yesterday has deigned to accept this request, and has fixed the feast of the nativity of Our Lady, Sunday, September 8, 1963, for the start of the second session'. This announcement was greeted with volleys of applause – despite the fact that Ruffini had tried to ban all applause on November 10, on the grounds that if expressions of approval were allowed, one could not rule out expressions of dissent (boos? catcalls? whistles?), which would be inappropriate in the august *aula*.

Though it won the approval of the Council, this decision must have cost Pope John a great deal. It meant that he was virtually certain not to see the second session. It was precisely at this moment that *l'Osservatore Romano* for the first time admitted that Pope John's health was giving trouble. It could not be concealed any longer. On November 29 the Vatican paper disclosed that on medical advice Pope John had been obliged to cancel audiences because 'the symptoms of gastric disturbance were getting worse; for some time the Holy Father has been on a diet and undergoing medical treatment that have led to rather severe anaemia'. This was seriously incomplete. It avoided the dreaded word 'cancer'. The truth was that by now there was no new treatment, only a close monitoring of his condition. 'From the doctors' words', wrote Giancarlo Zizola, 'Pope John could grasp that inoperable cancer left him with less than a year to live' (*Utopia*, English, p. 11). The remarkable result was that John became more than ever determined to write the encyclical about peace, conceived on October 25. If he were going to miss the second session of the Council, he could at least finish *Pacem in Terris*. It did not yet have this name.

No sooner had Pope John's illness been announced than it was said to be going away. He would struggle to appear at his window for the Angelus on December 2. Those who saw him were not reassured. Ottaviani, meanwhile, was presenting his last *schema*, significantly entitled *De Ecclesiae Militantis Natura* (On the nature of the Church Militant) which had ferocious chapters on authority and the absolute necessity of the Roman Church for salvation. But this was a different man from the confident and assured Ottaviani who had first spoken on October 14. He was now chastened and sad. It was difficult and unchristian not to feel some sympathy for him. Already half-blind, the butt of the cruellest lampoons, defending a concept of the Church he believed to be the only orthodox one, the baker's son from Trastevere knew that he was beaten. Pope John had persuaded him not to resign and would persuade him to work with Bea, but that was the limit of the concessions he was prepared to make. Ottaviani determined to go down in style. Introducing his hopeless *schema*, he said:

> I expect to hear the usual litanies from you all: it's not ecumenical and it's too scholastic, it's not pastoral and it's too negative, and similar charges. This time I will make a confession to you: those who are accustomed to say 'Take it away and replace it' are already poised for battle. And I will reveal something to you: even before this *schema* was distributed, an alternative *schema* was already prepared. So all that remains for me is to fall silent for, as scripture says, where no one is listening, there's no point in speaking (ASCV, I, 4, p. 9).

Ottaviani left the microphone beaming, amid general hilarity.

But his smile cannot have lasted very long. For that same morning his *schema* was demolished in a single speech which connoisseurs considered the most effective of the first session, if not of the Council. It was given by Bishop de Smedt of Bruges, but he was speaking in the name of the Secretariat for Christian Unity, which gave him added punch. De Smedt denounced three sinful attitudes: 'triumphalism' (the feeling as H. V. Morton said of the Saints on the facade of St Peter's that 'We have it in the bag'); 'clericalism' (the idea of the Church as a pyramid with the Pope at the apex), to which de Smedt opposed the Church as the people of God, filled with the gifts of the Holy Spirit and radically equal in grace; and 'juridicism' or the legalistic spirit.'No mother ever spoke in this way', he said, echoing Léger (ASCV, I, 4, p. 142). These defects would have been banished, de Smedt intimated, had the Secretariat for Christian Unity been allowed to work on the text.

Then, by one of those ironies in which conciliar history abounds, the next speaker after de Smedt was Archbishop Marcel Lefebvre, at the time superior general of the Holy Ghost Fathers, later head of dissident traditionalists with headquarters at Ecône in Switzerland, excommunicated in 1988, died in 1991 at 85. His main point in December 1962 was that the Council risked incoherence by pursuing too many goals:

> At one and the same time we have to propound true doctrine, extirpate errors, encourage ecumenism, and manifest the truth to all men. We are pastors, and we know perfectly well that we don't use the same language with those who know theology and with the laity. So how can we, in one and the same document, define doctrine so that contemporary errors are refuted and yet expound the faith intelligibly to everyone, even those who have no grasp of theological sciences (ASCV, I, 4, pp. 144–5).

What Lefebvre in 1962 regarded as a confused method, became by 1975 seen as 'neo-modernist and neo-Protestant tendencies that manifested themselves in the Second Vatican Council' ('Profession of Faith', in Congar, *Challenge to the Church*, p. 77).

The first session was not ending in total failure. On December 5, Montini spoke in the *aula*:

> Some are afraid that the conciliar discussion will be endless and that instead of bringing people together it will divide them even more. But that will not happen. The first session has been a running-in period. The second will progress much more swiftly, and there is already talk of concentrating the material in briefer drafts, and of laying before the Council only matters which are justified by today's pastoral needs and of general interest (Montini, GB, *Discorsi e scritti sul Concilio*, p. 197).

To avoid a repetition of the free-for-all in the preparations before the Council, Pope John set up a Co-ordinating Commission to oversee its continuation into 1963. Presided over by Cicognani, Pope John's trusty lieutenant, its members were Liénart, Spellman, Urbani, Confalonieri, Döpfner and Suenens (Caprile II, p. 259). But this was not announced until December 17, when most of the Fathers had gone home. The obvious 'conservatives' like Spellman of New York and Urbani, Pope John's successor in Venice, were there so that they could tug along their huge episcopal conferences. Confalonieri, we have already seen, was a curialist with an open mind. The 'golden triangle' of Lille, Brussels and Munich, in the persons of Liénart, Döpfner and Suenens, would organise the Council. Montini was not there because he was going to be pope. Ottaviani and Ruffini had completely lost control. Asked on Bavarian Radio what his hopes for the future of the Council were, Ottaviani replied: 'This question is too delicate' (Caprile, II, p. 292).

It is difficult to say exactly how much of this was known at the time. There were moments when secrecy was blown sky-high. In a homily at a journalists' Mass on November 25 Dom Helder Pessôa Câmara, then auxiliary of Rio de Janeiro, remarked that 'unofficial meetings at which Bishops from all the continents meet fraternally and talk' were just as important as the formal proceedings in St Peter's. He went on:

> It has been suggested that there should be a special commission with the task of studying the problems raised by the modern world, especially world peace and the relationship between the industrialised and under-developed countries (De Riedmatten, pp. 60–1).

This was obviously Suenens' Secretariat *ad extra*. Câmara was optimistic if he thought everyone already knew about this gleam in the eye, which was variously named the commission for charity, for peace or for the poor. Just over four years later it was actually set up on January 6, 1967, as the Justice and Peace Commission. It was another instance of the way the Council created its own organisations and set its own agenda.

Helder Camara belonged to another unofficial group presided over by Cardinal Pierre-Marie Gerlier of Lyons. They were concerned with 'the Church of the poor' (see Congar, *Power and Poverty in the Church*, p. 12). They took heart from, and constantly quoted, Pope John's September 11 broadcast in which he had said: 'Faced with the developing countries, the Church presents herself as she is and as she wishes to be, as the Church of all and especially the Church of the poor' (Alberigo, p. 357). This had theological implications for the exercise of authority in the Church. They were drawn out by Yves-Marie Congar in a lecture on 'The Historical Development of Authority' (*Power and Poverty*, pp. 40–79). So while in the morning session of the Council, the conservatives were beating the Counter-Reformation drum, in the afternoon Congar was telling those who wished to hear that all authority in the Church was for service. Although still not officially *periti* at the Council, Congar and Chenu were working their way back and made their presence felt. After an enforced absence of ten years, Congar's first lecture to his Dominican brothers at Le Saulchoir near Paris was in January 1963. It was on the first session of the Council.

It remained only to publish from the conciliar house-tops (that is, in the *aula*) what had already been whispered in private. It was a well-coordinated campaign which left the conservatives flummoxed. On December 4 Suenens gave the speech previously vetted by Pope John. He revived the distinction between the Church *ad intra* and the Church *ad extra*. He listed four topics that clamoured for attention under the second *ad extra* heading: everything concerned with human dignity – and that included 'the population explosion'; social justice; the Church of the poor; war and peace. The proper treatment of these subjects, Suenens went on, 'involves us in a threefold dialogue: with the faithful, with our separated brothers; and with the world' (Caprile, II, p. 247). The immense applause which followed meant that the vast majority of Council Fathers accepted Suenens' analysis of events at this first session: thanks to Pope John's opening speeches, it began well; then it meandered into frustration and deadlock; it was being saved at the last gasp by a return to Pope John's original intentions.

On December 5, Pope John struggled to his window at noon – the Council ended early so the bishops could see him – and put a brave face on things: 'As you see, my children, Providence is with us. There's progress from one day to the next, *piano, piano* (gently, gently). Sickness, then convalescence. Now we are convalescing'. Seeing the crowd made him feel better, and in a few faltering words he summed up the gist of what was later to be called his 'revolution': 'What a spectacle we see here today – the whole Church in all its fullness: behold its bishops! behold its priests! behold its Christian people! A whole family here present, the family of Christ'.

Pope John did not regard the first session as a failure, but as 'as a slow and solemn introduction to the Council - a generous willingness to enter into the heart and substance of the divine plan':

> Brothers gathered from afar took time to get to know each other; they needed to look each other in the eyes in order to understand each other's heart; they needed time to describe their own experiences which reflected differences in the apostolate in most varied situations; they needed time to have thoughtful and useful exchanges on pastoral matters (Caprile, II, p. 270).

Archbishop Roberts said the same thing more picturesquely: the children of God were able to slide down the banisters in the house of the Lord. So Pope John's judgement on the first session was positive. It may not have turned out as he had expected, but they were all in the hands of the Lord and would have to reckon on the surprises of the Holy Spirit.

Yet despite this spiritual optimism, the atmosphere at this closing meeting of the first session was oppressive, 'almost penitential'. What Pope John was saying was overshadowed by anxieties about his health. This was not the man who had so confidently walked, well, waddled, up the aisle of St Peter's on October 11. John was now a sick man. His face was sunken, his skin livid, his eyes looked under sedation. Many thought they were seeing him at the Council for the last time. 'What was intended as an *au revoir* turned into an *adieu*', said Karol Wojtyla when, as Pope John Paul II, he visited John's birthplace. There was sadness.

Yet this final speech had one very important function: it was designed to console those who were feeling hurt and defeated. Pope John did not rejoice over anyone's discomfiture, and he knew that Ottaviani and Ruffini, among his oldest friends, were feeling badly bruised. He offered them a healing olive-branch with several quite unnecessary references to Pius IX who had not only defined the Immaculate Conception, the day's feast, but opened the First Vatican Council on this very day in 1869.

What could it all mean? Was Pope John, in Gregory Baum's phrase, 'smiling in two directions' (Kaiser, p. 70)? It seems that he took seriously the project of beatifying Pius IX. A society existed in the Roman Curia to promote this curious aim. But Capovilla, from whom this information comes, adds that he used to ward off the zealots' demands for immediate action by saying: 'Tell me what the objections to concluding the cause are, and whether they can be overcome'. Those in the Curia who wanted to redo Pius IX's Syllabus of Errors, might just have found that encouraging. But despite such poultices for the bruised, Pope John continued to speak of Vatican II as a 'new Pentecost' and his deep-down optimism was undimmed. His last word on December 8 was that it seemed as though, in the Council, 'the heavens are opened above our heads, and the splendour of the heavenly court shines down upon us' (Caprile, II, p. 272).

Archbishop Heenan expressed astonishment that Pope John did not mention ecumenism or say farewell to the 'observers' at this final meeting (*Crown of Thorns*, p. 378). That puzzle is resolved once we grasp he was speaking to the defeated conservatives. In any case he had planned to meet the forty-six observers that same afternoon. At the last minute, he was forced to telephone and apologise for his absence. Cardinal Cicognani deputised for him. There was no discourtesy. Everyone understands illness. Lukas Vischer, observing on behalf of the World Council of Churches, made a speech in which he thanked the unavoidably absent Pope John for his welcome. 'From the very first day of the Council', he said, 'we realised the importance the Holy Father gave to the presence of observers from the Churches separated from Rome' (Caprile, II, p. 34). Nothing had been hidden from them. They had felt free to comment on everything. They had done some sliding down the banisters. They had formed friendships that would last a lifetime. Difficulties remained – every ecumenical speech has to recall this truism – but they could now be seen in different perspective.

That was not the least result of the first session of Vatican II. Astonishingly, it had lasted only sixty days. Pope John now had only another six months to live.

Chapter 23

Last will and testament

I never dared be radical when young.
For fear it would make me conservative when old.
(Robert Frost, *Precaution*, in *Complete Poems*, p.337)

Convalescence, Christmas and a message from Khrushchev came at about the same time.

In the excitement of the Council, Pope John had not forgotten about Metropolitan Josef Slipyi, still in a Soviet forced labour camp. The problem was to find some way of communicating with Khrushchev. It was Norman Cousins who made the breakthrough. As the first session of the Council drew to a close, he met Dell'Acqua and Cardinale with the news that he had a rendezvous fixed with Khrushchev for 11.30 a.m. on December 13. They told Cousins that Pope John would regard Slipyi's release as a clear sign of good will.

Within a few days Cousins' twenty-page report on his conversation was on Pope John's desk. Khrushchev told Cousins that he didn't know where Slipyi was now. But he said: 'I will have the case examined and if there are assurances that it will not be turned into a political case, I will not rule out liberation. I've had other enemies, and one more at large doesn't alarm me' (*Utopia*, English, p. 140). Khrushchev appeared genuinely grateful for Pope John's intervention in the Cuban missile crisis, and essayed a folksy comparison between himself and the Pope: 'We both come from humble origins and worked on the land in our youth'.

The new element to emerge was that Khrushchev wanted regular though private contacts with the Vatican; the Cuban emergency had shown how necessary this was. There was to be give and take in this new relationship: the Vatican should recognise the separation of Church and state, and the Soviet Union should recognise that the Catholic Church wishes to serve everyone. Cousins put the final point of agreement as follows: 'Khrushchev recognises that it was very courageous of the Pope to act as he did, given that he has problems within the Church, just as Khrushchev has in the Soviet Union' (*ibid.*, p. 139).

On December 19 the indefatigable Cousins had a forty-minute audience with Pope John. He delivered a personal message from Khrushchev:

To His Holiness Pope John XXIII. On the occasion of the holy season of Christmas, I beg you to accept good wishes for your health and energy to pursue efforts in favour of peace, well-being and prosperity for all humanity.

N. Khrushchev (*Lettere*, p. 439).

John said to Cousins:

I get many messages these days from people who are praying that my illness may be without pain. But pain is not my enemy. I have memories, so many marvellous memories. These memories bring me great joy, and fill up my life so that there is no room for pain. When I was young I was apostolic delegate to Bulgaria. I came to understand and love the Slav peoples. I tried to study Slavonic languages, including Russian. Do you know Russian?

Cousins did not know Russian. John went on:

A pity. You should learn it. You are much younger than I. It wouldn't take you too long. It is a very important language. The Russian people are a wonderful people. We must not condemn them because we don't like their political system. They have a deep spiritual inheritance which they have not lost. We can talk with them. We must always try to speak to the goodness that is in people. Nothing is lost in the attempt. Everything may be lost if men do not find a way to work together to save peace (*Utopia*, English, pp. 141-2: quoting Cousins, Norman, 'The Improbable Triumvirate', in *The Saturday Review*, October 30, 1971).

Back in New York Cousins saw to it that Pope John became *Time's* 'man of the year'. A tasteful drawing adorned the cover, and the fulsome article proclaimed: 'To the entire world Pope John has given what neither diplomacy nor science could give: a sense of the unity of the human family' (*Time*, December 31, 1962). Robert Kaiser, *Time's* man in Rome during the first session, was writing a book to explain it all and exalt the Pope (*Lettere*, p. 569: alas, Capovilla calls him Robert B. Piser). In February *Time-Life* invited Pope John to a spectacular summit lunch in New York, where the other guests would include Kennedy, Khrushchev, de Gaulle, Adenauer, Karl Barth and Pablo Picasso. It was to be most exclusive: only those who had made the cover of *Time* were asked. John didn't reject the idea out of hand, but thought it needed time to 'mature' (*Lettere, ibid.*). And a visit of Kennedy to the Vatican in that same month of May was also tentatively arranged. If Norman Cousins and *Time* cannot be said to have 'created' Pope John's American image, they certainly did their best to make it widely known.

Meanwhile, Pope John was wondering how to reply to Khrushchev's message. Rejecting the icy, anodyne draft proposed by the Secretariat of State, he typed out the message himself:

Cordial thanks for the courteous message of good wishes. We return them from the heart in words that come from on high: Peace on earth to people of good will.

We bring to your attention two Christmas documents from this year which call for the consolidation of a just peace between peoples.

May the good Lord hear and respond to the ardour and sincerity of our efforts and prayers. *Fiat pax in virtute tua, et abundantia in turribus tuis.* ['Peace within your walls, and security within your towers': Psalm 122.7].

Joyful good wishes for the prosperity of the Russian people and all the peoples of the world (*Lettere*, p. 438).

He enclosed his Christmas broadcast to be given the next day, December 22, and his address to the diplomatic corps. The Secretariat of State thought it was a mistake to use such a warm tone and to be quoting scripture - in Latin - when addressing an atheist dictator. So Pope John had to use Cardinal Bea's secretary, Fr Stjepan Schmidt SJ, to deliver his package to the Soviet ambassador. John sealed it with a picture of Our Lady by Tiepolo and the prayer 'Hail, Mary, hope of the world; hail, holy and meek Virgin, filled with God's love, gentle and serene'. Khrushchev was not to know that this prayer, attributed to Pope Innocent III, rhythmic as a mantra, had been used by John since his seminary days (*Rosario*, pp. 5–6). Khrushchev was being assaulted by prayer.

On December 22 Pope John broadcast the Christmas message he had just sent to Khrushchev. It was on the theme of *Gloria in excelsis Deo* (Glory be to God on high). These words, he said, had been sung at the Council in so many different languages – Greek and Slavonic, Armenian, Coptic, Syrian, Latin – and this diversity in unity summed up the experience of the Council (Caprile, II, p. 273). How wonderful it was, he went on, to hear the 'active participation' in the liturgy when over 2000 episcopal throats sang the *Gloria* at the final Mass on December 8. Death was never far from his thoughts these days. 'At the day of judgement', he declared, 'we won't be asked whether we realised unity, but whether we prayed, worked and suffered for it' (*ibid.*, p. 274). Then the 'glory of God' led him naturally to 'peace on earth' (*pacem in terris*). From now on John saw concluding the Council and working for peace as two complementary tasks.

The critics in the Secretariat of State were right in this: the presence of a Latin quotation from scripture in the message to Khrushchev was incongruous. But the Latin Bible was alive for John. Giacomo Manzù, the sculptor to whom he gave several sittings, says that John would declaim poetic passages from the Old Testament. When Manzù pointed out that he did not know Latin and was a man of the left, John would translate into Italian with equal gusto.

The work on *Pacem in Terris* was going well. John had set up a small editorial team headed by Mgr Pietro Pavan, professor of social doctrine at the Lateran. Now fifty-eight, Pavan was the son of a Venetian shopkeeper and anti-Fascist. His 1952 book on *Christianity and Democracy* followed Jacques Maritain in showing the affinities between the two – an unusual position for an Italian cleric. Right from the start, John insisted that there should be no condemnations in his projected encyclical. 'I can't attribute ill will to one side or the other', he told Pavan, 'if I do, there will be no dialogue, and all doors will be closed' (*ibid.*, p. 26). Pavan emerged from the papal library and said to Capovilla: 'What marvellous limpidity of mind he has'.

However, none of this meant that Pope John was 'blurring the difference between right and wrong' or 'naïvely falling into Khrushchev's trap' – to quote the commonest charges made against him. If John's critics could have read his diary for St Stephen's day, 1962, they would have been surprised to find him as concerned about 'the conversion of Russia' as Pius XII:

> December 26. A calm St Stephen's day. The liturgy made a great impression on me. My spirit continues to be concerned with whatever it is the Lord is mysteriously doing. Is not this Kroucheff – or Nikita Khrushchev as he signs himself – preparing some surprises for us? After a long meditation last night, and after reading the introduction to

Ettore Lo Gatto's *Russian Grammar* that Mgr Capovilla gave me as a Christmas present, I got out of bed and then, kneeling before the crucified Lord, I consecrated my life and the final sacrifice of my whole being for my part in this great undertaking, the conversion of Russia to the Catholic Church. I repeated it in the same spirit at holy Mass. At noon during the general audience in the Sala Clementina, still under the same inspiration, I put great fervour of heart and lips into the words, *Domine, tu scis quia amo te* (Lord, you know that I love you. John 21. 17) (*Lettere*, pp. 453-4).

But at the turn of the year, his immediate concern was with the Council. On January 1, 1963, he was up at 4 a.m. 'as usual' and working on his letter to 'the Bishops of the Council' (Caprile, II, p. 300). He was rather pleased with this new and collegial title, 'Bishops of the Council'. When the letter was finished and sent, he reflected that it had 'cost me quite a bit. But I wanted it to come wholly from the personal thought, the heart and the pen of the Pope, and I thank the Lord I managed it' (*ibid.*). The purpose of the letter was to remind bishops that although they were now having a rest from the Council, it was not over and they would soon have some documents to ponder. Working on the Council documents should take priority over all other work. It should be 'the apple of your eye'. Even the plea of 'urgent pastoral work' would not be accepted as an excuse for not answering swiftly requests for comments on draft texts.

After a shaky start, the Council had now found its feet. He described the role of the Coordinating Commission; it was to be the dynamo of the Council. He recalled that although conciliar decisions needed papal approval to be valid, until that final stage had been reached the bishops should not sit around waiting for the Pope to give them a lead (*Lettere*, p. 443). John's conclusion was very characteristic: the Council had exceeded all expectations by the interest it had aroused among the Catholic people, among the separated brothers and among people in the world at large (like 'Kroucheff'). The Letter to the bishops of the Council was published on January 6, the Epiphany, feast of Christ as the Light of Nations. It is bathed in light and common sense. It was not written by a man who was weary of the Council or disillusioned by it.

Pavan had been working fast. He delivered the first draft of *Pacem in Terris* on January 7, 1963. Pope John saw that it was the fifth and final section concerned with how to deal with unbelievers (euphemism for Communists) that would rock the foundations. But he wanted to keep open the possibility of 'prudent cooperation' with those of different views (*Pacem in Terris*, No. 100). He personally added a passage (*Utopia*, Italian, p. 35) which distinguishes between the 'error', always to be repudiated, and 'the person who falls into error', always to be respected. It was to become one of the most direct and forceful passages of the encyclical: 'A person who has fallen into error does not cease to be human. He never forfeits his personal dignity; and that is something that must always be taken into account' (*Pacem in Terris*, No. 158). This idea was essential if the ecumenical goals of the Council were to be achieved, and if his work for peace were to be effective. Though there was still a long and rocky road ahead, this was also to be the germ of the Council's declaration On *Religious Liberty (Dignitatis Humanae)*. Once again, completing the Council and making the world a more peaceful planet were two panels in the same diptych.

That is why Pope John attached so much importance to the first meeting of the Co-ordinating Commission, 21–27 January, 1963. It would prove whether or not a new and effective method had been found for guiding the future work of the Council. Cardinal Suenens had succeeded in reducing the number of drafts from seventy to twenty. He ordered those which remained according to the principles stated by Cardinal Montini and his own distinction between the Church *ad extra* and the Church *ad intra*. He proposed that genuine experts, including laymen, should be involved in the work. Some of the *periti* at the first session had been bogus. Cardinal Speliman's chauffeur was included on the grounds that 'Jack couldn't be left waiting outside'.

Pope John concluded another piece of unfinished business on February 10, when he officially opened the process intended to lead to the beatification of Cardinal Andrea Carlo Ferrari, archbishop of Milan. He had left it late. But recent historical research in Milan – in no way discouraged by Montini – made it quite clear that Ferrari had been scurvily treated by the Roman Curia and St Pius X. So by starting the process John was partly honouring his old friend and mentor, but also righting an injustice suffered by the diocese of Milan.

Mgr Jan Willebrands was now on his way to Moscow to negotiate the release of Metropolitan Slipyi. That involved accepting that his liberation would not be exploited for anti-Soviet propaganda. The right-wing would inevitably regard this as another instance of Pope John's 'weakness'. He lay down before Communism as the lamb before the lion. Moreover, it was clear that the political right-wing in Italy was allied with the 'opposition' within his own Curia. They were talking about him as though he were already dead, and thinking about the succession. John knew perfectly well what was being said behind his back, and talked about it frankly with Roberto Tucci, SJ, editor of *Civiltà Cattolica*, on February 9, 1963: 'Look, dear father, I know that I don't have very long to live. I must therefore be extremely careful in everything I do to prevent the conclave after my death being a conclave "against me", because then it might destroy the things I have not been able to achieve' (Roberto Tucci SJ, letter, April 25, 1991).

Metropolitan Slipyi had been ordained priest in September 1917, on the eve of the Russian Revolution. Now in February 1963 he was suddenly and without explanation hauled out of his prison camp and sent under guard to Moscow. On arrival he was taken to the Hotel Moscow where he was astonished to discover Mgr Willebrands who told him that he was being freed. But Slipyi's feelings of relief turned to horror when he realised that there were conditions. He would not be allowed to return to his beloved Lviv in the Ukraine, and would have to spend the rest of his days in exile. Negotiations dragged on, punctuated by awkward silences. Slipyi had the choice: permanent exile or back to the labour camp. Eventually, Slipyi fell to his knees and gave in. Slipyi hated planes, so they boarded a train and came back via Vienna and Venice (Lomax, Benedict, 'Pope John's Ostpolitik', in *The Month*, September 1974, pp. 691–6).

To avoid the press, it was arranged that the Alpen Express should stop at Orte, fifty miles north of Rome. Cardinale, chief of protocol, and Capovilla, bearing the gift of a pectoral cross, formed the reception committee. Slipyi was greeted and driven off to the nearby Abbey of Grottaferrata, accompanied by Cardinale, while Capovilla hastened back to Rome to tell Pope John. His light was out, so Capovilla hastily scribbled a note and slipped it under the door:

Holy Father! I got back at midnight. Metropolitan Slipyi arrived safely. He is very grateful to your Holiness. He admired your gifts. He said: 'If Pope John in his goodness hadn't brought this off, I wouldn't have lived much longer. Cancer was getting the better of me'. He gives the impression of being a wise man, strong and gentle at the same time. He's at ease in Italian. As they passed through Venice, they stopped to pray for you in the basilica – before the relics of St Mark and the Nicopeia Madonna. Don Loris (IME, p. 172).

Capovilla telephoned the deputy editor of *l'Osservatore Romano*, Cesidio Lolli, with the great news. Through him it appeared in the papers the following day. But no one guessed where Slipyi had arrived.

They met that same evening. John advanced with arms out-stretched to embrace him, but Slipyi fell to his knees and insisted on kissing the papal feet. 'Thank you, holy Father', said Slipyi, 'for all you have done to pull me out of the well'. What is there to say when one has been suddenly transported from a log-cabin in Siberia to the Vatican? They went to John's private chapel and recited the *Magnificat* together. Then they had a conversation lasting an hour and twenty minutes. John wanted to know about the labour camps – Slipyi had brought along his prison uniform – and about other priests and bishops to be found there. Slipyi gave him a map of the Soviet Union with all the camps marked – a guide to what Alexander Solzhenitsyn was soon to call 'the Gulag Archipelago'. John kept it beside him till he died. He wrote in the margin: 'The heart is closer to those who are further away; prayer hastens to seek out those who have the greatest need to feel understood and loved' (IME, p. 173).

But *Pacem in Terris* was not allowed to monopolise his attention or his time. On February 25, 1963, John received Pastor Roger Schutz, founder and prior of Taizé in Burgundy. Not only had Schutz been an observer at the first session, but he brought along members of his community to pray for the Council. Their modest fiat at via del Plebiscito 107 became an unofficial ecumenical centre in which the Latin Americans, who were interested in 'the Church of the poor', were particularly welcome (Caprile, II, p. 340). It may have been this background which led Schutz to surprise Pope John by saying that 'evangelically-minded people' were frankly shocked by the pomp and pageantry of the Vatican. He claimed that these apparently minor problems of sensitivity were more important than dogmatic differences. John was put out: 'Ah! *monsieur le pasteur*, just think to whom you are speaking. Our family is a poor family. Do you imagine that I don't suffer here in the Vatican? But reform takes a long time, and I can't change everything in a few years (Guitton, p. 16).

Two days later Pope John began the celebration of Lent by going to Santa Sabina, home of the Dominican master-general, for Ash Wednesday. Though increasingly breathless, he insisted on his usual round of parish visits throughout Lent. They were cheerful, chaotic affairs, more like a farewell party than anything else. The old *nonno* or grandfather was visiting his people. They loved him. Everyone wanted to catch a glimpse of 'good Pope John' before it was too late. By the time he came to visit Ostia, Borgata di San Basilio and Quarto Miglio, the general election campaign was well under way. But all political parties agreed to remove their posters and cancel meetings when Pope John came among them. It was as though his mere presence was enough to produce a truce, a moment of *convivenza*, of harmonious being together.

But it was easier to do that on the streets and squares of Rome than within the Vatican, as John was about to discover. Alexis Adzhubei, thirty-eight-year-old editor of *Izvestia*, arrived in Rome with his wife Rada on February 28. He let it be known that he had a gift for Pope John from his father-in-law and would like an audience to hand it over. Pope John, distressed at the way the Secretariat of State was refusing to help him but still anxious to go through the 'proper channels', consulted Cardinal Alfredo Ottaviani at the Holy Office on the wisdom of receiving Adzhubei. Ottaviani's answer was a qualified 'no'. In his judgement, the request was a propaganda move: it would suggest that agreements were being negotiated, would give rise to endless conjectures and arouse unrealisable hopes. Ottaviani opined that honour would be satisfied if Adzhubei were received by Augustin Bea at the Secretariat for Christian Unity or Gustavo Testa at Oriental Churches. Since Adzhubei was plainly not a Christian, this seemed a rather quixotic idea, and Pope John was not satisfied with it. Then Adzhubei helped him out. In a press conference he said: 'I haven't come to Rome to establish diplomatic relations with the Vatican'. Why had he come? 'I will visit St Peter's: I hear it is a great work of art'. Adzhubei also adroitly stressed that though he would like to meet Pope John – as a journalist one met all sorts – he wouldn't put any pressure on the Pope and was used to biding his time (*Utopia*, English, p. 152).

His wholly correct behaviour allowed Pope John time to devise a formula. John wrote a memo:

> I would be breaking my word and condemning all my previous behaviour if I refused to see someone who has courteously and sincerely asked to see me in order to bring a message and a gift. It should be recalled that, without any initiative on my part, three times the Russians have made courteous gestures towards the Pope: on his eightieth birthday, last Christmas, and on his nomination for the Balzan peace prize (*Utopia*, English, p. 154).

So he was now consulting Montini more than the Secretariat of State. The diplomatic solution devised was that Adzhubei, who was after all the editor of an important newspaper, could be present among the reporters at the announcement of the Balzan peace prize (awarded to Pope John for 'his activity in favour of brotherhood between all peoples') and would meet the Pope privately afterwards.

On the morning of March 7, 1963, the blond, chain-smoking Alexis Adzhubei was mobbed by photographers as he crossed St Peter's Square and entered the Vatican by the Bronze Gate. In the throne room he met Fr Alexander Koulič SJ, from the Oriental College, who was to act as interpreter. Adzhubei, in the second row of scarlet armchairs, listened carefully to Koulič's murmured translation of Pope John's words about 'active neutrality', and bowed solemnly for the papal blessing at the end. Then the other journalists were presented to the Pope. Pope John greeted Giancarlo Zizola, condemned by the alphabet to be last, and chatted amiably about *l'Eco di Bergamo*, his favourite paper, and then said: 'I'd like to talk to you at greater length, but I have another audience coming up'. He waved a blessing and added ironically: 'That's how much freedom and sovereignty the Pope has' (*Utopia*, English, p. 157). He vanished into his private library where the Russian couple were waiting for him. The doors closed. As far as press and public were concerned, that was that. Nothing would be reported.

Yet Pope John had given Capovilla, his 'historian', a full account of the audience, intending that it should appear in *l'Osservatore Romano*. But the Vatican newspaper did not see fit to publish it. Yet its substantial accuracy was confirmed by Fr Koulič's report submitted to the Secretariat of State the next day, March 8, 1963.

Rada Khrushchevska made a low bow; her husband bent his head over the Pope's hand, touching it with his brow, but not quite managing the homage of a kiss. Rada understood French, so John rattled on in French and explained the paintings and tapestries that decorated his library. He then sat them down on either side of him. With the ice broken, Alexis Adzhubei sketched a parallel between his father-in-law Khrushchev, considered a reformer in the Communist world, and Pope John, an innovator in the Catholic world (Koulič in *Utopia*, English, p. 159). Khrushchev wanted to have direct contact for solving problems as they arose. Pope John answered:

> The Bible says that God created the world and on the first day he created light. Then creation went on for another six days. But the days of the Bible, as you know, are whole epochs, and these epochs last a very long time. We are looking into each other's eyes and we see the light there. Today is the first day of creation, the day of light, the day of 'Let there be light'. It all takes time (*Utopia*, English, p. 158).

Then the conversation became more familiar. John talked about Bulgaria, the beauty of Slav music, and his own village of Sotto il Monte. Rada ventured in French: 'We come from a peasant family too. In Russia it is said that you are a countryman. You have hands that have been hardened by toil, like my father' (*Lettere*, p. 456). Had she been coached?

Finally came the presentations. John gave Rada a rosary, and said: 'Madame, I know that you have three children, and I know their names. But I would like *you* to tell me their names, because when a mother speaks the names of her children, something very special happens'. Rada said faintly and tremblingly: 'Nikita, Alexei, Ivan'. John said that Ivan, of course, was simply John, 'the name of my grandfather, my father, the name I chose for my pontificate, the name of the hill above my birthplace, the name of the basilica of which I am bishop'. He concluded 'When you get home, madame, give all your children a hug, but give Ivan a very special one – the others won't mind' (*Utopia*, English, p. 158). There were also stamps for the boys, coins for Alexis, and for the 'grandfather' Khrushchev medals struck by Giacomo Manzù. He did not reveal that Manzù was a man of the left. Koulič adds that Adzhubei asked Pope John if he could publish something, if only a couple of lines, about their meeting. John said 'no'. When the press gets involved, things become too complicated.

What was said during the Adzhubei visit remained a mystery until the following August, by which time Pope John was dead. This was not his intention. He wanted Capovilla's article and Koulič's memorandum published. But the 'first section' of the Secretariat of State would not hear of it. John's remark to Zizola – 'That's how much freedom and sovereignty the Pope has' – was now cruelly verified. His orders were simply not being obeyed.

On March 20, 1963, John wrote a note 'for history'. It makes it clear that disobedience at this level was incomprehensible to him:

I have told Dell'Acqua and Samorè repeatedly that the note written by Fr Koulič, the sole witness to my meeting with Rada and Alexis Adzhubei, should be published. But the first section [of the Secretariat of State] does not agree, and I'm unhappy about that. . . . When it is known what I said, and what he said, I think people will bless the name of Pope John. Everything should be carefully noted down. I deplore and pity those who in these last few days have lent themselves to unspeakable manoeuvres (*Utopia*, Italian, pp. 222–3; English, pp. 162–3).

Pope John's 'note' was written just three days before *Pacem in Terris* was sent to the printers. Even the first section of the Secretariat of State could not suppress an encyclical. John was in a hurry. On the death of a Pope all his projects are halted. A Pope has no authority beyond the tomb. Some of John's opponents wished he were already there.

John's opponents were not stupid or wicked men. Historians still argue about how far Khrushchev really changed Russian society and foreign policy. For the curialists who opposed Pope John the issue was much simpler: the Italian general election was due on April 28. If 'good Pope John' was seen talking in friendly fashion with a Communist leader like Adzhubei, then it would be impossible to prevent Italian Catholics from voting Communist. For Pope John had taught them that Communists could be 'men of good will'.

One cannot blame the Secretariat of State for its interpretation of events. But John was deeply hurt. They were thinking of short-term political consequences; he was thinking in epochs . . . They were calculating; he was dreaming . . . This was why *Pacem in Terris* made such a powerful impact on public opinion. It was what Pope John had been trying to say all along. The misunderstandings of those who should have been his collaborators and his physical sufferings – all the time this lump in the gut was growing – made it more than ever necessary to speak before it was too late. So *Pacem in Terris* became his last will and testament.

Pope John was bubbling over and announced it on March 31, 1963. He signed the first five copies of *Pacem in Terris* in his private library before the television lights on the Tuesday of Holy Week. He wore a stole to indicate that this was a religious event. The press had the text the next day and it was officially dated, as John had wished, Maundy Thursday, April 11, 1963.

Pacem in Terris completes and carries further the process begun in *Mater et Magistra*. Pope John felt free to take the modern world seriously and to appraise it positively. Even though he builds his encyclical on the contrast between the 'order' willed by God and the 'disorder' that is sin, he finds much to praise in the contemporary world. He starts, for example, with a confession of faith in science that is worthy of Teilhard de Chardin: 'That a marvellous order prevails in the world of living beings and in the forces of nature is the clear lesson to emerge from progressive modem scientific research' (No. 2).

Then, in the section called 'Order among human persons' (Nos. 8–38) John develops the idea that respect for the dignity of the human person provides the norm of morality. That the dignity of the human person should be respected had been a principle of Catholic social doctrine at least since *Rerum Novarum* in 1891. John's originality lay in the range and number of rights he deduced from it. When John declared that 'every human being has the right to worship God in accordance with the rights of his own conscience, and to profess his religion both in private and in public' (No. 14), he was saying something *new:* in the nineteenth century Protestants were conceded no such liberty. When he defended the right of developing nations to determine their own future, he was again saying something *new:* in the nineteenth century both Catholic Poland and Ireland were ordered by the papacy to be obedient to legitimate authority, however foreign or unpleasant it might be. *Pacem in Terris* also has a preference for democracy that was novel: persons have a right to take an active part in public life (No. 73).

Again, while the nineteenth century was suspicious of the language of 'human rights' as the slogan of the French Revolution ('Only God has rights', as Archbishop Marcel Lefebvre insisted), John saw human rights as fundamental to the preaching of the Gospel. And while the nineteenth century *magisterium* thought Catholicism should unashamedly use the state to maintain its dominance where it could, John envisaged a pluralist society in which Church and state are distinct, and therefore could be well-disposed towards each other.

The real originality of *Pacem in Terris* and its true starting point are to be found in Nos. 39–45. It begins, unarrestingly: 'There are three things which characterise our modern age'. In previous encyclicals this would have been a prelude to the denunciation of three evils (like laicism, materialism and scientism). John's three features, however, are all positive. First he noticed 'a progressive improvement in the economic and social conditions of working people' who insist on being treated as human beings (No. 40). Next 'the part that women are now playing in political life is everywhere evident' and 'women are gaining an increasing awareness of their natural dignity' (No. 41). Thirdly 'imperialism is rapidly becoming an anachronism' since 'all people have either attained political independence or are on the point of obtaining it' (No. 42). All these were instances of emancipation or liberation.

But it was not enough merely to register what was going on. John gave a positive evaluation of these three features of the modern age because he believed them to be 'signs of the times'. The Holy Spirit has to be discerned at work in the trends and tendencies of the age. It would be idle to pretend that the Church had single-handedly promoted the social advance of the working class or feminine emancipation or decolonisation. So the Church had to admit that sometimes the 'world' was ahead and could teach the Church lessons. The Vatican II pastoral constitution, *Gaudium et Spes*, would adopt Pope John's 'signs of the times' approach explicitly: 'With the help of the Holy Spirit, it is the task of the entire people of God, especially pastors and theologians, to hear, distinguish and interpret the many voices of our age, and to judge them in the light of the divine word' (*Gaudium et Spes*, 44). *Pacem in Terris* showed how one could respect tradition while being open to the action of the Holy Spirit in the now of history. This was John's bequest.

On one major question *Pacem in Terris* advanced further than previous papal teaching. Pius XII had talked a great deal about peace. As Graham Greene remarked '*Pax, pacem, pacis, pace* – the comforting word, in all its declensions, tolled like a bell throughout his long pontificate' ('Pius XII', in *The Month*, December 1951, p. 329). Here is what Pope John said about nuclear weapons: 'In this age which boasts of its atomic power, it no longer makes sense to maintain that war is a fit instrument with which to repair the violation of justice' (No. 127). Pope John was not saying that an atomic war was hard to imagine: he said it was '*alienum a ratione*', that is, irrational or even insane. In the nuclear age, the choice was between dialogue or catastrophe or permanent international tension. *Pacem in Terris* caught the world's imagination because it came from someone who had no power in the conventional sense. So whatever authority it had come from the cogency of what it said and the hope it inspired. It remains the only encyclical that has been set to music – by French composer Darius Milhaud.

For Pope John *Pacem in Terris* was a supreme effort. It cost him a lot. On Maundy Thursday he talked about the encyclical to the diplomatic corps, and had to struggle to conceal the torment he was in. Through the pain, the passion, his words reached a new level of simplicity:

> I'm glad that the encyclical has been published today, the day on which the lips of Christ pronounced the words, 'Love one another' [John 13. 14]. For what I wanted to do above all was to issue an appeal to love for the people of this time. Let us recognise the common origin that makes us brothers, and come together! (DMC, V, p. 196).

The long ceremonies of Holy Week were a trial. On Good Friday the doctors stood by in St Peter's during the veneration of the cross, fully expecting him to collapse at any moment (IME, p. 194). But somehow he came through.

On Holy Saturday at noon, John gave an audience to Giacomo Manzù. The sculptor felt reasonably satisfied with three of his bronzes – those he disliked he destroyed – and they were set out like soldiers on parade for John to inspect them. 'So many Pope Johns', said the subject of the bronzes, 'isn't one enough?' They laughed. But Manzù, with his sculptor's eye for physical detail, was appalled and broken-hearted. The face he had tried to recapture was no more. 'Most of it had fallen, except the big hooked nose and the immense ears which were left to ride above all else like an alarming sentinel, gaunt towers of a crumbling castle' (Pepper, pp. 212–13). It was that ravaged face that was seen on the balcony of St Peter's the next morning, Easter Sunday, blessing the city and the world.

Chapter 24

Eastertide

On the natural level the death of a man is an absurd phenomenon,
something that denies all the promise man bears within himself in his
earthly life and shatters all his inmost hopes.

(Edward Schillebeeckx OP 'The Death of a Christian' in *Vatican II, a Struggle for Minds*,
p. 65)

April 14, Easter Sunday. Mass at 7 a.m. A bad morning. Very fatigued. But is able to walk to the central *loggia* of St Peter's at noon and says: 'The Easter message is full of light – not death but life, not conflict but peace, not lies but truth, not whatever depresses and casts down but the triumph of light, purity, mutual respect' (DMC, V, pp. 212-13). He looks at the children and says: 'Here is tomorrow's Rome! I stretch out my arms to embrace you, but my words can scarcely express what my heart feels'. In the afternoon sees John Casserly's television film about the Vatican. No comment. He writes in his diary:

> I came though Easter well enough, though with considerable pain . . . A peaceful Mass at home, then abandonment to God. St Peter's Square was simply triumphal, as is usual on special occasions . . . Final greetings in twenty-six languages: peace and joy spread visibly through the crowd. The encyclical *Pacem in Terra* [*sic*] acclaimed more than ever . . . Unbroken pain that makes me seriously wonder about my chances (IME, p. 195).

April 20, Saturday. Exhausted. Audiences start at 10 a.m., and he finds it impossible to stick to the allotted ten minutes each. Doesn't finish till 1.45 p.m. At 5 p.m. the annual concert of the RAI orchestra. What ought to be a pleasure becomes 'seventy-five minutes of pain'. But Rimsky-Korsakoff's *Russian Easter* reminded him of the church music he had heard in Bulgaria in the 1920s. He goes straight to bed as soon as it is over.

April 25, Thursday. Mass at 7 a.m. Recites, on his knees, the litany of the saints. Works on the new draft documents prepared for the second session of the Council with the help of his confessor, Mgr Alfredo Cavagna. Appears at his window at noon for the Angelus and to greet the *Bersaglieri*, the sympathetic regiment who wear feathers in their hats and trot where others march. 'I didn't make such a bad sergeant', he tells them.

April 26, Friday. A flash of anger as he rejects the proposal to hold the Balzan Peace Prize award in St Peter's. 'I will not go down to St Peter's', he says firmly, 'it isn't right to honour a pope on the tomb of the crucified St Peter' (*Utopia*, English, p. 112).

April 28, Good Shepherd Sunday and election day. Wakes at 2 a.m. and prays till 6.30 a.m. Meets Cardinal Gustavo Testa and Metropolitan Slipyi. There seems to be a faint hope of rescuing Cardinal József Mindszenty from the US Embassy in Budapest, where he has been immured since 1956.

April 30, Tuesday. The election results show that, compared with five years ago, the Communists have gained over a million votes. They now have a respectable 7,700,000 votes which makes it difficult to disregard them completely. The wildest theories circulate to explain these figures. The right-wing says that Aldo Moro's Christian Democrats are being punished by the electorate for their 'opening to the left'. But according to some papers, the real culprit is Pope John and his encyclical. An evening paper in Milan changed its title to *Falcem in Terris* ('The Sickle on Earth'). In Germany *Die Welt* published an open letter from a German Catholic who apostrophises the pope with the charge: 'You have misused the Chair of Peter'. There is much more in the same vein.

May 1, Wednesday. Loses his place during Mass. Memory going. Mgr Martin O'Connor, rector of the North American College, interprets for John McCone, top spy. There is no meeting of minds. McCone tries to warn him against Khrushchev who is not to be trusted. The success of the Communists in the Italian elections is grist to his mill (and the reason why he is here). Afterwards John, incorrigible, remarks: 'I'm not going to put off my stroke by the unseemly fuss that some people try to impress churchmen with. I bless all peoples, and withhold my confidence from none' (IME, p. 200).

May 2, Thursday. Mass at 8 a.m. An unwonted burst of fresh energy sees him through the new conciliar texts. Cavagna is always by his side. The liturgical commission is in session: it started on April 28 and will go on till May 10. John approves of its democratic methods and appeal to a wide range of genuine experts (Caprile, II, p. 406). But twelve other *schemata* are sufficiently far advanced to be sent out to the bishops in mid-May.

It is evident that Pope John wants very much to be able to conclude his Council. The notion that he became disenchanted with it is a baseless right-wing piece of wishfulfilment. Twenty years after the event, Malachi Martin will state it in classical form: 'Roncalli changed his mind before the end. Already in the spring of 1963, when an inoperable cancer was slowly killing him, he came to the conviction that it had all been a mistake' (Malachi Martin, p. 243). John did not change his mind about the Council. It took him down unexpected paths, but that is another question.

May 5, Sunday. Mass at 8.30 a.m. Spends the afternoon in the tower and welcomes the Venetian architect, Lorenzo Barbato, and his wife, who bring along their ten-month-old son, Luca, Luke. John jokes: 'Luke, the beloved physician (Colossians 4.14). Do you want him to be a doctor? or a lawyer? or . . . an evangelist?' (IME, p. 201).

May 7, Tuesday. Hurt by what the Italian and international press is saying about the April 28 elections. Finds it hard to understand why Catholics cannot accept the pastoral instructions in Part V of *Pacem in Terris*. Still more pained by the way the encyclical and the Adzhubei visit are being yoked together to explain the increase in the Communist vote. When Capovilla asks whether it would have been better to have delayed publication of *Pacem in Terris* until after the election, John replies:

The doctrine expounded in the encyclical is in accord with the Lord's Gospel and in harmony with the papal *magisterium* of the last sixty years. The meeting with Adjoubei fitted in with the overall line of my ministry. I've said it clearly enough, several times already, that one could publish the text of our conversation in perfect tranquillity (IME, p. 202).

May 9, Thursday. Mass at 7 a.m. At 8 consultation with Professor Antonio Gasbarrini, a specialist from Bologna. Receives François Marty, archbishop of Rheims.

From 5 p.m. to 6.45 talks with Cardinal Stefan Wyszyński in the Torre San Giovanni. The Polish bishops have proposed that qualified lay people should take part in the Council as *socii Concilii* (companions of the Council). In the event, they were known as *auditores* (listeners) (Caprile, II, p. 413). Discusses the welcome given to *Pacem in Terris* in Eastern Europe. In playful mood, John thinks up some recondite Latin names for his tower, '*oppidulum, casula, tugurium, gurgustium* [roughly village, cottage, shack, hovel]' (IME, p. 203).

May 11, Saturday. John spends two hours on his knees in the afternoon. He says: An exceptional event is going to take place — we must pray'. The 'exceptional event' is his visit to President Segni at the Quirinale Palace fixed for 5.30 p.m. His illness dispenses him from the obligation of a return visit, but John insists on this final act of respect towards Italy.

John is in great pain in the car. He tells Capovilla that he is going 'as an act of deference towards my country, because I owe so much not only to Bergamo but to Italy'. Passing the tomb of the Unknown Soldier in the Piazza Venezia, he raises a hand in salute to the men he had helped to die well more than forty years ago. President Segni greets him, and tactfully steers him first to the Pauline Chapel. Then they go out onto the balcony, from which the dome of St Peter's can be seen.

John sits slumped in a chair, while President Segni greets him, with what observers take for a strange smile on his lips: in fact he is trying to dominate the pain. He makes a simple speech in reply, rejoicing at the way he has been welcomed 'in this historic place', a welcome that 'is but the echo of public opinion'. Segni is deeply moved and falls to his knees. John raises him to his feet and embraces him saying: 'For you and for Italy'. With this embrace, the reconciliation of the Holy See and Italy was finally sealed.

On the way back he feels drained of all strength. He has pushed himself to the limit. He is in great pain and keeps coming back to this contrast, obsessively: 'Out there the world exalts me, while here the Lord rivets me to this bed'.

May 14, Tuesday. Mass at 7 a.m. As he is putting on the amice, he winces and grows pale. Capovilla asks how he feels. 'Like St Laurence on the grid-iron', he says.

May 16, Thursday. His newly married niece, Maria, and her bridegroom, Luigi Gotti, are present at Mass.

In the evening has a two-hour long conversation with Mgr Agostino Casaroli, undersecretary at the Secretariat of State, just back from Hungary and Czechoslovakia. Much later Casaroli said of this journey:

> One thing struck me in my meetings in Prague and Budapest: it was quite evident that these Communist leaders were convinced that the Pope was sincere, trustworthy and loved them as well. These feelings of warmth and affection melted the miles of ice-floes that had kept us apart for so long. Their judgement on Pope John was always positive (Casaroli in *Famiglia Cristiana*, April 4, 1971).

May 17, Friday. At 7.30 a.m. John says his last Mass, and knows that it is his last Mass.

May 18, Saturday. A very disturbed night. Vomiting. Stays in bed and from now on Mgr Capovilla will say Mass for him and give him Communion in the room next door; it has the 'window of the Angelus'. Flicks through the Secretariat of State press review. The attacks on him as a naive dupe of the Communists continue, adding moral suffering to his already intense physical sufferings. I forgive and put it out of my mind, he says. However, he is greatly consoled by a message from President John F. Kennedy. Through Cardinal Richard J. Cushing, archbishop of Boston, Kennedy says: 'The Pope should know that the US administration deplores and regards as unfounded the insinuations made in the press and in certain political circles'.

May 19, Sunday. Slept well through the night. Reviews the proofs of his apostolic exhortation, *Novem per dies*, in which he invites the whole Church to a Novena of prayer for the Council in the days before Pentecost. He appears at his window for the Angelus, and blows paternal kisses to the crowd below (Capovilla, IME, p. 209).

May 20, Monday. Exhausted. In the diary is an audience for Wyszyński and four Polish bishops. Dell'Acqua says: 'You could perfectly well receive them in your bedroom – they would be honoured by this mark of confidence'. John replies: 'We're not that far gone yet. Anyway, if I died during the audience, what a wonderful way to go' (IME, p. 209). It is John's last audience. 'Good-bye until September', says Wyszyński. John is not fooled. 'In September you'll find me or . . . someone else. It only takes a month, you know: the funeral of one and the elevation of another . . . If it weren't for this blessed protocol, I'd come down with you to the bronze door' (*ibid.*, p. 210).

Minor haemorrhages in the afternoon, but he responds to treatment and in the evening makes plans for the future. Says: 'If the Lord grants me life, after the Council I want to visit all the parishes of Rome – and all the municipal offices as well' (IME, p. 210). 'After the Council' is his horizon, his mirage.

May 21, Tuesday. A restless night. Communion at 6 a.m., after which he says:

> I'm ready to go. I've said all my breviary and the whole rosary. I've prayed for the children, for the sick, for sinners. (IME, p. 210).

Yet Dr Pietro Valdoni doesn't think the end is near. He even believes there could be a partial recovery.

May 22, Wednesday. Audiences cancelled.

May 23, Ascension Thursday. A much better night. Gets up to receive his nephew Flavio Roncalli. The red of his cape heightens the pallor of his face. At noon he intones the *Regina Coeli* from his window in a voice that is still musical and strong. The applause of the crowd almost prevents him giving his blessing.

At 6.30 p.m. he receives Cardinal Gustavo Testa, who had been 'entrusted' to him in 1905 at the age of nineteen. Seeing John's condition, Testa begins to blubber uncontrollably, like a child. John says:

> Dear Don Gustavo, we have to take things as they are. I've had a long life and served the Church and left some sort of mark on history. By God's grace I haven't behaved badly: so, not a day more. If the Lord wants me to remain a little longer, well and good, otherwise – we're off (IME, p. 212).

But the rack of pain is screwed up another notch. 'I wish I could say Mass', he says to the Augustinian friar, Frederico Belotti from near Sotto il Monte, who is acting as night-nurse. 'But this bed is your altar', says Brother Frederico (who remembers the incident very well:

letter of Fr Thomas A. Hunt OSA, June 19, 1983). John liked this. 'You are right: this bed is an altar, an altar needs a victim, and I'm ready. I wouldn't mind going tonight on the feast of the Ascension' (IME, p. 212).

May 24, Friday. Feels his strength ebbing away. Says: 'It is not that the Gospel has changed: it is that we have begun to understand it better.'

May 26, Sunday. Still more haemorrhages. But he gets up. The doctors forbid him to appear at the window, and the *Regina Coeli* of the Ascension is broadcast instead. The medical bulletin goes on about 'gastric troubles'. But few believe it.

May 30, Thursday. A good night at last, the 'peaceful night and quiet ending' that he had so often invoked at Compline. Night and death. Dawn and light.

At 11.30 a.m. he is wracked by a violent abdominal pain. Dr Pietro Mazzoni thinks that there could be a perforation of the tumour, in which case an operation will be impossible. John's days are counted. He is given sedatives. Ironically enough, none of this gets into the 1 p.m. medical bulletin which asserts that the Pope is responding to treatment. Antonio Gasbarrini, the specialist from Bologna, is so confident that his task is over that he goes home. Throughout the night the newspapers follow the optimistic lead of the medical bulletin.

May 31, Friday. The doctors confer. There is nothing more they can do. As has been agreed in advance, Capovilla has the task of breaking the news. 'Holy Father', he begins solemnly, fighting back the tears, 'I'm keeping my promise: I have to do for you what you did for Mgr Radini at the end of his life. The time has come. The Lord calls you'. John, not in the least put out, reflects for a moment and says: 'It would be good to have the doctors' verdict'.

'Their verdict, holy Father, is that it's the end. The tumour has done its work'.

'So, as with Mgr Radini . . . there will be an operation?'

'It's too late. The cancer has at last overcome your long resistance'. Capovilla falls to his knees, weeping, and buries his face in the bed-covers while John calmly gives instructions about his last hours. He says simply: 'Help me to die as a bishop or a pope should' (IME, p. 218).

At 11 a.m. in the presence of Cicognani, Dell'Acqua and Samorè (representing the Secretariat of State), the pontifical household, the doctors, the nurses, and the three Bergamo sisters who had been his housekeepers, he receives the Viaticum, food for the final journey, from Mgr Alfredo Cavagna. John is sitting up, in a white shirt and a white stole. The papal sacristan, Bishop Peter Canisius Van Lierde OSA, is about to anoint his five senses when John speaks:

> The secret of my ministry is in that crucifix you see opposite my bed. It's there so that I can see it in my first waking moment and before going to sleep. It's there, also, so that I can talk to it during the long evening hours. Look at it, see it as I see it. Those open arms have been the programme of my pontificate: they say that Christ died for all, for all. No one is excluded from his love, from his forgiveness.
>
> What did Christ leave to his Church? He left us 'that all may be one' (John 10.16) . . .
>
> For my part, I'm not aware of having offended anyone, but if I have, I beg their forgiveness; and if you know anyone who has not been edified by my attitudes or actions, ask them to have compassion on me and to forgive me. In this last hour I feel

calm and sure that my Lord, in his mercy, will not reject me. Unworthy though I am, I wanted to serve him, and I've done my best to pay homage to truth, justice, charity, and the meek and humble heart of the Gospel.

My time on earth is drawing to a close. But Christ lives on and the Church continues his work. Souls, souls. That they may be one! That they may be one! (Synthesised from many witnesses, including IME, pp. 218–19; Pepper, pp. 228–9).

Van Lierde then anoints his eyes, ears, nose, mouth, hands and feet. Overcome by emotion, he forgets the right order. John helps him out.

After that John has a personal word for all the by-standers. There are about twenty of them. Some are weeping. He shares a memory with each one, as though reviewing his whole life for the last time. From 4.30 p.m. Roman cardinals and members of the Curia begin to troop through his room, and the farewell audiences continue in the same style. He briefly alludes to the forthcoming conclave: 'I'm sure the sacred college will provide for the succession without any difficulty, and I'm sure the Bishops will bring the Council to a happy conclusion' (IME, p. 220). But he also made a more precise prediction: 'In my opinion my successor will be Montini. The votes of the sacred college will converge on him' (*ibid.*).

Montini has been summoned, but has not yet arrived from Milan. At 6 p.m. the second series of audiences is concluded. He says to Capovilla his secretary for the last ten years: 'We've worked together and served the Church without stopping to pick up and throw back the stones that have sometimes blocked our path. You've put up with my defects, and I've put up with yours. We'll always be friends ... I'll protect you from heaven' (IME, p. 221). John knows that the secretary of a deceased Pope has no further role in the Vatican. He entrusts his family at Sotto il Monte to Capovilla. 'When this is all over', he advises, 'get some rest and go and see your mother'. Outside in St Peter's Square a huge crowd is quietly praying.

At 7 p.m. more spasms of pain. He is put under sedation and is asleep when Montini ushers in John's brothers, Zaverio, Alfredo, Giuseppe and his sister Assunta. They kneel at his bedside, watching and praying.

June 1, Saturday. At 3 a.m. John wakes up and imagines he is in France. He starts talking in French, as though to his Paris doctor. Then he pulls himself together and greets his family. He sits up, drinks a cup of coffee, is revived. 'I'm still here', he says cheerfully, 'when yesterday I thought I was gone.' Then, in a different tone, he comments on Jesus' question to Martha, 'Do you believe that I am the resurrection and the life?' (John 11.25–6). He dozes off again. At 3.45 he wakes up and there are more brief encounters with the bishop and the mayor of Bergamo and Andrea Spada, editor of *l'Eco di Bergamo;* and then with the parish priest and mayor of Sotto il Monte. The cycle of his life is complete. Though his own world is narrowing down, messages of good will are pouring in from the five continents. There is one from Khrushchev. There is one from Plovdiv in Bulgaria from someone who remembered him from the earthquake of 1928. But he has drifted off into unconsciousness again. From two American children: 'Dear Pope John, we love you'. From Anglicans: 'Our Australian hearts are more than ever with you'. From a Buddhist: 'May God love you'. From an atheist: 'In so far as an atheist can pray, I'm praying for you' (IME, p. 222).

June 2, Whitsunday. The Novena of prayer for the Council has become a Novena of prayer for 'the Pope of the Council', as he liked to define himself. Throughout the night 20,000 young people are praying in the cathedral of Milan. Cardinal Montini is among them. We need, says Montini, to 'gather up his inheritance and his final message of peace'. 'Perhaps never before in our time', says Montini, 'has a human word – the word of a master, a leader, a prophet, a pope – rung out so loudly and won such affection throughout the whole world' (IME, p. 225).

At 8 p.m. Pope John takes a turn for the worse, but medication brings him some relief. At 9 p.m., Cardinal Fernando Cento, grand penitentiary, starts the prayers for the dying, the liturgy of death. But John is tough or – as the official bulletin puts it – 'has exceptional physical strength'. It sees him through another day, another night, to another dawn, his last.

June 3, Whitmonday. John wakes up at 3 a.m. and says twice, with great emphasis, 'Lord, you know that I love you'. At 5 p.m. a vast crowd begins to fill St Peter's Square. Cardinal Luigi Traglia, pro-vicar of Rome, is saying the Mass *pro infirmo*, for the sick bishop of Rome. At John's bedside are the members of his family, Cicognani, Cavagna, Capovilla, the doctors, the Gusso brothers, Brother Frederico, the Bergamo nuns. They say the prayers for the dying while the Mass proceeds in the square. Towards 7.45 the Mass is over. In the Pope's bedroom, the words of dismissal, *Ite Missa Est*, can be clearly heard over the microphone. Pope John gives a last shudder. His breathing becomes faint and, after a barely audible death-rattle, stops. The doctors bow reverently and shrug. It is 7.49 p.m.

Those present knelt and recited the *In paradisum* from the office of the dead: 'The angels lead you into paradise'. Then they said the great hymns of Christian thanksgiving, the *Magnificat* and the *Te Deum*. John's brow was ritually tapped to make sure he was really dead. The 'window of the Angelus' was suddenly illumined, and the crowd knew the truth. Giacomo Manzù, hastily summoned, took a plaster cast of John's face and right hand, the blessing hand. Next day, contrary to custom John's body was carried through the grieving crowd in the square and then into St Peter's to await burial in the crypt.

He had lived eighty-one and a half years, been a priest for fifty-eight years, a bishop for thirty-eight years, and pope for less than five years – the shortest pontificate of the century so far. Yet in him the Church and the world were prodigiously blessed.

Bibliography and sources

AAS = *Acta Apostolicae Sedis* (the official collection of papal and curial documents).

Abbott, Walter J., SJ, ed., *The Documents of Vatican II*, Geoffrey Chapman, London, 1966.

Actes et documents = *Actes et documents du Saint-Siège*, edited by Pierre Blet SJ, Robert A. Graham SJ, Angelo Martini SJ and Burkhart Schneider SJ, Libreria Editrice Vaticana. Eleven volumes. The following are relevant for Roncalli:

    vol. 4: *Le Saint-Siège et la situation religieuse en Pologne et dans les pays Baltes 1939–1945*, part 11 (1967).

    vol. 6: *Le Saint-Siège et les victimes de la guerre, mars 1939–décembre 1940* (1972).

    vol. 7: *Le Saint-Siège et la guerre mondiale, novembre 1942–décembre 1943* (1973).

    vol. 8: *Le Saint-Siège et les victimes de la guerre, janvier 1941–décembre 1943* (1981).

    vol. 9: *Le Saint-Siège et les victimes de la guerre, janvier–décembre 1944* (1975).

    vol. 10: *Le Saint-Siège et les victimes de la guerre, janvier 1944–juillet 1945* (1980).

    vol. 11: *Le Saint-Siège et la guerre mondiale* (1981).

Acton, Lord, *Essays on Church and State*, edited by Douglas Woodruff, Hollis and Carter, London, 1952 (Acton learned history in the house of Ignaz Döllinger in Munich, and survived the experience to become Regius Professor in Cambridge).

ADAP = *Akten zur Deutschen Auswärtigen Politik 1918–1945*, Vandenhoeck and Ruprecht, Göttingen, series E, volume 7 (1979).

Aimé-Azam, Denise, *l'Extraordinaire Ambassadeur*, La Table Ronde, Paris, 1967 (splendidly anecdotal account by a Jewish convert of Roncalli's time in Paris).

Alberigo = *Giovanni XXIII, Profezia nella fedeltà*, by Giuseppe and Angelina Alberigo, Queriniana, Brescia, 1978 (after a long, 100-page introduction, an extensive anthology of Roncalli's writings from all periods of his long life: for Italian readers the best possible introduction to Pope John).

Alberigo, Giuseppe, 'Dal bastone alla misericordia, in *Cristianesimo nella Storia*, October 1981, pp. 487–521 ('From the rod to Mercy' shows how the exercise of authority changed between Gregory XVI and John XXIII).

Alexander, Stella, *Church and State in Yugoslavia since 1945*, Cambridge University Press, 1979 (a ground-breaking work that has no competitors).

Algisi, Leone, *Giovanni XXIII*, Marietti, Turin, 1959 (was checked for accuracy by Pope John himself: but he found it too flattering).

Andreotti, Giulio, *A Ogni Morte di Papa – I Papi che ho conosciuto*, Rizzoli, Milan, 1980 (a peculiarly Italian form: Andreotti, Foreign Minister in 1984, knew all the Popes from Pius XI and had some important conversations with Pope John).

ANSA = the Italian news agency.

ARCIC = The Anglican Roman Catholic International Commission, *The Final Report*, SPCK and CTS, London, 1982.

ASCV = *Acta Synodalia Concilii Vaticani II*, Vatican Polyglot Press, 4 vols, 1970–1 (the 'Hansard' of the first session: even if the 'real' Council was happening somewhere else, the indispensable record against which immediate journalistic accounts have to be checked).

Gli Atti della visita apostolica di S. Carlo Borromeo a Bergamo (1575), edited by Angelo Giuseppe Roncalli and Pietro Forno, Leo. S. Olschki, Florence, in two parts and five volumes, 1936, 1937, 1938, 1946 and 1957 (Roncalli's life-work, begun in 1906 when Achille Ratti – the future Pius XI – photocopied the material for him; completed just before he became pope).

Avvenire d'Italia. Italian Catholic daily. Its pale ghost survives in *Avvenire*.

Bacci, Antonio, *Con il Latino a servizio di quattro papi*, Studium, Rome, 1964 (memoirs of a Latinist, once defined as 'someone who doesn't know enough Greek to be a classical scholar': unfair to Bacci).

Baltimore Sun, The (one of the world's oldest newspapers: in the eighteenth century it announced that it would appear weekly – or more often 'if there were a glut of occurrences').

Baronio = *Il cardinale Cesare Baronio*, by Angelo Giuseppe Roncalli, Storia e letteratura, Rome, 1961 (Roncalli's 1907 lecture republished).

Batelli, Giuseppe, 'Francesco Pitocchi', '*La formazione spirituale del giovane Angelo G. Roncalli. Il rapporto col redentorista Francesco Pitocchi*' in *Fede Tradizione Profezia*, edited by Giuseppe Alberigo, Paideia, Brescia, 1984.

Bedeschi, Lorenzo, *Buonaiuti, il Concordato e la Chiesa*, Il Saggiatore, Milan, 1970 (much unpublished material which reveals Buonaiuti, hitherto the arch Italian 'Modernist', to have been a prophetic figure).

Bedeschi, Lorenzo, *Modernismo a Milano*, Pan, Milan, 1974 (more *inédits* throwing light on renewal movements in Milan under Cardinal Ferrari).

Bell, George K., *The Kingship of Christ, The Story of the World Council of Churches*, Penguin, Harmondsworth, 1954 (the Anglican Bishop of Chichester reflects on the international ecumenical movement that had brought him into contact, *inter alios*, with Roncalli's Bulgarian Orthodox Christians and Dietrich Bonhoeffer).

Bergerre, Max, *Six Papes, un journaliste*, Téqui, Paris, 1979 (the unpretentious memoirs of the *doyen* of the Vatican press corps).

Bertoli, Bruno, *La Questione Romana negli Scritti di Papa Giovanni*, Morcelliana, Brescia, 1970 (a short – 42 pp. – study of Roncalli and the Lateran Pacts).

Bertrand, Dominique, SJ, gave information about Fr Alfred de Soras SJ, who 'preached' the retreat made by Roncalli at Clamart, a suburb of Paris, December 8–13, 1947. Roncalli wrote of de Soras: 'Good doctrine, expounded in an interesting way, but quite modern in construction, language and imagery' (*Journal*, p. 288). Bertrand scotched the notion that this might have been a 'directed' retreat.

Bevilacqua, Giulio, 'Ii Concilio', in *Vita e Pensiero*, 1960, p. 513 and following (important article by the Brescia anti-Fascist Oratorian who was Montini's mentor: became a cardinal under Paul VI).

Binchy, D. A., *Church and State in Fascist Italy*, Oxford University Press, 1941 (the best book on its subject, written by an Irish diplomat turned academic: the 1970 edition has a new preface).

Bishops and Writers, edited by Adrian Hastings, Anthony Clarke, Wheathampton, 1977 (a *Festschrift* for and worthy of Mgr Garrett Sweeney, historian of Vatican I: includes outstanding essay by Professor Nicholas Lash on 'Modernism').

Blessing of Years, A, The Memoirs of Lawrence Cardinal Shehan, Notre Dame Press, Notre Dame and London, 1982 (relatively frank confessions of a tiny and bewildered US bishop who, however, later redeemed himself with good interventions on religious liberty).

Bologna Archives: this refers to the material gathered at the Istituto per le scienze religiose in the University of Bologna. Thanks are due to its director, Giuseppe Alberigo.

Bonisteel, Roy, *Man Alive: The Human Journey*, Collins, Toronto, 1983 (a CBC TV interviewer for over twenty years who persuaded Cardinal Paul-Emile Léger, former archbishop of Montréal, to talk about Pope John).

Bonnot, Bernard R., *Pope John XXIII, an Astute Pastoral Leader*, Alba House, New York, 1979 (grew out of a thesis: a careful and largely unappreciated study of the pontificate).

Borghese, Il, right-wing scurrilous magazine, edited in the relevant period by Mario Tedeschi (its regular feature, 'Through the Bronze door', picks up and embroiders Curial gossip).

Boudens, Robrecht, of Leuven University, Belgium, provided information on the relationship between Cardinal Mercier and the Vatican, most of it drawn from his book, *Karl Mercier en de vlaamse beweging*, 1970. In 1913 Mercier sprang to the defence of the Bollandists, the Jesuit Church historians, who were being threatened with the Index. Mercier pleaded: 'At least consult the Belgian Bishops first'. Though the scare turned out to be a false alarm, Merry del Val, Secretary of State, assured Mercier that 'the Pope did not feel obliged to consult anyone when dealing with false teachings against which half-measures achieve nothing'. Roncalli admired both the Bollandists and Mercier.

Bugnini, Annibale, *La Riforma Liturgica 1948–1975*, Edizioni Liturgiche, Rome, 1983 (this enormous volume traces the continuity in liturgical reform from Pius XII onwards; attacked as a 'termite' gnawing away at tradition, Bugnini had the misfortune to become Apostolic Delegate in Teheran where he was abused by student partisans of Ayatollah Khomenei; this hastened his death).

Burgess, Anthony, see *Earthly Powers*.

Butler, Cuthbert, OSB, *The Vatican Council*, two vols, Longmans, Green & Co, London, 1930 (classic English account of Vatican I – it was not so numbered when the book was written – that relies on the letters and diaries of Archbishop William Ullathorne, Yorkshireman, Benedictine and apostle of Australia).

Campbell-Johnston, Michael, SJ, 'The Social Teaching of the Church', in *Thought*, autumn, 1964 (shows the 'French' and *Semaines Sociales* background to *Mater et Magistra*).

Caprile, Giovanni, SJ, *Il Concilio Vaticano II*, Civiltà Cattolica, Rome:
  vol. I, part 1: *Annunzio e preparazione 1959–1960* (1966);
  vol. I, part 2: *Annunzio e preparazione 1961–1962* (1966);
  vol. II, *Prima Periodo* (1968) (no one interested in the Council can do without this veritable mine of information; even his omissions are interesting).

Caprile, Giovanni, 'Pio XII e un nuovo progetto di Concilio Ecumenico', in *Civiltà Cattolica*, August 6, 1966, pp. 209–27 (the first article on the-Council-that-never-was).

Caprile, Giovanni, reviews *L'Utopia di Giovanni XXIII*, by Giancarlo Zizola, *Civiltà Cattolica*, February 16, 1974.

Caprile, Giovanni, 'Ancora su Giovanni XXIII', in *Civiltà Cattolica*, April 5, 1980, pp. 50–4.

Carbone, Vincenzo, 'Genesi e criteri della pubblicazione degli Atti del Concilio Vaticano II', in *Lateranum*, XLIV, 1978, pp. 579–95.

Cardinale, Igino, *The Holy See and the International Order*, Colin Smythe, Gerrards Cross, 1976 (the standard work on Vatican diplomacy).

Cardinale, Igino. In a long meeting at the Brussels Nunciature on March 30, 1980, Archbishop Cardinale answered with frankness every question that I put to him about Pope John. May he rest in peace.

Cartier, Raymond, *La Seconde Guerre Mondiale*, vol. 5, juin 1944–février 1945, Presses Pocket, Paris, 1976.

Chiesa e Stato nell'Ottocento, Miscellanea in onore di Pietro Pirri, 2 vols, Antenore, Padua, 1962 (*Festschrift* for a Jesuit historian: much light on nineteenth-century Church problems).

Chronicle = *The Chronicle of the Worker-Priests*, preface by André Latreille, translated and edited by Stan Windass, The Merlin Press, London, 1966 (though Emile Poulat says that it is 'chock-full of errors' – *fourmille d'inexactitudes* – a useful compilation if checked against other sources).

Church = *The Church*, by Giovanni Battista Montini, Palm Publishers, Montréal, 1964 (lectures and pastoral letters on the Council while Pope John was still reigning).

Church in the Power of the Spirit, The, by Jürgen Moltmann, SCM Press, London, 1977 (the rediscoverer of 'the theology of hope' finds Pope John's treatment of 'signs of the times' too optimistic).

Ciano's Diary 1939-1943, edited with an introduction by Malcolm Muggeridge, foreword by Sumner Welles, Heinemann, London, 1947 (Mussolini's son-in-law and foreign minister, opposed Italian participation in the war, was executed by order of his father-in-law).

Civiltà Cattolica, Rome, the fortnightly review of the Rome Jesuits founded in 1849: it became the prototype of other Jesuit reviews – *Etudes, Stimmen der Zeit, Razón y Fe, The Month* etc.; but while they went their own way, *Civiltà* allowed only Jesuits to write in its pages and was censored by the Secretariat of State.

Collin, Richard, *The De Lorenzo Gambit: the Italian Coup Manqué of 1964*, Sage Research Papers in the Social Sciences, Beverly Hills/London, 1976 (though General De Lorenzo did not attempt his coup till 1964, he was preparing it from long before as head of the Secret Service – SIFAR).

Combat pour la liberté', Lettres inédites de Georges Bernanos, 2 vols, Plon, Paris, 1971.

Congar, Yves-Marie, OP, *Challenge to the Church*, Collins, London, 1977 (translation of a 1976 pamphlet, *La Crise dans l'Eglise et Mgr Lefebvre*, Cerf).

Congar, Yves-Marie, *Dialogue between Christians*, Geoffrey Chapman, London, 1966.

Congar, Yves-Marie, *Power and Poverty in the Church*, Geoffrey Chapman, London, 1964 (Jennifer Nicholson's translation of *Pour une Eglise servante et pauvre*, Cerf, 1964, Paris: most of the book grew out of lectures given in Rome during the Council).

Corriere della Sera, influential Milan paper that for good or ill has reflected Italian life faithfully for over a century.

Council and Reunion, by Hans Küng, Sheed and Ward, London, 1961 (English translation of *Konzil und Wiedervereinigung. Erneuerung als Ruf in die Einheit*. The Americans – Doubleday, 1965 – called it *The Council, Reform and Reunion*).

Cousins, Norman, 'The Improbable Triumvirate', *The Saturday Review*, October 30, 1971 (the trio was Kennedy, Khrushchev and Pope John).

Cristianesimo nella storia. The journal of the Istituto per le scienze religiose, Bologna. Edited by Giuseppe Alberigo.

Critic, The, Chicago.

Croix, La, Paris. During the Council edited by Antoine Wenger AA.

Cronologia = pp. 515–765 of *Giovanni XXIII, Quindici Letture*, by Loris Capovilla, Storia e

Letteratura, 1970 (indispensable starting point for any biographer: expanded and corrected in later works).

Crown of Thorns, A, An Autobiography 1951-1963, by John Carmel Heenan, Hodder & Stoughton, London, 1974 (a sequel to the earlier volume, *Not the Whole Truth:* in the *New Statesman*, the review was headlined: 'Too Clever by a Quarter').

Cugini, Davide, *Papa Giovanni nei suoi primi passi a Sotto il Monte*, Istituto Italiano d'Arti Grafiche, Bergamo, 1965 (an art-historian friend of Roncalli on his childhood and time in Venice).

Daly, Gabriel, OSA, *Transcendence and Immanence. A Study in Catholic Modernism and Integralism*, Clarendon Press, Oxford, 1980 (the most thorough and 'revisionist' Catholic study of 'Modernism').

De Gasperi, Alcide, *Lettere sul Concordato*, Morcelliana, Brescia, 1970, with an introduction by Maria Romana De Gasperi and a long essay by Giacomo Martina SJ on the background and the consequences of the Lateran Pacts (also contains family snaps of De Gasperi and a photograph of the desk he sat at in the catalogue room of the Vatican Library).

De Gaulle, Charles, *Mémoires de Guerre*, vol. 2, Plon, Paris, 1954.

De la Bedoyère, Michael, *The Life of Baron von Hügel*, Dent, London, 1951 (courageously broke new ground: dedicated to the Duke Gallarati Scotti, then Ambassador at the court of St James, London, and a friend of Roncalli).

De Luca, Giuseppe, *Altar, Gift and Gospel*, St Paul Publications, London, 1967 (with an important introduction by Mgr Igino Cardinale, De Luca's nephew, who compares him to Mgr Ronald Knox).

De Luca, Giuseppe, *Il Cardinale Bonaventura Cerretti*, Istituto Grafico Tiberino, Rome, 1939.

De Riedmatten, Henri, OP, 'Histoire de la Constitution Pastorale', in *L'Eglise dans le Monde de ce Temps, Schema XIII, Commentaires*, Maime, Paris, 1967 (along with Roberto Tucci's booklet, essential reading on the origins of *Gaudium et Spes).*

Decimo anniversario = *X anniversario della morte di Papa Giovanni*, by Loris Capovilla, Storia e Letteratura, 1973 (unpublished letters on the charge of 'Modernism').

Disquisitio, Vatican Polyglot Press, 1950 (the historical study for the beatification of Pius X: while defending Pius, it throws a flood of light on his methods: Pope John read it through in 1959 and corrected a few misprints: Giancarlo Zizola now possesses this copy, gift of Loris Capovilla).

DMC = *Discorsi, messaggi, colloqui del Santo Padre Giovanni XXIII, 1958–1963*, five volumes plus index, Vatican Polyglot Press, 1960-7 (the official collection of all Pope John's public utterances: not entirely reliable, since he was frequently over-edited).

Documenti Segreti della Diplomazia Vaticana, Società Cooperativa Operaia, Lugano, 1948 (a fraud: but thanks to Roland Hill for lending it, and to Emil Poulat who pointed out that forgeries could be more interesting and revealing about 'what was perceived' than authentic texts).

Dodicesimo anniversario = *XII anniversario della morte di Papa Giovanni* (essential reading for Roncalli's relationship with Cardinal Ferrari and Ernesto Buonaiuti).

Dreyfus, Paul, *Jean XXIII*, Fayard, Paris, 1979 (fast-moving French biography with seventy pages of learned appendices and yet, strangely, no references in the text).

D–S = *Enchiridion Symbolorum, Definitionum et Declarationum de rebus fidei et morum*, by H. Denzinger and A. Schönmetzer, Freiburg im Breisgau, 1965.

Earthly Powers, by Anthony Burgess, Penguin, Harmondsworth, 1981 (like myself an old boy of the Xaverian College, Victoria Park, Manchester, Burgess was kind enough to imagine that I was in Rome during the 1958 conclave and wrote a book about it, *Rebirth of a Church*, p. 548).

Elliott, Lawrence, *I will be called John*, Reader's Digest Press, New York, 1973, and Collins, London, 1974 ('It began on a day when the summer had slipped almost imperceptibly into golden autumn. It began in the olive hills southeast of Rome . . . There, Pius XII died.., exhausted by the burdens of holy office in a world of skepticism and rage' *etc.).*

Epoca, Rome, Italian weekly.

Erikson, Erik, *Identity, Youth and Crisis*, Faber and Faber, London, W. W. Norton, New York, 1968 (breviary of the 1960s).

Exercises = The Spiritual Exercises of St Ignatius, edited by Louis J. Puhl SJ, Loyola University Press, Chicago, 1951.

Falconi, Carlo, see *Popes of the Twentieth Century.*

Famiglia Cristiana. Italy's most widely diffused Catholic magazine.

Familiari = Giovanni XXIII, Lettere ai familiari, two vols, edited by Loris Capovilla, Storia e Letteratura, Rome, 1968 (727 letters from Roncalli to his family at Sotto il Monte: he kept carbon copies).

Fappani-Molinari = *Gianbattista Montini Giovane*, by Antonio Fappani and Franco Molinari, Marietti, Turin, 1979 (essential documentation on the 'young' Montini; the authors, serious historians, still regard him as young at 47; full of surprises).

Felici, Pericle, *Il Lungo Cammino del Concilio*, Ancora, Milan, 1967 (the former Secretary General of the Council tells his story).

Fonzi, Fausto, *I Cattolici e la Società Italiana dopo l'Unità*, Studium, Rome, 1977 (surveys the Vatican and Italian politics from Roncalli's childhood and youth to 1929).

Fox, Matthew, OP, *Religion USA*, Listening Press, Dubuque, Iowa, 1971 (originally a doctoral thesis on the way 'religion' is presented in *Time:* a joyous romp through a delicious field).

Frost, Robert, *Complete Poems*, Jonathan Cape, London, 1967.

Gill, Joseph, SJ, historian of the Council of Florence, was Rector of the Oriental Institute in Rome when the Council was announced. He supplied precisions about the Roman ecumenical scene in 1959–60.

Giornale dell'Anima, see *Journal.*

Giudici, Marco, 'Il Coraggio della Speranza', in *Vita e Pensiero*, February 1980 (a report on the 'prophetic' figure, Don Primo Mazzolari).

Gogol, Nicolas, *Lettres spirituelles et familières*, Grasset, Paris, 1957.

Gorresio, Vittorio, *La Nuova Missione*, Rizzoli, Milan, 1968 (useful for Cardinal Giacomo Lercaro's early misjudgement of Pope John).

Graham, Robert A., SJ, 'Quale pace cercava Pio XII?, in *Civiltà Cattolica*, May 1, 1982, pp. 218–33 (particularly interesting because the author had written in *America*, June 24, 1944, on the same theme: 'What peace does the Pope want?' How journalism becomes history).

Gran Sacerdote = Papa Giovanni XXIII, Gran Sacerdote, come lo ricordo, by Loris Capovilla, Storia e Letteratura, Rome, 1977 (includes unpublished diaries from the pontificate and a selection of letters: useful for Roncalli's time at Propaganda).

Greene, Graham, 'Pius XII', in *The Month*, December 1951, pp. 327–39 (the editor, Fr Philip Caraman, was reprimanded by the Vatican for this allegedly 'disrespectful' but actually blameless article. Writes Greene: 'It is a long time since a Pope has awoken even in those of other faiths such a sense of closeness' – p. 338).

Grootaers, Jan, 'L'Attitude de l'Archevêque Montini au cours de la première période du Concile', a paper given at the Paul VI Conference, Milan, September 23–25, 1983. MS.

Guarducci, Margherita, *Saint Pierre Retrouvé*, Editions Saint-Paul, Paris, 1974 (complains that Pope John was not interested in the excavations).

Guarnieri, R., *Don Giuseppe De Luca tra cronaca e storia*, Bologna, 1974 (a biography of this enigmatic priest, the Orvietan Giuseppe De Luca: his nephew, Mgr Igino Cardinale, called him 'the Mgr Ronald Knox of Italian Catholicism' – but that overlooks his 'Fascist' phase and his secret dealings with Communists later).

Guitton, Jean, *Paul VI secret*, Desclée de Brouwer, Paris, 1979 (memories of the only Catholic layman present at the first session of the Council: says key word for John was *rajeunir* while Paul's key word was *approfondir).*

Hales, E. E. Y., *Pope John and his Revolution*, Eyre and Spottiswoode, London, 1965 (far and away the best study in English of the pontificate of Pope John, and especially of his 'social teaching').

Hamilton, Elizabeth, *Cardinal Suenens, a Portrait*, Hodder and Stoughton, London, 1975 (hagiography).

Helmreich, Ernst Christian, *The German Churches under Hitler*, Wayne State University Press, Detroit, 1979 (shows that Hitler's policy towards the Catholic Church *varied).*

Heppel, Dr Muriel, checked up on my Bulgarian history.

Hill, Michael, *The Religious Order*, Heinemann, London 1973 (discusses how the 'institutional personality' is formed in prisons and seminaries).

History of Vatican II, edited by Giuseppe Alberigo, English version edited by Joseph A. Komonchak, Orbis Books, Leuven, Belgium (volume 1, 1996; volume 3, 2000; volumes 2, 4 and 5, forthcoming).

Hoffmann, Paul, *O Vatican! A Slightly Wicked View of the Holy See*, Congden and Weed Inc., New York, 1984 (somewhat better than its title would suggest).

Holmes, J. Derek, *The Papacy in the Modern World*, Burns and Oates, London, 1981 (a solid and dependable survey).

Hornby, Col. Robert, formerly press officer to the Archbishop of Canterbury, supplied material on Dr Geoffrey Fisher's visit to Pope John on December 2, 1960.

Hurn, David Abner, *Archbishop Roberts SJ, His Life and Writings*, Darton, Longman and Todd, London, 1966 (the bizarre *nom de plume* conceals Margaret Rowland of *The Universe).*

IME see *Ite Missa Est.*

Infallibile? by Hans Küng, Collins, London 1971 (a provocative work that is less 'controversial' for those who know any Church history: makes Pope John a hero).

Irénikon, an ecumenical review founded by Dom Lambert Beauduin OSB in 1926: published from Amay-sur-Meuse and, from 1939, the Abbey of Chevetogne in Belgium.

l'Italia, the Milan newspaper to which Cardinal Montini contributed during the first session of the Council.

Ite Missa Est, by Loris Capovilla, Messaggero, Padua and Grafica e Arte, Bergamo, 1983 (invaluable documentation on Roncalli's childhood, his time in Venice, and certain key episodes in the pontificate; with a reworked account of the last two months; sumptuously illustrated).

Jaeger, Lorenz, *The Ecumenical Council, the Church and Christendom*, Geoffrey Chapman, London, 1961 (discussed in Chapter 18).

Jemolo, Arturo Carlo, *Chiesa e Stato in Italia negli ultimi cento anni*, Marietti, Turin, 1963 (classic work by the *doyen* of Italian Church historians).

Johnson, Paul, *Pope John XXIII*, Hutchinson, London, 1975 (the author's last book before swinging, vigorously, to the right).

Journal =Journal of a Soul, Pope John XXIII, introduced by Loris Capovilla, translated by Dorothy White, Geoffrey Chapman, London, revised edition 1980 (this edition has been referred to throughout: to find passages in other editions, consult the dates; the White translation has been revised where necessary, and her omissions have been remedied with reference to the *Giornale dell'Anima*, Storia e Letteratura, Rome, fifth edition, 1967).

Kaiser, Robert B., *Pope, Council and World, the Story of Vatican II*, Macmillan, New York, 1963; and Burns and Oates, London, 1963 (one of the first books to 'open the windows of the Vatican' by the *Time* magazine correspondent).

Keneally, Thomas, *Schindler's Ark*, Hodder and Stoughton, London, 1982.

Kerr, Fergus, OP, provided information on how *Humani Generis* affected French Dominicans.

KNA = Katholische Nachrichten Agentur, the German Catholic News Agency, which used to have a special interest in the Vatican's *Ostpolitik*.

Küng, Hans, see *Council and Reunion* and *Infallible?*

Lai, Benny, *Les Secrets du Vatican*, Hachette, Paris, 1983 (supersedes the author's previous books such as *Vaticano sotto voce*, Longanesi, Milan, 1961, and retells the old stories. The 'prelate' who smashed his episcopal ring as he thumped the table on hearing that some wanted Montini to be elected in 1958 is revealed as Cardinal Giovanni Siri, p. 60).

Larkin, Maurice, *Church and State after the Dreyfus Affair*, Macmillan, London, 1974.

Latreille, André, *De Gaulle, la libération et l'Eglise Catholique*, Cerf, Paris, 1978 (gives balance to the much mythologised story of Roncalli and the French bishops).

Lawrence, Sir John, Roman Diary, February–March 1959 (unpublished: offers a unique insight into the atmosphere in Rome in the weeks after the announcement of the Council).

Lettere = Giovanni XXIII, Lettere 1958–1963, edited by Loris Capovilla, Storia e Letteratura, Rome, 1978 (217 letters, private and public, written by Pope John during his pontificate followed by 131 'notes' and memoranda: fully annotated by Mgr Capovilla, this volume is essential to the understanding of the pontificate).

Letture = Giovanni XXIII, Quindici Letture, by Loris Capovilla, Storia e Letteratura, Rome, 1970 (fifteen lectures on Pope John, the first given on January 17, 1959 and the last on June 3, 1967; with appendices on the *Journal of a Soul*, the last days of Pope John and the 'Chronology' of his life; a monumental work that becomes part of the story it has to tell; much unpublished material).

Levi, Primo, *If this is a Man*, Penguin Modern Classics, Harmondsworth, 1979 (*Se questo è un uomo* appeared in 1958; Levi survived Auschwitz and came home via Russia and Poland).

Levillain, Philippe, *La mécanique politique de Vatican II, La Majorité et l'unanimité dans un concile*, Beauchesne, coll. *Théologie Historique*, Paris, 1975 (applies the categories of political science to the Council, with interesting results; based on the notes of Henri de Lubac, SJ).

Linee = Giovanni XXIII, Linee per una ricerca storica, by Giacomo Lercaro; with an appendix by Gabriele De Rosa on *Angelo Roncalli e Radini Tedeschi*, Storia e Letteratura, Rome, 1965 (the first plea for a serious historical study of Pope John).

Loisy, Alfred, *Mémoires pour servir à l'histoire religieuse de notre temps*, 2 vols, Paris, 1931.

Lomax, Benedict, 'Pope John's Ostpolitik', in *The Month*, September, 1974, pp. 691–6 (I can now reveal that Benedict Lomax was a *nom de guerre* for Peter Hebblethwaite).

McGregor, Geddes, *The Vatican Revolution*, Macmillan, London, 1958 (an assault on Vatican I from the point of view of a Scottish theologian: there was a 'revolution' because the definition of infallibility represented a departure from tradition; anticipates Bernard Hasler and Hans Küng).

Machiavelli, Niccolò, *The Prince*, translated by George Bull, Penguin Classics, Harmondsworth, 1961 ('Old Nick', as he was sometimes known in England in Shakespeare's time, was never the cynical monster he was presented as; alas no ruler ever availed himself of his political wisdom).

Mack Smith, Denis, *Mussolini*, Weidenfeld and Nicolson, London, 1981 (comfortably the best biography of Mussolini who 'having been once praised to excess, was now being blamed for doing more harm to Italy than anyone had ever done').

Magister, Sandro, *La Politica Vaticana e l'Italia 1943-1978*, Editori Riuniti, Rome, 1979 (excellent study of a period that is more complex than it looks).

Manzoni, Alessandro, *I Promessi Sposi*, Mursia, Milan, 1966 (Roncalli's favourite novel, quoted by him more often than any other literary work).

Manzoni, Alessandro, Tutte le Poesie di, edited by Giovanni Titta Rosa, Ceschina, Milan, 1966 (Manzoni's *inni sacri* – sacred hymns – contain a poem on Pentecost which is dated 1817–1822).

Marrou, Henri-Irenée, *Crise de notre temps et réflexion chrétienne (de 1930 à 1975)*, Beauchesne, Paris, 1978 (collected pieces of a historian whose concern with St Augustine and the collapse of the Roman Empire did not blind him to the iniquities of French colonialism; also, under the pseudonym Henri Davenson, music critic for *Esprit* while Roncalli was in Paris).

Martin, Bryan, *John Henry Newman*, Chatto and Windus, London, 1982.

Martin, David, *The Religious and the Secular*, Routledge and Kegan Paul, London, 1969 (this most literate of sociologists writes two rather unexpected chapters on Bulgaria).

Martin, Malachi, *The Decline and Fall of the Roman Church*, G. P. Putnam's Sons, New York, 1981 (in which the author eats his earlier informed judgements and now alleges that Pope John 'created the circumstances in which the authority and unity of his Church were destroyed'; tells us more about Malachi Martin than Pope John).

Medvedev, Roy, *Khrushchev*, translated by Brian Pearce, Basil Blackwell, Oxford, 1983 (accepts that there was some 'change' in Khrushchev's Soviet Union, but also shows that in the closing down of churches and contemptuous treatment of Christians, the later Khrushchev years were *more* authoritarian than the post-war Stalin period).

Memorie = Giovanni XXIII, *Memorie e Appunti 1919*, in *Humanitas*, Number 6, June, 1973, pp. 428–87, with an introduction by Loris Capovilla (substantial extracts from Roncalli's diary and notebooks for the year 1919).

Merry del Val, Rafael, *Memoirs of Pius X*, Newman Press, Westminster, Maryland, 1951 (very brief and self-justifying: at the age of thirty-seven, Merry del Val became Pius X's Secretary of State; after the death of Pius in 1914, his faithful henchman drifted into an ineffectual limbo).

Mission = *Mission to France 1944–1953*, by Angelo Giuseppe Roncalli, Geoffrey Chapman, London, 1966 (English translation of *Souvenirs d'un Nonce 1944–1953*, Storia e Letteratura, Rome, 1963: a collection of letters, homilies and addresses during Roncalli's French period).

Moignt, Joseph, SJ, invited me to give a paper at his conference on the *Magisterium*, Chantilly, June, 1982: it appeared as 'Le discours de Jean XXIII à l'ouverture de Vatican II' in *Recherches de Sciences Religieuses*, avril–juin, 1983, pp. 203–12.

Momigliano, Arnaldo, *Terzo contributo alla storia degli studi classici*, Storia e Letteratura, Rome, 1966

(Polyglot Jewish scholar from Turin who found a haven in Oxford: keenly interested in Italian historiography and therefore in Roncalli on Baronius and Charles Borromeo).

Monaco, Franco, 'Montini a Milano', in *Vita e Pensiero*, Milan, November, 1983, p. 61 and following (a report on the second meeting of the Paul VI Institute held in Milan 23–25 September, 1983: argues that Milan 'explains' Montini).

Mondrone, Domenico, SJ, 'L'Episcopato del Card. Andrea C. Ferrari in uno studio di Carlo Snider', in *Civiltà Cattolica*, July 18, 1981, pp. 154–61 (admits that a study of the relationship between Ferrari and Pius X will show 'how far a well-orchestrated campaign of calumny can win over the mind and discernment of a saint': which seems to let Pius X off the hook).

Month, The, review of the English – now British – Jesuits.

Morris, James, *Venice*, Faber and Faber, London, 1960 (the author later claimed a sex-change and became Jan Morris: the prose remained as vivid as ever).

My Bishop = *My Bishop, a Portrait of Mgr Giacomo Maria Radini Tedeschi*, by Angelo Giuseppe Roncalli, English translation by Dorothy White, Geoffrey Chapman, London, 1969; a much abbreviated version of *In Memoria di Monsignore Giacomo Radini Tedeschi, Vescovo di Bergamo*, Sant Alessandro, Bergamo, 1916; second edition, Storia e Letteratura, Rome, 1963 (only comes to life when one has seen what questions were being asked by Italian Catholics before the First World War).

Nash, Margaret, *The Ecumenical Movement in the 1960s*, Ravan Press, Johannesburg, South Africa, 1975 (a useful work by an Anglican, no doubt neglected because of its place of publication; in his preface Dr W. A. Visser 't Hooft calls it 'a significant contribution'; has forgivable errors).

Natale 1970, Capodanno 1971, edited by Loris Capovilla (in effect Mgr Capovilla's Christmas and New Year greetings: contains correspondence relating to Roncalli's move to Rome in 1921, and also a photograph of his study when Pope).

Natale 1975, Capodanno 1976, edited by Loris Capovilla (devoted to Pope John's thoughts on ecumenism, with a complete list of his ecumenical encounters).

National Catholic Reporter, The, Kansas City, Missouri (I declare an interest: I first wrote in NCR in 1967 and have been its 'Vatican Affairs Writer' since September 1979; its successive editors, Arthur Jones and Thomas C. Fox, encouraged this book and in effect subsidised it; may they be blessed).

Negro, Silvio, the leading Vaticanologist of his day; worked for *Corriere della Sera*, Milan.

Newman, John Henry, *Sermons, chiefly on the theory of religious belief*, Oxford, 1843.

Nicolini, Giulio, *Il Cardinale Domenico Tardini*, Messaggero, Padua, 1980 (insider's book by young – fifty-four – curialist who knows more than he lets on and reveals more than he intends).

Novak, Michael, *The Open Church*, Darton, Longman and Todd, London, 1964 (based on articles in *The New Republic* etc, tried to do for the second session what Robert B. Kaiser had done for the first; denounced 'non-historical orthodoxy'; changed his tune twenty years later).

Nowell, Robert, *A Passion for Truth, Hans Küng: A Biography*, Collins, London, 1981 (believes that Küng is more sinned against than sinning).

Observer, The. Though its news editor once assured me that '*The Observer* is a humanist newspaper', it employed Patrick O'Donovan, the great, the good, to report on the Council.

Orga, Irfan and Margarete, *Atatürk*, Michael Joseph, London, 1962.

Orient Express, by John Dos Passos, Jonathan Cape, London, 1928 (vivid description of a journey on the famous train at the time when Roncalli began to use it regularly).

l'Osservatore Romano, Vatican daily. Indispensable. 'Compared with it', *The Economist* once wrote, '*Pravda* positively bristles with gossip'.

Owen, Wilfrid, 'Anthem for Doomed Youth', in *Poems since 1900*, edited by Colin Falck, Macdonald and Jane's, London, 1975, p. 69.

Panorama, 'Rapporti tra Moro e Giovanni XXIII', by Giancarlo Zizola, in two parts, May 10 and May 17, 1982 (essential reading on Pope John and his relationship with Aldo Moro, then Secretary of the Christian Democrats; with unpublished documents provided by Capovilla).

Pasqua, 1976 = Pasqua di Risurrezione, edited by Loris Capovilla (Roncalli on the strike at Ranica in 1909 and his sermon, in the presence of the Fascists, in 1924 on the tenth anniversary of the death of Radini Tedeschi).

Pasqua, 1978 = Pasqua di risurrezione con Papa Giovanni XXIII, edited by Loris Capovilla (detailed chronicle and diary extracts from November 1952 to April 1953, from Paris to Venice).

Pastore = Giovanni XXIII, il Pastore, edited by Giambattista Busetti, Messaggero, Padua, 1980 (a revelation: Roncalli's correspondence from 1911 to 1963 with the diocesan religious congregation to which he belonged, the Priests of the Sacred Heart).

Pawley, Bernard and Margaret, *Rome and Canterbury through Four Centuries*, Mowbray, London, 1974 (the first 'personal representative of the Archbishop of Canterbury' at the Vatican joins with his Russian Orthodox wife to record his candid impressions).

Péguy, Charles, *Oeuvres Poétiques complètes*, Pléiade, Paris, 1948 (to understand the importance of Péguy in John's circle, here is a passage from Don Giuseppe De Luca in a letter to Mgr Loris Capovilla, January 29, 1962: 'Read Péguy. He is the greatest poet of socialism and then of Catholicism – but not the Catholicism of the '*curés*'. You follow? The wife he loved was an unbeliever and wouldn't agree to a religious marriage, so he couldn't frequent the sacraments. But he used to walk around Paris saying his rosary, and made three pilgrimages on foot to Chartres. What a poet, monsignore, what a poet! . . . I send you a copy of his *Un nouveau théologien, M. Fernand Laudet*: it is the most ferocious and passionate Christian polemic of the last few centuries – perhaps since Dante'. In *Pur che l'alba nasca*, edited by Loris Capovilla, Grafica e Arte, Bergamo, 1983, pp. 4–5).

Pensiamo al Concilio, a Pastoral letter for Lent, 1962, by Cardinal Gianbattista Montini. Published by the Archdiocesan Press, Milan, 1962 (a bad English trans. is found in *The Church*, Palm Publishers, Montréal, 1964, pp. 149–92).

Pepper, Curtis Bill, *An Artist and the Pope, based upon the personal recollections of Giacomo Manzù*, Peter Davies, London, 1969 (the left-wing sculptor from Bergamo was introduced to Pope John by Don Giuseppe De Luca; Manzù's memorial is seen in the new doors of St Peter's; *Newsweek's* contribution to the Pope John saga; it sure is vivid).

Per Crucem ad Lucem, Lettres Pastorales etc, by Cardinal Mercier, Bloud et Gay, Paris, no date but on internal evidence probably 1916 (though it was the Christmas 1914 pastoral, 'Patriotisme et endurance' that made Mercier the spokesman for 'gallant little Belgium', his Lent 1915 pastoral, called simply 'Pius X and Benedict XV' is a masterpiece of litotes in which, properly read, Pius X is largely demolished).

Politics = The Politics of the Vatican, by Peter Nichols, Frederick A. Praeger, New York, 1968 (the Rome correspondent of *The Times*, of London, presents the Vatican with his usual charm and perspicacity).

Pollard, John, *The Vatican and Italian Fascism 1929–1932: a study in conflict*, Cambridge University Press, 1985 (shows that the signing of the Lateran Pacts, far from making peace between Church and State, intensified the conflict).

Popes of the Twentieth Century, by Carlo Falconi, Weidenfeld and Nicolson, London, 1967 (Falconi, a priest who resigned from his ministry, retained the friendship of some of his peers; a witty, engaging, and often penetrating view of the Vatican in this century; officially frowned upon).

Poulat, Emile, *Catholicisme, Démocratie et Socialisme*, Casterman, Paris, 1977 (many unpublished documents and psychological analysis of Umberto Benigni, Roncalli's professor of Church History, who ran the anti-modernist spy ring).

Poulat, Emile, *Intégrisme et Catholicisme intégrale*, Casterman, Paris, 1969 (discusses, among other things, whether the historical study prepared for the beatification of Pius X was fairly conducted; concludes that it was not).

Poulat, Emile, *Naissance des Prêtres Ouvriers*, Casterman, Tournai, Belgium, 1965 (magisterial).

Poulat, Emile, appears again as a friend who has constantly encouraged this book which has aimed to match his high standards of evidence and argument.

Pravda, Soviet Party newspaper. Pope John made the page one headline on October 26, 1962. See p. 231 above.

Prima Romana Synodus, Vatican Polyglot Press, Rome, 1960 (a deservedly rare work containing the 755 decrees of what Pope John called, correctly, the First Roman Synod).

I Promessi Sposi, The Betrothed, see Manzoni, Alessandro.

Quale Papa? by Giancarlo Zizola, Borla, Rome, 1977 (apart from asking 'what kind of Pope is needed in what kind of Church in what kind of world' just before the death of Pope Paul VI, provides the best account of what happened in recent conclaves).

Quindicesimo anniversario = *XV anniversario della morte di Papa Giovanni*, edited by Loris Capovilla, Storia e Letteratura, 1978 (includes 33 unpublished letters 1918–57).

Ragionieri, Ernesto, *Storia d'Italia*, vol 4, *Dall'Unità a oggi*, tomo terzo, Giulio Einaudi, Turin, 1976 (the standard history of Italy for Italians; the accompanying volume of photographs is a revelation).

Ramsey, Archbishop Michael, made some interesting remarks about Cardinal Bea in a letter dated February 25, 1984.

Repubblica, La, Rome daily (except Monday) post-war, left-leaning.

Riccardi, Andrea, *Roma città sacra? Dalla Conciliazione all'operazione Sturzo*, Milan, 1979.

Righi, Vittore Ugo, *Papa Giovanni sulle rive del Bosforo*, Messaggero, Padua, 1971, with preface by Loris Capovilla (detailed account of Roncalli's work in wartime Turkey and Greece; some unpublished texts; useful despite its persistently 'edifying' tone).

Rocca, magazine edited from Assisi by Don Giovanni Rossi.

Rosario = *Il rosaria con Papa Giovanni*, edited by Loris Capovilla, Storia e Letteratura, Rome, 1979 (texts by Roncalli on mariological themes from his student days to the pontificate).

Rotundi, Virgilio, 'Padre Lombardi', in *Civiltà Cattolica*, February 2, 1980.

Rouquette, Robert, SJ, *Vatican II, la fin d'une Chrétienté*, 2 vols, Cerf, Paris, 1968 ('*chroniques*' republished from *Etudes* with afterthoughts; volume I is relevant to Pope John, and includes the famous essay '*Le Mystère Roncalli*' in which he attacked the 'personality cult' growing up around Pope John and denounced the danger of 'dreaming of a Church of angels presided over by angelic men').

Rynne, Xavier *Letters from Vatican City*, Farrar, Straus & Co, New York, and Faber and Faber, London, 1963 (based on his *New Yorker* articles, Rynne 'took the lid off' the Vatican; Fr Francis Xavier Murphy has never admitted to writing the book, but – with help – he did; his mother's maiden name was Rynne).

Saggia = *Giovanni e Paolo, due Papi, Saggio di Corrispondenza (1925–1962)*, edited by Loris Capovilla, published for the Istituto Paolo VI, Brescia by Studium, Rome, 1982 (91 items – letters, telegrams – exchanged between Roncalli and Montini; they had great respect for each other; it is highly unlikely that Pope John ever spoke about Montini's 'Hamletism').

Saturday Review, The, see Cousins, Norman.

Schillebeeckx, Edward, OP, *Vatican II, a Struggle of Minds and other Essays*, Gill and Son, Dublin, translation of *Het ambts-celibaat in de branding*, Nelissen, Bilthoven, 1966 (not really vintage Schillebeeckx, but a good attempt to trawl the tradition).

Schillebeeckx, Edward, OP, *Vatican II, a Struggle of Minds and other Essays*, Gill and Son, Dublin, 1964.

Schlesinger, Arthur M., jr, *Robert Kennedy and his Times*, Deutsch, London, 1978 (as the latest of the many Schlesinger books on the Kennedys one expected some mention of Pope John's role in the Cuban missile crisis: in vain).

SD=*Scritti e discorsi*, by Cardinal Angelo Giuseppe Roncalli, Edizioni Paoline, Rome, 1959–62 (the speeches and writings of Patriarch Roncalli in his Venice period; would probably have escaped publication had he not become Pope; the best of them are in Alberigo).

Secolo =*Papa Giovanni, un secolo*, by Loris Capovilla, Grafica e Arte, Bergamo, 1981 (a good reconstitution of Pope John's childhood on the hundredth anniversary of his birth; colour pictures of Sotto il Monte).

Seton-Watson, Christopher, *Italy from Liberalism to Fascism*, Methuen and Co., London, Barnes and Noble Inc., USA, 1967 (the incomparable work on Italian political life between 1870 and 1925).

Siri, Cardinal Giuseppe, address to the Roman Synod on the 25th anniversary of the death of Pope Pius XII, October 9, 1983 (Vatican Press Office).

Snider, Carlo, *L'episcopato del cardinale Andrea Carlo Ferrari*, vol. I, Neri Pozza, Vicenza, 1981 (the first volume of an immense and learned work which will restore Ferrari to his historical context and rehabilitate him; Roncalli should appear in volume II).

Soldati, *La Messa dei Villeggianti*, Mondadori, Milan, 1959.

Spain = Central Intelligence Agency (CIA) staff memorandum No. 27–63, 'Change in the Church', by James W. Spain, May 13, 1963. Declassified March 9, 1978 (Spain wrote to the author on April 8, 1984, and explained how he came to write his report; he was an academic rather than a 'spy', and in any case he soon moved to the State Department).

Spiritual Profile, edited by Stjepan Schmidt, SJ, Geoffrey Chapman, London, 1971 (notes from Cardinal Augustin Bea's spiritual diary; a labour of love from his former secretary).

St John-Stevas, Norman, *The Agonising Choice, Birth Control, Religion and the Law*, Eyre and Spottiswoode, London, 1971 (correctly traces the origins of the 'birth-control commission' to Pope John's pontificate though it was, so to speak, Cardinal Suenens' baby).

Stehle, Hans-Jakob, *Eastern Politics of the Vatican 1917–1978*, Ohio University Press, Athens, Ohio, 1981; translation with additional material of *Die Ostpolitik des Vatikans*, Piper, Munich, 1975 (a scrupulous and solid work, with much original material, from a reporter who was in Warsaw before going to Rome; not well served by his translator, who ominously gets the title wrong: it should be *policy*).

Tempo, Il, right-wing Roman daily.

Tillard, Jean, OP, *The Bishop of Rome*, SPCK, London, 1983 (documents the various 'titles' of the pope, and confirms from history the rightness of many of Pope John's intuitions).

Time, New York.

Tomlin, E. W. F., shared his memories of war-time Istanbul.

Tramontin, Silvio, *Un secolo di storia della Chiesa*, 2 vols, Studium, Rome, 1980 (a calm and balanced survey of the last century of Catholic Church history; Italy-centred, but not obsessively so).

Transizione = *Giovanni XXIII, Papa di Transizione*, edited by Loris Capovilla, Storia e Letteratura, Rome, 1979 (Capovilla reflects on the irony of the sobriquet, 'transitional Pope', and in an interview comments on some of the problems posed by John's pontificate; then texts on Pope John from, among others, Albino Luciani – the future Pope John Paul I, Paul VI, Marie-Dominique Chenu and the novelist Mario Soldati).

Trevor, Meriol, *Pope John*, Macmillan, London, 1967 (on the basis of the material available at that time, the best biography in English).

Tucci, Roberto, SJ, my first *maestro* in Vaticanology and sometime director of Vatican Radio; would have been embarrassed if this book had been dedicated to him – as it ought to have been.

Unity of Christians = *The Unity of Christians*, by Cardinal Augustin Bea, edited Bernard Leeming SJ, introduced by Archbishop Gerald P. O'Hara, Apostolic Delegate in Great Britain, Geoffrey Chapman, May 1963 (the publication of this book just before Pope John died was an important event, intended to make ecumenism acceptable in the English-speaking world; Bea never wrote a proper book, and these occasional pieces, lectures, radio and TV interviews gain enormously in interest when read in historical context; the original *Civiltà Cattolica* edition bore the title, *L'Unione dei Cristiani*, which is subtly different).

L'Uomo che non divenne Papa, by Carlo Falconi (this *roman à clef is* a useful complement to the same author's *Popes of the Twentieth Century*).

Utopia = *L'Utopia di Papa Giovanni*, by Giancarlo Zizola, Cittadella Editrice, Assisi, 1973, second edition; translated by Helen Barolini, *The Utopia of Pope John XXIII*, Orbis Books, New York, 1978 (persuaded me that with help from Mgr Loris Capovilla, a biography of Pope John was perfectly feasible; it is a splendid, passionate and somewhat disorderly book; unfortunately the English translation is so bad as to be unreadable and unusable; so whichever edition is referred to, I have always retranslated).

Vent'Anni = *Vent'Anni dalla Elezione di Giovanni XXIII*, edited by Loris Capovilla, Storia e Letteratura, Rome, 1978 (the conclave and the first three months of John's pontificate, illumined through his private diaries).

Villain, Maurice, *Introduction à l'Oecuménisme*, Casterman, Paris, 1961 (veteran ecumenist who wrote the life of the abbé Paul Couturier, founder of ecumenism in France, and translated Lancelot Andrewes into French).

Vita e Pensiero, monthly review of the Catholic University of the Sacred Heart, Milan.

Wall, Bernard, *A City and a World, a Roman Sketchbook*, Weidenfeld and Nicolson, London, 1962 (observations of an English man of letters with good portrait of Cardinal Domenico Tardini).

Walsh, Michael, librarian at Heythrop College, London, chased up every bibliographical enquiry and offered me space in which to work.

Wasserstein, Bernard, *Britain and the Jews of Europe 1939–1945*, Clarendon Press, Oxford, 1980 (punctures British self-esteem).

Weber, Francis J., 'Pope Pius XII and the Vatican Council', in *The American Benedictine Review*, September 1970 (has a useful bibliography: its chief interest, however, is that it provides a remarkable illustration of the arch-conservative thesis that Vatican II was 'really' the dream-child of Pius XII: thanks to Dom Alberic Stacpoole OSB for drawing my attention to it).

Wenger, Antoine, A. A., *Vatican II, Chronique de La première session*, Centurion, Paris, 1963 (best account of the first session in any language, which was hardly surprising since the author, the Editor of *La Croix*, was the only journalist inside St Peter's; he also chanced to be a scholar with a good knowledge of Orthodoxy).

West, Morris, *The Salamander*, Heinemann, London, 1973 (a fictional account of the failed *coup* of General De Lorenzo in 1964; see Collin, Richard).

Willebrands, Cardinal Jan, *'Papa Giovanni e l'ecumenismo'*, lecture at the Lateran University, Rome, November 10, 1981, MS (quotes and gives evidence for Dr Visser 't Hooft's statement: 'I am convinced that Pope John will go down in history as the pope who made dialogue possible').

Williams, George Huntston, *The Mind and Heart of Pope John Paul II*, Seabury Press, New York, 1981 (a gallant attempt to understand Karol Wojtyla with much useful material on inter-war Poland).

Woodhouse, C. M., *Modern Greece, a Short History*, Faber, London, 1968.

Worlock, Archbishop Derek, 'The Sharing Church', in *The Tablet*, October 9, 1982, pp. 1005–6 (a short, amusing, and ill-titled article); also *'Aggiornamento* in Embryo, Vatican II to date', in *The Wiseman Review* (formerly *The Dublin Review)*, Winter, 1963–4, pp. 316–34 (Archbishop Worlock has also consulted his memories and answered my questions on the Council and its preparation; but he prefers his presence to be like that of 'the Scarlet Pimpernel').

Zizola, Giancarlo, see *Panorama* and *Utopia*. In *Oggi*, April 13, 1983, he reported on the present state of the beatification cause (historical work completed; miracles abounding in Italy). It is fitting that the alphabet permits me to end with thanks to Zizola who not only completed my education in Vaticanology but gave me the run of his Rome apartment and his remarkable collection of books.

Appendix: The Roman Curia at the start of the Council, October 1962

Pope John XXIII, 81

Papal Household
Mgr Igino Cardinale, 47, Chief of protocol
Mgr Loris F. Capovilla, 48, private secretary

Curial Departments (Dicasteries)

Seminaries and Universities
Card. Giuseppe Pizzardo, 86
Sec. Abp Dino Staffa, 57

Rites (= Liturgy)
Card. Arcadio Larraona, 76
Sec. Abp Enrico Dante, 79

Religious
Card. Valerio Valeri, 80

Discipline of the Sacraments
(dispensations etc.)
Card. Benedetto Masella, 84

Oriental Churches
(i.e. Uniates)
Card. Gustavo Testa, 77

Consistorial Congregation
(selected bishops)
Card. Carlo Confalonieri, 70

Secretariat of State[4]
Card. Amleto Cicognani, 80
Sec. Abp Antonio Samorè, 58
Under Sec. Abp Agostino Casaroli, 49
Substitute Abp Angelo Dell'Acqua, 60

Conciliar Commissions etc.

Seminary Studies and Catholic Education,[1]
Pizzardo
Sec. Fr Augustin Meyer OSB

Liturgy, Larroana[2]
Sec. Fr Ferdinando Antonelli OFM

Religious, Valeri
Sec. Fr Giuseppe Rousseau OMI

Sacraments, Masella
Sec. Fr Raimondo Bidagor SJ

Oriental Churches[3]
Pres. Card. Amleto Cicognani
(made up mostly of Oriental patriarchs)

Bishops and Dioceses
Pres. Card. Paolo Marella, 68

The Holy Office
Card. Alfredo Ottaviani, 73
Sec. Abp Pietro Parente, 72

Congregation of the Council
(i.e. Trent: deals with priests and
catechisms)
Card. Pietro Ciriaci, 78
Sec. Abp Pietro Palazzini, 51

Propaganda Fide
(i.e. missionary work)
Card. Pietro Agagianian, 68
Abp Pietro Sigismondi, 55

On the Doctrine of Faith and Morals[5]
Pres. Ottaviani
Vice-pres. Card. Michael Browne OP, 68

*On the Discipline of the Clergy and the
Christian People*
Pres. Ciriaci
Sec. Fr Alvaro del Portillo, Opus Dei

Missions, Pres. Agagianian[6]
Sec. Mgr Saverio Paventi

Secretariat for Christian Unity[7]
Pres. Card. Augustin Bea 51, 81
Sec. Mgr Jan Willebrands, 54
also Mgr Jean-François Arrighi
Fr Tom Stransky CSP

Commission 'For the Lay Apostolate'[5]
Pres. Card. Fernando Cento, 80
Sec. Mgr Achille Glorieux

Secretariat of the Council[9]
Abp Pericle Felici, 52

Secretariat for Extraordinary Affairs[10]
(Cardinals Sin, Wyszynski, Montini,
Confalonieri, Döpfner, Meyer and
Suenens)

Notes

1. Produced *Veterum Sapientia:* theology to be taught in Latin.
2. Drew up only draft to survive first session.
3. Produced draft on Church unity — heavily criticised, hastily withdrawn.
4. Not formally involved in the Council, but Cicognani, Secretary of State, was President of the co-ordinating work and in overall charge of the Council.
5. Produced four draft texts – all rejected. 'Two Sources of Revelation' treated with great severity. Yet claimed a veto over all texts
6. Concentrated on logistic and financial problems of housing some 800 Missionary Bps.
7. Decisive in shaping the Council. After struggle, attains parity with Holy Office – works on Church and the relationship to other Christians, hosts the 'Observers'.
8. Timidly considers lay participation (by 1963); controls dealings with the media.
9. Brings order out of chaos and keeps the paper moving.
10. This body rather than the Council of Presidents took the vital decisions in consultation with Pope John.

Index